AMERICAN BASEBALL

Volume II

From the Commissioners
to
Continental Expansion

DAVID QUENTIN VOIGT

Foreword by
Ronald A. Smith

The Pennsylvania State University Press
University Park and London

Library of Congress Cataloging in Publication Data

Voigt, David Quentin.
American baseball.

Vol. 1 foreword by Allan Nevins; v. 2 foreword by Ronald A. Smith; v. 3 foreword by Clifford Kachline.
Vol. 1–2 are reprints. Originally published: Norman : University of Oklahoma Press, 1966–1970.
Includes bibliographies and indexes.
Contents: v. 1. From gentleman's sport to the commissioner system—v. 2. From the commissioners to continental expansion—v. 3. From postwar expansion to the electronic age.

1. Baseball—United States—History—Collected works. I. Title.
GV863.A1V65 1983 796.357'64'0973 83-2300
ISBN 0-271-00331-6 (v. 1)
ISBN 0-271-00334-0 (pbk. : V. 1)
ISBN 0-271-00330-8 (v. 2)
ISBN 0-271-00333-2 (pbk. : V. 2)
ISBN 0-271-00329-4 (v. 3)
ISBN 0-271-00332-4 (pbk. : V. 3)

Printed in the United States of America

With the publication of Volume 3 of Voigt's *American Baseball*, Penn State Press reissues Volumes 1 and 2 in order to complete the series.

Third printing, 1992

Foreword

The second volume of David Voigt's trilogy on baseball in America covers the period from the turn of the century into and through the 1960s. While there was some questioning in that era as to whether baseball continued to be the "National Pastime," author Voigt has no doubt that baseball remained the "Great American Game." As the leading scholar writing on the history of baseball, Voigt entertains and educates, bringing the reader through the game's Silver Age of the early twentieth century, into the second Golden Age of the 1920s and 1930s, and up to the dawn of the post-World War II Plastic Age. From dynasties like the Chicago Cubs and the New York Giants, to performers such as the zany Rube Waddell and the saturnine Ty Cobb, Voigt tells the baseball story, starting with the National League-American League rivalry that raged in the first years of the century and concluding at the midcentury advent of televised games.

Baseball, more than any other sport in American history, has reflected the larger social milieu of the country. Voigt's thorough research reveals the impact upon baseball of labor unrest, Sabbatarianism, big business ethics, desegregation pressures, technological progress, nationalism, wars, and depression. Description of the sportscasting of Graham McNamee in the 1920s and the Paul Gallico newspaper write-up of a double play are both included, in addition to entertaining anecdotes about players, owners, managers, and umpires.

Voigt's sojourn through early and midcentury baseball catches the game's high peaks, exemplified by the domination of the New York Yankees and the introduction of blacks into the game; it also captures the low ebbs of American baseball, such as the Black Sox Scandal and the untimely fatal paralysis of Lou Gehrig. In the process he reproduces the essence of a trio of demigods: Commissioner Judge Kenesaw Mountain Landis, Branch Rickey, and Babe Ruth.

Historian Jacques Barzun once wrote that "whoever wants to know the heart and mind of America had better learn baseball." No better start can be made than by reading David Voigt's *American Baseball*. His story tells us much about ourselves and our society.

Ronald A. Smith

Introduction

"AMERICA'S TRAGEDY," as George Bernard Shaw peevishly dubbed our national obsession, baseball, did not come into being spontaneously. Rather, it evolved from various forms of childish games and play and grew to fit the leisureways of an increasingly urban America where an ethic of fun was gaining at the expense of such values as religious sobriety and commitment to toil. Certainly by the 1840's, and probably earlier, the basic pattern of the game was shaped in the snobbish gentlemen's clubs which vied with one another for championship honors in several eastern cities. By 1845 one of these clubs, the New York Knickerbockers, established the dimensions of the baseball diamond and thus created the familiar battlefield for all baseball games to this day.

As other aspiring gentlemen formed exclusive clubs in America's northeast and old northwest, they adopted the "New York Game" of the Knickerbockers, thereby making it the basis for intercity competition. Such contests attracted throngs of urbanites, and by 1860 a national mania surrounded these clubs as they battled for the mythical championship of the United States. With heightening public interest in the game, newspapers provided regular coverage of contests, thus further broadening the appeal of the sport. The Civil War dampened enthusiasm for a time, but with the return of peace the baseball mania mounted until it topped the prewar excesses.

In a land growing ever more competitive and individualistic, the weak code of gentlemanly mores that regulated play crumbled under a ruthless ethic of win or else. This emphasis on competitive

A dramatic moment in a game between a pair of local rivals, the Phila delphia Club and the Philadelphia Athletics, played on April 30, 187; Because action photography was undeveloped, baseball stories of th nineteenth and early twentieth centuries were illustrated with line draw ings and sketches. This one appeared in the New York Daily Graphic (Courtesy The New-York Historical Society, New York City)

success drew the attention of professional and commercial interest whose leaders sniffed the profits to be wrung from baseball promo tion. By the late 1860's, undercover commercialism was rampan with many clubs bidding for husky proletarian stars whose service would insure victories. Seeing in this a mandate for professionalism Harry Wright, the English-born son of a cricket professional, i 1869 fielded the first all-salaried team. Called the Cincinnati Reds the team dominated play in 1869 and inspired other promoters t move toward open commercialism.

With sights set on cash and glory, the professional interests me in New York in 1871 and established the first professional major league. Known as the National League of Professional Base Ball Players, it was a rickety structure that never solved such knotty problems as how to make players live up to contracts or how to force clubs to live up to scheduling obligations. Yet despite such crippling disadvantages, this first major league lasted five years and broadened the game's appeal. However, its inability to control clubs and players, together with the domination of Harry Wright's brilliant Boston Red Stockings, winners of four consecutive pennants up to 1875, led to its demise.

Sensing that greater profit might come from better organization, Chicago promoter William Hulbert joined with pitching superstar Al Spalding and managed the 1876 coup that created the modern National League. Under its rules, members were tightly disciplined and players were bound to one club by its ingenious reserve clause. Although financial success came slowly, the new league functioned, and it carried major-league baseball into its first golden age.

In the decade of the 1880's, major-league promoters found the elusive formula that solidified the grip of the game on the nation. Perhaps most important of all the ingredients was the development of the heroic superstar whose very presence lured eager city dwellers to the parks where they might worship and identify with him. Among the heroes of the 1880's were men like the charismatic Irish-American star, Mike "King" Kelly; the slugging Adrian "Pop" Anson, playing manager of the Chicago Nationals; the debonair John Ward, leader of the Giants; and the durable Charles "Hoss" Radbourne, pitching phenomenon of the Providence Grays. With such titans in camp, the National League ruled the major baseball scene, but beginning in 1882 the rival American Association mounted a lively challenge and furnished such heroes as the stars of the perennial championship St. Louis Browns.

The heroic deeds of the superstars delighted loyal fans, and countless others identified with them via the baseball columns of American newspapers. New specialists in American journalism, baseball writers, came to stay in the eighties, and their stories helped make major-league baseball a million-dollar industry. Al-

An artist for the New York Daily Graphic *uses baseball clichés as pegs for his action sketches in order to whet the appetites of baseball fans for the forthcoming 1874 season. The sketches depict the action in an American Association game played between the Philadelphia Club and the Philadelphia Athletics on opening day.* (Goulston Baseball Collection, The New York Public Library)

though dominated by Henry Chadwick, a prolific writer whose career spanned the entire nineteenth-century history of major-league baseball, younger writers departed from his stilted style and created the lively, cliché-ridden pattern of reporting that still characterizes this form of American literature.

Arthur Irwin, captain of the Philadelphia "Phillies" of the 1880's, strikes an infielder's pose in a photographer's studio. Similar posed photos of the era testified to the slow pace of action photography during the early years of baseball growth. (Spalding Baseball Collection, The New York Public Library)

Nor did writers and promoters fear to create villains if such wretches could sell papers and fill ball parks. Thus, the 1880's saw the systematic vilification of the baseball umpire, a necessary and long-suffering functionary whose presence and pontifications evoked constant criticism. In time, this ritualized hostility became important byplay to the spectacle; it was as seductive as the player idols and as enticing as the "hot dog," a baseball lunch popularized in this golden age.

During the golden age, baseball strategy also came of age, and ever since managers have debated the merits of two styles of play—the brawny, slugging game of big rallies versus the "scientific"

A sketch of skaters playing a game of baseball on ice in New York's Central Park in the winter of 1884. American baseball's golden age of the 1880's saw the public's love of the game reach its greatest heights. (Harper's Weekly)

game which combines tight pitching with clever fielding and an offense geared to the tactics of bunting and base stealing. By the end of the golden decade, the latter style carried the day, and throughout the next decade two "scientific" teams, the Baltimore Orioles and Boston Beaneaters, fought for supremacy. In this, fortune favored the Orioles, whose ranks included John McGraw, a tough "mug," whose skill at skulduggery enhanced his club's scientific strategy.

By the 1890's, when McGraw's Orioles were dashing to fame, the National League enjoyed a clear monopoly of the major-league enterprise. Not that victory came easily, for in 1890 National leaders had to battle the Players League, an organization of major-league players who were out to balk owners' plans to reduce their salaries. When the Players League collapsed in 1890, the National turned on the American Association and crushed this rival in 1892.

A Pyrrhic victory, it put an end to the colorful postseason World Series spectacle between these two leagues, a rivalry that accounted for much of the game's popularity in the preceding decade. Denied this important attraction, besieged by continuing business depressions, and engulfed in the Spanish-American War of 1898, baseball profits and salaries tailed off alarmingly in the grim 1890's. Moreover, egotistical owners styled themselves "magnates" after the captains of industry of the era, a move that further alienated fans. Thus, the dawn of the twentieth century saw major-league baseball facing a desperate struggle to maintain its claim to being America's national game. Nor was financial survival the only threat, for in 1900 a determined rival, soon to be named the American League, demanded recognition as a major league. There followed two years of bitter interleague warfare which ended in 1902 with an uneasy settlement that grudgingly recognized President Byron Bancroft Johnson's American League as a major-league circuit.[1]

That 1903 was to be a turning point toward a new age of peace and prosperity was beyond the ken of the most sunny optimist among baseball men. On the contrary, most promoters in both the National and American camps stood by their guns and waited for an act of treachery that would renew hostilities. Especially militant were the American leaders, who well remembered the dismal fate of past invaders with too much trust in National promises of peace and unity. Knowing the bitter record, American sentiment echoed Mohammed's ancient warning about keeping company with Christians: "God fight them, what liars they are!" And because American chiefs like Johnson, Connie Mack, and Charles Comiskey had suffered firsthand from this duplicity, they kept their powder dry and watched for the slightest breach in the new National Agreement.

Adopted early in 1903, after two days of hard bargaining, the latest National Agreement gave major-league status to the Americans and bound both leagues to a common system of playing rules, player contracts, and schedules. Territorial rights for the sixteen major-league franchises were reallocated, and the Americans won

1 David Quentin Voigt, *American Baseball: From Gentleman's Sport to the Commissioner System.*

the right to move into New York. For their part, the Americans promised to stop raiding National playing rosters, which by 1902 had suffered eighty desertions. Although the raids were costly because they broke forever the old $2,400 salary limit rule, they paid off at the gate. From a total of 1,683,000 fans in 1901, American attendance climbed to 2,200,000 in 1902, while their rivals saw attendance drop to 1,683,000 in 1902.[2] This humiliation, along with rising costs and fears of bankruptcies, prompted weary National leaders to sue for peace.

Of the National's trinity of woes, the leadership crisis was the most decisive factor in their capitulation. Late in 1901, the Nationals dropped tired, aging Nick Young from the presidency only to plunge into a bitter struggle over his successor. Such bickering weakened their ability to resist outside attack. Not until late in 1902 did tempers cool enough to allow a commission headed by Barney Dreyfuss of Pittsburgh and August Herrmann of Cincinnati to secure the election of young Harry C. Pulliam as president. Fresh and for the moment uncontroversial, Pulliam convinced his American counterpart, Johnson, that peace was wanted. Out of their ensuing negotiations came the new National Agreement and its enforcement body, the National Commission, which henceforth consisted of Pulliam, Johnson, and Herrman. Convinced that the Commission might keep the peace, Johnson staked his career on his own confidence that he could control its decisions. Time would verify Johnson's faith in his abilities, for he used the Commission to guarantee the hard-won independence of his American League.

In 1903, although understandably hopeful for the stability of the marriage bed after the unease of the chaise longue, Johnson was too much the realist to expect eternal fidelity from his new partner. Under his urging, American clubs remained on a war footing throughout 1903. It was well they did, for in that year pockets of resistance flared, especially in cities where National and American teams coexisted.

In Chicago, Jim Hart of the Chicago Nationals tried to prevent

[2] *Spalding's Official Base Ball Guide,* 1902, pp. 99–102. See also *National League Green Book,* 1964, p. 24; *Reach's Official Base Ball Guide,* 1911, p. 27.

After the American League War ended, American baseball found peace and prosperity for eighteen years under the National Commission. Top, August Herrmann of Cincinnati, the at-large member of the triumvirate who was regularly elected each year during the life of the Commission. Left, Henry C. Pulliam, National League president, an ex officio member. His death in 1909 and the National League's problem in finding a successor weakened the league's influence on the Commission. Opposite Pulliam is Ban Johnson, president of the American League. Like Herrmann, he served the entire eighteen-year period and was the influential force behind the Commission. John E. Bruce, below, was the nonvoting secretary. (Reach's Official American League Base Ball Guide, 1908)

his American rival, Charles Comiskey, from using the word "Chicago" as a team designation. Although the tactic was absurd, it kept Comiskey on his toes and spurred him to field a team that would outshine Hart's Cubs. Not until 1905, the year the Cubs passed into new ownership, did tension ease between these two clubs. By then Comiskey felt secure enough to appropriate the proud "White Stocking" label, which formerly had been worn by his rivals.[3]

Much more serious was the guerrilla war in New York, where John T. Brush, new owner of the Giants and a stubborn warrior, harried the Americans. In 1903, his hometown rival was a forlorn franchise bravely dubbed the "Greater New York Club of the American League" and jointly owned by a gambler and a police chief. Under the 1903 peace pact, owners Frank Farrell and William Devery won the right to operate in New York, but their hasty efforts to plant a park atop a Washington Heights promontory were menaced by Brush, who tried unsuccessfully to get the city to cut a street through the center of the site. Stoking Brush's hostility was Giants manager John McGraw. Once a Johnson ally and manager of the American's Baltimore club, the old Oriole turned on Johnson after a dispute over McGraw's umpire baiting. Jumping to the National in 1902, McGraw was to be a vicious enemy. Indeed, in 1904 he persuaded Brush to refuse to engage the American League champions in the World Series. Small wonder that for years afterward Johnson cautioned his owners to deal carefully with "that old Oriole crowd"![4]

Although Chicago and New York remained the crucial points of stress between the embattled leagues, there was trouble in Philadelphia, Boston, and St. Louis. Of these embattled areas, the first two suffered most from American incursions; they provided ample grounds for American fears of vengeful counterattacks. However, neither outpost was in any condition to fight. In both places, aging or timorous owners, noting losses and dwindling

[3] Ed Fitzgerald (ed.), *The Book of Major League Baseball Clubs: The American League,* 40, 158, 165.

[4] Ed Fitzgerald (ed.), *The Book of Major League Baseball Clubs: The National League,* 95, 200.

attendance, chose to sell out. The passing of such influential leaders as Al Reach and John Rogers of Philadelphia and Arthur Soden and James Conant of Boston only added to National disunity. Because both sites passed into the hands of conservative newcomers, Johnson saw both towns as opportunities for developing promising American strongholds. Thus, in 1904, he convinced John I. Taylor, a son of a powerful Boston newspaper family, to invest money in a Boston franchise. With the Boston territory financially secured, Johnson and his lieutenants now concentrated their limited capital on other trouble spots.

Fortunately, the St. Louis battleground was less threatening than Boston, Philadelphia, or New York. Since 1902, the American's St. Louis Browns were in the capable hands of Robert Lee Hedges, a Cincinnati carriage manufacturer. A liberal spender for the moment, Hedges stocked his club with stars pried loose from the rival St. Louis Nationals. But his real coup came when he secured a lease to famous old Sportsman's Park, the only good ball field in town. By his enterprise, Hedges won the hearts of St. Louis ball fans, many of whom resented the syndicate baseball dealings of Cardinal owner Frank Robison.

Elsewhere, as in Detroit, Cleveland, and Washington, Americans relaxed as no established National team challenged them. But there were other problems. Most discouraging was the bad baseball reputation of these three sites, each having been rejected as profitless by major-league clubs in the past. Indeed, so doubtful was Johnson over Detroit's potential that he considered moving the franchise to Pittsburgh. But at the peace conference this move was quashed by Dreyfuss, who exacted a promise that the Americans would stay out of his smoky city.

Also regarded as "dead rabbit" towns were Cleveland and Washington. In 1900, both were dropped by the National League when that circuit cut back from twelve to eight clubs. Planting new teams in such places was risky, and Johnson counted heavily on new players to win fans. His hopes were not shared by smart money men; not until 1904 did each team win independent sponsorship. Until then, they were carried by special subsidies from the American League war chest. When Charles W. Somers finally decided to finance Cleveland, he was pleasantly surprised to find that Napoleon Lajoie, a rising superstar, was able to win popularity for the team. Soon, increasing attendance vindicated the faith of Johnson and Somers in Cleveland, but Washington remained weak. Not until the early 1910's, when Clark Griffith moved in to manage and acquired pitching star Walter Johnson as his chief attraction, did the Senators pay their own way.

With such gaps in its framework, peace came none too soon for the shaky American League structure. By 1903 financial aid was drying up. Somers was personally financing four clubs with help from the league reserves. Sorely needed were local owners with fat wallets, but to get them was to convince them that profits could be made. For the latter, peace was vital. Now at last, the peace of 1903 handed Americans the chance to show what they could do, and the 1903 season would test Johnson's boast that his league would "furnish a better article of base ball than the National League." More than this, it would test his brash decision to make American League admission prices the equal of the National's.[5] Thus the issue was joined, and the battle for popularity shifted to the playing fields, the turnstiles, and the World Series parks. None doubted that a decision regarding American League survival was imminent, but that verdict rested with the fans.

And so 1903 marks the beginning point of the present narrative. It was the dawn of baseball's silver age, an era of returning prosperity inspired by the scientific style of such legendary performers as Christy Mathewson, the peerless pitcher, and the brilliant all-round hitting and running of Ty Cobb. A colorful era, it marks the beginning of modern baseball, and, together with the rise of the home-run style popularized by the great "Babe" Ruth in the 1920's, its mythic grip on the imagination of sports-minded Americans lasts until this day.

[5] Fitzgerald (ed.), *The American League*, 58–69, 95.

Contents

Illustrations

I. *Baseball's Silver Age*

1

Deadball Dynasties: The American League

DETERMINED TO WIN the battle of the turnstiles, American League clubs worked to perfect the "scientific" style of play that dominated baseball in the 1890's. As a recipe for victory it demanded strong pitching, sturdy catching, and fast base running. As perfected by the Beaneaters and Orioles of the old big league, it was baseball's parallel to top military strategy, and as such it ruled the National League. Hence prudence dictated that the Americans master it as well as their rivals. Because the strategy produced so many low-scoring games, tactics called for playing for a couple of runs, and fans and managers came to appreciate the arts that produced the runs. Although later generations denounced the "deadball" era as dull, nobody at that time seemed offended. Complaints came only when comparisons were available, and these were possible with the introduction of a lively, cork-centered ball in 1909. But even when the new ball showed the marked differences between quick and dead play, clubs abandoned the familiar style reluctantly. Because all clubs were committed to the older pattern of play, it took another decade for the "big bang" style of high scores and long-ball hitting to take hold.

With such a strong consensus, it was not surprising that the history of the silver age is a tale of domination by a few powerful dynasties in each league, all of which excelled in the application of a familiar formula. Indeed, each rising dynasty followed the same developmental pattern of a buildup phase followed by successful dominance, after which a decline was followed by a vigorous rebuilding phase.

The chief difference between the two leagues was that the American League record showed a complete pattern of domination by four powerful clubs. So exclusive was their rule that there was no place for the four outsiders. Locked in this four-way struggle for supremacy were teams from Chicago, Philadelphia, Boston, and Detroit, and because of their control it was 1920 before a wallflower like Cleveland entered a World Series. Until that time, however, the silver age, as viewed from American League battlements, is a history of four tyrannical contenders battling for each successive pennant.

Chicago's emergence as the first American dynasty resembled a Horatio Alger plot. It began in 1900 when President Ban Johnson changed the name of his minor Western League to the more pretentious "American League." At the same time, Johnson persuaded his chief lieutenant, Charles A. Comiskey, to move his St. Paul club to Chicago. Fully aware of his precarious position, the forty-one-year-old "Commy" determined to strengthen his foothold in order to glorify the American League and to protect his own modest investment.

With a loan from a banker, Commy built a modest-sized park at Thirty-ninth Avenue and Wentworth Street. This was a major breakthrough, but it brought Comiskey to face the bitter hostility of Jim Hart of the Chicago Cubs. Exercising his authority as senior occupant of the territory, Hart forbade the use of the word

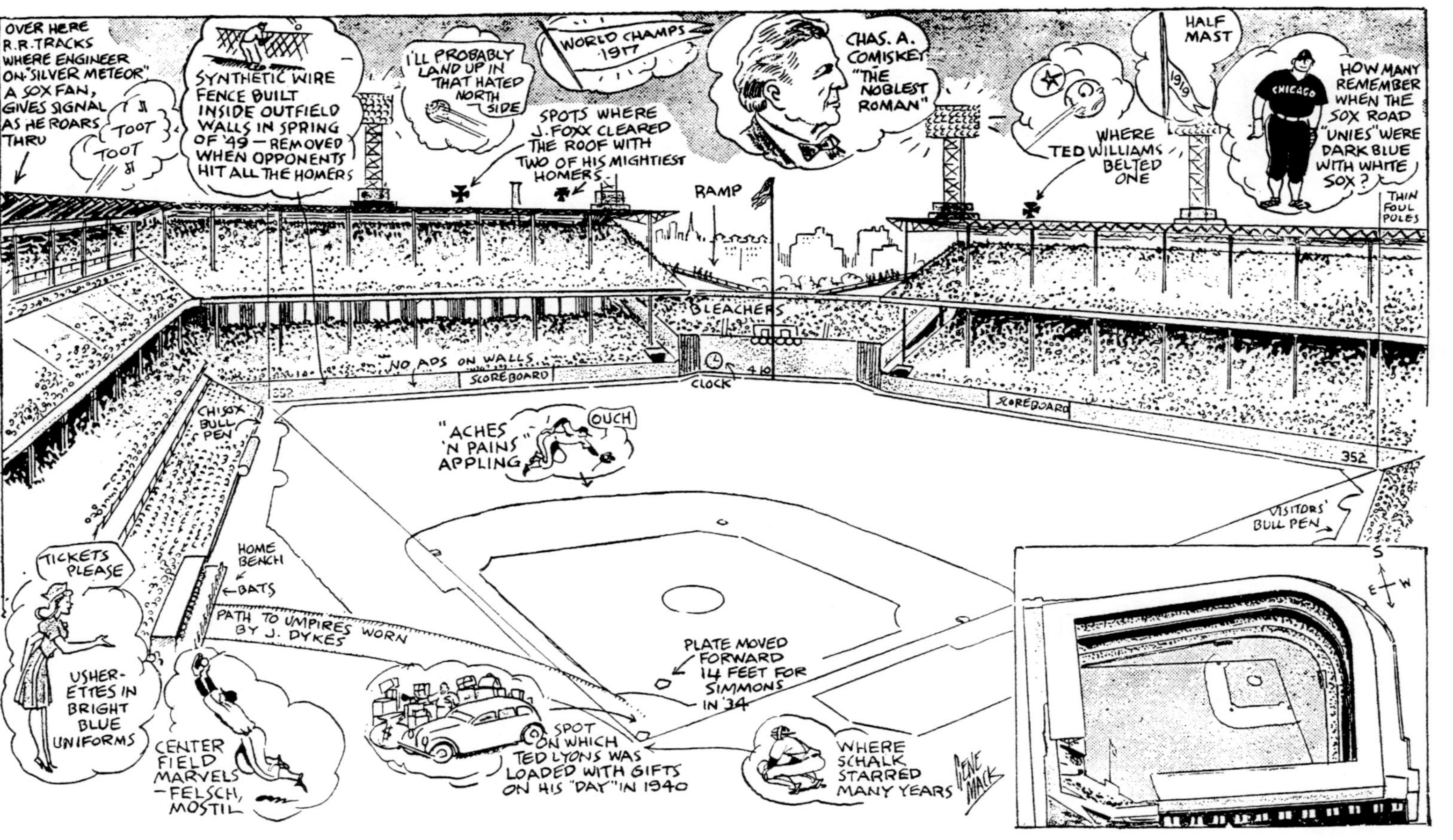

Comiskey Park, Chicago. Gene Mack's Hall of Fame Cartoons, Major League Ball Parks. (Copyright 1950. Gene Mack. Courtesy Eugene G.

"Chicago" in Comiskey's promotional schemes, and sought to draft players from Comiskey's teams on the ground that his rival was still a minor-league club.

But Comiskey was a veteran operator whose acumen had been sharpened by years of successful experience as a major-league player, captain, and manager. Using all of his experience, Commy in 1900 assembled a team of mixed major-league castoffs and rising youngsters to capture the first American League pennant. A modest achievement at the time, this victory was important to the future of Johnson's league. By its scrappy play, Commy's team established the new league in a major city, and, by scoring a modest triumph at the box office,[1] Commy demonstrated to investors the bright financial future of the American venture. On the strength of this success, Johnson in 1901 announced that his league was now a major circuit which would no longer bow to National player drafts or exclude itself from other big cities.

Naturally, this meant war, but the time was propitious for taking on the neighborhood bully. Badly crippled by chronic gate losses, ineffective and aging leaders, and embittered players, the National League reeled under Johnson's assault. American clubs in 1901 quickly occupied such former National cities as Boston, Baltimore, Washington, Cleveland, and Philadelphia. To hold these strongpoints, Johnson took advantage of widespread disenchantment among National players and the fact that numbers of good players were available after the National League's cutback from a twelve- to an eight-club circuit. Helping to facilitate the shifts was the National's unpopular $2,400 salary limit, which made possible easy seductions by the offer of a few hundred dollars more pay. Hence, in 1901, more than one hundred National leaguers joined American ranks, and this number included some outstanding stars.

One of these stars, Clark Griffith, a top pitcher for the Cubs, jumped to Comiskey, who quickly appointed him playing manager. With Griffith came another Cub pitcher, Jim Callahan, and this pair accounted for thirty-nine victories, enough to earn Comiskey's

[1] *Sporting Life,* October 27, 1900; Gustav Axelson, *"COMMY": The Life Story of Charles A. Comiskey,* 121–34.

team its first major-league flag. Altogether Griffith's team won eighty-three games to top the new Boston entry managed by Jim Collins, a deserter from the Boston Nationals, by four games. A close race, and a profitable one, it encouraged the invaders to press on.[2]

The following year, Griffith's team led at midseason, but after a lively second-half battle it fell to fourth. While Chicago floundered, a new dynasty, the Philadelphia Athletics, climbed to the top under Connie Mack. A tall, slim, ex-catcher who joined forces with Johnson back in 1896, Mack was the son of an Irish immigrant named McGillicuddy, who shortened the family name. To escape a lifetime as a Massachusetts factory worker, Mack chose baseball, and in 1886 at the age of twenty-four he joined the Washington club to begin a career that would span sixty-six years. Never a consistent hitter, Mack was a good fielder and leader, and in 1894 he became playing manager at Pittsburgh. Released in 1896, he gambled on a chancy future as manager and entrepreneur with Milwaukee in Johnson's Western League. Five years later, in company with owner Matt Killilea, Mack moved the club to Philadelphia to battle the entrenched Phillies for local favor. A risky move at the time, it took on a tragic aspect when Killilea died of tuberculosis before the year was out. At the time, Mack held only a quarter of the stock, but the energetic Johnson came to the rescue by persuading Benjamin Shibe to pick up the majority stock. This was a successful venture because Shibe was a partner with Al Reach, who for years had backed the Phillies. Not only did this move mean stability for the "White Elephants," but it freed the invaders from fears of costly interference on the part of their local rivals. Emboldened by this stroke, Mack proceeded to lure Napoleon Lajoie, their star slugger, from the Phillies for only a modest increase in salary.

With Lajoie batting .422 in 1901 and young Eddie Plank, a pitcher from Gettysburg College, winning sixteen games and showing signs of coming greatness, Mack drove his club to a strong

[2] *Sporting Life,* March 24, 1900; Axelson, *op. cit.,* 143–59; Lee Allen, *The American League Story,* 8–10, 18–20.

George "Rube" Waddell, star left-handed pitcher for manager Connie Mack's Philadelphia Athletics, was one of the most coloful and least manageable characters of baseball's silver age. When at his best, he was superb as a strikeout artist, and his record of sixteen strikeouts in a single game stood for many years. (George Brace, photographer)

fourth-place finish behind Comiskey's winners. It was enough to make the "White Elephants," a derisive epithet chosen by Mack as the team symbol, the darlings of Philadelphia.

But then came the counterblow. Colonel John Rogers of the Phillies, a tough-minded lawyer, obtained a court injunction barring Mack from using Lajoie in 1902. This cruel blow prompted Johnson to advise Mack to trade Lajoie to Cleveland, where the injunction had no effect. But Mack recovered quickly and lured the eccentric pitcher George "Rube" Waddell from the Chicago

Cubs. A pitching genius, Waddell was incredibly difficult to handle, and his impulsive antics became Mack's despair. Nevertheless, in four turbulent years he won ninety-six games for Mack, including a 23–7 record in 1902. That year, pitching, including Plank's 20–15 record, enabled the Athletics to win eighty-three games, five more than the Browns, and to hand Philadelphia fans their first major-league flag since the 1880's.[3]

Two of the four dynasties were thus onstage by 1902; a third rose to power in 1903. The Boston team, dubbed the Pilgrims or Puritans, like their rivals drew power from raids on a hometown neighbor. Hastily founded in 1901 with financial help from Johnson, Somers, and Mack, the club was located close to the South End grounds of the rival Beaneaters. Because the Beaneater players were chafing under the $2,400 salary limit, American promoters easily enticed a covey of stars to jump. For $4,000 in salary, the Americans got Jimmy Collins, a star third baseman, to take over as playing manager. With him came such established stars as outfielder Chick Stahl, slugging first baseman Buck Freeman, and ace pitchers Bill Dinneen and Ed Lewis. Meanwhile, another raid lured the fabulous pitcher Cy Young and his catcher Lou Criger from the St. Louis Nationals. With Young winning thirty-two games, this new team attracted some 527,000 fans, more than double the attendance of their rival.

After a disappointing third-place finish in 1902, Collins's team caught fire in 1903, winning by fourteen and one-half games over the tough Athletics. Superb pitching told the story as Young led the staff with twenty-eight wins, followed by Tom Hughes and Dinneen, both twenty-one-game winners. Although the team made a shambles of the American League race of 1903, it captured Boston rooters, including an all-weather throng of former National League partisans. These self-styled "royal rooters" even had a fight song, "Tessie," which was led by colorful, mustachioed "Nuf Sed" McGreevy. Bolstered by this crew, fans set up an August clamor to revive the World Series.

[3] *The Sporting News,* October 4, 1902; Allen, *American League Story,* 13–24; *Sporting Life,* March 2, 1901.

Although hesitant, Johnson consented, and a five-out-of-nine-games test was devised. The Pirates won early victories, but the Puritans closed fast with Dinneen and Young winning five games between them. By winning the Series five games to three, Boston handed Johnson a timely public relations coup. At the American meeting in December, a joyous group of owners toasted this success, raising Johnson's salary by $2,500 and awarding him a gift of $5,000.[4]

Even more important, the club's success prompted John Taylor, son of the Boston *Globe* owner, to purchase the club, thus ending its stepchild status in the American League. But Taylor's impulsiveness soon led to some costly player trades that nearly wrecked the team in 1904. Fortunately, these came too late to upset the team. Although closely trailed by the New York Highlanders, a shaky franchise which Johnson helped stock with good talent such as pitchers Clark Griffith and Jack Chesbro, Boston won the race by defeating New York on the last day of the season. A crushing blow to the Highlanders, whose hometown rivals, the Giants, were winning the National championship easily, the victory gave Boston its second straight pennant. However, the Giants alienated many fans by refusing Taylor's offer to meet the Puritans in the World Series. Widely criticized, McGraw's refusal led to an interleague conference which devised the "Brush rules" for the future conduct of World Series matches under the supervision of the National Commission. This important agreement stabilized relations between the two leagues and went far to end the guerrilla warfare that marked the early years of the National Agreement.[5]

By banishing lingering fears of sabotage, the latest rapprochement between the two leagues focused attention on the pennant race of 1905. The Highlanders seemed poised for a championship after their fine 1904 showing. With Boston suffering the loss of key players and Chicago rebuilding under a new manager, the path to glory seemed open. But Chesbro followed up his forty-one-

[4] Allen, *American League Story,* 30–35; Fitzgerald (ed.), *The American League,* 213–247.

[5] *Boston Daily Globe,* October 11, 1904; Fitzgerald (ed.), *The American League,* 3–36, 88–121; *Reach's Official Base Ball Guide,* 1905, pp. 13–23, 71, 280.

victory season with a mere twenty, and the Highlanders floundered. So into the breach moved the Athletics behind great pitching from Plank, Albert "Chief" Bender, and Rube Waddell. Of this trio Waddell was best, and his record of 26–11 included seven shutouts while Plank followed closely with 26–12.

In 1905, Mack needed every win from his formidable trio as the Chicago team, openly flaunting the new name "White Sox," fought to the end. For much of the campaign the two teams exchanged first place, but late in September the A's took two of three crucial games and went on to post a 92–56 record, enough to win by two games. The hero of the season was Waddell with forty-four consecutive shutout innings in September and the season's strikeout mark. His heroics were tempered by his off-field antics, however, including drunken sprees and a publicized brawl with his in-laws. Oddly, he won redeeming praise for carrying a blazing stove out of a burning house to avert a major fire. Perhaps the "Rube" might have regained Mack's favor had he not suffered a needless injury in some railroad-car horseplay that kept him out of the World Series. Without the Rube, the Athletics went down before the Giants and Christy Mathewson, losing four games to one and batting less than .200.[6]

By 1906 it was evident that victory in the deadball era depended on first-rate pitching. For this reason, the A's looked like good choices to repeat, except that their brilliant pitching staff collapsed. But the edict that good pitching conquers all still held true as the White Sox, blessed by good pitching and cursed by their legendary weakness at the bat, won the pennant. Ever since 1901, Chicago's team batting average had declined until it sank to .228, lowest in the league in 1906. Called the "hitless wonders," Fielder Jones's team proved its gameness despite suffering sixteen shutouts and scoring only 570 runs. Overcoming repeated humiliations, the team was brought back time and again by the pitchers. That year Frank Owen won twenty-two, the clown-faced Nick Altrock won twenty, dental student "Doc" White won eighteen, and big, handsome, spit-

[6] *Reach's Official Base Ball Guide,* 1906, pp. 43–54; Allen, *American League Story,* 36–47; Fitzgerald (ed.), *The American League,* 122–35; Axelson, *op. cit.,* 165.

ball-throwing Ed Walsh won seventeen. Led by Walsh with seven, this quartet accounted for nineteen straight victories in August, enough to put the team in contention. After that, the club had to fight the revived Highlanders, who were actually outdrawing the Giants for the first time. Battling into late September, the Sox took the lead on the twenty-fourth and hung on to win. This unexpected triumph for Comiskey was not welcomed by Johnson. Recalling how the "hitless wonders" fell before the Cubs in the 1905 Chicago city series, Johnson anticipated a humiliating massacre at the hands of the same Cubs.

Needing a miracle, the White Sox managed to combine tight pitching with unexpected and timely hitting. Altrock and Walsh pitched brilliantly, but it was providential the way neophyte George Rohe filled in for an injured player and made key hits. As a result, the Sox tied the Series at two games apiece. In the crucial fifth game, Sox pitching faltered, but Frank Isbell doubled four times to carry the team to an 8–6 win. After that, Doc White held the Cubs to an 8–3 score in the deciding game, which Johnson followed by publicly kissing Comiskey. A totally surprising victory, it sent American League spirits winging; combined with another attendance victory, it inspired jubilation at the annual league meeting. Meanwhile, the now legendary "hitless wonders" were spending shares of a $15,000 bonus from the grateful Comiskey.[7]

Although spitballer Ed Walsh touched Olympian heights in 1907–1908, Comiskey's team faded to third, trailing behind the rising Detroit Tigers. Led by fiery Hugh Jennings, an old Oriole distrusted by Johnson, the Tigers mounted a hitting attack that belied the opinion that the deadball era was a pitcher's paradise. In the 1907 season, the established Tiger star was big Sam Crawford, a nine-year veteran from Wahoo, Nebraska, who would perform well for still another decade. A fast runner and power hitter, "Wahoo Sam" led the National League in homers in 1901 as a slugger twenty years ahead of his time. Most of Crawford's long

[7] Axelson, *op. cit.*, 165–79; Fred Lieb, *The Story of the World Series*, 43–51; *Reach's Official Base Ball Guide*, 1907, pp. 17–29; Fitzgerald (ed.), *The American League*, 3–15, 37–47.

hits went for a record number of triples. Combined with a .312 lifetime average, these feats eventually won him membership in baseball's Hall of Fame.

But it was Crawford's fate to have to play in the shadow of Ty Cobb, the superstar of the silver age. Born Tyrus Raymond Cobb in Cobb City, Georgia, this tall, combative youth came to baseball with a chip on his shoulder. A scion of aristocratic slave-holding ancestors, he was the son of a mathematics teacher who stressed this heritage and urged the son to honor it. Cobb fumed at the uncouth jibes at southern players. After brief seasoning in a Georgia minor league, Cobb came to the Tigers in 1906 with a price tag of $750. It was a wrenching transformation for this humorless young man, and his early days were marred by fights with his mates, and an unimpressive performance on the field. He showed brief flashes of greatness, but managed only a .240 batting average in 1906. This failure stung him, and his temper worsened in 1907 when resentful mates tried to drive him from the team with cruel hazing; they locked him out of the hotel bathroom, hid his clothes, and sawed his bats.

But Cobb gave as good as he got, and as the year wore on he battled his way back into the lineup. A keen student of pitchers' styles, he learned to steal bases on their motions. As a batter, his spread-handed grip and smooth swing gave him uncanny control and enabled him to bunt or hit to any part of the field. Time would show that this style was the key to batting mastery in the deadball era. In 1907 it propelled Cobb to the batting title, the first of a long string that enabled him to eclipse Honus Wagner, his National rival. But in shooting to overnight stardom, Cobb paid the price in a lifelong moody temperament that tolerated no rivals, and, at this time, especially Crawford.[8]

The year Cobb broke in, another outfielder, Davy Jones, joined the club on the rebound from the minors. It was his lot to room with Cobb during these championship years, and long afterward Jones still recalled Cobb's "rotten disposition." But in 1907 the

8 Lawrence S. Ritter, *The Glory of Their Times,* 47–69; Ty Cobb and Al Stump, *My Life in Baseball: The True Record,* 9–48.

A familiar scene in the silver age was the peerless Ty Cobb sliding spikes first into home plate. This photograph was made in St. Louis before 1920. The shin guards and chest protector worn by the unidentified catcher are crude by today's standards. Note the absence of identifying numbers on the uniforms. Not until the 1920's did numbered uniforms appear. (Courtesy Detroit Tigers, American League)

light-hitting Jones and the slugging Crawford flanked Cobb in the Tiger outfield. In the infield, Jennings posted Claude Rossman on first, Herman (Germany) Schaefer at second, Bill Coughlin at third, and Charley O'Leary at short. Burly Charley Schmidt did the catching, and Bill Donovan, George Mullin, and Ed Killain headed the pitching staff.

With Jennings infusing some old Oriole spirit and Cobb taking on the world in general, the Tigers became the brawling club of the circuit. Although the pitching was good, other teams had better, including Washington with its fire-balling Walter Johnson. Nevertheless, the batting of Cobb and Crawford carried the day although the race was close—Detroit outlasted the Athletics by two and one-half games. That year Cobb took base-stealing honors with forty-nine and his first batting title with a .350 mark. Unquestionably, the exciting race helped the Americans to another box-office victory, but the general increase in baseball attendance even in the face of a national business depression underscored the soundness of the two-league system. Moreover, the National League shared some of the glory when the powerful Cubs ripped Tiger pitching and held Cobb to a mere .200 average in winning the Series.[9]

The next two campaigns duplicated the 1907 pattern. Although Detroit won both times, each contest was close, especially the one in 1908 which editor Richter of the *Guide* said was more exciting than Taft's presidential campaign. That year Mack released the troublesome Waddell and rebuilt his squad, a move that consigned the young Athletics to sixth place. But the slack was taken up by Chicago and the Cleveland "Naps," a nickname honoring the club's great playing manager, Nap Lajoie. Cleveland harried the Tigers to the end. So close was the race that it hung on the outcome of a final game between Detroit and Chicago. With Donovan pitching a two-hitter, Detroit won the game 7–0 and clinched the title.

Meanwhile, the National race was equally close, for it was the year of the "Merkle boner" and the gallant drive of the Cubs that tied the Giants. In an unprecedented postseason playoff, Chicago won, although the Giants set a major-league attendance record

[9] *Reach's Official Base Ball Guide,* 1908, pp. 5-37, 90–95.

with 910,000 admissions. Another depression-defying year of prosperity for American baseball, it ended with more glory for the Nationals as the Cubs again downed the Tigers in the Series, after which snide National jibes were heard to the effect that the American was only a good minor league.[10]

But the final arbiters of such exchanges were the baseball fans, and in 1909 they favored the Americans. In another cliff-hanging race, Jennings's Tigers topped Mack's reconstructed A's by three and one-half games. Except for a reshuffled infield, the Tiger team was the same, with fair pitching and a superb outfield. For the third straight year, Cobb won both stealing and batting honors and established himself as the team's star attraction.

For most of the season it seemed that the Tigers were to enjoy a relaxed campaign, but in August Mack's young lions came on strongly behind the pitching of his veteran stars. While the Tigers slumped, the A's kept on, and as the pace grew hotter, tempers flared. Late in the year, the hard-running Cobb spiked young Jack Barry of the A's, the incident nearly triggering a riot. With Barry out, the A's fell back, but their surge convinced observers of their bright future.

If Cobb was a villain to the Athletics, he was the star of the Series with Pittsburgh. That fall he hit brilliantly, but the Pirates won a tense Series four games to three. It was a third consecutive defeat for the Americans and it infuriated Johnson. Recalling the McGraw defection, Johnson was heard to mutter that maybe Jennings was in cahoots with McGraw to sabotage the American league.[11] The emotionalism of this episode has to be taken into account, but it nevertheless indicated a growing resentment of the Tiger domination. Many wondered, after observing Cobb's tireless zeal, if that would go on forever.

But only a few knew the extent of Mack's determination to win. Only forty-eight in 1910, he was now known as the "dean of American League managers," and in an age of uniformed playing man-

[10] *Ibid.*, 1909, pp. 7–63.

[11] *Ibid.*, 1910, pp. 7–49, 129; Fitzgerald (ed.), *The American League*, 157–89; Lieb, *op. cit.*; Allen, *American League Story*, 58–68.

agers he was a strange presence in austere, civilian clothes. Some jeered at him, and hard-nosed Hugh Jennings ridiculed his mania for signing college-bred players. Still others thought him foolish and overly optimistic in 1909 for opening the great Shibe Park with a seating capacity far beyond that of most other parks.

Mack in 1910 faced a crisis, but the superb manner in which his well-drilled team responded established him as the foremost American League manager of the silver age. In a ruthless stampede, the white elephants won 102 games, 14½ games ahead of the Highlanders who were being dubbed the "Yankees." Pitching was Mack's chief weapon; young Jack Coombs led the staff with thirty-one victories, followed by Bender with twenty-three, Morgan, eighteen, and Plank, sixteen. Pacing a batting onslaught which produced a .265 team average was young Eddie Collins, a second baseman already being compared to the great Lajoie. The key to the great defensive infield, soon to be celebrated as the "$100,000 infield," Collins was flanked by Barry at short and Frank Baker at third, with young John "Stuffy" McInnis soon to take over at first. The outfield of Amos Strunk, Rube Oldring, Dan Murphy, and Ed Murphy was adequate, and the catching of Jack Lapp and Ira Thomas was superb.

A youthful team, it was also the most highly educated one in baseball history, sprinkled as it was with college graduates. To some critics this was a fatal sissiness, but such talk faded with the club's walkaway victory and its four game to one triumph over the Cubs in the Series. In the eyes of exuberant president Johnson, now showing the effects of his three hundred pounds, it was a neat victory, done by dignified men, in the best traditions of middle-class American values.[12]

The Athletic stampede of 1910 heralded a new style of play in major-league baseball. Although the old style of using power pitching to protect a few runs craftily teased home by short hits, stolen bases, and sacrifices still dominated, the newly introduced cork-centered ball promised greater offensive outbursts. Coinciding with the big-park building boom pioneered by Mack in Philadelphia

12 *Reach's Official Base Ball Guide,* 1911, pp. 7–71.

and Dreyfuss in Pittsburgh in 1909, the new style was written on the wall, and managerial Belshazzars needed no Daniels to interpret its meaning. Public approval came suddenly and convincingly in 1911 when an unprecedented ten million fans crowded into the eighteen major-league parks. Interpreted by promoters as a vote of confidence in the two-league system and the new park movement, all but the most fainthearted of them began building.

As rivals rushed to catch up, Mack forged still further ahead. He groomed his A's for another successful sortie. With McInnis at first and hitting .300, the $100,000 infield was set. After a slow start, the young elephants overhauled the Tigers and lumbered home. Winning by thirteen and one-half games, the team, led by Collins's .365 average, posted an awesome .297 team average.

This triumph underscored the new offensive style as did Cobb's herculean .420 mark and the .408 mark of "Shoeless Joe" Jackson, an illiterate southern-born outfielder who played with Mack in 1909. Because Jackson was alienated from his literate teammates, Mack released him to Cleveland. Ordinarily, losing such a star would have been disastrous to a manager, but Mack rode out the loss because of his team's remarkable balance. For Mack's team led all in hitting, pitching, and fielding and, if this were not enough for redemption, beat the hated Giants in the Series. In avenging his 1905 setback, Mack triumphed in a closely fought struggle marred by spiking incidents, highlighted by strong pitching, and powered by Baker's two dramatic hits which won him the nickname of "Home Run" Baker.[13]

But the all-out drive to avenge 1905 exacted its toll. Mack's ace pitcher, Coombs, begged to pitch in spite of a bad groin injury, but his effort only aggravated the condition. Coombs rallied to win twenty-one in 1912, seven off his previous year's effort. Similarly, injuries, aging, and complacency caught up with others. The usually reliable Bender was chastised for drinking, and two pitchers were released for ineffectiveness. Fortunately, Mack's scouts were signing a trio of future pitching greats in Herb Pennock, Joe Bush, and Bob Shawkey, along with a fine catching prospect in Wally

[13] *Ibid.*, 1912, pp. 7–65, 155–203; Lieb, *op. cit.*, 70–84.

Schang. However, none of these were ready in 1912, and although the team won ninety games, it finished third, fifteen games behind the winning Red Sox.

The victory of the Red Sox was a reminder to all smug dynasts of the uncertainties of baseball. Since scoring back-to-back victories in 1903–1904, Boston's chief distinction was its appropriation of the proud "Red Stocking" emblem. Its name shortened now to "Red Sox," the floundering team was fifth in 1911. Bitterly disappointed at this and haunted by fear that his new park was a bad investment and his judgment of players inadequate, owner Taylor sold the club to a Washington financier with Johnson's blessing. The incredibly ill-timed move came just as Taylor's earlier efforts bore fruit. One of his most remarkable proteges was a twenty-three-year-old pitcher, Joe Wood, with a fast ball rated the equal of Walter Johnson's. Moreover, Taylor already had recruited Tristram Speaker, Duffy Lewis, and Harry Hooper, an outfield often rated as the finest ever assembled. Of these Speaker was best, but like his knightly namesake he was overshadowed by the Lancelot of the age, Ty Cobb.

Managed by the veteran first baseman, Jake Stahl, and cheered by "royal rooters" still singing "Tessie," the team won 105 games. The brightest star was Wood, who won 34, lost 5, and vied with Johnson as the best pitcher. That year both scored sixteen straight wins, and the highlight of the rivalry came when Wood snapped Johnson's streak in a 1–0 duel fought before a Boston crowd so vast that Wood scarcely had room for warming up. Saving enough to dazzle the Giants, Wood won three games in the hard-fought Series, made legendary by Giant outfielder Fred Snodgrass's muff of an easy fly ball. Coming in the last inning of the last game, it led to a winning Boston rally and preserved Wood's third victory. Aside from being another welcome slap at McGraw, the victory put the Americans ahead in the annual test of strength;[14] never again would the American League fall behind.

But the redeemers of American League pride were toppled the

[14] *Ritter, op. cit.,* 131–46; *Reach's Official Base Ball Guide,* 1913, pp. 6–71, 138–201.

very next year. Like the collapse of the Athletics of 1912, theirs followed an injury to their best pitcher. Some maintained that Joe Wood threw his arm out in 1912, but Wood later said that he returned to pitching too soon after fracturing a thumb. When he pitched in 1913 he was effective, as his 11–5 record indicated, but every pitch brought sickening pain. The chronic condition forced him to quit pitching in 1916, but later he made a comeback in the majors as a better-than-average outfielder.

As Boston faded, Griffith's Senators moved in along with Mack's revitalized A's. Now the owner of half of the club's stock, Mack had a great incentive to rescale the heights. As usual, pitchers Bender and Plank led the way, but support came from rookies Shawkey, Pennock, and Bush. Backed by good hitting, the A's won by six and one-half games and easily trampled the Giants in the Series.[15]

Once again there was joy in major-league countinghouses as nearly all clubs made money. But, as baseball history indicates, the click of turnstiles is a powerful lure to interlopers anxious to cash in on the bonanza. Ever since 1910, rumors warned of new major-league invaders, and to forestall them *Reach's Guide* ceased publishing attendance figures after 1910. But the big Series profits of 1911–12 convinced promoters of the new Federal League that the time was at hand. And so in 1913 the majors faced a rival supplied with funds by such noted captains of industry as oilman Albert Sinclair and the Ward baking family of New York. In 1913, Federal representatives made lucrative offers to major-league stars and there were takers. Thus smiles of prosperity gave way to frowns of fear: fear of war with the Federal League, fear of international war in Europe, and fear of American involvement in a war with Mexico.

Against a gloomy backdrop, Mack drove his club to an easy eight and one-half game victory over the Red Sox. As usual Mack's pitching staff and infield carried the load. Rated an overwhelming favorite to crush the ugly duckling Boston Braves in the Series, the Athletics shocked the nation by losing four straight.

Mack publicly denounced his team for arrogance and com-

[15] "Mack's Great Expectations," *Literary Digest,* March 8, 1913.

placency. While nursing hurt feelings, Mack was weighing such negative factors as the Federal threat, the European war, and (above all) a $60,000 loss in 1914. He was convinced that the times demanded retrenchment and began shedding his stars. Over the winter he made headlines by releasing Plank, Bender, and Coombs and by selling Collins to the White Sox for $50,000. Once again, Mack deliberately broke up a winning combination, but this time he was unwilling to invest in promising youngsters. Indeed, in a disastrous miscalculation he turned down the chance to get Babe Ruth and Ernie Shore from Jack Dunn of Baltimore for $10,000. And this time Mack paid the full price for his managerial sins; like the Biblical peoples who faced a period of famine after a time of plenty, Mack's elephants were to dwell in the league cellar for seven years.[16]

For the next few years, the grim financial picture in the majors vindicated Mack's pessimism. The blackest year since the 1890's came in 1915 as only seven major-league clubs made minimal profits; the other nine, along with six Federal clubs and most of the minors, lost money. In a pathetic attempt to explain the situation, a *Guide* blamed external forces such as the "unwise Democratic tariff," the Mexican conflict, the European war, the automobile, and an intangible called "the mercenary spirit of commercialization."[17]

Yet even in the grimmest of times there were some optimistic bulls amidst the bears. Two of them, canny Charles Comiskey and neophyte owner Joe Lannin of Boston, elected to invest in superstars at bargain-basement prices. As a result, their clubs won the next five American pennants. In 1915 both splurged simultaneously and took advantage of Mack's gloom to buy his stars. Lannin bought Jack Barry from Mack, and then Ruth and Shore, both of whom Mack had snubbed.

With Bill "Rough" Carrigan as catcher-manager, the Red Sox groomed a fine pitching staff and backed them with the tight inner defense of Dick Hoblitzel at first, Barry at second, Everett

16 Fitzgerald (ed.), *The American League,* 122–56; *Reach's Official Base Ball Guide,* 1915, pp. 1–31; Lieb, *op. cit.,* 101–107; Allen, *American League Story,* 69–89.

17 *Reach's Official Base Ball Guide,* 1916, pp. 9–18.

Scott at short, and Larry Gardner at third. As usual, the outfield of Speaker, Hooper, and Lewis was conceded to be the league's best.

In spite of its formidable appearance on paper, this team was clawed and pursued to the end by Jennings's Tigers, whose hitting was sparked by Cobb's ninth consecutive batting title. But the race ended with Boston in front by two and one-half games. A cliff-hanging victory, it initiated rookies like Babe Ruth and Ernie Shore. Both responded well, with Ruth winning eighteen games and batting strong as a pinch hitter, and Shore winning nineteen. After the fight with the Tigers, the National League Phillies posed less trouble, falling 4–1 in Series games, although all Boston victories were eked out by a single run.

Such high-pressure experience supported the Red Sox in 1916 as they faced another nerve-jangling campaign with the White Sox. It might have gone easier for Boston had not Lannin, in the wake of a salary dispute with Speaker, traded the great outfielder to Cleveland for $50,000. Fortunately for Lannin, Speaker's loss was partly offset by the performance of newcomers and by even sturdier pitching from Ruth, Shore, Dutch Leonard, and Carl Mays. In his new Cleveland environment, "Spoke" finally won a batting title, thus ending Cobb's skein of nine straight. Nevertheless, Boston's strong arms carried the club to a two-game triumph over Chicago, then to an easy four to one game victory over the Dodgers in the Series.[18]

This battle-hardened team collapsed in 1917 because of a leadership crisis that came when Manager Carrigan suddenly decided to quit baseball for the business world. Hard after this, Lannin sold out to Harry Frazee and Hugh J. Ward. Frazee was a prominent theatrical producer whose credits included the runaway success "No, No, Nanette," which was enough to convince Lannin to accept a promissory note. Within three years Frazee fell victim to the feast and famine world of the theater and Lannin was obliged to sue for his money. Time would show the Frazee years to be the grimmest in Red Sox history.

[18] *Ibid.*, 1916, pp. 9–18, 65–70, 1917, pp. 7–17; Lieb, *op. cit.*, 107–17; Fitzgerald (ed.), *The American League*, 88–121.

Meanwhile, Carrigan's 1917 replacement, Jack Barry, drove his ex-mates hard but was overmatched by the wise and insistent Comiskey. Desperate after an eleven-year pennant drought marked by heartbreaking near-misses, one of which he blamed on Johnson for disciplining a player at a critical time, Comiskey was buying and building. In 1914 he loosed his purse strings in a massive talent hunt that turned up pitcher Ed Cicotte, catcher Ray Schalk, and infielder Buck Freeman. A year later, an unprecedented $130,000 outlay brought Eddie Collins from Mack and Joe Jackson from Cleveland.

Always a meddler, Comiskey was notorious for his difficulties with his field managers, but since 1915 he had settled on little-known Clarence "Pants" Rowland. Up to 1917, Rowland's record showed a third-place finish and a very close second in 1916. With his job most certainly at stake in 1917, Rowland at last fitted the expensive parts into an efficient machine. In so doing, he delegated broad powers to Captain Collins, an effective but unpopular leader with a strong cabal that resented his collegiate polish, his authority, and his high salary. Led by first baseman Chick Gandil, the clique made life miserable for Collins and Rowland; at the same time, its off-field contacts with gamblers portended trouble for Comiskey.

But in 1917, as the drums of war echoed throughout the land, Rowland's team stormed the league, winning one hundred games and finishing nine and a half ahead of the Red Sox. Cicotte, a master of trick deliveries such as the knuckle ball and the spitter, led Rowland's pitching staff, while the offense-minded team won easily in spite of subpar performances from Collins and Jackson. That fall, with the aid of another classic Giant blunder, the White Sox handed McGraw a fourth Series defeat. It came in the sixth and final game when the Giant catcher left his post, thus forcing the third baseman into the ludicrous position of chasing home the fleet Eddie Collins. The incident hung a clown label on third baseman Heinie Zimmerman and left McGraw fuming at the luck of his "bush-league" rival.

Although it was baseball as usual in 1917, the deepening war effort signalled problems for 1918. Just as certain forces worked to bring down European dynasties, others worked to end the American League dynasties. In the topsy-turvy campaign of 1918, Boston won, but the season was affected qualitatively and quantitatively by the war effort. Thus Boston's winning log of seventy-five wins in a short campaign seemed forlorn in comparison with past campaigns, and the departure of many players to the ranks gave a synthetic quality to the game.

Until special dispensation came from Washington, it even appeared that there would be no Series. Boston responded to the special concession and defeated the Cubs in a ritual that seemed, like the season, to be curiously irrelevant. Certainly wartime was no time for baseball; attendance flagged, active players were called slackers, and those who sought to escape military service by taking defense jobs were treated with contempt.[19]

Small wonder that some club owners despaired and sold out. Even with the Armistice in November, few expected a normal season in 1919. But demobilization proceeded faster than most thought possible, and American fans stormed the ball parks that year. If the eager faces seemed familiar, however, their moods and tastes were different. For the war years had wrought profound changes in American life in general and in baseball in particular. Some were devastating, like the get-rich spirit that led to the scandal which overwhelmed the tidy dynastic pattern of Johnson's league.

Other changes held promise of a bright new future. After all, it was the wartime doubling-up solution that sent colorful Babe Ruth to his first home-run title in 1918. A familiar aftermath of wars is this bittersweet blend of upheaval and promise. Such times called for bold men to pick up the wreckage of the old and build anew. This time of rebuilding would be remembered as a new golden age.

[19] *Reach's Official Base Ball Guide,* 1919, pp. 8–17, 38; Axelson, *op. cit.,* 201–18.

2

Deadball Dynasties: The National League

THE NATIONAL LEAGUE of the 1890's first perfected the deadball style of play. Mastered in succession by the Baltimore Orioles, Boston, and Brooklyn, the style brought fame and flags to these early leaders. The three clubs dominated play for a decade, but then came the war with the American League, which wrecked playing rosters and forced major changes in the league's balance of power. As early as 1901, power had shifted to three new centers under a new breed of owners and managers who carried the fight against the invading Americans. For thirteen years thereafter, National League pennants were monopolized by Pittsburgh, Chicago, and New York, as this dominant trio rewrote the history of the senior circuit.

When the National League re-formed under an eight-club pattern in 1900, owner Barney Dreyfuss of the disaffiliated Louisville franchise seized an opportunity to buy half ownership in the Pittsburgh Pirates. An energetic German-Jewish immigrant, Dreyfuss was driven by love of baseball and a determination to profit from the game. His careful study of Pittsburgh attendance patterns convinced him that fans would only support a fighting first-division team. Henceforth it was his obsession to grab one of the top four places each year, and he forced this demand on his managers. For his part, Dreyfuss willingly supplied the necessary financial backing to make the policy bear fruit. In the years 1900–1913 his Pirates won four flags and never sank lower than fourth; and from 1918 to his death in 1931 his teams added two more pennants to fulfill his stern demand.

Dreyfuss escaped the usual fate of newcomers by bringing with him from Louisville a hand-picked cadre of first-rate players, led by player-manager Fred Clarke. A fine, hard-hitting outfielder, Clarke was already battle-tested and quickly welded the Louisville men with Pittsburgh players to make a strong baseball machine. In fashioning his juggernaut, Clarke selected Louisville infielders John (Honus) Wagner, Tom Leach, and Claude Ritchey, along with catchers Charles Zimmer and Cliff Latimer and pitchers Charles "Deacon" Phillippe, Rube Waddell, and Pat Flaherty. These he joined to a Pittsburgh contingent of pitchers Jack Chesbro, Jess Tannehill, and Sam Leever, infielders John Williams and Fred Ely, and outfielders Clarence "Ginger" Beaumont and Tom McCreery. From the minors came Bill "Kitty" Bransfield to take a four-year lease as first baseman.[1]

Sparking this formidable machine was "Honus" Wagner, a versatile player regarded by some as the greatest in baseball history. A tall man, this son of a Pennsylvania coal-mining family was solidly built, but with bowed legs that belied his stature. Craggy-faced, hook-nosed, with a huge pair of hands hung on long arms, the awkward-looking Dutchman was a brilliant fielder and champion batter. He employed a wide-open stance, gripping his bat, like Cobb, with one hand well above the other. Using this style he

[1] *Spalding's Official Base Ball Guide,* 1902, pp. 42–63; Fitzgerald (ed.), *The National League,* 44–46.

Charles L. "Deacon" Phillippe was a mainstay on the Pittsburgh Pirates pitching staff during the early years of the silver age. In thirteen years with the Pirates, beginning in 1899, the Deacon won over twenty games five times. In that same span, manager Fred Clarke's Pirates, ranked as one of the National League's three contending dynasties. (George Brace, photographer)

set a league record for most hits that still stands. He was so versatile as a fielder that Clarke posted him everywhere before stationing him permanently at shortstop. There he performed "with cumbersome grace" over a fifteen-year period during which the popular superstar won four consecutive batting titles.[2]

In 1901, Clarke's team rode to the first of three straight championships. This was the first victory by a western National outpost

[2] *Spalding's Official Base Ball Guide,* 1902, pp. 36, 42–65; *Baseball Magazine,* September, 1913, October, 1916; *The Sporting News,* March 2, 1911.

Two of the greatest stars of baseball's silver age were Napoleon Lajoie (left) of the American League and John "Honus" Wagner of the National. In 1916, Lajoie ended a twenty-one-year career with a .339 lifetime batting average, and the following year Wagner ended his twenty-one-year career with a .329 average. (MacGreevy Collection, Boston Public Library)

since Detroit won in 1887. Acclaimed by the venerable Henry Chadwick for its clean-cut play, Clarke's team scored ninety victories; of these sixty-one were won by pitchers Phillippe, Chesbro, and Tannehill. To the surprise of those who thought Wagner slow of foot, he led the league in stolen bases.[3]

The Pirates were spared from the devastating American League raids that depleted rival rosters, and easily won a second championship in 1902 with 103 victories. That year Chesbro led the league's pitchers with twenty-eight wins; Beaumont, the hitters with .357; Leach, the sluggers with six homers (all inside-the-park blows); and Wagner, the base stealers with forty-three.

That fall, however, the raiders caught up with the Pirates. Dreyfuss's hired detectives once had to chase Johnson out of a hotel where Wagner was staying, but other American raiders snared Chesbro, Tannehill, Leach, and Conroy. Although this was a paralyzing blow, Clarke rallied his forces and won a third pennant in 1903. Wagner led all hitters with a .355 mark, and Sam Leever surpassed all pitchers with twenty-five wins. With their help, the Pirates scored ninety-one victories and outlasted the revitalized Giants. This courageous effort was overshadowed, however, when the Pirates fell before Boston in the first of the modern World Series tests.[4] The defeat signalled an end to Pirate rule. Next year, plagued with shortages of pitchers, and fading veterans, the Pirates fell to fourth place behind McGraw's surging Giants.

To New York fans, who suffered through so many shabby performances in the 1890's, the new look in the Giants was refreshing. Impotent since 1894, when John Ward led the club to a Temple Cup win, the Giants had suffered eight famine years, finishing last in 1900 and again in 1902.

But now there was room for optimism. The new hand at the club tiller belonged to owner John T. Brush, a veteran baseball enthusiast who pushed hard for victory. This native New Yorker had spent most of his life in Indianapolis making a fortune as a clothing

[3] *Spalding's Official Base Ball Guide,* 1902, pp. 42–45; Leach's recollections of his Pirate days are to be found in Ritter, *op. cit.,* 20–33.

[4] *Spalding's Annual Base Ball Record,* 1908, pp. 61–62; Fitzgerald (ed.), *The National League,* 44–46.

merchant. While he was there he also indulged his love of baseball, using all his resourcefulness to win a National League franchise for that city. When, in the aftermath of the Brotherhood War of 1900, the city lost its membership, Brush took over the Cincinnati franchise and ran it from 1891 to 1902. Although he won no pennants, his leadership impressed his colleagues, who offered him the chance to redeem the Giants in 1902.

While laying plans to restore this once lucrative center, Brush was felled by a crippling stroke. Refusing to quit, he determined to crush the American League and made a portentous decision by naming John McGraw as manager. Like Brush, McGraw nursed a hatred for the Americans, having just been disciplined by Johnson for umpire-baiting. Avid for revenge, in 1902 he leaped at Brush's offer, leaving the American League Baltimore club in the lurch with four of their best players in tow.

As the third Giant manager in 1902, McGraw's best insurance was his three-year contract. With no chance to escape the cellar, he concentrated on fashioning a smooth-running machine that would function flawlessly at defense, pitching, and the hit-and-run offensive style. It was to be the classic deadball style, and until his men were capable of acting on their own, McGraw made most of the tactical decisions. Under this system, McGraw became a little Napoleon, but he proved his ability by leading Giant teams to ten pennants in his thirty-year tenure, thus turning the franchise into the league's most profitable one.

Possibly because of his own experiences with the pitching-poor Orioles of the 1890's, McGraw seemed obsessed with a desire for superb pitching. When he came to New York, he immediately terminated a predecessor's experiment aimed at converting Christy Mathewson into a first baseman. And because he saw potential greatness in the husky young Bucknell graduate, McGraw roomed with him on the road trips. One result was a lifelong friendship and a constant dialogue between two dedicated baseball students. "Matty" profited enormously from this interchange and soon became one of the superstars of American baseball.

In 1903, McGraw used Matty and Joe McGinnity, the great

A great competitor, pitcher Christy Mathewson made the New York Giants the dominant dynasty of the National League's silver age. "Matty" joined the Giants in 1900, and by the time he retired his combination of speed, control, and tricky "fadeaway" curve brought him 373 victories and a place in baseball's Hall of Fame. (George Brace, photographer)

pitching star who left Baltimore with McGraw, as the nucleus for an effective six-man hurling staff. Backing it were catchers Roger Bresnahan, Frank Bowerman, and Jack Warner. Bresnahan, dubbed "the Duke of Tralee," was the natural leader of this trio and an inventive genius both in catching tactics and innovations in equipment. If ruthlessness was needed to complement the Duke's intellectuality, McGraw could count on Bowerman, a surly man who once reputedly raced a woman for the last seat on a ferryboat.

In the infield, where McGraw himself still played third base, were Dan McGann, Bill Gilbert, and Steve Brodie. The outfielders included George Van Haltren, Sam Mertes, and George Brown. Emboldened by this team's upswing in 1903, McGraw turned to the trading market for five key men who he thought would insure the 1904 pennant. Among these, George (Hooks) Wiltse became a dependable pitcher, Art Devlin and Bill Dahlen added infield strength, and Moose McCormick and "Turkey" Mike Donlin fortified the outfield.

McGraw directed play from the bench and berated weaknesses as the 1904 Giants raced to the pennant, winning 106 and finishing 13 games ahead of the Chicago Cubs. Overpowering pitching was the major factor as "Iron Man" Joe McGinnity won 35 games, topping the 30 mark for the second straight year. Mathewson also won more than 30, and began a three-year mastery that produced

96 victories to class him with Cy Young, Jack Chesbro, Grover Cleveland Alexander, and Walter Johnson as the pitchers of this era to turn in 90 victories in a three-year span. But the season closed in discord as McGraw and Brush refused to meet the American League winner in the World Series. The decision embittered Giant players who wanted the extra money, but McGraw stubbornly refused to engage the "bushers."

To feud with the Americans was trouble enough, but in 1905 an intraleague battle pitted the Giants against the Pirates. With the latter showing signs of regaining their mastery, rivalry between these titans grew more heated. In Pittsburgh, newspapers called Mathewson a "sissy," and the Giants were bombarded by vegetables on the field and en route to their hotel. When McGraw protested, charges and countercharges mounted until the Pirates persuaded president Pulliam to suspend him. But Brush went to the courts and forced Pulliam to lift McGraw's suspension.

Meanwhile, the Giants kept on winning and by midseason controlled the race. At the end they posted 105 wins, 9 better than the Pirates. Once again, pitching was the deciding factor as Matty led the league with 31 wins, including a no-hit victory over the Cubs. During the year, the Giant offense improved, and Art Devlin led the base stealers with fifty-nine. To round out the year, the team scored a decisive Series victory as Giant pitching four times shut out the A's, with Matty accounting for twenty-seven scoreless innings.[5] This Series marked the beginning of a long and profitable regulated rivalry, under the new joint agreement, between the two leagues.

Flushed by success, McGraw ordered new uniforms for 1906 with the words "World Champions" emblazoned over the chests. The same proud slogan decorated the horse blankets that went with the team carriage. But if the purpose of this was to make rivals feel inferior, it backfired badly. Indeed, it may have been a challenge to the rising Chicago Cubs.

[5] Mrs. John McGraw, *The Real McGraw* (ed. by Arthur Mann), 193–211; Christy Mathewson, "How I Became a Big League Pitcher," in C. H. Claudy, *The Battle of Baseball,* 315–57; *National League Green Book,* 1962; *Spalding's Annual Base Ball Record,* 1908, pp. 63–65; Fitzgerald (ed.), *The National League,* 217–44.

Like the Giants and Pirates, the Cubs had undergone a sweeping organizational change. In the twenty years since Chicago's last pennant, wholesale changes in personnel had been tried without success. Neither owner Jim Hart's 1900 decision to change the club name to "Cubs," nor engaging successful Frank Selee as a manager helped. When both magical ploys failed, Hart sold out to ex-sportswriter Charles W. Murphy who was financed by Charles P. Taft, brother of the future American president.

Murphy took over in the midst of the 1905 race and released Selee, handing the management to Frank Chance, a solid-hitting first baseman. Chance knew the game and was a follower of the brainy "inside-play" gospel, as practiced by his two young infielders John Evers and Joe Tinker. "A bundle of nerves with the best brain in baseball" was sportswriter Hugh Fullerton's description of the wispy Evers. His lantern-jawed asceticism could easily have fitted into an El Greco grouping. Brilliant and opinionated, Evers feuded with mates and rivals, and for years his only communication with Tinker was a testy, "Give me the ball,—— ——!"[6] In spite of this, the pair combined with Chance and third baseman Harry Steinfeldt to evolve some of the headiest plays of the era. One tactic, designed to break the back of enemy sacrifice plays, called for the pitcher to throw outside, then for Chance to rush in and field the bunt while Evers covered first and Tinker guarded second. The usual elimination of the runner at second made the combination of Tinker-to-Evers-to-Chance a legendary one. Double plays sometimes resulted, but even this expert crew made few such plays. As a familiar defensive tactic, the double play awaited the coming age of the lively ball, when sharply hit balls, and resultant faster fielding made this electrifying play commonplace.

Chance's early strategy showed a sound grasp of realities and was popular with his players. In a bold move, he traded pitcher "Tornado Jake" Weimer to Cincinnati for Harry Steinfeldt, a hard-hitting third baseman. After that, another deal brought

[6] *Baseball Digest*, September, 1950; John J. Evers and Hugh S. Fullerton, *Touching Second: The Science of Baseball*, 56–72.

The most acclaimed infield in American baseball was that of the Chicago Cubs of the 1900's. From left to right, Harry Steinfeldt, third base; Joe Tinker, shortstop; John Evers, second base; and Frank Chance, first base and playing manager. In celebrating the artistry of the Tinker to Evers to Chance fielding combination, newsman Franklin P. Adams once described them as "a trio of bear cubs, fleeter than birds." (George Brace, photographer)

pitcher Orval Overall and catcher Pat Moran to Chicago, and a later trade with Brooklyn secured outfielder Jim Sheckard. These were key deals, but the club's best supply came from scout George Huff, then athletic director at the University of Illinois. It was Huff who put Chance on the trail of pitchers Jack Pfeister, Carl Lundgren, and Ed Ruelbach. Huff also alerted Chance to Frank "Wildfire" Schulte, a great outfield prospect.

With Chance directing the team from first base, the club in 1905 finished a distant third. Because standout pitching was lacking, few expected more of 1906, but early that year the baseball public heard talk about the wizardry of Mordecai Brown. Called "Three Finger" by the press because of a mutilating childhood accident, Brown turned his handicap into a pitching asset. A hard thrower, his unorthodox grip made for bewildering breaking pitches that he had taught himself to control. A shy man, at twenty-eight he was old by baseball standards, but once established he lasted to become an all-time great.

In 1906, Brown was practically invincible as he amassed a 26–6 record. With Pfeister and Jack Taylor each winning 20, Cub pitching ranked with that of any rival. Yet not until June did the Giants believe the Cub threat. Then came three straight victories over the Giants; the last was a 19–0 romp which one writer called "a disgrace to the National League." Giant fans also took offense, and soon the lowly American League Highlanders were outdrawing the Giants. Desperately, McGraw rallied his club, driving them to 13 straight wins in August, but the Cubs topped them with 14. Chance never let up; that year he drove the club to an all-time record of 116 wins and 36 losses—twenty games ahead of the Giants and twenty-three more than the Pirates.[7] It was an explosive debut for the third and last major dynasty of the silver age.

Now the National stage was set and the major characters announced; except for three brief forays by the supporting cast, the next fifteen pennants went to one of the three titans. But in 1906 the Cub superiority contributed to falling league attendance. Mean-

[7] *The Sporting News,* June 16, August 18, September 29, 1906; *Spalding's Annual Base Ball Record,* 1908, pp. 65–67, Evers and Fullerton, *op. cit.,* 60–70.

A crowd of 9,600 watches the Chicago Cubs play the New York Giants on August 18, 1906, in Chicago. Whether at home or on the road, the Cubs that year were invincible. Under manager Frank Chance, the team won a record 116 times and lost only 36, but, incredibly, dropped the World Series to their cross-town rivals, the "Hitless Wonders," the Chicago White Sox. (George Brace, photographer)

while, the American League staged a lively three-cornered fight finally won by the Chicago White Sox. The Cubs expected to make short work of these lightweights, but in the Series the Sox beat the Cubs four games to two. A popular victory, its David and Goliath aspect spiced many a Sunday School lesson and enshrined the "hitless wonders" as an American folk legend.

That winter, many old-time Chicago fans drew parallels between the recent Cub failure and the failures of Anson's Colts of the 1880's. But Chance came back grimly determined, and once again his club scaled the heights, winning without a .300 hitter on great pitching by Overall and Brown. The team record of 107 wins and 45 losses was 17 better than Pittsburgh's. Against the Tigers that fall, the Cubs swept the Series in four straight games.

Next year, 1908, the Cubs dropped behind the hard-driving Giants. By September Chance faced the formidable task of winning eleven of the last twelve games just to gain a tie. On the twenty-third the Cubs met the Giants at the Polo Grounds in a crucial game. In the last inning of a 1–1 game, the Giants broke through as Moose McCormick took base, and then "scored" on singles by Fred Merkle and Al Bridewell. However, Merkle failed to touch second on the Bridewell hit, turning short and running joyously to his dugout instead. Having been involved in a similar play only two weeks before, the alert Evers screamed for his outfielder to return the ball. To this day no one knows for sure if he got *the* ball, but he tagged second with *a* ball, then appealed to umpire Hank O'Day, the same arbiter whose judgment on the earlier play had been overruled. With fans and players milling around, O'Day called Merkle out, then ruled the game a tie because of darkness and the uproar.

The decision startled the baseball world. All the rest of his life, McGraw would say that this pennant had been stolen from him. As for the inconsolable nineteen-year-old Merkle, to his dying day he was known as "Bonehead." More tragic than this was the macabre reaction of league President Pulliam; public scorn for upholding the umpire probably contributed to his suicide in 1909.

The outcome of this frantic contest would have meant little had the Cubs not rallied to win eleven out of twelve games. By doing so, they tied the Giants and forced a play-off. The game was held on October 17 before a frenzied gathering of Giant fans at the Polo Grounds. As the game began, Mathewson opposed Pfeister, who was quickly replaced by Brown. With Brown pitching coolly in spite of the wild crowd, whose excesses caused police and firemen to bring in and use fire hoses, the Cubs rallied to win by a score of 4–2. Thus ended the most memorable campaign in American baseball history; the Cubs's follow-up Series victory over the Tigers was an anticlimax. But the two victories made for a National League love feast, and owner Murphy sweetened his players' share of the Series with an extra $10,000. It was well earned.[8]

In a much calmer race in 1909, the Cubs won 104 games to lead the Giants by 12 games, but Clarke's Pirates took the pennant with 110 victories. Except for a brilliant rookie pitcher, Charles "Babe" Adams, the Pirates' pitching staff was the same; other holdovers included Wagner, Clarke, and Leach. Among the newcomers were George Gibson, a durable catcher who caught in 151 games; Bill Abstein, "Dots" Miller, and Bob Byrne in the infield; and "Chief" Wilson in the outfield. For owner Dreyfuss, the victory was most welcome since he had just built Forbes Field, a triple-decker stadium seating 25,000. Much criticized for his baseball bullishness, Dreyfuss was vindicated on opening day when 30,338 jammed his new park. Equally bright was the campaign's ending when Adams won the decisive game of a hard-fought Series with the Tigers.

By 1910, popular interest in major-league baseball had soared so high that the league sought to extend the schedule from 154 to 168 games. When the Americans demurred, the Nationals returned to the now-classic 154-game format. In other ways, the format was familiar as Chance's Cubs regained the pennant on 104 victories, good enough to beat the runner-up Giants by 13 games. In topping the 100-game mark for the fifth straight year, Chicago entered the record books as baseball's first "500" club. This was a remarkable achievement won by the same combination of players first inducted back in 1906. But as so often happens when a baseball team becomes overconfident, a rival slapped them down. This time the young Athletics did it, downing the Cubs 4–1 in Series games. The defeat widened the growing rift between Chance and owner Murphy. Two years later Chance was fired, and a year after that Evers

[8] *Spalding's Annual Base Ball Record,* 1909, p. 36; Evers and Fullerton, *op. cit.,* 79–86; Lee Allen, *The National League Story,* 113–22.

and Tinker were released. Murphy himself was the next casualty.[9]

Because at this time the Pirates were affected by the same erosion processes, the Giants faced a golden opportunity. McGraw was completing a major rebuilding project in 1910. Gone by now were stars like McGinnity and Bresnahan, replaced by new faces like Fred Snodgrass and Josh Devore in the outfield; Art Fletcher, Larry Doyle, and Charles Herzog in the infield; and pitchers like "Rube" Marquard and catchers like John "Chief" Meyers.

Hand-picked, youthful, and educable, the young team was drilled in McGraw's system. Above all, he demanded submission to his will and after that long practice in sliding, place-hitting, and running. At McGraw's signalled command, pitchers altered their deliveries, runners broke for bases, and fielders shifted positions. This "inside baseball" made for efficiency, but the price was mechanical conformity. Bullied by McGraw until he shaped up, a surviving player knew automatically how to respond to a given situation. Under the circumstances there were few super heroes on the Giants, for McGraw alone stood out as the dictator.

Yet few could deny that the system won pennants. In the years 1911–13, McGraw's teams dominated the league. In those years Mathewson piled up seventy-three victories including twenty-five each in 1911 and 1913. Behind Matty were two other veterans from 1905, Wiltse and Red Ames, but there were also younger players. Rounding out the staff were pitchers Jeff Tesreau and Richard "Rube" Marquard. Like Matty, the Rube won seventy-three in these years.

To back these pitchers, the Giants unleashed a formidable batting attack, leading all rivals with team averages of .279, .286, and .273. Only in fielding did the Giants of 1911–13 yield to a rival. With such power the 1911 team won 99 to defeat the Cubs by 7½ games; the 1912 team won 103 to best the Pirates by 10; and, in 1913, 101 victories outdistanced the Phillies by 12½ games.

Ironically, this powerful aggregation failed to win a single World Series. Three times it collapsed, twice before Mack's Athletics, and

[9] *Spalding's Annual Base Ball Record,* 1911; Allen, *National League Story,* 135–36; Fitzgerald (ed.), *The National League,* 44–67, 101–27; *Spalding's Official Base Ball Guide,* 1925, p. 19.

once before the Red Sox. Nevertheless, the Giants ruled the National League. After finishing a successful world tour as a baseball missionary, McGraw basked amidst his acclaim as the prince of baseball managers.[10]

A turning point came in 1914. Ever since 1903, National League history had been written by these three great dynasties. So powerful was their sway that only three times in that era did an outside club climb as high as third place. The Phillies did it twice and even managed a distant second in 1913, an event that gave hope to the also-rans.

In retrospect, the world of 1914 was generally a time of hope for battered outsiders. In that year the death knell of the old royal dynasties of Europe had already begun to toll. If the guns of August shattered the old ruling pattern of the Western world, at least the aftermath of the ordeal opened an era in which the benefits of industrialism were available to more people.

In an odd way, the same theme of dying dynasties and rising little people was mirrored in the baseball war of 1914. At the outset, the three central baseball powers appeared solidly entrenched, but a closer look showed weaknesses. In Chicago, the disintegration of the famous Cub team had become increasingly evident. It began in 1912 when owner Murphy fired Chance and named Evers to succeed and culminated in the easing-out of Murphy himself. His passing in 1914 added to the Cubs's disorganization.[11]

Meanwhile, in Pittsburgh, manager Clarke now came under hostile criticism. Aging was the key factor in the Pirate decline. By 1914, Clarke's playing career was fading, and worse, so was Wagner's. In two years the Pirates would be looking for a new commander and crew.

Only New York seemed to weather the winds of change. Owner Brush died in 1912, but the club fell to his heirs, who named his son-in-law, Harry Hempstead, as president. Otherwise, with

[10] *Spalding's Annual Base Ball Record,* 1912, 1913, pp. 89–92, 1914, pp. 141–43, 170–75; *Spalding's Official Base Ball Guide,* 1925, p. 21; Fitzgerald (ed.), *The National League,* 217–44; Mrs. John McGraw, *op. cit.,* 226.

[11] *Baseball Magazine,* September, 1913, pp. 358–60.

McGraw in command, with Matty and Marquard as able pitchers, and with the acquisition of the All-American athlete, Indian Jim Thorpe, the dynasty looked impregnable. When McGraw returned from his world tour aboard the superliner, *Lusitania*, his world at least appeared to be right side up.

About 1910, Indian Jim Thorpe was considered the greatest athlete in American history. He began his big league baseball career with the New York Giants in 1913, but never made the regular lineup. In six seasons, ending in 1919, Thorpe posted a .252 batting average. (George Brace, photographer)

The Giants took an early and decisive lead in 1914. Matty was still a big winner and Marquard looked very strong. From the beginning the big "Rube" won steadily, and at midseason he won a twenty-one-inning pitching duel with Babe Adams at Pittsburgh, but after this tremendous effort he faded sharply, losing twelve straight. And now outsiders moved into contention.[12]

At the halfway point in July, the Giants still led, but the race was so close that even the last-place Boston Braves, ten games out, had hopes. Not since the 1890's did Boston fans have anything to cheer about. The American League War had left grievous wounds that had resisted the curative powers of a succession of Boston owners. Some of the owners tried changing the club's name. Since 1903, the club had been called "Beaneaters," then "Nationals," then "Doves," the latter a pacifist designation that became the butt of sportswriters' jokes. After that the team was named "Rustlers" in honor of an owner named Russell, but in 1911 under James Gaffney and John M. Ward the club took the more militant name of

[12] Mrs. John McGraw, *op. cit.*, 237–55; *The Sporting News,* July 23, 1914.

"Braves." However, two last places and a fifth-place finish made a mockery of the bold label.

Nevertheless, some Boston players lived up to the name. Bravest of all was the manager, George Stallings, a courtly Dr. Jekyll off the field, but a veritable Mr. Hyde in the dugout. Never a winner in the majors, he had bobbed up and down since the 1880's, acquiring in the process a vast store of baseball knowledge and a reputation as a hard-driving leader.

When Stallings picked up discarded John Evers for $25,000, it was like adding a war chief to the Braves. Appointed captain, Evers quickly took charge and tightened the inner defense by teaming up with shortstop Walter "Rabbit" Maranville. Maranville was a born actor whose funny antics time and again lifted team spirits. Always good for a laugh were his pantomime routines aimed at goading slow-working pitchers and harassing enemy fielders. A laughing jumping jack on the base paths, he once dived safely back to first between an umpire's legs.

Among ordinary warriors of the Braves, the pitching trio of Dick Rudolph, Bill James, and George Tyler stood out, as did catcher Hank Gowdy and infielders Charles Schmidt and Red Smith. The others were undistinguished; indeed, the outfield was so uncertain that Stallings platooned eleven different men at various times during the season.[13]

On the nineteenth of July, this nondescript tribe stood last, eleven games behind the Giants. But with Stallings and Evers as sachems, the team massacred its opponents, winning sixty of its last seventy-six games for a total of ninety-four victories. It was good enough to top the second-place Giants by ten and a half games. Stallings fought rivals, umpires, and his own men in working the miracle of 1914. Sometimes loyal fans lent assistance, as on Labor Day when they nearly mobbed Snodgrass of the Giants for thumbing his nose at "Lefty" Tyler.

The Boston legend reached epic proportions when Stallings whipped his tribe into an avenging mood in the World Series. With Evers's connivance, Stallings told his players that Manager Mack

[13] *Baseball Magazine,* August, 1914, p. 32; Allen, *National League Story,* 134–42.

had refused to allow them to practice at Shibe Park. This blatant lie infuriated the men, who went out and beat the Athletics four straight. The victory, gained in approved American fashion, brought typical lavish rewards like a five-year contract for Stallings, a Chalmers auto for Evers, and a brand-new ball park named "Braves Field" for this team of many names.[14]

The trouble with miracles is that they are beyond human control. Next year's baseball miracle was not destined to happen in Boston's new park. Instead, this supernatural force shifted to dilapidated Baker Field, home of the Philadelphia Phillies. A showplace when it was built in 1887, the field became a pitcher's chamber of horrors with the advent of the lively ball. Nor were its penurious owners about to replace the tiny park. The club had never won a pennant, and after 1903 its fortunes sank as those of Mack's Athletics soared. Discouraging to profits and hopes, such competition persuaded Reach and Rogers to sell. However, the club fell into weaker hands, including those of Horace Fogel, a man whose enthusiasm was unaccompanied by necessary building capital. Naturally the club foundered, and if we are to believe a Philadelphia sportswriter the most memorable event between 1903 and 1911 was the birth of a baby boy in the ladies' room of the park.

After Fogel's ouster in 1911, the club passed into the hands of William Baker. Only moderately wealthy, his reluctance to part with even a little won him a reputation as a penny-pinching owner. Yet in 1915 there were enough good players on hand to respond to a good leader, and there was one in the person of Pat Moran. Known as "Whiskey Face" for good reason, Moran was a first-rate strategist and an irritating "jockey," who reviled opponents with clever insults. Moran prescribed diets, forced exercise, and exacted obedience to build a fighting team around a great pitcher, Grover Cleveland Alexander, and slugger George "Gavvy" Cravath. After a strenuous southern training program, the Phillies grabbed an early lead and finished seven games ahead of the miracle Braves,

[14] *The Sporting News*, August 20, September 10, 24, October 1, 15, 1914; Fitzgerald (ed.), *The National League*, 68–100; *Spalding's Annual Base Ball Record*, 1915, pp. 22–23, 44–46, 97.

led by Alexander's thirty-one victories which included 12 shutouts and 241 strikeouts. Although Alexander's pitching was the big story, outfielder Cravath took aim at Baker Field's short fences and hit twenty-four home runs, an unprecedented total that heralded the coming "long ball" style of play. Another strength was the tight infield play of Fred Luderus at first, Bert Niehoff at second, Milton Stock at third, and Dave Bancroft at shortstop. Such was the making of the first Phillies championship, but the miracle ended there. For in the Series, the Red Sox methodically cut the Phillies down in four straight games.

Like the Braves of 1915, the Phillies battled hard the next year to retain their title. In winning thirty-three games, the superb Alexander finished a three-year skein of ninety-one victories for a new record. Nevertheless, his mates were beaten by the pennant-starved Brooklyn Robins amidst charges that the Giants played dead in a late-season series with the Robins to help their crosstown mates land the pennant.[15]

In 1916 the Robins were managed by Wilbert Robinson, McGraw's old Oriole sidekick whose popularity accounted for the club's name. Before his hiring in 1913 by owner Charles Ebbets, the team had been variously known as "Bridegrooms," "Dodgers," or "Superbas." Never a rich man, Ebbets had scrimped and saved to build a modern park which was called Ebbets Field. The park was opened in 1908 on the site of "Pigtown," a notorious slum; it was considered a white elephant until Robinson began to draw fans with his antics. As a manager, he was a walking sideshow, but his buffoonery masked a keen baseball sense, including unsurpassed skill in developing pitchers.

Not surprisingly, pitching was the strongpoint of the 1916 Robins. Ed Pfeffer won twenty-five games to pace a reconstructed squad that included castoffs Jack Coombs and Marquard. Supported by solid hitting from Casey Stengel, Zack Wheat, and Jake Daubert, the team topped the Phillies and the resurgent Giants. But it was the Giants, winners of two stretches of seventeen and

[15] *Spalding's Annual Base Ball Record,* 1916, pp. 59–63, 108–17; Fitzgerald (ed.), *The National League,* 128–49; Lieb, *op. cit.,* 95–139.

twenty-six consecutive games in 1916, who helped the Robins win. By dropping a crucial series to the Robins, the Giants raised cries of "fix." Even McGraw stalked off the field calling his men "quitters." This incident, coupled with the Robins' defeat in the World Series, left a lingering odor in Brooklyn.[16]

America's involvement in the World War hurt baseball in 1917. So all-absorbing was America's preparation that fainthearted owners like Baker of the Phillies despaired of profits. Despite a close second-place finish in 1916, he snapped at an offer to sell Alexander to the Cubs. Regarded by fans as a supreme act of treason, the sale of Alexander started the Phillies on a thirty-year exile into the depths of the second division. Other owners also feared the prospect of losses from baseball promotion during wartime; even the great dynasts shuddered. In 1918, Giant owner Harry Hempstead sold out to Charles Stoneham, and as part of the aftermath, in 1921 Chicago owner Charles Weeghman sold to William Wrigley, the chewing-gum king.

Nevertheless, the great dynasties were in the best position to survive. In New York, McGraw doggedly continued to rebuild after dropping aging stars like Mathewson. After a last-place finish in 1915, his 1916 team rebounded sharply with the help of newcomers like pitcher Ferdie Schupp and hitters George Burns and Benny Kauff. By 1917, the Giants were strong enough to post ninety-eight wins for an easy victory, but in the World Series the team was beaten by the White Sox. This fourth consecutive Series defeat took much of the gloss from McGraw's reputation.

The full impact of wartime austerity hit baseball in 1918. For a time, the very continuance of the game was in doubt; as it was, the season was shortened and the Series only belatedly and grudgingly tolerated. Played under the handicaps of declining attendance, scarcity of talent, and player demands for more money, the season of 1918 was a nightmare for owners. The over-all quality of play was down, but the Cubs, under the management of Fred Mitchell, took an early lead and won by ten and one-half games.

[16] *Spalding's Annual Base Ball Record*, 1917, pp. 37ff.; Fitzgerald (ed.), *The National League*, 3–43; Allen, *National League Story*, 145–46; Mrs. John McGraw, *op. cit.*, 259–60.

John J. McGraw, the "Napoleonic" manager of the New York Giants, surveys his charges at the Polo Grounds in New York. In McGraw's thirty-three years as Giants manager, his teams captured ten National League pennants but won only three world championships. (George Brace, photographer)

Having the only twenty-game pitchers, Jim Vaughn and Claude Hendrix, helped that year, but the team fell before the pitching of Babe Ruth of the Red Sox in the Series. This was the fourth consecutive time an American League team had humbled the Nationals.[17]

That fall, the gloom of a dismal season mingled with the gloom of war. Then came the Armistice and quick demobilization, yet baseball owners remained pessimistic. They jointly decided to play a shortened season, a decision soon to be regretted in the light of the great resurgence of baseball interest. This was a pleasant surprise that would soon be mixed with others, pleasant and unpleasant, including the great scandal arising from the 1919 World Series and the great public interest in a new free-swinging style of play.[18] As baseball men came to understand the postwar world of change, they would realize that the style of the silver age had disappeared as completely as the old European dynasties.

[17] *Spalding's Annual Base Ball Record,* 1918, pp. 31–42, 1919, pp. 30–60; Allen, *National League Story,* 150–57; Fitzgerald (ed.), *The National League,* 101–27.

[18] *Spalding's Annual Base Ball Record,* 1920, pp. 96–147.

3

Heroes of the Silver Age

At least one baseball observer would have welcomed the face-lifting changes wrought by the First World War. Even before the outbreak of the war, sportswriter William A. Phelon complained about the deadly boring style of baseball play. Writing in the testy style of one who sees at last that his best years were devoted to a spurious activity, Phelon declared that baseball was fossilized. Except for minor changes in equipment and pitching tactics, he saw no changes in the sport in twenty-five years.

It is possible that personal dissatisfactions may have provoked his outburst, but Phelon had a point. Since the 1890's all major-league teams had followed the gospel of scientific baseball. Phelon warned that unless forceful changes were introduced, bored fans would turn to livelier spectacles like football and basketball.[1]

1 *Baseball Magazine,* June, 1914, pp. 53–55.

Optimistic voices were louder, however, and Jeremiahs like Phelon were ignored. How much more satisfying to listen to Walt Whitman sing the praises of American baseball: "I see great things in baseball, it's our game—the American game. It will take our people out of doors, fill them with oxygen, give them a larger physical stoicism . . . and be a blessing to us."

Whitman's description was couched in lofty terms, a literary privilege unfortunately appropriated by the 1907 historical commission. Convened to settle the matter of baseball's origins, the delegates discarded Chadwick's reasonable evolutionary argument and sanctioned the Doubleday myth which proclaimed Cooperstown, New York, to be the game's birthplace. Incredibly, the explanation was widely accepted and continues to be touted by many sportswriters of today.[2]

Along with the professional mythmakers, other baseball missionaries sought to sanctify the silver-age style. In 1913, McGraw and Comiskey launched baseball's third major revival by heading a mission to spread the game to foreign lands. Ignoring the previous failures of Wright and Spalding, these two later emissaries won at least one staunch convert. Cordially welcomed in Japan, they are to be credited with boosting baseball's growing reputation in the Land of the Rising Sun. But in Europe there was the usual polite, bored reception, and the teams returned only months before increasing unrest was to break out into sharp conflict.

Myths and missionaries aside, the best refutation of Phelon's doleful forecast was the popularity of the World Series. Revived in 1903 almost as an afterthought, the Series was originally designed to serve as a gesture of good will and faith in the National Agreement. To the surprise of owners, it generated an annual baseball delirium. Dazzled by profits that climbed to half a million dollars in 1912, owners voted to impose a division. In 1918, owners and players on the second-, third-, and fourth-place teams in each league won shares of the pie.[3]

[2] *Ibid.,* April, 1911, p. 84; *Spalding's Official Base Ball Guide,* 1908, pp. 35–49; *Spalding's Annual Base Ball Record,* 1910, pp. 261–64; Voigt, *American Baseball: From Gentleman's Sport to the Commissioner System,* 5–7.

[3] Ted Sullivan, *History of the World's Tour, Chicago White Sox and New York*

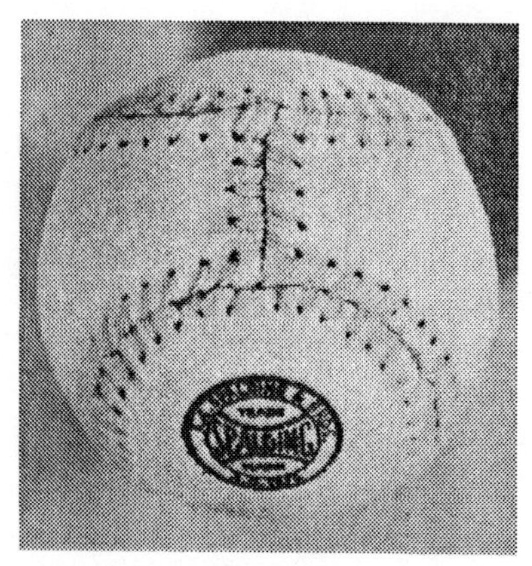

When A. G. Spalding & Bros. was founded in 1876, the company produced baseballs of this type. Under a "putting-out system" of piece labor, the balls were hand sewn by women in their own homes, with poor quality control. (Courtesy A. G. Spalding & Bros.)

But poetry and profit notwithstanding, baseball remained a stereotyped spectacle. Indeed, resistance to change was a *leitmotiv* of the silver age. Certainly the rules stayed the same, except for a 1901 change that found the Americans accepting the National code and thus adopting the foul-strike rule. In that same year, both leagues agreed that a runner was out if he passed another on the bases and that a batter was out if he jumped from one side of the plate to another in order to harass a pitcher. Not only did rules remain largely the same, but in one sense both leagues turned the clocks back ten years when they returned to the single-umpire system with all its evils. Happily, umpires were not lonely for long; the double-umpire system was penitently restored before the first decade of the silver age was out.

Despite all the resistance to change, innovations in equipment forced alterations in playing style. Like most Americans, baseball men liked new gadgets, and better gloves and livelier balls found their way into the game. Although both played their part, it was the lively ball with its rubberized covering and cork center that helped most to end the scientific style of the silver age.

One of the most criticized aspects of the silver-age style was the weak offense. According to Johnny Evers, a batter of this age was supposed to "push, poke, shove, and chop" at the ball to push across the run or two needed for victory. If this made for low batting

Giants, 5–89; *Spalding's Official Base Ball Guide,* 1914, pp. 40–51; *Baseball Magazine,* November, 1914, pp. 85–88; *The Sporting News,* October 10, 1907, October 19, 26, 1911; Lieb, *op. cit.,* 84–86, 100.

In 1910, Spalding introduced the first cork-centered baseballs for the World Series. Continued use of these balls over the next decade ended the "deadball" era and began the "big bang" style of play. By 1926 the "cushion cork center" ball was officially adopted by both leagues. From then on, generations of fans watched home runs aplenty as the style of play shifted dramatically. (Courtesy A. G. Spalding & Bros.)

averages, managers accepted the drawback and often fined free swingers for disobeying orders. Mostly, managers wanted only to get a man on, even if it meant his walking, getting hit by a pitch, or faking the experience of being hit. Once the runner was on base, the standard managerial stratagem was to advance him to second by bunting, sacrificing, or stealing. The bunt was the favorite tactical weapon. Joe McCloskey of the Cardinals once ordered seventeen consecutive bunts against a Cub pitcher. Whatever this tactic lacked in imagination, the stubborn determination involved eventually forced the Cubs to commit errors which handed the Cardinals the two runs that won the game.

Some players chafed under the discipline of this style, but unless a man was a masterful hitter, he either obeyed or faced release. Even under so stifling a system, some batters cherished their hits and the clubs that made them. To big Ed Delehanty, his favorite bat "Big Betsy" was almost a living thing, and a serious hitter like Cobb not only selected the wood for his bats, but supervised their construction, and then spent loving hours "honing" them with "a steer bone." It was probably the tight discipline imposed on most batters that explains why they lavished so much care on their bats.

A psychologist might have explained this in terms of sublimation. Certainly, it was an age which favored pitching and defense above free-swinging batting.[4]

The predominance of defense over offense evoked protests from writers such as Hugh Fullerton who argued that the game "needs more dash, less mechanical work, more brains by individuals, and fewer orders from the bench."[5] If these were not forthcoming, Fullerton feared that baseball, like the California Condor, would be heading toward extinction. But batters were a tough breed, and a few were aggressive enough to resist the deadening discipline. Among them were sluggers like Delehanty, Wagner, Sam Crawford, and Lajoie, all of whom swung for distance. Yet it was their fate that their hardest blows fell for doubles and triples because of the dead ball. Most batters preferred to challenge the infield defenses by chopping, poking, and pushing at the ball, counting on deception and speed to beat out hits. Among the masters of this style were men like Bobby Veach, "Dummy" Hoy, "Rabbit" Maranville, and Evers.

2. The Age of Ty Cobb

Fortunately for the future of American baseball, there was a giant among the batting pygmies. In this age, nobody stood taller than Tyrus Raymond Cobb, whose batting prowess and fiery personality provided thrills aplenty for baseball fans. As a batter, Cobb terrorized pitchers for twenty-three years while he rewrote all previous records in compiling a lifetime average of .367. This feat easily put him at the head of the army of ten thousand major leaguers who had performed since 1871. Cobb's daring as a base runner also produced the amazing total of 892 stolen bases.

[4] *Spalding's Annual Base Ball Record,* 1911, pp. 31–35.

[5] Evers and Fullerton, *op. cit.*, 140–80; Claudy, *op. cit.*, 4–23, 29–58.

With Ty Cobb and Sam Crawford as partners, Bobby Veach made Detroit's outfield one of the most formidable offensive units in baseball history. Shown here wearing a Tiger road uniform in 1915, the left-handed-hitting Veach lines one out. His .310 average in sixteen years of play ranks him as one of the game's great unsung heroes. (Courtesy Detroit Tigers, American League)

"Tyrus the Greatest" poses at Detroit's Bennett Park soon after 1910. As a batter, the left-handed Cobb had no equal. His lifetime batting average, the highest of any Hall of Fame member, was .367. Cobb played twenty-two years with the Tigers and finished his career in 1928, at the age of forty-one, hitting .323 for Mack's Athletics. (Courtesy Detroit Tigers, American League)

More than this, Cobb had a driving, combative spirit that galvanized teammates, rivals, and fans. When he took the field, everybody reacted either favorably or unfavorably to his daring *élan*. So cunning was he that none of the classic scientific defenses held him down. If opponents played back against him, he choked up on his bat and bunted; if they moved up on him, he slashed long hits. Once on base Cobb upset pitchers and infielders by his base stealing. He was the sovereign player of the silver age—a master of all the arts and tactics of offensive play.

On the other hand, his driving zeal for perfection gave him no rest. As the game's chief drawing card, he was exalted over all others, but his fierce pride earned him alienation and envy. Although both are the lot of any superstar, Cobb occupied a special niche as the hot-tempered devil of baseball. His early years with Detroit were friendless and punctuated by bruising fist fights; even his roommate recoiled at his "rotten disposition."[6] As a rookie in 1906, he suffered severely because nobody sought to understand what prompted his rebelliousness. Had they tried, they might have learned how hard he had taken his father's tragic death. He had been shot down by Cobb's mother, who mistook him for a burglar. The loss of this father brought a heavy burden of grief on the rookie who always doubted the manner and motive for his father's death. Cobb shouldered his intolerable burden alone, along with hazing by his mates and his fear of failure. It was not surprising that he batted poorly in 1906, but his humiliation only drove him to try harder.[7] He ceaselessly learned, unlearned, studied, and

[6] Evers and Fullerton, *op. cit.*, 168–80; Ring Lardner, "Tyrus the Greatest," *American Mercury*, June, 1915.

[7] Ritter, *op. cit.*, 47–69.

taught himself the tricks of the game. Eventually his mastery won the rangy six-footer a star's salary which he prudently invested in the Coca-Cola company, a move that eventually made him a millionaire. Most men would have mellowed at such a turn of fortune, but Cobb in retirement was embittered to the point of doubting his choice of a career. At this stage, he told James T. Farrell that if he had his life to live over, he would have chosen a medical career.[8]

That such a man became an idol of the fans and the personification of silver-age baseball is an index to the changing values of the American people. In Cobb the public had a hero in the style of the urban industrial age—a combative personality with a ruthless win-or-else spirit, who was, above all, a financial success. Certainly in Cobb, President Theodore Roosevelt's doctrine of the strenuous life found its athletic fulfillment. Perhaps this explains why he towered over Wagner or Cy Young. Both were brilliant, as was the graceful and flashy Lajoie,[9] but none did so much so well and with such dash. So successful was the Cobb formula that even brilliant rivals seemed ordinary by comparison.

Because lesser figures resented Cobb's towering personality, they tried to drag him down. In 1910, as he pursued his fourth consecutive batting title in a hot race with Lajoie, members of the Browns conspired to help Lajoie win the honor. In a final doubleheader with Cleveland, the Browns deliberately handed Lajoie the opportunity to bunt his way to the title. Happily for baseball, Cobb won by a narrow margin, but the flagrant display hurt the American League and led to disciplinary action from President Johnson.

Anti-Cobb sentiment welled up in other ways. Roasted by fans and players alike, Cobb fought them both hand to hand. Once an ugly feud with two Giant players threatened to lead to bloodshed. On another occasion, Cobb rushed into the stands and struck an insulting fan who turned out to be physically handicapped. Cobb was suspended for this act, and his mates went on strike in his

[8] Interview, James Farrell with D. Voigt; Interview, Lee Allen with D. Voigt; Cobb and Stump, *op. cit.*, 9–13, 32–48; Allen, *American League Story,* 63; *Baseball Digest,* April, 1946, pp. 57–58; *New York Times,* January 28, 1966.

[9] *New York Times,* February 8, 10, 1959.

defense. After the shorthanded Tigers lost one game, the incident ended with the strikers having to pay heavier fines than Cobb's.

That so much heroism and villainy were combined in one human being underscores the complexity of modern American hero worship. No longer, it seemed, could one man embody all the qualities the fans were seeking; instead what was needed was a variety of qualities, and baseball provided these in overwhelming abundance.

For the rural-minded fans there were strong farm-boy types like Crawford or Wagner; for the romantics seeking a dashing French musketeer there was the flashy, handsome Lajoie;[10] for those who admired grace and power there was Ed Delehanty; for those seeking collegiate sophistication there was Eddie Collins of the Athletics; for the primitivists there was the highly touted Indian athlete, Jim Thorpe, who failed to land a regular berth with the Giants. For raw naked power there was Joe Jackson, a foul-mouthed, illiterate "linthead" from a southern milltown. Unkindly characterized as "Ty Cobb—from the neck down," Jackson was often goaded by fans who asked him to spell simple words, a cruel treatment that drove him to unprintable replies. Finally, the anti-hero seekers found identity in zany pitchers like the unmanageable Waddell and later in the equally difficult "Bugs" Raymond. In short, the silver age offered a cafeteria line of hero-types, but Cobb was the one matchless hero of the era.[11]

Had there been no Cobb to rule the silver age, some pitcher would probably have become the superstar, since brilliant pitching otherwise dominated the era. In adapting to the extended pitching distance forced on them in the 1890's, pitchers used a variety of natural and artificial tricks to cow batters. Among the natural tools were speed, curves, and trick deliveries like the knuckle ball. These were baffling enough, but the artificial devices were even more bewildering. Pitchers boldly circumvented the rule forbidding the soiling of balls and utilizing spitballs, shine balls, emery balls, and paraffin balls. Not that all of these were needed, for as Ed Walsh

10 Arthur Daley, "The Big Frenchman," *ibid.,* February 10, 1959.

11 *Baseball Magazine,* May, 1915, p. 56, March, 1916, pp. 53–67; "Thorpe in Baseball," *Literary Digest,* February 15, 1913; Arthur Daley, *Times at Bat. A Half Century of Baseball,* 30–33; Ritter, *op. cit.,* 50–51.

discovered, one could get by with a good "spitter." As others learned the truth of this discovery, the pitch became the most practiced and protested of all artificial deliveries.[12]

As with many a baseball innovation, it is futile to search for the inventor of the spitter. Walsh, one of the most successful users, credited an obscure teammate for teaching him the "cuspidorious curve." For maximum efficiency, Walsh threw the moist pitch hard, which made it break unpredictably on both batter and catcher. Catching Walsh was an unforgettable experience according to Bill Sullivan, who suffered to learn the puzzling down and out break. But batters suffered more, and in 1908 Walsh used the pitch to win forty games, a mark untouched since. Others rushed to learn the weapon and, in contrast to Walsh, used slippery elm or tobacco juice to stimulate the flow of saliva.[13]

By 1908 so many spitballs were flying that John B. Foster, editor of the influential *Spalding's Guide*, held a "spitball symposium" to protest the menace. For the most part, objectors decried the ugliness of the pitch, but weakened their case with terrible puns. Moreover, in urging a ban on "the salivated shoot" or "slobber-coated sphere," few could say how to abolish it. "Into the cuspidor with it," was the best suggestion, but to this day pitchers continue to smuggle it in.[14]

What made the spitter so controversial was that it spawned other artificial deliveries. By 1909 pitchers and infielders used a variety of "doctoring" devices to make a ball break freakishly. Included were sanding with emery paper, soaking with licorice or tobacco juice, waxing with paraffin, greasing with hair oil, and cutting with sharpened belt buckles. All of these produced abnormally breaking pitches. Not surprisingly, these were the first to be outlawed, but not until 1920 were enough votes marshalled to ban the spitter. Even then the ban was not retroactive, and practitioners

[12] National Broadcasting Company, "Today Show," June 9, 1967.

[13] *Baseball Magazine*, March, 1913, pp. 41–59, May, 1913, p. 68, August, 1913; *Baseball Digest*, September, 1950, pp. 71–72. Still offered for sale are "Thayer's Slippery Elm Lozenges," which the author used to determine the effect on saliva flow.

[14] *Spalding's Official Base Ball Guide*, 1909, pp. 35–51; *Baseball Magazine*, November, 1913.

like Jack Quinn and Burleigh Grimes were allowed to ply their moist trade until they retired in the 1930's.[15]

The banning of artificial pitches helped bring on a batting revolution in the 1920's. Badly battered, pitchers countered with legal trick deliveries like the knuckle ball and palm ball. Called the "dry spitter," the knuckle ball was a slow-breaking ball that baffled batters. In throwing it, a pitcher gripped the ball with his knuckles or fingernails; either way, the effect was to take the spin off the ball and make it break erratically, sometimes changing directions more than once as it floated toward the plate. Mixing these deliveries with bread-and-butter pitches like a fast ball or a curve enabled crafty hurlers like Ed Cicotte to remain the equal of any batter.

Actually, at no time did artificial tricksters outdo the great natural pitchers. After all, it was the fast ball and curve that made super heroes out of Young, Alexander, Wood, McGinnity, and Mathewson. Matty also used a variation of the curve, his devastating "fadeaway," which he learned as a sandlotter. To throw it, Matty used a two-fingered grip and slid the ball off the thumb with a sharp leftward twist of the wrist, causing the pitch to break in on the fists of a right-handed batter.[16]

Mathewson was at his peak when the hard-throwing sidearmer, Grover Cleveland Alexander, broke in with the 1911 Phillies at twenty-four years of age. Despite an epileptic condition which sometimes attacked him while on the mound, and despite a growing taste for liquor, Alexander pitched eighty shutouts and 250 victories in the years 1911–21. His winning formula was a blend of good control and a "live" sidearm fast ball. A workhorse, Alexander lasted until 1930, and by then his victory total of 373 wins tied him with Mathewson.[17]

Alexander's debut coincided with the retirement of the great

15 Cobb and Stump, *op. cit.*, 85–86; *Spalding's Official Base Ball Guide*, 1921, p. 17.

16 *Baseball Magazine,* July, 1908, pp. 7–8; *Reach's Official Base Ball Guide*, 1911, p. 69; Claudy, *op. cit.,* 315–51; Evers and Fullerton, *op. cit.,* for descriptions of pitches thrown.

17 *Baseball Bat Bag,* 1921; Mrs. G. C. Alexander to Editor, *Time,* October 14, 1967.

Denton True "Cy" Young, whose total of 511 major-league victories is unsurpassed. Like Charles "Kid" Nichols, Vic Willis, and several others, Young was a holdover from the feudal age. As a rookie, he depended on a fast ball that was so hot his catcher used a piece of beefsteak to cushion its impact. Later, when his fast ball lost some of its smoke, Young depended on control and an uncanny ability to keep batters off stride with his changing speeds. Because of his adaptability, the Ohio farmer lasted as a winning pitcher until he was more than forty-five. Even though he was a hero to fans in Cleveland and Boston, Young was colorless, imperturbable, and ruthlessly efficient. A stickler for sobriety, he drank coffee and kept the sort of hours that vindicated the advice of Sunday School teachers. A gentleman farmer during the off-season, Young shunned publicity and invested his savings in order to live comfortably until well into his eighties. As a hero-type, he kept alive the rural, Protestant life-model so often subverted by the earthy antics of pitchers like Alexander or Waddell.[18]

In 1907, as Young celebrated his fortieth birthday by moving toward another twenty-victory season, youthful Walter Perry Johnson joined the Senators. Signed by an injured catcher on scouting duty for Griffith, Johnson was a hard-throwing farm boy in the same heroic mold as Young. Like Young, he entered the majors with little more than a blazing fast ball, but after two years of maltreatment by bunting batters, Johnson learned his trade. By 1910 his blazing speed and fielding agility aroused the baseball world. When the American League began keeping earned-run averages in 1913, Johnson posted a 1.09 mark for 346 innings, a record that still stands. He won twenty games that season and was to better that mark for the next nine years. A giant on a team of pygmies, Johnson waited until 1924 to enter a World Series. But he was always a hero to Washington fans, and his lifetime total of 414 victories is second only to that of the great Young.

To bat against the fireballing Johnson was a test for the bravest batter, but to a rookie it was an unforgettable experience. Facing

[18] *Baseball Magazine,* September, 1908, pp. 38–45; *The Sporting News,* January 21, 1945; *Baseball Digest,* January, 1949, pp. 75–76.

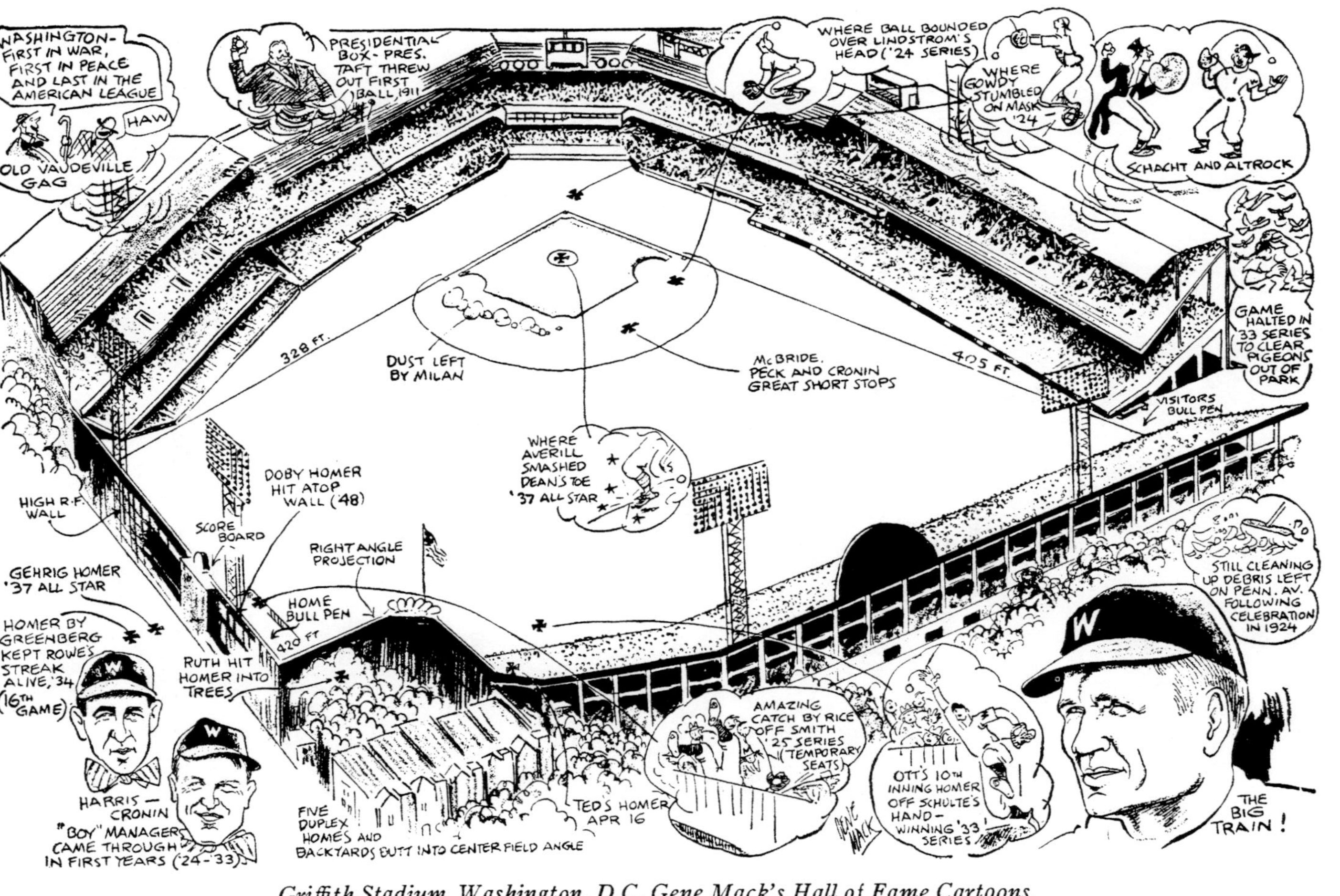

Griffith Stadium, Washington, D.C. Gene Mack's Hall of Fame Cartoons,

the "Big Train" for the first time in 1916, Jimmy Dykes never saw the first pitch and was amazed when told by the umpire to take his base. When Dykes asked why, the umpire pointed to his cap, which had been clipped by the pitch and knocked completely around so that the bill faced backwards.[19]

Johnson's only rival as a speedball pitcher in 1908 was nineteen-year-old Joe Wood who joined the Red Sox that year. Called "Smokey Joe," Wood was nursed along until 1911, when he won twenty-three games. The next year he hit his peak, winning thirty-four and equalling Johnson's sixteen-game winning streak, while pitching Boston to the pennant. Acclaimed the best right-handed pitcher in the game, Wood developed arm trouble the following year. When his arm failed to respond, he switched to outfielding and later became a regular with Cleveland. His outfielding never matched his pitching, but his successful switch made him a model of the virtues of hard work and determination.[20]

An authentic, if meteoric, hero of the silver age, Wood has yet to be inducted into baseball's Cooperstown shrine. Nevertheless, it is safe to use Hall of Fame admissions as an indicator of the most popular heroes of this era. That it was a pitcher's age is evidenced by the selection of Young, Mathewson, McGinnity, Alexander, Chesbro, Brown, Walsh, Griffith, Bender, and Plank. All were well-known heroes on pennant-winning teams, but also elected were such standouts as Eppa Rixey, Alexander's teammate on the Phillies, spitballers Burleigh Grimes and Urban "Red" Faber, and that brilliant anti-hero, Rube Waddell.

Only two catchers won places in this age of outstanding catchers. These were Roger Bresnahan of the Giants, Cardinals, and Cubs, and Ray Schalk, the peppery catcher of the White Sox who battled valiantly but unsuccessfully to right the pitchers who were bent on throwing the 1919 World Series.

Naturally, the Hall of Fame lists Wagner at the head of the great infielders of the silver age. But the Dutchman shares honors with

[19] *Baseball Magazine,* December, 1912, pp. 25–28, 104–106; *The Sporting News,* December 18, 1946; *Baseball Digest,* January-February, 1957, p. 54; Morris A. Bealle, *The Washington Senators,* 72.

[20] *Baseball Magazine,* September, 1920, pp. 61–67; Ritter, *op. cit.,* 146–61.

men like Baker and Collins of the Athletics, Maranville of the Braves, Tinker, Evers, and Chance of the Cubs, and Lajoie of the Cleveland "Naps."

Cobb leads all outfielders of the time, but two of his mates, Crawford and Harry Heilmann, are enshrined with him. The latter owed a great debt to Cobb who managed the Tigers as he struggled to make the grade. It was Cobb who corrected Heilmann's batting faults and helped him become a four-time batting champion in the 1920's. Thus, Cobb overshadows all, including Speaker, who ended Cobb's string of nine straight batting titles, and Elmer Flick, the batting hero in the years before Cobb arrived. Indeed, the Tiger management once nearly traded Cobb for Flick, a deal that if consummated would certainly have ranked as the boner of the century. Finally, even the lone National League outfielder of the Hall of Fame of this age, Max Carey, who achieved renown as a base stealer, was outstripped by Cobb in that specialty.

Such a plenitude of heroes suggests that the silver age was a distinctive epoch in baseball history, but it should be remembered that all these heroes were evolutionary products of nineteenth-century practices. Indeed, the first decade of the era was dominated by stars whose best marks came during the feudal age. As tutors to Cobb, Mathewson, and Wagner, such Hall of Fame heroes as Nichols, Hugh Duffy, Willie Keeler, Jess Burkett, and Ed Delehanty deserve mention, along with infielders like Jennings, McGraw, and Bobby Wallace.[21]

But our focus upon baseball's brightest galaxy ought not to obscure the lesser stars who sparkled brightly for brief periods, or even in a single crucial game. After all, it was just one game that stamped Fred Merkle as the anti-hero of the century. Indeed, that black day of September 23, 1908, introduced the epithet "bonehead" into the American language. It had previously been "an anemic and almost meaningless word"; but shortened to "boner" it became a favorite description of a pathetic performance.[22] For what it was worth, Merkle at least was not alone. Joining him

21 Robert Smith, *Baseball's Hall of Fame,* 27–132.

22 Mark Sullivan, *Our Times: The United States, 1900–1925*, III, 540–42.

were anti-heroes like Heinie Zimmermann, for his ludicrous World Series performance, and Carl Mays, the pitcher whose errant delivery struck and killed Ray Chapman of Cleveland in 1920.

Far more in tune with the dreams of aspiring players were the brief but heroic performances of men like Stan Coveleskie of the Phillies, whose pitching earned him the title of "Giant killer." Nor were the Giants excluded from the roll call of lesser heroes. A darling of the Broadway set was "Turkey" Mike Donlin, a good hitter, who married one of the most beloved actresses of the day, Mabel Hite. For this achievement, fans screamed, "Oh, you Mabel's Mike!" even when Donlin made a routine play. But the story has a sad ending as Mike took to drink and tuberculosis took his beloved Mabel.[23]

In this era, an estimated 2,750 boys followed dreams of playing professional baseball to the majors, but for each success at least four failed. Those who succeeded came from all sections of the nation, but Pennsylvania, with 327, led all states, and New York's 200 was the next highest total. Regionally, the northeastern states sent most of the players, with well over 1,000 from that section, and with 885 the Midwest was becoming an important talent area. The South (with 357) and the far West (with 234) lagged behind the other sections. Missing in this age were the beards and moustaches of the nineteenth century, but increasingly noticeable were the names of foreign born (81) and second generation Americans.

Few of those who aspired to a career in baseball came from impoverished backgrounds. Most were small-town residents with lower middle-class backgrounds, and nearly all had at least an elementary school education. Indeed, 493 were college men, a type much sought by managers like Mack and Branch Rickey, who urged their scouts to scour the campuses for promising talent.[24]

Sensing the ephemeral character of baseball glory, most players strove for the monetary rewards, and the slow upward trend in salaries reflected this pragmatic emphasis. In this age, rising attendance stimulated several sharp increases in salary. The first

[23] *The Sporting News,* January 19, 1950.
[24] Lee Allen, "Notebooks containing statistical data on baseball players."

came when the American League challenge erased forever the old $2,400 limit and sent salaries soaring to peaks untouched since the 1880's. By 1906, Bobby Wallace, a star infielder of the Browns, was the highest paid player at $6,500. However, a recognized star like Hal Chase, the first baseman of the Highlanders, got only $2,500, and Joe Tinker, a measly $1,500.[25]

But better days were coming; in 1908, increasing revenues encouraged good players to pressure owners by the technique of the salary holdout. At that time, Mike Donlin demanded $6,000 and Jake Stahl $5,000. Although both failed, others who held out were more successful, including Lajoie who signed a three-year pact for $36,000. By 1910, Wagner and Mathewson headed a list of ten with five-figure salaries—a group topped by Wagner's $18,000 and ranging downward to Matty's $10,000. Without doubt, such success boosted the earnings of lesser men; the 1909 Cub payroll of $90,000 showed how levels were rising. A 1910 estimate reported salaries ranging from a low of $2,000 for substitutes, to $5,000 for able regulars, and up to five figures for superstars.[26]

That estimate was disputed by David Fultz, an ex-player turned lawyer, who headed the 1912 Players Fraternity. According to Fultz, some players in 1912 got as little as $900 and one pitcher was held to $1,200 by a penny-pinching owner in spite of his winning record. Fultz's figures also showed a broad gap between salaries of superstars and those of ordinary players. However, in 1913, reporter Frank C. Lane counted fifty major leaguers, his "baseball's 400," all of whom earned better than $4,500.[27]

In 1912, the second and greatest upsurge came under the Federal League threat when owners were forced to pay unprecedented sums to keep stars from deserting. This period of "inflated salaries" saw Cobb's go from $9,000 in 1910 to $11,332 after a famous 1913

25 *Spalding's Annual Base Ball Record*, 1912, pp. 8–12; *Spalding's Official Base Ball Guide*, 1914, p. 23; *Baseball Magazine*, September, 1908, pp. 51–52; *The Sporting News*, February 9, 1907, March 12, 1913.

26 *The Sporting News*, February 23, 1907, October 29, 1910, October 29, 1931; *Spalding's Annual Base Ball Record*, 1910, pp. 10–15, 1912, p. 8; *Baseball Magazine*, June, 1909, April, 1911, pp. 69–70, November, 1912, p. 31.

27 *Baseball Magazine*, January, 1913, p. 48, April, 1913, pp. 45–62; for an opposite view of these figures, see *The Sporting News*, February 22, 1950.

holdout, to $20,000 in 1915—the largest sum paid to a player of the silver age. At the same time, Walter Johnson's rose from $7,000 in 1910 to $8,000 in 1911, and on into five figures after he threatened to jump to the Federals. Meanwhile, this same bluff won Speaker a two-year contract at $36,000. Those who actually jumped to the Federal League won lucrative, if short-lived, rewards as illustrated by Tinker's $10,000, John Kling's $7,500, Mordecai Brown's $6,000, and Jim Sheckard's $3,500. Although owners fought back with blacklist threats, the general effect was to make $70,000 the average sum for a twenty-five-man major-league team.[28]

Some owners flatly refused to be coerced by players. Blaming greed and intrigue for the poor performance of his 1914 champions, Connie Mack chose to sell his high-priced stars, thereby consigning his Athletics to long years in the league cellar.

If owners sighed with relief at the Federal surrender in 1915, they soon learned it was no time for vengeance or salary rollbacks. When the Red Sox management tried to renegotiate Speaker's contract, the great outfielder held out until he was sold to Cleveland where his demands were met. Only the weaker clubs successfully rolled back salaries, and in 1919 they were obliged to pay more in order to cash in on the wave of popular interest in baseball.[29]

At the close of the silver age in 1920, a third advance in salaries was under way. Nevertheless, inequities remained, as did niggardly owners. Considered to be the cheapest, the Phillies' owners tried to entice Alexander with a low base-salary offer and the promise of an extra $1,000 if he won more than twenty-five games. But Rube Waddell's treatment in 1913 stands as a monument to avaricious exploitation. Playing with the Browns, Waddell ended the season in debt, as he was billed $1,000 for breaking a no-drinking pledge, another $750 loaned him for his wife's alimony and $700 for miscellaneous disciplinary fines.

[28] *Baseball Magazine,* March, 1914, p. 57, November, 1914, p. 53, January, 1915, May, 1915, p. 74, May, 1916, pp. 19, 28; *Spalding's Annual Base Ball Record,* 1912, p. 8; *The Sporting News,* December 28, 1960.

[29] U.S. House of Representatives, *Organized Baseball,* Report No. 2002 to accom-

Along with increases in player salaries came increases in sums involved in player sales. Before 1908, no sale matched the $10,000 paid for either Kelly or Clarkson, but in that year the Giants paid Indianapolis $11,000 for pitcher "Rube" Marquard, and in 1912 the Pirates broke this record by paying the same club $22,500 for pitcher Marty O'Toole. After that, records toppled regularly; the White Sox paid Mack $50,000 for Collins, Cleveland paid the Red Sox $55,000 for Speaker, and the 1920 Yankees paid the Red Sox $125,000 for Babe Ruth.[30]

While such sales were portraying ball players as valuable slaves, the short-lived Baseball Players Fraternity was attempting to achieve greater player freedom and dignity. Created in 1912 under President Fultz, it was the third attempt to unionize players. As with its predecessors, success depended on its ability to exploit unrest. Its chief aim was to insure that no major-league player earned less than he could command in the high minors. To their credit, stars like Mathewson took leading roles in the crusade and seven hundred members were enrolled by 1913. With the Federal League war raging, the timing was excellent, and Fultz aimed seventeen demands at major-league owners. Although Ban Johnson called them blackmail, owners forced him to listen to requests for clarification of policies on player releases, contracts, and severance payments. At the time, 90 per cent of all players never held copies of their contracts, an omission that was speedily remedied. Another concession called for the publication of waiver lists so that discarded players could learn something about their forthcoming fate. In addition, veterans of ten or more years of service won unconditional releases, enabling them to work out their own deals with interested clubs.

Still other concessions brought improved playing conditions by making owners pay for uniforms and for travel expenses to spring training camps, and by requiring them to justify all fines or suspensions. In all, the Fraternity won eleven of seventeen demands,

pany H.R. 95, 82 Cong., 2 sess., 1952, pp. 1091, 1393; *Baseball Magazine,* May, September, 1916; *The Sporting News,* February 26, 1914.

30 *The Sporting News,* July 6, 1910, April 13, September 21, 1916; *Baseball Magazine,* January, 1915, p. 70, May, 1916, p. 78; *Reach's Official Base Ball Guide,* 1920, pp. 29–30, 94.

losing only three and winning three others in modified form, including five day's severance pay and free-agent rights for fifteen-year veterans. Although the Fraternity hung on for a few years after this victory, this was the high point in its existence. Its chief success was that it opened the way for collective bargaining. Players continued to bargain as individuals, however, and the rising salaries of the affluent 1920's killed their interest in the organization. Nevertheless, the Fraternity set a precedent that would be revived in powerful form in the years following the Second World War, an era when players were to recognize the value of a permanent bargaining agency.[31]

For the time being, owners with a horror of unions were spared by the continuing self-interest of players. The free-lancing, money-seeking star had opportunities to endorse proprietary products or to pick up $50 and some brief fame for hitting the Bull Durham sign on outfield fences. In 1917, Phillies' outfielder Gavvy Cravath hit the sign four times, but his reward was trivial compared with the money to be made from World Series play. In an age of dynasties, repeated Series opportunities made wealthy men out of certain stars. By 1919 Jack Barry had earned an extra $17,930 for his Series play; Eddie Collins, $14,500; and Larry Doyle, $7,165. For many years, only players on pennant-winning teams received the windfall, but at the end of the era regulations required that a portion be divided among players on first-division clubs, a precedent that continues to this day.[32]

Buoyed by more money and professional recognition, players still faced a problem of a negative "image." Many fans idolized them, but others regarded players as rowdy bums who ought to be confined to second-rate hotels and restaurants. Because of this frustrating dual image, players were unable to shake off the hostilities that persisted to the end of this era. Years later, Sam Crawford remembered the indifference of hotelkeepers, which inspired

[31] *Reach's Official Base Ball Guide,* 1913, pp. 79–81, 1914, pp. 197–202; *Spalding's Official Base Ball Guide,* 1914, p. 144; *Baseball Magazine,* March, 1914, pp. 11–14, October, 1914, p. 85, November, 1914, pp. 85–92, April, 1915, p. 13.

[32] *The Sporting News,* June 30, 1906, October 15, 1914, October 18, 25, 1917; Claudy, *op. cit.,* xii.

rookies like "Kid" Elberfeld to smash dishes in order to get attention. Likewise, a player-turned-sportswriter, Stan Baumgartner, recalled how the Edgewater Inn at St. Petersburg, Florida, offered the Phillies cheaper rates and patronizing treatment. When a player ordered steak, the waiter yelled, "baseball steak," a contemptuous call for a poor cut. Incensed at this kind of treatment, Grover Alexander once looked at the offering, dashed it to the floor, and stormed out to a better eating place.[33]

Lest one be moved to pity, it should be noted that players often brought much of this on themselves. Although a poor club like the Phillies negotiated for rock-bottom rates, this was sometimes done to force players to eat a reasonably balanced meal. If they were given an allowance of three dollars a day, many would spend only a part of it for room and board, "knocking down" the remainder either for savings or for liquor and accompanying adventures. The ballplayer's chief problem was that he was young and easily stimulated to rowdyism in the company of other lusty bachelors. Boorish escapades occurred regularly, especially in hotel lobbies. To while away the hours, pitcher Lee Meadows of the Phillies caused consternation to doormen with his oral imitation of an auto tire going flat. And Lefty Tyler of the Braves learned to propel a BB shot orally by means of a toothpick launcher. Pretending quiet repose in a lobby armchair, Tyler chose as targets room clerks and comely ladies in registration lines. On the field he potted enemy players and umpires, until the latter barred him from using toothpicks.[34]

Such pranks clouded the professional image of players, but many of them took a childish delight in the antics. Long years after his boyhood experiences of traveling with the Tigers of 1901, young George Stallings, Jr., was still enchanted by their brawling behavior. Most of the trickery began at the hotel when the horse-drawn bus delivered its sweaty human cargo at the dollar-a-day establishment. Storming onto the primitive elevator, players raced for first place in the communal bathtub. Usually the winner hid the soap or lathered the floor to trip up latecomers. Under the

[33] Ritter, *op. cit.*, 51–65; Lieb and Baumgartner, *op. cit.*, 135, 150.
[34] Lieb and Baumgartner, *op. cit.*, 150.

American plan, the last ones to the family-style meal got the leavings. Experience always favored the veterans while rookies like Jameson Harper, whose suitcase nametag bore the proud title "Ballplayer," were hazed mercilessly. Not only did Harper lose the contests for food, but veterans broke his bats and hid his clothing. One lonely night he was awakened by a strange scratching sound coming from the floor; looking down, he saw what appeared to be a dozen playing cards walking across the floor. After he had recovered from his shock, he learned the cause; each card was glued to the back of a three-inch cockroach.

Had players confined their antics to cheap hotels, they might have escaped notice. But the jokesters performed at other public places, including Pullman trains where they badgered porters, smoked cheap cigars, ogled pornographic pictures, and played noisy poker endlessly. Sometimes to get extra food, tricksters used the tactic of placing a fly on a plate of half-eaten food, then demanding the replacement of the "contaminated" food.[35]

Although many were sober, serious, faithful husbands or devoted sons, all were stamped as rowdies. Perhaps more than anyone else, it was the great sportswriter, Ring Lardner, who portrayed ballplayers as they were. In a series of articles entitled "Pullman Pastimes," Lardner recorded the language and diversions of traveling players. If, on the one hand, his candid sketches humanized players by smashing romantic myths, they also hurt by exposing the narrow range of player interests and tastes.[36] Meanwhile, scandalmongering writers greedily exploited the drunken antics of unfortunates like Waddell and Raymond, suggesting that such behavior was widely typical.[37] In a similar manner, by scolding players for buying autos, the editor of *Baseball Magazine* gave the impression that most players were wastrels.[38]

Partly to counteract the rowdy image, Mack tried to build his teams with players from colleges, while McGraw's policy was to

[35] George Stallings, Jr., "I Was Buddy-Buddy With the Rip Roaring Players of My Dad's Teams," *Baseball Digest*, July, 1957, pp. 79–92.

[36] *The Sporting News*, December 21, 1910; *Baseball Magazine*, March, 1915, p. 70.

[37] Ritter, *op. cit.*, 80–87; *The Sporting News*, November 24, 1906, December 24, 1914.

[38] *Baseball Magazine*, May, 1914; *The Sporting News*, May 25, 1911.

maintain decorum by fines. Whatever their methods, managers sought to open middle-class doors to their men.[39] Both league presidents fought to eliminate rowdyism, succeeding enough by 1910 to convince Hugh Fullerton that players now showed "higher levels of social and educational development." Yet Fullerton continued to urge the National Commission to use its authority to enforce discipline.[40]

Few bothered to weigh the cost of the Commission's harsh imposition of fines and suspensions. Such restrictions amounted to the denial of the basic civil rights of players. Indeed, the patriarchal code was accepted by them without serious challenge. Undoubtedly it would have been better had the Commission tried to understand the background of players and the conditions under which they played. Today, such probings are regularly undertaken by social scientists, but in the silver age these infant disciplines were only beginning to investigate human behavior. Only a few crude studies were available, including a 1915 study of the backgrounds of 146 "crack" players done by a criminologist. Among other findings, the survey showed that 61 per cent were rural born and raised. The average height was five feet, nine and one half inches, but pitchers and catchers averaged five feet, eleven inches. Interestingly, the smaller men excelled the taller ones in batting and fielding. But this was as far as the study went, and the author's purpose in undertaking the study was to probe baseball's potential as a "moral tonic" for deterring crime.

To understand baseball players of this era is to appreciate the courage with which they faced daily hazards. Most common were injuries like bruises, breaks, and strains, with head injuries and spike punctures as grim possibilities.[41] To these must be added social dangers from contact with shady characters and designing females. Called "baseball Sadies," the latter sometimes trapped or blackmailed those who enjoyed their favors. In a tragic incident, Chick Stahl of the Red Sox, distraught over fear of exposure,

[39] Mrs. John McGraw, *op. cit.*, 233.

[40] Evers and Fullerton, *op. cit.*, 25–65.

[41] "Why is a Baseball Player?" *Literary Digest,* June 12, 1915; *Reach's Official Base Ball Guide,* 1908, p. 344, 1910, pp. 189–91, 1926, p. 42; *Baseball Digest,* September, 1947, pp. 57–58.

swallowed carbolic acid and died in agony at the age of thirty-four.[42]

The biggest burden a player shouldered was fear of failure. Next to rookies, the most pressured group were the pitchers, one of whom found words to tell how lengthened schedules, road trips, and bigger crowds taxed his mind and stamina. Because of increasing demands, pitchers worked less often and more clubs used relief pitchers.[43] Likewise, infielders and catchers and outfielders won occasional relief from the daily grind with the help of "utility" men.

In addition to injury and failure, players feared growing old, and, because they felt they would be considered too old after age thirty, many lied about their age. But as American society developed more complete records, this tactic became less credible; besides, most managers automatically assumed that a player was at least twenty-two at the time he reached the majors.[44] Forced to stand alone, to extend themselves physically and mentally each day, it is not surprising that veterans also banded together against newcomers.

Always a superstitious lot, players continued to read the future in ordinary happenings like the passing of a load of barrels or a load of hay. Because both were divined as omens of good hitting, McGraw occasionally hired drovers to pass by the hotel with the magic loads. Even highly educated men like Collins invoked charms; when batting, Collins wore the same old sweatshirt and always placed his chewing gum on the button of his cap. Had the anthropologist Sir James Frazer been a fan, he could have gleaned many examples of imitative and contagious magic to add to those included in his *Golden Bough*. Among imitative devices was pitcher Doc White's insistence that his last warm-up pitch be a curve, and Lajoie's habit of drawing a line outside the batter's box. Men like Cobb and Crawford invoked the principle of contagion by spend-

[42] Al Stump, "Dames are the Biggest Headache," *Baseball Digest*, September, 1959, p. 63; *Reach's Official Base Ball Guide*, 1908, p. 393.

[43] Addie Joss, "The Strenuosity of Pitching," *Baseball Magazine*, October, 1908; *The Sporting News*, November 24, 1906.

[44] *Baseball Magazine*, November, 1908, p. 21; *The Sporting News*, November 11, 1915.

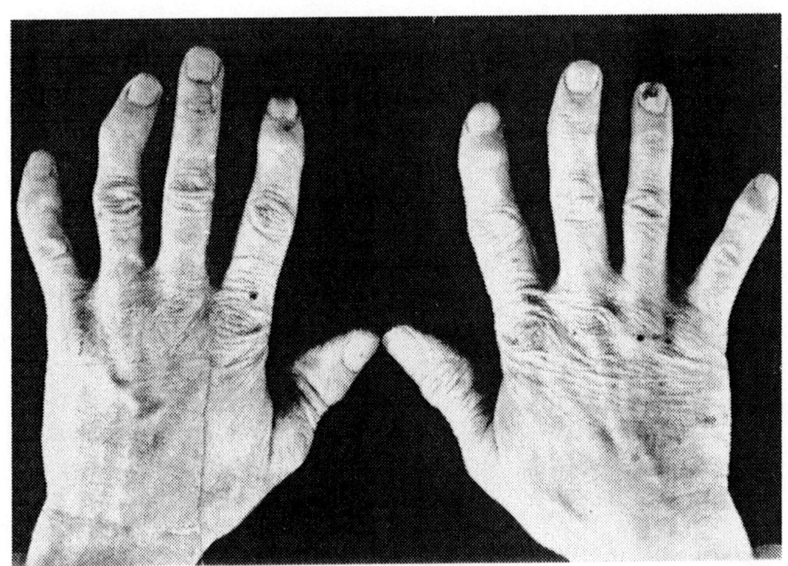

Even with improved gloves, the hands of a baseball player of the silver age took a fierce beating. These photographs of a baseball player's hands were taken in the early 1920's for the U.S. Surgeon General's office. (The New York Public Library)

ing hours bone-rubbing their bats. Moreover, some teams, like the 1912 Athletics, used group magic when they begged Mack to billet them in the same second-rate hotel which was theirs for the 1911 Series.[45]

Notwithstanding their passion for magic, players were pragmatic enough to accept changes in equipment. This was especially true of gloves, which grew in size and flexibility until they became veritable ball traps. By 1919, the Rawlings Company offered three different types of gloves including a big padded mitt for catchers, a shovel-shaped first baseman's glove, and an efficient five-fingered fielder's model. In all these, the big improvement was the multi-thonged web between the thumb and forefinger. Designed in 1919 by Bill Doak, an ex-player, its adoption sent fielding averages up twenty points over 1898 figures.[46]

45 *Literary Digest,* May 9, 1914; *Baseball Digest,* March, 1947, pp. 43–48.

46 "You've Got to Hand it to the Glove," *Baseball Digest,* March, 1959, pp. 35–41; *Baseball Magazine,* October, 1913, pp. 46–48.

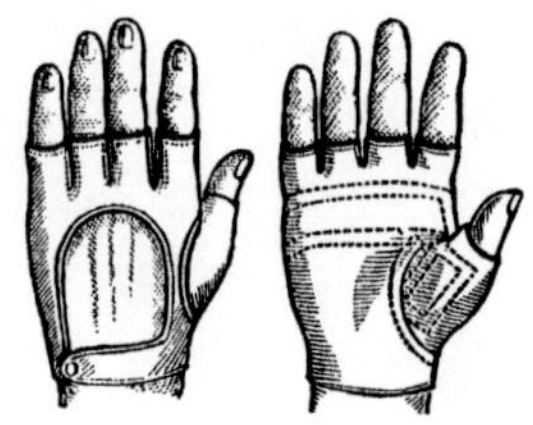

a. 1885

Gloved players were usually tagged as sissies for daring to wear the primitive, half-fingered gloves of the 1880's (a). *Designed for wear on one hand or both, the gloves sold for a dollar apiece.*

*By 1893, with the evolution of overhand pitching from the present distance of sixty feet, six inches, and with catchers stationed behind batters, baseball's rugged style of play demanded protective gloves. Gloves worn by infielders of the nineties closely followed the catcher's mitt in design (*b*). As more players used gloves, purists, including even George Wright, who manufactured them, were afraid that they would give fielders an unfair advantage. To be gloved in the nineties was still socially risky.*

b. 1890

By 1900, gloves for infielders and outfielders were an accepted part of the

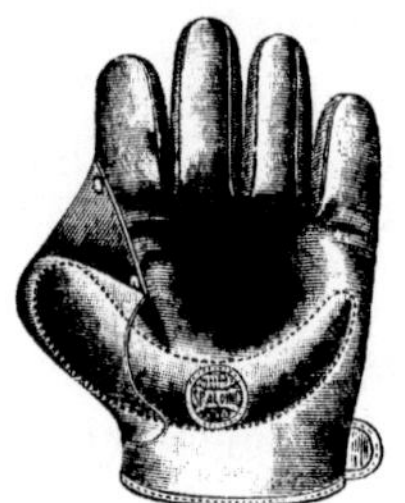

c. 1901

d. 1906

major-league scene (c) and could be purchased for $2.50.

Because fans more readily conceded a catcher's right to gloved protection, the catcher's mitt evolved rapidly. The "Decker Patent" model (d) was equal to the task of catching speedsters like "Cy" Young.

Like catchers' mitts, first basemen's mitts were evolving in a distinctly specialized direction by the early 1900's. A black leather model (e) cost $4.00.

In baseball's prosperous era of the 1920's, gloves adapted to cope with sharply batted "lively" balls (f), and were commonly used by infielders and outfielders. Although some balls were caught in the primitive "web," most players depended on the "pocket" of the glove. To develop a good pocket required much

e. 1906

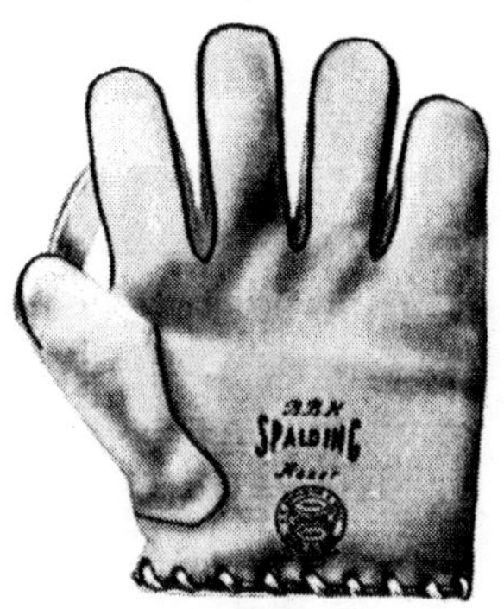

f. 1920

g. 1924

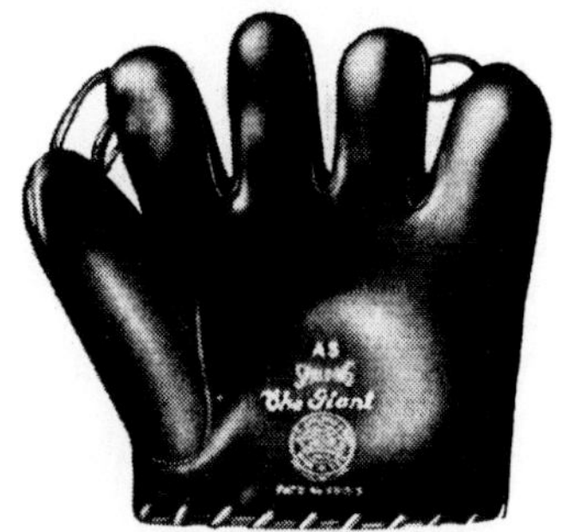

h. 1933

i. 1938

breaking in, including a trick of binding a ball inside the glove and soaking glove and ball together. By the twenties, such gloves as these cost ten dollars.

*A trend toward the efficient traplike gloves of today came in the late twenties and thirties (*g, h*). Figure* g *shows a trend toward a bigger web, and* h *shows a trend toward stringing the fingers together for better snaring of line drives. The latter model took only a timid step in this direction, and, as figure* i *shows, it was briefly reversed in 1938. However, the 1938 model shows a marked improvement of the webbed pocket between thumb and forefinger.*

*By the end of World War II, the webbed pocket trap was rapidly exploited. In 1944, the first baseman's mitt (*j*) used a double webbed trap to snare thrown balls. Well named "the Trapper,"*

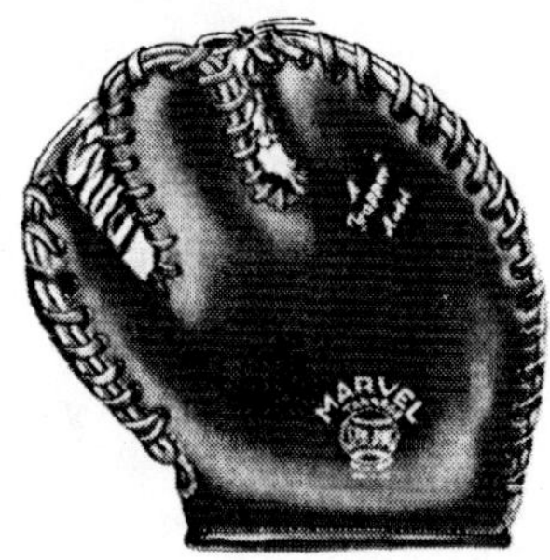

j. 1944

k. 1948

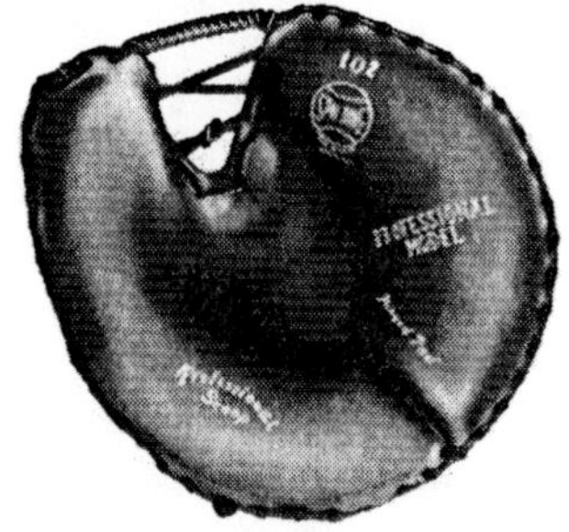

l. 1950

it allowed the first baseman to scoop grounders and snag thrown balls with lessened shock.

Rapid exploitation of the webbed pocket has served infielders and outfielders alike (m, n, o, p). *So effective is the webbed pocket trap that most balls are now caught in the webbing. Today, the "pocket" begins at the base of the web, and the rest of the glove is artfully constructed, often with built-in heels, to cause an almost automatic closing of the glove when the ball strikes it. The growing efficiency of gloves seems to verify Wright's earlier fear. Although no restrictive action has yet been taken, the hitting famine of 1968 has prompted suggestions for curbing the size and design of gloves in order to restore hitting to the game.* (Courtesy A. G. Spalding & Bros.)

m. 1950

n. 1955

o. 1964

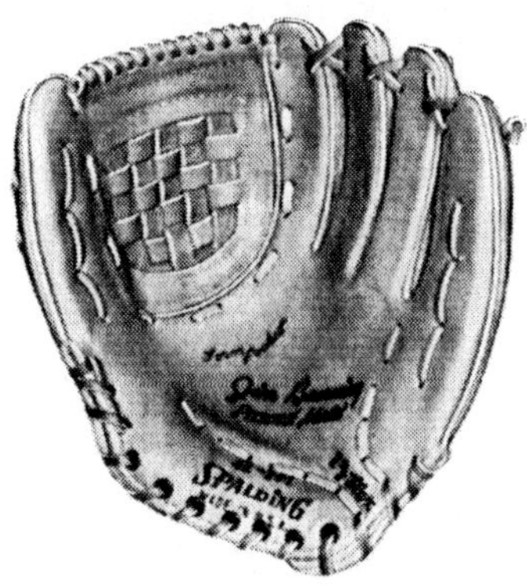

p. 1969

Another player-innovator, Roger Bresnahan, knew firsthand how easily a tipped ball could collapse a flimsy wire mask and drive the broken wires into a catcher's face. Equally dangerous were the low foul tips that bruised legs and sometimes crushed genitals, a threat minimized by the invention of the "cup" athletic supporter. To lessen the danger of bodily injury, Bresnahan persuaded a sporting goods firm to build a stronger mask, while he himself devised padded shin guards and a batting helmet. But only the shin guards won adoption; the cumbersome helmet was rejected and this necessary innovation awaited the development of plastics.

Slightly less frightening than "beanballs" were the spike wounds which threatened infielders and catchers. Because of the primitive state of antiseptics, the danger of blood poisoning magnified the fear. In 1910, a minor-league manager designed a safety spike which won some acceptance, but the menace was largely overcome by teaching infielders how to get out of the way of sliding runners.[47]

To teach such skills and to condition men for a 154-game ordeal, most teams by 1910 regularly maintained spring training camps in the South. Players may have recognized the value of such a conditioning program, but they hated the separation from families, the dull life, and above all, the unpaid donation of their time. A few stars like Edd Roush regularly avoided the sessions, but most submitted.[48] For many it was a fine opportunity to learn baseball, especially under a manager such as Branch Rickey. Rickey was a tireless student of the game and used methods that combined theory and practice, blending gadgets like batting cages, which he designed, with illustrated lectures.[49]

At spring training it was the rookies who worked hardest and who were most exploited by experienced veterans. Gullible ones were hazed and tormented, making survival a test of determination as well as talent. Naturally, mortality was high, and one study gave a minor leaguer of that time one chance in a thousand to make

[47] *Baseball Magazine,* June, 1908, p. 66, August, 1910, pp. 54–58; Evers and Fullerton, *op. cit.,* 87–99, 168–80.

[48] *Baseball Magazine,* March, 1914, pp. 27–30; "Big Leaguers in Training," *Literary Digest,* March 30, 1912; *Baseball Digest,* March, 1947, pp. 3–8.

[49] *The Sporting News,* February 26, 1914.

the majors. To land a berth against these odds took luck, talent, and some way of winning the manager's attention. But injuries and aging inevitably opened doors for determined rookies. A study in 1913 showed a 90 per cent turnover in the majors every ten years. But if hopes were raised by such an account, another account telling of "professional minor leaguers" sobered hopes. This was a tag hung on players still waiting for a call to the majors after ten years in the minors. There were enough who fitted the label by 1914 to attract attention.[50]

The chosen few who made the big leagues came to know the mixed cheers and jeers of a career that sooner or later led to declines and rejection. Dreaded by all players, such a process often began with a sustained "slump." According to one writer, a slump resembled a gambler's bad luck streak. When it dragged on, a player pressed, lost confidence, and sulked until driven by fear to try all sorts of magical devices to save his job. It was true that all players slumped, but only stars were given understanding extensions of time; for the ordinary player, any prolonged slump ended with his dismissal.[51]

Once rejected, a veteran might return as a coach, but these scarce jobs usually went to friends of the manager. Sooner or later, most men had to readjust to civilian life, a grim challenge for those who knew only baseball. To avoid it, many played on minor-league teams where the presence of eager youngsters was a further reminder of their inadequacy. With doors slammed in their faces at every turn, many former big leaguers faced a difficult adjustment with no help from those who had cut them loose.[52]

Sometimes adjustment was aided by baseball-minded local politicians who handed out jobs with the garbage disposal service, the police, or the fire department. Those who had money to invest sometimes opened saloons, although this outlet was dammed up for a decade by national prohibition. Other favored investment

50 *Baseball Magazine,* February, 1914, pp. 55–59, April, 1914, pp. 57–58.

51 J. R. McDermott, "The Psychology of a Slump," *Baseball Magazine,* July, 1913, pp. 33–40.

52 G. F. Sawyer, "Famous Big League Favorites in the Minors," *ibid.,* September, 1920.

outlets included sporting goods stores, bowling alleys, and auto and tire agencies. A few tried sportswriting and some opened baseball schools. But these were the lucky ones; experiences were often grim and traumatic as evidenced by the high rate of suicides and violent deaths for ballplayers.[53]

To improve the lot of retired players was one of the goals of the Players Fraternity. Objectives included severance pay, pension plans, and a home for indigent players. But in the silver age, players were obliged to live on dreams and comfort themselves with hopes that their deeds would not be forgotten. Mostly because fans and writers maintained a lively interest in the history of the game and its heroes, there was some small consolation for the rejects of the silver age.

[53] Lee Allen, *The Hot Stove League,* 234–40.

4

Silver Age Auxiliaries

1. The Fans

FROM THE BEGINNING of the silver age, successive waves of popular enthusiasm constantly refired dreams of glory for players and owners. Beginning with a major-league attendance of three and a half million in 1902, the total climbed to 4,500,000 in 1903, and in each of the following four years bettered the five million mark. Included was an encouraging figure of 5,900,000 in the depression year of 1907. Nor did the increase stop there; in 1908–1909 attendance topped the 7,000,000 mark, and in 1910–11 it averaged 6,500,000.

Then came a slump triggered by the Federal League war; major-league attendance dipped below six million in 1912–13 and then to a low point of 4,100,000 in 1914. This was only a temporary setback, however. When the Federals capitulated, attendance for 1916 briefly rebounded to the six million mark. The impact of the First World War lowered attendance to five million in 1917, then dropped it still lower to three million in the short season of 1918. This discouraging drop-off was mercifully brief, and those owners who hung on were rewarded by a new surge of interest which sent attendance above six million in 1919 and on to a new peak of nine million in 1920. That year the American League alone drew a record five million — a feat matched only five times up to 1945.[1]

Baseball gained a massive vote of confidence during the silver age, and public enthusiasm was further manifested by the popularity of the World Series. Reborn in 1903, the Series annually attracted more than 100,000 fans; in 1912 and 1919 over 200,000 attended.[2]

Dazzled by the profits that accompanied the waves of popular excitement, baseball owners were too busy planning bigger parks to take time to understand the trend. However, sportswriters like W. A. Phelon of *Baseball Magazine* were curious enough to try. In Phelon's opinion, fans had a compulsion to identify with player heroes—a psychological need that was intensified by the upsetting forces of industrialization, urbanization, and immigration. Although psychologists had yet to set forth theories about a search for identity under such conditions, Phelon hit upon a similar explanation when he talked about the adulation given to super heroes like Cobb, and the equally intense devotion of minority groups toward men like Wagner, Coveleskie, and "Ping" Bodie.[3]

Certain evidence substantiates Phelon's hero-worship theory. In Detroit, attendance lagged dismally until Cobb came along, whereupon it picked up dramatically. Meanwhile, the great dynastic championship teams of both leagues attracted large followings; proof enough that hero-worshipers liked nothing better than to identify with winners. From these winning teams, fans chose

[1] *American League Red Book*, 1962, p. 34; *National League Green Book*, 1964, p. 24; *Reach's Official Base Ball Guide*, 1911, p. 27; U.S. House of Representatives, *Organized Baseball*, pp. 1616–19.

[2] *Baseball Magazine*, November, 1915, pp. 57–64.

[3] *Ibid.*, October, 1910, p. 32; In *ibid.*, August, 1908, p. 20, see Rabbi Fleischer's article crediting baseball for helping workers adjust to dull industrial jobs.

as special favorites durable performers like Wagner or Mathewson, and wherever they performed attendance figures rose. Given a chance to show their admiration for their heroes, fans showered them with gifts, money, and floral tributes at honoring ceremonies.

Sensing the commercial opportunities in this phenomenon, the Chalmers Auto Company four times awarded autos to the season's most valuable player. Cobb, of course, was a recipient along with super heroes Collins, Wagner, and Lajoie. Not everyone agreed with the choices; in 1911 disgruntled fans of the Phillies held a ceremony of their own and awarded an auto to Sherwood Magee for winning the 1910 National League batting title.[4]

Often fickle in their choice of diamond heroes, fans sometimes worshiped with religious fervor. In Cleveland, the death of pitcher Addie Joss from a lung disease in 1911 had such an effect, as did the death of Chapman in 1920. Shocked by Chapman's death, Clevelanders wore crepe as thousands came to the funeral, officiated over by twenty-four priests.[5]

The hero-worship theory was not the only explanation offered for baseball's popularity at this time. Another view held that its reputation came from the fact that most males had played the game at some point in their lives. In 1910, sportswriter Joe Campbell polled Congressmen and found that all but two had played, the exceptions being a blind man and a cripple. Certainly such broad familiarity enhanced baseball's appeal, and smart politicians knew enough to defer to the game. In an age of rising nationalism, American Presidents recognized the sport as a symbolic expression of Americanism. Early in this era, Theodore Roosevelt, who disliked the game, accepted a lifetime pass and acknowledged with thanks a tribute from owners for his work in elevating "the Christianity of good health."[6] President Taft regularly attended games and began the annual custom of lending the Presidential presence to each opening day game in Washington. With the President on hand, this game resembled an annual renewal rite dedicated to American patriotism, and if a hymn was needed to sanctify the

4 *The Sporting News,* April 20, 1911.

5 *Ibid.,* April 20, 1911, August 26, 1920.

6 Evers and Fullerton, *op. cit.,* 14–24; *The Sporting News,* May 25, 1907.

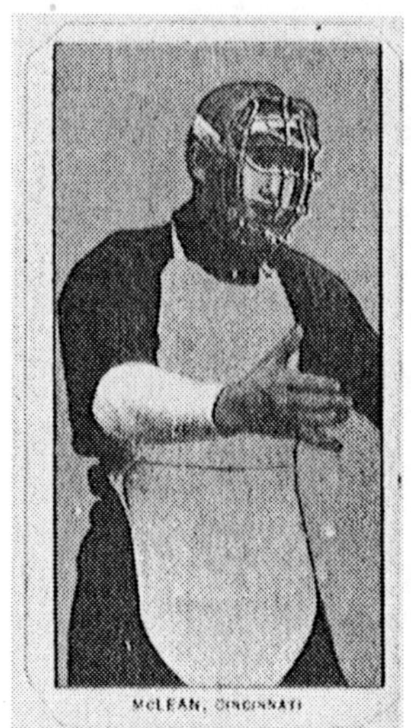

A collection of baseball cards eagerly sought by hero-worshiping young fans of the early 1900's. Because youngsters of the last three generations have been accustomed to getting baseball cards in bubble gum packages, it comes as a surprise to learn that youngsters of the early years got theirs from their fathers' cigarette packages. In that pre-cancer-scare era (when tuberculosis was the big

killer), Sweet Caporal cigarettes sold briskly by capitalizing on the popularity of baseball heroes. The cards in the cigarette packages, like the cards of today, were printed in full color and were eagerly hoarded and bartered. Nor was this the first appearance of the fad, for the history of ballplayer pictures goes back at least to the 1870's. (Goulston Collection, The New York Public Library) rite, it came in 1908 with the publication of the ever popular "Take Me Out to the Ball Game."[7]

Nevertheless, baseball men were constantly reminded of the fugitive quality of the game's appeal. Certainly other outdoor spectacles were gaining ground and posing threats to baseball's popularity. Above all, college football gained in attraction and its Saturday games in the early fall intruded on the end of the baseball schedule, while the new indoor spectacle, "basket ball," cut in on the beginning. Prize fighting and horseracing continued to offer formidable competition. Baseball more than held its own, however. As measured by listings in the *Reader's Guide to Periodical Literature,* popular articles on baseball always outnumbered those on rival spectacles.[8]

America's booming industry unleashed other powerful competitors for baseball's pre-eminent position as a recreation. As Americans slowly gained more time free from work, they were tempted both to buy automobiles and to spend time in the wonderworld of movie houses. In this age the auto threw the biggest scare into baseball men and for good reason. Certainly the call of the open road hurt the minor leagues, but major-league owners soon understood that like bicycles in the 1890's, motor cars could help get people to the parks. Nevertheless, the prospect of greatly increased numbers of cars was not taken into consideration in the park building boom of this era. Instead, most newly built parks were located within reach of streetcars and subways, leaving a growing problem of inadequate parking space to strangle the new parks.[9]

Neither radio, which developed too late in this era to be regarded as a problem, nor movies matched the challenge of the auto. Indeed, movie-going became a popular off-field diversion for players, except for perfectionists like Ty Cobb and Rogers Hornsby who thought that watching movies would ruin batting eyes.

Aside from making lonely road trips more bearable, movie-going

[7] *Baseball Magazine,* June, 1915; Sullivan, *op. cit.,* III, 406.

[8] David Q. Voigt, "Baseball's Pre-Eminence in Popular Literature," unpublished essay.

[9] *The Sporting News,* May 25, 1911, January 8, 1914; John B. Rae, *The American Automobile, passim.*

put an end to some hotel lobby antics and served as a useful training aid. Baseball owners also discovered a publicity value in movies. In 1911, a company was authorized to film and circulate a World Series movie, and players were ordered to co-operate fully in its filming. A few of the players were dimly aware of the film's money-making potential and unsuccessfully sought a share of its profits.[10]

A small group of owners believed that movies would cut into baseball attendance. To head off the threat, some tried a promotional gimmick called the dollar baseball plan, which offered any seat in the park at that price. But rising costs of movie admissions made this sacrifice unnecessary. Still, baseball undoubtedly gained future fans by such promotional devices as the "Knot Hole Gang" program, which made free tickets available for youngsters. Fear of movie competition also inspired more doubleheaders and intensified the drive for Sunday baseball games.[11]

To win the battle for Sunday baseball meant bitter fights with deeply entrenched Protestant religions, engagements charged with emotion and fraught with dangers. Baseball partisans had scored initial successes, but in the 1890's they had given ground under counterattacks from Sabbatarians. By 1902 only Chicago, St. Louis, and Cincinnati permitted Sunday games. Elsewhere, state and local laws barred such games. Usually the laws were quasi-secular in nature and aimed at promoting peace and quiet; hence violaters were punished for unlawful assembly, trespassing, or indecent gatherings.[12]

Cutting through the thicket of repressive laws was a herculean task, but baseball men had the support of a powerful liberal movement in American religion. Known as the "social gospel," one of its beliefs was that industrial man had a right to recreational leisure. By 1918 this secular activity helped bring Sunday baseball to Cleveland, Detroit, and Washington, although in the East opposition banned such games in greater New York, Boston, Philadelphia,

[10] *The Sporting News,* October 26, 1911.

[11] *Ibid.*, August 22, 1907, March 23, 1916; *Baseball Digest*, July, 1956, pp. 42–43.

[12] James Hodgson, "Digest of Laws Prohibiting Sports or Baseball on Sunday," New York Public Library Pamphlet, February, 1917; L. A. Wilde, "Baseball and the Law," *Case and Comment,* August, 1912, pp. 155, 162.

and Pittsburgh, thus creating a nightmare for baseball schedule makers.

Throughout the silver age, *Baseball Magazine* crusaded against the parochialism of New York Sabbatarians, sometimes using arguments resembling the anticlerical rhetoric of the Industrial Workers of the World. Certainly William Kirk's poem, "Sunday Baseball," caught some of the fervor of Joe Hill, the songman of the "Wobblies":

The East Side Terrors were playing the Slashers,
Piling up hits, assists and errors.
Far from their stuffy tenement homes
That cluster thicker than honeycombs.
They ran the bases 'neath shady trees,
And were cooled by the Hudson's gentle breeze.

Mrs. Hamilton Marshall-Gray,
Coming from church, chanced to drive that way.
She saw the frolicking urchins there,
Their shrill cries splitting the Sabbath air.
"Mercy!" she muttered, "this must stop!"
And promptly proceeded to call a cop,
And the cop swooped down on the luckless boys,
Stopping their frivolous Sunday joys. . . .

The Terrors and Slashers, side by side,
Started their stifling subway ride.
Down through the city, ever down
To the warping walls of Tenement Town.
Reaching their homes, the troublesome tots,
Crept away to their shabby cots.
They thought of the far off West Side trees,
And the cool green grass, and the gentle breeze,
And how they had played their baseball game,
Till the beautiful Christian lady came.[13]

Armageddon came in 1918 and ended with the rout of the Sabbatarians in New York. That year Al Smith's gubernatorial cam-

[13] *Baseball Magazine,* May, 1908, p. 29, October, 1909, pp. 38–40. In his counterattack, Billy Sunday, an ex-ballplayer turned vaudevillian-revivalist, said, "when [baseball] usurps the day of the Lord, it has overstepped itself and must be curbed."

paign was tied to Sunday baseball and his victory led to a hot legislative battle in which James Walker masterminded the passage of a bill permitting Sunday games. Lending solid support to Walker as a lobbyist was Judge Francis X. McQuade, a Giant stockholder. Their victory opened the Sunday gates in Brooklyn and Manhattan and the rush was so great that the Giants evicted the Yankees as tenants so as not to lose some Sunday dates. Thus Sunday baseball was partly responsible for the construction of Yankee Stadium, the most magnificent ball park of the first half of this century.[14]

Although routed, the Sabbatarians, led by the "Lord's Day League" of Boston and strong Pennsylvania forces, fought a strong rearguard action. Not until 1929 did Boston capitulate, and local option laws kept Sunday games out of Pittsburgh and Philadelphia until 1933. By 1934 the war was largely over. Only in Pennsylvania did irritating blue laws disrupt scheduling by requiring the early completion of Sunday games, an annoying problem that lasted until the 1950's.[15]

In retrospect, the coming of Sunday baseball was an inevitable accompaniment of heightened American appetites for material comfort. Sensing this, profit-minded owners built bigger and more comfortable parks. First to open was Forbes Field in Pittsburgh, and its commercial success spurred a building boom which culminated in 1923 with the opening of the 74,000-seat Yankee Stadium.

Although owners were most interested in size, safety consciousness was forced on them by a tragedy at the Phillies' park. Built in 1887 with seats for 20,000, it once was the palace park of America. However, just before a game in 1903, one of its overhanging galleries collapsed, dropping hundreds onto the bleacherites below. In this disaster, 12 were killed and 282 injured, and public reaction forced stricter building codes in park construction. Incredibly, the Philadelphia park was not replaced, but only rebuilt without balconies. It thus became the smallest park with the smallest playing area in the majors. In this happy hunting ground for power hitters,

14 *The Sporting News,* November 14, 1918, May 20, 1920; Frank Graham, "How New York Got Sunday Games," *Baseball Digest,* June, 1955, p. 60.

15 *Reach's Official Base Ball Guide,* 1929, p. 193; *The Sporting News,* August 5, 1920, February 8, 1923, November 16, December 21, 1933.

foul shots sometimes struck ancient iron girders, showering spectators with rust. Finally, after thirty years' service as the National League's garbage dump, the "Baker Bowl" was condemned and abandoned in 1934.[16]

Mingled in with the more mercenary dreams of owners was the added hope that the comfortable new parks might improve fans' behavior. To implement this dream, builders provided an expanded buffer zone between players and spectators. Separate dugouts and separate dressing rooms for umpires and players further reduced chances for hostile confrontations. Loudmouthed fans still zeroed in with insults, but sheer distance reduced most yawps to a wall of blurred noise.

After 1910, anyone seeking to recapture the barbarian flavor of old-time baseball had to go to Philadelphia. Until its abandonment, the Baker Bowl remained a symbol of the old days of intimate contact between fans and players, a small arena that helped to brand Phillies' fans as the league's most abominable.[17] The Philadelphia scene was dominated for years by "the bug, the bug, the hootin', rootin' bug," with "pocket full of change and heart full of gingerine," who "sassed" the umpire and sometimes punched his "mug." Fans sometimes fought players, and their most lethal missiles were pop bottles. To deny the weapon without losing profits challenged owners who acted to do so only when goaded by threats from the National Commission.[18]

In the midst of the pop bottle controversy, some penurious owners worried more about the loss of flying foul balls. Today, fans scramble for every foul ball, and the successful scrambler proudly displays his prize to all. But in 1911 this was defined as stealing; fans were denounced for catching and hiding balls and for pretending innocence when confronted by park police. *Sporting News* reported in 1916 that an average club lost fifty dozen balls a year. Eventually, the idea of "finders, keepers" forced owners to

16 *Baseball Magazine,* October, 1920, p. 527; *Reach's Official Base Ball Guide,* 1910, p. 121, 1911, pp. 99–109; 1912; Lieb and Baumgartner, *op. cit.,* 23–24, 105–109.

17 Fred Schwed, Jr., *How to Watch a Baseball Game,* 31–40.

18 *Reach's Official Base Ball Guide,* 1908, p. 49; *The Sporting News,* July 11, August 1, September, 1907, May 6, 1920; *Baseball Magazine,* December, 1908, p. 62, August, 1913, p. 90.

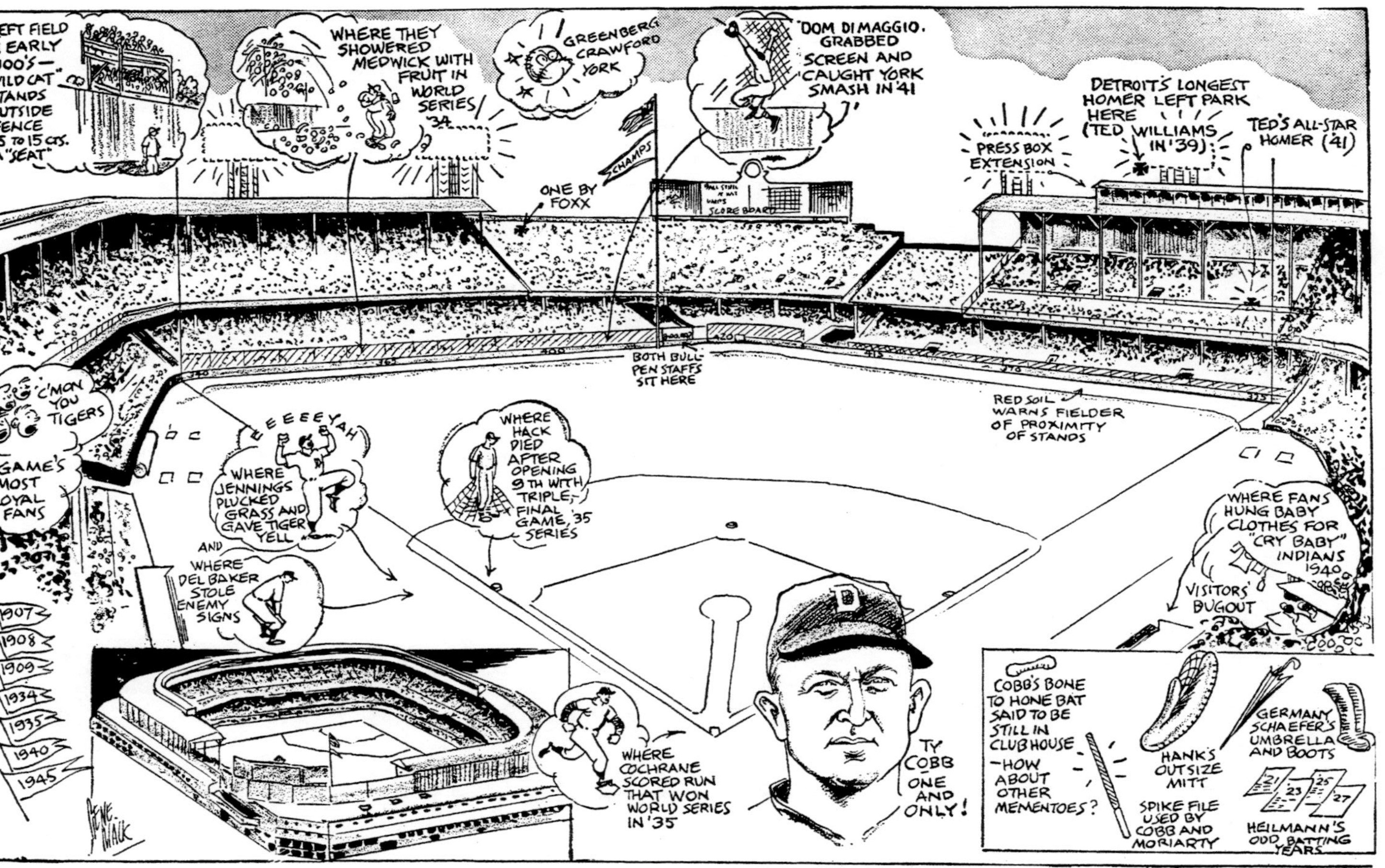

Briggs Stadium, Detroit. Gene Mack's Hall of Fame Cartoons, Major

abandon recovery of this tiny part of their profits. They did receive some relief when league officials persuaded manufacturers to furnish clubs with more free balls.[19]

Another form of intrusion opposed by the clubs was the practice of owners of adjacent properties who built and sold seats on rooftops in direct competition with the club. At Shibe Park this practice drove Mack to try legal action. After he failed this, his only recourse was to raise the height of the wall.[20]

One ray of hope amidst such headaches was the improved behavior of fans. They still jeered, cursed, and at times acted like mobs, but compared with fans of the 1890's they seemed better behaved and more sophisticated. Some observers noted that there was less swearing; that umpires were now mere "robbers" instead of whoresons. One owner credited the greater numbers of female fans for this change. Others thought that the new sophisticates were intolerant of old-fashioned, loudmouthed cheering. Now when fans whooped aloud, they might be disciplined by catcalls telling them to "choke," or "hire a hall." If the loudmouth persisted, he might be showered with debris. Certainly this hostile spirit helped put an end to organized rooting clubs such as Boston's Royal Rooters.

Of course, fans continued to yell and cheer, but the noise now resembled a disciplined, blended "crowd roar" tied to exciting events. Perhaps baseball fans were growing in sophistication, but one observer found them to be "almost unanimously eager, knowledgeable, and friendly." And because so many were avid students of box scores, this "petty form of communication" provided a bond for common experience and brief friendships.

Certainly the "personality" of each crowd differed, varying from day to day and from city to city. Although no systematic studies were made of silver age crowds, observers focused on easily noticed elements like the "bleacherites," so called because their unsheltered seats were the cheapest. Every park, even those in St. Louis, with its notoriously hot summers, had "bleacher bugs."

[19] *Baseball Magazine*, April 1911, p. 42; *The Sporting News*, February 2, December 21, 1911. Today clubs use as many as 150 balls in a single game.

[20] *The Sporting News*, October 15, 1914.

They were earthy folk who liked sunbathing and baseball. Discovered by reporters in 1909, this subculture was investigated with all the zeal anthropologists used in studying a primitive tribe. Like primitives, these subjects were overromanticized so that baseball mythology still labels "bleacherites" as "true baseball fans." One of the contributors to this myth, Franklin P. Adams, deserves much credit (or blame) for this rhapsody:

With other men and wastrel hounds
I walk into the Polo Grounds,
And cursing hard at the expense,
I bought a seat for fifty cents.
By cripes, I thought do human creatures
Sit out here in the bloody bleachers?

I heard them argue and exclaim
An hour or so before the game:
"Brooklyn's some team."
"Some team is right."
"You said a face full."
"Aw, good night!" . . .

I left these loud, loquacious louts,
Their tenuous talk of ins and outs;
Their fruitless talk of hits and errors,
What do they know, I asked of Sport?
They haven't the slightest feeling for't.
They talk and yell and swear and shout,
But they don't know what sport's about.
What is it? I said, By cripes, I'll show em!
So I went down town and pulled this poem![21]

A vivid word picture of bleacher life in the silver age was painted by novelist James T. Farrell. As an Irish-American boy growing up in Chicago, Farrell found the bleachers at Comiskey Park an

[21] F. P. Adams, "The Ball Game," in Edward B. Lyman, *Baseball Fanthology: Hits and Skits of the Game,* 55–58; See also, A. Sayre, "Fans and their Frenzies: the Wholesome Madness of Baseball," *Everybody's Magazine,* September, 1907; C. Van Loan, "Baseball as the Bleachers Like It," *Outing,* September, 1909; "Baseball From the Bleachers," *Colliers,* May 8, 1909; *Baseball Magazine,* August, 1910, pp. 67–69, October, 1910, pp. 63–66.

earthly paradise. Although bad eyesight precluded a playing career, Farrell collected cigarette pictures and inspected players in the flesh at the park. On ladies' days he went with his strong-willed grandmother, who knew little of the game but idolized players with Irish names. With his formidable escort, Farrell was able to get in free on ladies' days. If the gatekeeper objected, the doughty woman threatened to report him to "Alderman Willie O'Toole." Usually that did the trick, and the triumphant grandmother then placated the gatekeeper by adding sweetly, "God will bless you and your wife!"

For the Farrell boys, it was an unforgettable experience to rise at four in the morning and join the long waiting line for Series bleacher seats. The wait was always exciting and friendly; it was often warmed by good-fellowship, bonfires, and hot coffee peddled by vendors. After a while, latecomers made cash offers to buy places in line, and the Farrells managed to pick up a few dollars without relinquishing their spots until objections from those behind warned that enough was enough. At last came the opening of the gates at ten o'clock, and the boys were off to a glorious day of picnicking and worshiping their idols.[22]

Fans like the Farrells were twice blessed because they could see their heroes in person and follow them in the sporting pages. But for many, newsprint was the only access to the magical world of baseball. Probably the majority of American fans depended on newspapers, dime paper-backed books, or magazines for baseball sustenance; this vicarious adjunct of the baseball spectacle is thus well worth examining.[23]

2. Baseball's Second Dimension

Because they considered themselves most responsible for shaping the "second dimension," sportswriters never tired of protesting baseball's failure to honor them. Whenever reporters got together, in the pressboxes or saloons, this complaint, already old in the 1880's, was repeated. Yet their claim had some merit. By 1910

[22] James T. Farrell, *My Baseball Diary*, 3–59.

[23] *Baseball Magazine,* August, 1908, p. 20; "Newspaper Fan," *Atlantic,* April, 1908.

whole sections of metropolitan papers were devoted to baseball. Complete with features, photos, cartoons, and reminiscences, the coverage was of such scope and dollar value as to make baseball's bill for paid advertising look inconsequential.

The job of baseball reporting was a nine-month activity and was followed by a three-month winter stint aimed at promoting interest for the coming year. Measured in terms of reporters' fees, averaging about $7.50 for a thousand words, this was a million-dollar outlay with up to ninety full-time writers assigned to regular games. This number swelled to an army of two hundred at Series time. Except for press passes and pressbox maintenance, all of this cost baseball owners nothing.

Despite some friction, a symbiotic relationship existed between baseball clubs and newspapers. Like Gilbert and Sullivan, they needed each other, and the hard economic fact was that baseball coverage sold newspapers. Certainly William Randolph Hearst knew this, for when he bought the *Chicago's American* he immediately hired Al Mitchell to turn out five pages of sports a day with the aid of an 18-man staff. Ban Johnson, a former sportswriter, also knew the value of newspapers and never failed to encourage his clubs to co-operate fully with reporters and photographers.[24]

With the rise of large publishing empires like the Hearst and Scripps-Howard chains, smaller papers fell by the wayside. The giants simply overpowered them in quantity and quality of news coverage. This pattern also resulted in broader baseball coverage, including more box scores, features, and photos. Above all, games were covered in a slick, breezy style, a vital factor in the making of new fans.[25]

A new development in this age was the use of action photos to supplement baseball news. By 1909, photography was a recognized tool of reporting, but its application to baseball took time. In covering games, photographers had to learn to position themselves and often they were rebuffed by superstitious players or made the butt of practical jokes. But success came from learning about the

[24] *Baseball Magazine*, March, 1909, p. 30, October, 1910, pp. 67–70.
[25] John Tebbel, *The Compact History of American Newspapers*, 209–19.

One of the earliest extant action photographs of a baseball game is this one by R. Hoe Lawrence showing a National League contest played between Boston and the New York Giants at the old Polo Grounds in New York City in May, 1886. (Courtesy The New-York Historical Society, New York City)

game, and by the end of the silver age baseball photography was becoming a fine art.[26]

Although baseball writing had the advantage of half a century of continuity, its growth was stunted under the longtime conservative influence of pioneers like Chadwick, Murnane, and Richter. But by 1920 this trio had passed on, and new names like Ring Lardner, Hugh Fullerton, Franklin P. Adams, and Grantland Rice dominated the by-lines. In an age of routinized sportswriting, these men stood out as individual stylists.

In the opinion of many, Lardner was the best of silver age base-

[26] *Baseball Magazine,* August, 1909, pp. 43–45.

ball writers. "Tall, solemn-looking, dark-haired, dark-skinned, big-eyed," Ringgold Wilmerding Lardner majored in "football and dentistry" at the University of Michigan, then worked at a variety of semiskilled jobs before breaking into journalism. By the time he joined the *Chicago Tribune,* he was familiar with human foibles in general and those of ballplayers in particular. Cynical, pessimistic, iconoclastic, he had an odd sense of humor which was nurtured by years of travel with the Chicago teams.[27] The over-romanticized image of ballplayers was not for him, as his short stories "Alibi Ike" and "Lose With a Smile" showed. Both of these exposed the all-too-human blend of triumph and defeat, kindness and selfishness, hope and despair, and both testified to Lardner's cynical belief in the power of fate over human will which was to be exemplified in his later works. In one, he told of a girl choosing between two suitors, a decision that left her in lifelong agony as to the wisdom of her choice. After fifty years she is reunited with her former suitor, whereupon Lardner mercilessly drove home the point that she could have chosen either and her life would have been the same.[28]

Because Ring Lardner had an eye and ear for the unusual, baseball fans glimpsed the vital "dark side" of players' lives through his "stenographically true" reports of what players actually said and did. Especially amusing were his accounts of the "table breaking" of a rookie whose only knowledge seemed to be how to put on a baseball uniform. Perhaps the best introduction to Lardner's realistic style is his "Pullman Pastimes," a feature series on the White Sox in which he recounts the interests, activities, and words of a major-league team.[29]

A Voltaire among sportswriters, Lardner's devotion to baseball writing rested on his faint hope that the sport might offer a refuge from life's phoniness. The Black Sox scandal disillusioned him forever and prompted him to seek broader literary fields. This was a gain for American letters, but baseball fans were poorer for it.

Others followed Lardner's lead, including a trio of Chicago colleagues, Hugh S. Fullerton, Cy Sanborne, and Charles Dryden.

[27] *The Sporting News,* October 5, 1933, November 21, 1941.

[28] William R. Burnett, *The Roar of the Crowd,* 108.

[29] *The Sporting News,* December 21, 1910, November 13, 1941.

Fullerton's work is the most memorable, especially his book *Touching Second,* which he co-authored with Johnny Evers. Well-written, wide-ranging, and deeply probing, the book touches on topics like baseball law and justice, never before presented to the public.

As a working reporter and columnist, Fullerton's specialty was making predictions from the statistical analysis of performances. He won fame by forecasting victory for the "hitless wonders" in 1906, but his later errors as a forecaster convinced him that baseball writing was more art than science. However, in 1919 it was Fullerton's detective work that unraveled the web of fact and rumor and exposed the crooked work of the "Black Sox."[30]

New York City was also a center for talented writers. Here, the master stylist Damon Runyon was the first baseball writer to make large sums of money and the first to use a portable typewriter. An artist at drawing caustic and witty word portraits of baseball characters, Runyon was often snobbish and contemptuous of other writers. Occasionally his practical jokes angered others. One example was his 1916 telegram telling colleagues to abandon baseball reporting and go to Mexico to cover Pancho Villa. Perhaps this elaborate effort signaled his personal dissatisfaction with sportswriting; at any rate, given an opportunity to work as a war correspondent, Runyon seized the chance to sever his connections with baseball forever.[31]

The best explanation for the defections of talented writers like Lardner and Runyon is that baseball writing was too stereotyped, too stylized, and too confining to challenge such keen observers of human behavior. Indeed, William Phelon claimed in 1908 that baseball writing had reached its peak as a literary form in 1892 and had not grown since.[32] Phelon's statement was true inasmuch as the reporting style, the clichés, and the anecdotes had not changed much. Under the circumstances, a baseball writing career appealed mostly to immature writers who were often frustrated ballplayers and who could accept the narrow confines of the diamond. Yet

30 "Baseball Reporters Who Broke Into Literature," *Literary Digest,* April 9, 1921; Evers and Fullerton, *op. cit.,* 42–55; *Literary Digest,* February 17, 1944.

31 *The Sporting News,* November 21, 1941.

32 *Baseball Magazine,* September, 1908, pp. 29–42.

many noted American writers, including James T. Farrell and the historian Lloyd Lewis, freely admitted a great debt to their baseball writing experiences.

Fortunately for curious fans, enough men were content to be baseball writers for life. Some, like Grantland Rice, were unashamed romantics. Rice was a college-trained southerner whose love of Latin poets moved him to lace his columns with the countless verses that became his trademark. They drew sneers from those who believed that reading a poem was effete, but Rice's style was popular enough to earn him a highly paid job with the *New York Evening Mail.* New York life and daily contacts with men like Adams, Heywood Broun, and Rube Goldberg, sharpened Rice's talents. Rising amidst such competition was difficult, but Rice held his own and his syndicated column "Sportlight" made him a national favorite by 1920.[33]

If Rice's formula of optimistic verse and adventurous sagas struck a popular chord, other writers found different but equally satisfying approaches. One such competitor was Joe Vila of the *New York Sun*, a Harvard graduate and dedicated baseball writer, who specialized in the sensational exposé and the baseball "scoop." It was Vila who broke the story on the Players Fraternity, who first reported the surrender of the Federal League, and who scooped everybody on the planned site of Yankee Stadium. A man of many contacts, Vila gloried in his reputation as the Richard Harding Davis of baseball writers.[34]

A profession big enough to accommodate such diverse talents as Lardner, Rice, and Vila also had room for other personalities. Since fans loved to pore over records and statistics, "figure filberts" such as Ernie Lanigan commanded a responsive market. Noting the chaotic state of baseball records, Lanigan labored many years to produce in 1920 the first systematic encyclopedia of baseball statistics.

In the same tradition as Lanigan was Fred Lieb, whose thorough

[33] Grantland Rice, *The Tumult and the Shouting: My Life in Sport,* 20–21, 41–47, 224–25.

[34] *The Sporting News,* February 7, 1929; For Vila's attack on "Muggsy" McGraw, see *ibid.,* July 4, 1907.

but unimaginative style evoked a sound sense of baseball history. In the years before 1920 he attended nearly every World Series game, stockpiling observations all the time. From his notes came many informal histories of teams and events that serve as a basis for critical inquiries into American baseball.

Occasionally good fortune allowed writers to take an active part in baseball, and at least two writers became club owners for a time. One, Charles Murphy, headed the Cubs in the glorious days of Chance and Evers. For a while he rode out the Cubs's victory string, although he made many enemies with his unsolicited advice. In time, errors in judgment humbled him and enabled his adversaries to force his retirement. A similar fate overtook Horace Fogel, a veteran writer who managed the Giants before McGraw. Ridiculed by McGraw for trying to make a first baseman out of Mathewson, Fogel bounced back as president of the 1912 Phillies. But altercations with umpires soon led to his dismissal on charges of misconduct. Fogel returned to writing, but his vengeful attacks, such as demanding a federal antitrust suit against baseball, alienated him all the more.[35] In contrast with Fogel and Murphy, ex-writers Ban Johnson and John Heydler succeeded brilliantly as baseball leaders.

Meanwhile, the silver age offered players a chance to become writers. With the assistance of "ghost writers," a term applied to financially harassed sportswriters who did the real work, stars like Mathewson, Chance, Cobb, Evers, and McGraw won by-lines. Usually they were hired to comment on World Series games, but a working newsman always did the actual writing.

In the years before 1920, baseball reporters spent most of their energy attacking poor working conditions. Bad press facilities headed the list, followed by protests over procedures for scoring games, a task traditionally handled by reporters. In hopes of improving these conditions, writers in 1908 formed the Baseball Writers National Association. By 1913, 187 members were enrolled, and there were active chapters in each league city.[36] Because

[35] *Baseball Magazine,* June, 1913, pp. 21–23.

[36] *The Sporting News,* October 19, 1916, October 18, 1917, October 9, 1941; *Baseball Magazine,* November, 1912, pp. 55–60.

most of its goals were realized by 1920, Association members contented themselves with attendance at annual dinners highlighted by satirical skits parodying baseball leaders and events, but seldom their own odd plight. To this day, the New York chapter remains the acknowledged leader in such theatrical enterprises.

3. Baseball's "Men of the Cloth"

As players gained in prestige, fans in sophistication, and reporters in objectivity, the status of umpires gradually rose. Branded as baseball's archvillains by fans of the 1890's, umpires carried the stigma well into the silver age. Moreover, the peace that ended the American League war brought no noticeable peace to umpires. In the National League of 1904 there were mob scenes as club presidents continued to curry public favor by using umpires as scapegoats. Even in the more enlightened American League, President Johnson's edict against umpire-baiting was openly defied by McGraw. In a *cause célèbre* of 1901, McGraw protested Johnson's suspension of pitcher McGinnity for spitting in an umpire's face and called Johnson a "Czar." Although this incident was smoothed over, McGraw's continuing harassment of umpires soon forced further disciplinary action which in turn prompted his defection to the National League.[37]

Cursing players and bottle-tossing fans continued to be a severe menace to umpires. In 1907 at Sportsman's Park, a bottle thrown by a clerk in the office of the German consul fractured the skull of young Billy Evans. As the umpire lay between life and death, Johnson issued an order telling owners to patrol their stands or face fines.[38] As for verbal abuse, umpires always accepted the curses, the boos, and the waves of maniacal laughter that came whenever an umpire was hit by a foul tip. All of this was a familiar part of the silver age ritual of umpire-baiting; indeed, it found musical expression in the popular song, "Let's Get the Umpire's Goat."[39]

[37] *Reach's Official Base Ball Guide*, 1902, pp. 36–37; *The Sporting News*, August 3, 31, 1901.

[38] *The Sporting News*, September 19, 1907.

[39] *Spalding's Official Base Ball Guide*, 1909; Burnett, *op. cit.*, 38.

In the early years of the silver age, umpires faced attacks from several directions. On one flank were fans, on another hostile newsmen like the writer who used a fan's fatal heart attack as inspiration for the headline, "Umpire Klem Kills Innocent Fan." But the toughest onslaughts came when umpires confronted players. Umpires usually came off second best in this war of swearing, kicking, spiking, and spitting. Occasionally, umpires fought back in kind, but most learned to accept the advice of league presidents who urged them to walk away and later file a report, trusting the league to right the wrong by fines. This legal remedy slowly reduced the number of physical assaults, so that a 1904 study found that 85 per cent of the trouble amounted to verbal abuse. However, umpires were sneered at as cowardly and eunuchoid for using the tactic, a painful reminder of their new status as "men of the cloth."[40]

In reality, the conditions under which an umpire worked more than vindicated his masculinity. Stationed behind the catcher, he shared the same bruises and blows. Indeed, his risk was twice as great because a catcher spent half of each inning in the shade of the dugout while an umpire had no respite. In addition, because umpires worked alone in the early years of the era and could not be on top of every play, players got away with tricks like doctoring balls, fouling base runners, and prancing impudently around bases without touching them. These intolerable working conditions lasted until 1911, when the National League finally restored the dual-umpire system.[41]

The loneliness of the working umpire also made his off-duty hours more burdensome. With no assurance of tenure and no association to fight for his rights, his life was a constant siege of insecurity in which the votes of five owners could end his career. With their lives and performances under daily scrutiny, umpires learned to shun the company of owners, players, managers, gamblers, and fans, lest suspicions arise. For most, this spelled a mo-

[40] James M. Kahn, *The Umpire Story,* 107–17; *The Sporting News,* June 29, 1911.

[41] Tyrus R. Cobb, *Busting 'Em,* 70–91; Kahn, *op. cit.*, 75.

nastic, lonely existence, but for some it resulted in closer marital relationships. Bill Klem freely acknowledged his debt to his wife, and Silk O'Loughlin's last moments on earth testified to the depth of his devotion. When he was dying of flu during the 1919 epidemic, O'Loughlin's last request was for one more embrace from the wife who lay beside him stricken with the same disease.[42]

An umpire's life was always hectic, and included a long season of traveling with no certain knowledge of the itinerary. Not before 1911 were umpires paid travel expenses, and when the leagues finally provided allowances, payment came on a reimbursement basis. Umpires also paid the full costs of their uniforms and protective equipment. But the biggest cost was to a man's pride. To fans nothing was sacred, certainly not an umpire's name. When an earnest young neophyte named Colliflower joined the American League staff, he was cruelly mocked for the name. He changed his name to James, but this was a bad choice since antagonists took to calling him "Jesse."[43] Under such conditions, survival demanded that a man have tough moral fiber. Grantland Rice once playfully recommended the Theodore Roosevelt try umpiring for two weeks, promising that "it will curb your rash, headlong stren-u-os-i-tee."[44]

Umpires' salaries lagged far behind the upward trend of player pay. In the early 1900's, salaries for umpires ranged from $1,500 to $2,000; in 1910 the top salary in the National League was $3,000 with only four of seven topping $2,000. For all the officiating that year, the league paid only $25,000, a sum including $8,000 in travel expenses. Such bargain prices continued for years, and in 1920, under the double-umpire system, the combined costs came to only $41,000.

By contrast, World Series duty offered umpires a bonanza, and their chances of getting Series duty were good. Nevertheless, until Klem in 1917 demanded and got $650 for such an assignment, the most any umpire collected was $400. Emboldened, Klem went for

42 *The Sporting News,* October 16, 1919, February 8, 1923; Kahn, *op. cit.*, 216–23.

43 *Baseball Magazine,* June, 1948, p. 36.

44 *Ibid.*, May, 1948.

$1,000 in 1918 and won, but President Johnson stubbornly held the other three umpires to $650.[45]

One of the ironies of American baseball was that these despised lackeys carried the integrity of the game on their ill-paid shoulders. Although this was vaguely appreciated by silver age owners, it took the Black Sox scandal to drive the fact home. It was paradoxical that they were daily exposed to angry emotions and vengeful actions but were expected to maintain their objectivity at all times. Fascinated by this paradox, writer Hugh Fullerton challenged the prevailing trust in the honesty of baseball's umpires. In raising the question, Fullerton was more concerned about psychological dishonesty than overt corruption. After all, to be loved is an important human drive, and even umpires shared it. As Fullerton saw it, some umpires gratified their need for regard by being "homers," a term describing those who gave close decisions to the home team. On the other hand, a few were "bullheads," so-called because self-love motivated them to buck home crowds. To Fullerton, Umpire Hank O'Day, who decided for Chicago in the Merkle case, was a notorious bullhead.

Since neither stance was objective, Fullerton urged the Commission to keep careful and critical watch over umpiring, since the most able judges had off days. The crying need was to maximize good days, and Fullerton urged that umpires be subject to fines for misbehavior.[46]

Quite advanced in his psychological insight, Fullerton was too far ahead of contemporaries. League officials generally entrusted silver age umpiring to even-tempered men who seemed to know the rules. Much admired for his knowledge and discipline was Bill Klem. A mature man of thirty-one when he joined the National League in 1905, Klem was toughened by earlier jobs as steelworker and bartender. He was proud of his honesty and his knowledge of rules, and he made telling use of both. Fully aware of President

[45] Kahn, *op. cit.*, 120–21, 219–20; U.S. House of Representatives, *Organized Baseball*, pp. 1321–25.

[46] Evers and Fullerton, *op. cit.*, 181–95; *Baseball Magazine*, February, 1911, pp. 2–4, July, 1913, p. 71; *The Sporting News*, August 21, 1924.

Pulliam's inability to protect umpires from powerful owners, Klem determined to enforce discipline in his own way.[47]

A charismatic figure, Klem awed players with his knowledge and cowed them with fines. Only McGraw consistently fought him, and often the pair purpled the air with cries of "Catfish" and "Muggsy." Usually Klem avoided arguments by his tactic of drawing a mark in the dirt and warning a player not to cross it. He popularized a close-fitting chest protector worn inside the coat and colleagues learned from him where best to stand to call balls and strikes. As others followed his lead, Klem accepted plaudits with scornful arrogance. Not until late in life did he admit to making mistakes; then he explained that his much-quoted claim "I never called one wrong," really meant "in my heart I never did." A proud martinet, he lectured everybody, including veteran Tim Hurst whom he rebuked for insulting the profession. Retiring in the 1940's he became the senior National League umpire, a post he took so seriously that he wrote a pamphlet on umpiring etiquette which included a warning that an umpire must not point his rear end toward the fans when sweeping the plate.[48]

Other National League umpires achieved some measure of fame. With a career dating back to the 1890's, Bob Emslie received the first umpire's pension in 1919 and later came out of retirement to serve as adviser to the National staff. Another holdover from the feudal age, the colorful O'Day could read the sign language of the deaf and once fined "Dummy" Taylor of the Giants for signaling a silent curse. O'Day's passing after 1910 opened the way for Klem's long reign.[49]

During the same period, under Johnson's iron rule, American League umpires lived more securely. From the start, Johnson fought rowdyism as a threat to the security of his league. To win the war he hired good men, paid them well, and backed their decisions. He raided the National League for men like O'Loughlin,

[47] *The Sporting News*, August 18, September 8, 15, 1906.

[48] *Ibid.*, August 21, 1924; Kahn, *op. cit.*, 77–89.

[49] Henry O'Day, "A Big League Umpire's View," *Baseball Magazine*, June, 1908, pp. 30–32, November, 1908, p. 17; *The Sporting News*, December 21, 1910, February 8, 1923.

Hurst, Jack Sheridan, and Tom Connolly. His scouts also approached Billy Evans and Klem. But because Klem had a vague verbal promise from the National League, he felt obliged to honor his commitment.

As "Czar" of his league, Johnson set standards of decorum at games and allowed umpires to uphold them with fines. Because Johnson was fighting their fight, his "big five" staff of Connolly, O'Loughlin, Sheridan, Hurst, and Evans generally welcomed his leadership. Hurst alone chafed under Johnson's authority. Tough, outspoken, sarcastic—excellent qualities for umpiring in the 1890's—Hurst could not adjust to the new professional approach. A collision was inevitable, and it finally came when Hurst spat in the face of young Eddie Collins. When he was asked why, Hurst told Johnson, "I don't like college boys." This was a typical Hurstian remark, but this time it led to his dismissal.

Except for the difficulties with Hurst, Johnson's star system worked well, and each luminary retired honorably. The most outstanding was Tom Connolly, who enjoyed a long tenure. An expert on rules, his judicious handling of cases won him recognition as the leading American League umpire and a niche in baseball's Hall of Fame.

Another master of rules was Billy Evans, the boy umpire whom Johnson apprenticed to grizzled Jack Sheridan. It was Evans's beaning that led to Johnson's tough edict against pop bottle throwing. Recovering, Evans worked with honor until the mid-1920's when he left to become a general manager. After retiring, he published a remarkable pamphlet, "The Billy Evans Course in Umpiring," an excellent guide for rookies. Among 51 points listed was advice to avoid arguments and conversation with fans and to practice diplomacy by watching the ball instead of looking for trouble. He also urged greater tolerance for star players and told rookies to take time before calling a play.[50]

Evans's tutor, the veteran Sheridan, later became Johnson's

[50] William Evans, "The Billy Evans Course on Umpiring." (Privately published in 1926. In the Spalding Collection of the New York Public Library); *The Sporting News*, December 21, 1910.

chief scout. In an article written in 1910, he praised Johnson for treating umpiring as a profession, and his best advice to neophytes was to keep quiet and smile.[51] Such advice, however, was not for Silk O'Loughlin. Called "Silk" because of his pleasant voice, O'Loughlin loved to match words and wits with players. Nor did he suffer for his debates as, alone among umpires of 1906, his fame led to his appearance in an early soft drink ad.[52]

Compared with their low estate in 1900, umpires gradually attained greater prestige during the silver age. They might not expect cheers, but at least they made a few tangible gains beyond the short hours. By 1920 they no longer had to make announcements by megaphone, keep the batting order, or summon police for control.[53] Some fans called this "coddling," but these were well-earned concessions for baseball's "men of the cloth," who shouldered so much of the burden of the game's integrity.

4. The Owners

The general public's image of the baseball owner was that of a grasping skinflint with a public-be-damned attitude. Owners contributed to this image themselves back in the 1890's by their petty intrigues and mania for publicity. This was a heavy burden to shoulder and owners had difficulty in lightening it. But in 1913 William Phelon tried to introduce fans to the "new magnates," who he claimed were dedicated to the game, to the people, and to a gospel of wholesome leisure.[54]

Phelon's approach de-emphasized the profit motive and suggested that many owners even lost money in baseball. No doubt Phelon was out to counteract a widely read article of 1912 which portrayed silver age owners as monopolistic profiteers.[55] If so, he chose a difficult task because muckrakers were pushing the thesis that baseball was a bonanza for profit-seeking owners.

51 John Sheridan, "Umpiring for Big Leaguers," *Baseball Magazine,* May, 1908, pp. 9–12; *The Sporting News,* August 11, 1910.

52 *Baseball Magazine,* July, 1908, p. 11.

53 *The Sporting News,* May 20, 1920.

54 W. A. Phelon, "The Great American Magnate," *Baseball Magazine,* January, 1913, pp. 17–23.

55 A Club Owner, "The Base Ball Trust," *Literary Digest,* December 7, 1912.

In July, 1912, the *Literary Digest* cited four cases of baseball profiteering. The outstanding one was that of John T. Brush, who began with a $25 investment in a weak Indianapolis franchise in 1887 which he sold out for $16,000 in 1890. He then moved to Cincinnati, sold that franchise for $146,000 in 1900, and moved to New York as owner of the Giants, a club that by 1912 fetched annual profits of $100,000 to $300,000. Almost as meteoric was the rise of Charles Murphy, who with a $100,000 loan bought the Cubs in time to cash in on the prosperous days of the Chance era to the tune of $165,000 in profits a year. The same quick success came to Barney Dreyfuss, a German-born distiller, whose original $16,000 investment in Louisville blossomed into more than $100,000 annual profits with the help of his $750,000 Forbes Field park.

The fourth in the quartet of profiteers was Frank Navin, who joined forces with a Detroit millionaire, William H. Yawkey. Hired as Yawkey's bookkeeper, Navin's loyalty won him a half interest in the Tigers, a team valued at only $35,000 in 1906. The following year the pennant-winning Tigers returned Navin $50,000 in profits, and by 1912 he had earned a total of $365,000 from baseball. By then the value of his team, which he now owned completely, had soared to $650,000.[56]

Such selective accounts gave a distorted impression of baseball owners. Although some of them maximized profits, there were those who invested as gentlemen-sportsmen with little thought of profit. This complex mixture of avarice and altruism moved the Supreme Court in the early 1920's to decide that major-league baseball ought to be shielded from attack under antitrust laws. Nevertheless, the conflict between these motives confused most Americans, especially those who suspected all rhetorical appeals to gentlemanly sportsmanship and pride in the national game.[57]

Certainly baseball's silver age showed that considerable money could be made by promoting a major-league club. In the years 1901–1908, attendance in each major league averaged better than

[56] "Fortunes Made in Base Ball," *ibid.*, July 20, 1912.
[57] *Baseball Magazine*, March, 1915, pp. 13–14.

2,000,000 a year, providing a gross operating income of over $17,000,000 for each league in that period. Profits were modest at first, but they rose sharply in the five-year period after 1909, when attendance averaged better than 3,000,000 a year, returning a $20,000,000 gross operating income for each league. This upsurge prompted owners to build the great ball parks which served fans until midcentury and which had the immediate effect of further increasing attendance. Thus, in the five-year period 1911–16, gross operating income reached $23,000,000, but this was followed by the slump during World War I. However, the silver age ended on an optimistic note as the 1920 season returned a million-dollar profit for each league.

Nevertheless, there were great differences in income between the two major leagues and between member clubs in each league. As an example, the Yankees in 1920 topped all with $373,000 in profits, whereas the lowly Phillies netted $63,000. Such a gap was a function of many factors including park size, city size, Sunday baseball, team rosters, and team standing. In concert, such forces worked to give certain clubs greater "attendance strength" than others. Throughout the silver age, the greatest attendance strength fell to the American League in general and the great championship dynasties in particular. Yet this was not always the case; from 1901–10, New York joined with Chicago, Boston, and Philadelphia to collect 56 per cent of the American's gross earnings. And in 1911–20, six American clubs shared 79 per cent of the wealth, showing a rather unusual balance, although hardly comforting to the "have-not" Browns and Senators.

Meanwhile, the great National League dynasties were garnering the biggest slices of profits; in the period 1901–10 McGraw's Giants took 18 per cent of the league's earnings, a record for the silver age. This pattern also held for the 1911–20 period, as the Giants took 17, the Cubs 14, and the Phillies 12 per cent, leaving the lowly Braves with the gleanings.[58]

It is worth noting that these figures were assembled thirty years after the silver age had passed, when a Congressional investigating

58 U.S. House of Representatives, *Organized Baseball,* pp. 1599, 1615–20.

committee threatened the majors with antitrust legislation. Forced to divulge earnings, baseball men of 1951 gave information on profits that was not available in the silver age. Baseball leaders of that time, fearing incursions, argued that such information was not a matter of public record.

Unhappily for major-league owners, their embargo on information failed to deter the invading Federal League and was only partly successful in putting a stop to the sportswriting practice of printing wild stories of profiteering. The dog-in-the-manger attitude stimulated guessing by sportswriters who spun yarns about profits based on hearsay. Such tales as the high prices paid for players, the annual reports of World Series profits, and rumors of high prices paid for franchises all worked to keep alive the myth of a baseball El Dorado.[59]

While such tales kept alive the image of the avaricious owner, other stories promoted an image of owners as public servants. Indeed, the latter gained currency in this era, especially after the passing of the great villains of the feudal age; men like Freedman, Hart, Soden, and Rogers. They were replaced by more neutral characters, while such former villains as Brush and Robison were seen in a more favorable light. How could one hate tough old John Brush, who sat crippled in his wheelchair? Instead, he captivated Giant fans by his courage and by the success of his teams. Yet he never lost his love of controversy, and with Dreyfuss and Charles Ebbets he continued to battle umpires and league presidents.[60] Always resentful of the power of the National Commission, Brush led a guerrilla war against it. Although he did not live to see it, his dissent eventually helped to put baseball under the even stronger rule of Judge Landis.

The passing of the nineteenth-century "magnate" brought other controversial personalities forward, and for a time Charles Murphy of the Cubs was a favorite whipping boy. Outspoken, crass,

[59] *Reach's Official Base Ball Guide*, 1913, 1915, pp. 7–8, 1916, p. 9, 1920, p. 194; *Spalding's Official Base Ball Record*, 1911, p. 7, 1918, p. 5; *Base Ball Blue Book*, 1915, p. 10.

[60] *Baseball Magazine*, January, 1913, pp.57–61, August, 1913, p. 30; Mrs. John McGraw, *op. cit.*, 201–22, 236–38.

ruthless, he was harried out of baseball in 1914, but not without a lucrative payoff. He left exulting, "I didn't think there was so much money in the world."[61] Like Murphy, Fogel of Philadelphia was ousted as a troublemaker, and his club passed into the hands of William Baker who gained a reputation for cheapness, best symbolized by the park which bore his name.

The difficulty of classing National League owners as saints or sinners was increased by the presence of a woman in the ranks. In 1910, the death of Robison put the Cardinals in the hands of his attractive daughter, Mrs. Schuyler Britton. Because nobody expected her to work at the role, she was given courtly treatment at the league meeting that year, and she charmed sportswriters by claiming greater interest in Christmas shopping. However, she soon hired and fired Roger Bresnahan as manager, and went on to challenge a host of successive managers before selling out in 1918. By then, the Cardinals had become the weakest franchise in the league. In time, however, the capable combination of owner Sam Breadon and his general manager, Branch Rickey, revived the club and made it great.[62]

In the silver age writers often contrasted the truculence of National owners with the tolerance of the Americans. In Phelon's opinion, Johnson's genius lay in his ability to handpick co-operative owners. But even Johnson had an opponent; in 1910 his old friend Comiskey rebelled at Johnson's discipline and his vengeful opposition eventually broke Johnson's power. As owner of the American's most lucrative franchise in this era, Comiskey was a formidable power. A man whose sole income came from baseball, he battled hard to field a team that would attract fans to his expensive park. Because his fortune depended on the support of fans, he pandered to them, thereby becoming baseball's most popular owner. On opening his new park, he offered its use free for any worthy project, saying, "The fans built the park, didn't they?" He was also popular for such policies as letting bleacherites move to the grandstand

61 *Baseball Magazine*, March, 1913, pp. 26–28, April, 1914, p. 14; *Spalding's Official Base Ball Record*, 1913, pp. 20–21; *The Sporting News*, February 26, 1914.

62 *Baseball Magazine*, January, 1913, pp. 110–12; *The Sporting News*, June 9, 1910, April 6, December 21, 1911, July 18, 1918.

when it rained. Although he was liked by the fans, others took differing views of Comiskey. To his players he was a cheapskate, and to Johnson he was a rowdy umpire-baiter. But as vice-president of the league in 1916, he carried on a vendetta with Johnson which helped to break Johnson's power in 1921.[63]

Like Comiskey, other ex-players worked their way into the ranks of American owners, and depended heavily on baseball earnings for their livelihood. Because Connie Mack and Clark Griffith both battled a feast and famine existence, they were forced into conservative policies and were often branded as skinflints by fans and players.[64]

In 1915, as Mack and Griffith struggled to complete the purchase of their teams, Johnson's strongest supporters included Charles Somers of Cleveland, Frank Navin of Detroit, and Robert Hedges of St. Louis. These were his stable outposts while Boston and New York were disappointingly chaotic. In spite of its pennant successes, Boston reeled under a succession of vacillating owners, while New York suffered under the lightweight leadership of Frank Farrell. Always close to bankruptcy, Farrell finally gave up in 1914, allowing a relieved Johnson to seek the kind of free-spending owners needed to compete with the popular Giants.

The search for reliable owners was a major task of Johnson's leadership, and his efforts lend insight into the clubby world of owners. Johnson demanded that a candidate put love of baseball and loyalty to the league above profit-seeking. Not that an owner had to play Santa Claus, but he had to understand that his franchise was linked with seven others and that his policies affected those others. Obviously, the success of the system demanded cooperative owners, and newcomers had to learn the inside rules of the system. Johnson's effort was to bar "troublemakers," but his choices had to be approved by others. By 1910, both leagues had devised an elaborate and secret policy for screening applicants. It began by ordering any applicant to submit his qualifications in

[63] Axelson, *op. cit.*, 186–95, 207, 308–10; *Spalding's Official Base Ball Record,* 1920, p. 187.

[64] *Baseball Magazine*, January, 1913, pp. 77–112; *The Sporting News*, February 16, 1907, November 9, 1911, January 19, 1922; Bealle, *op. cit.*, 3–4, 108–12.

writing. If all owners approved, he was admitted unconditionally; if two dissented, his admission was subject to review after a year. Moreover, the 1910 agreement allowed seven owners to expel another by their unanimous vote. If ousted, the owner was reimbursed, but he was pledged to sell the franchise only to the league. Moreover, owners gave their word not to resist league policy by suing in the civil courts.[65]

Although the utility of this brotherly code can be defended, its legal status was shaky. To subvert the system a maverick with one or two allies could stir up a hornet's nest of dissent. And this was precisely what happened in the American League. In 1914, Johnson induced Jacob Ruppert, a wealthy New York realtor and brewer, to take over the New York franchise. With a partner, Tillinghast Huston, Ruppert moved in and undertook a lavish spending program to build the Yankees. At first Johnson was delighted, but when Ruppert began dealing exclusively with Harry Frazee, the latest Boston owner, Johnson was irritated by the adverse publicity that followed. When protests followed the sale of pitcher Carl Mays to the Yankees, Johnson used the 1910 code to nullify the deal. But Ruppert and Huston broke the rules by going to the courts where they got an injunction against Johnson. At this point Johnson might have evoked the ouster clause of the 1910 agreement, but Ruppert had the support of Frazee and two of Johnson's enemies, Comiskey and Phil Ball of the Browns.[66] The episode was a shocking blow to Johnson's power, marking the end of an era in baseball, and setting in motion a search for a new political equilibrium.

[65] U.S. House of Representatives, *Organized Professional Team Sports*, Report No. 1720, 85 Cong., 2 sess., 1958, pp. 1352–57, 1388–91.

[66] *The Sporting News,* November 9, 1916, September 11, 1919, February 12, 1920.

5

Baseball's Time of Troubles

1. The Federal League War

Haunted by memories of business depressions and baseball wars, owners moved into the silver age with varying degrees of confidence. The more timorous adopted an attitude of "watchful waiting"; their bolder colleagues built the first of the modern ball parks. Caution was an understandable reaction. After all, the nation had undergone a business recession in 1904–1905 and a "panic" in 1907–1908, but baseball survived both periods easily. The vitality of the game led not only to expanded investment, but to attempted incursions by outsiders.

To ward off these raids, owners tried to conceal evidence of baseball's prosperity. After 1911, no attendance figures appeared in the *Guides,* and other information on earnings was withheld. But it was too late; the park building boom and World Series crowds were evidence enough to whet the appetites of outsiders.

Indeed, poachers were already on the major-league preserve in 1911. That year, William Whitman and Harry Boyer, of Reading, Pennsylvania, hastily established the "United States League" with outposts in Baltimore, Philadelphia, Reading, New York, Newark, Washington, and Lynchburg. Although they banked on expanding urban populations to support more big-league baseball, the interlopers did a wretched job of planning. After only three games in 1912, the jerry-built circuit failed, leaving unpaid players and a harvest of ill will. That same year, a similar fate overtook the "Columbian League," an abortive attempt by John T. Powers of Chicago, who hoped to stock his western circuit with major leaguers.

Editor Richter of *Reach's Official Base Ball Guide* viewed these failures as evidence of organized baseball's impregnability, warning that the "salvation, stability, or existence" of any league must take place within the National Agreement of 1903. But his pronouncement impressed no one, certainly not Powers, who quickly rebounded and in 1913 promoted the Federal League in the midwest. The new league finished the season, but with unknown players and profits. This inauspicious beginning led to talk of disbandment in the fall.[1]

But at this point a savior appeared. A Chicago iron manufacturer, James A. Gilmore, or "Long Jim" to his cronies, presented himself at the meeting of the disconsolate Federal owners and painted a bright word picture of an expanded operation with expanded profits. Incredibly, Gilmore persuaded the Federal leaders to drop Powers and place himself as their head. This coup passed largely unnoticed until Gilmore announced that the Federals now had the support of a wealthy Chicago restaurant owner, Charles Weeghman. With the Weeghman name at his command, Gilmore lined up stronger backers from Kansas City, Indianapolis, Baltimore, Buffalo, St. Louis, and Toronto.

While investigating the Toronto territory, Gilmore met Robert B. Ward of Brooklyn, the baseball-minded president of the Ward

1 *Baseball Magazine,* January, 1911, p. *Reach's Official Base Ball Guide,* 1913, p. 9, 1914, pp. 521–27.

Baking Company. A genuine friendship quickly developed, and Ward became Gilmore's most dependable source of wealth. For the moment, Ward was handed the Toronto territory to disguise his real plan, which was to plant a franchise in Brooklyn. The ruse worked well, and Ward dropped a bombshell in 1914 by announcing that old Washington Park would be the home of his "Tip Tops," a team name taken right off the label of his best selling bread loaf.

Gilmore's amazing powers of persuasion helped him line up other influential men, such as the St. Louis pair of Phil Ball, an ice machine manufacturer, and Otto Stifel, the brewer. Both were wealthy, but seemed impoverished alongside oil king Albert Sinclair, whose 1915 entrance as holder of the Newark franchise frightened all major-league owners. The greatest scare was given to Harry Hempstead, Brush's successor with the Giants; he was afraid that Sinclair was out to do him in for having spurned the oilman's offer to buy the Giants at the time of Brush's death. Ball and Weeghman seemed similarly motivated, for each had made generous offers to buy big-league franchises, and each had met with a rebuff. Vengeance also motivated the pathetic Horace Fogel to join with the Federals, but his effectiveness was lessened by lack of money. On discovering his plight, his colleagues dropped him in favor of a pair of conservative investors who sponsored franchises in Baltimore and Buffalo.[2]

The shock of Gilmore's Federal coup soon gave way to panic in the established leagues as the invaders built parks and tempted major-league players with fantastic offers. By now everybody knew that it was to be war to the death, in the classic style of past wars waged by the Unions or the Players. This time the stakes were to be higher.

Beginning in 1914, Federal agents stalked major- and minor-league clubs in search of talent and found a receptive quarry. They quickly signed an estimated seventy-five by offering salary boosts and bonuses. Among them were forty-two big leaguers, including

[2] *Baseball Magazine*, November, 1913, p. 81, March, 1914, pp. 14–18, 108, April, 1914, pp. 21–22; *The Sporting News*, January 22, April 2, 1914.

well-known players like Tinker, who traded a $5,500 Cincinnati offer for a $12,000 Federal offer; Hal Chase, who moved from $6,000 to $9,000; Russ Ford, who signed for $10,000; and "Three Finger" Brown, who signed for $10,000.

The major-league owners retaliated with blacklists and expulsion threats, yet Federal offers were real enough to force raises in salaries. When Walter Johnson threatened to jump, a frantic Griffith reminded him of his debt to fans. Although Johnson was flattered, he neatly converted the praise into a $12,500 salary as his price for staying home. Meanwhile, other stars like Cobb, Speaker, and Evers asked for raises, and the publicity that greeted each coup made bludgeoning owners a favorite winter sport.

Some owners refused to participate, including Mack who chose to sell his stars rather than submit. If he expected support in the form of an owners' boycott, he was disappointed, as colleagues greedily snapped up his stars. Mack became a short-term profiteer but a long-term loser, and his crippled teams were to spend the next several years in the cellar. It was small consolation that everybody lost money in 1915. At the close of that gloomy season, the only comfort was that the Federals suffered more and faced gate losses in addition to a $300,000 outlay for players.[3]

While their enemies listened for the death rattle, Federal leaders desperately tried to keep their league going, since merely finishing the season could be hailed as a vital sign. Although the pathway was rough, the league survived 1914 with Indianapolis winning the flag. Their franchise was then transferred to Newark under Sinclair. In 1915, Joe Tinker's Chicago "Whales" won behind stars like Bender, Plank, and Ford, edging St. Louis and Pittsburgh in a torrid race. Yet not even the surefire combination of a close race and a ten-cent minimum admission generated fan interest in the Federal venture. The end of the 1915 season found the Federals in a panic. Among its owners, the fainthearted listened to press criticisms that ridiculed its proposals and sneered at the

[3] "The Federal League's Chances," *Literary Digest,* February 7, 1914, 279–82; Bealle, *op. cit.*, 96–98; *The Sporting News,* December 24, 1914, March 26, 1947; *Baseball Magazine,* May, 1914, pp. 43–48, June, 1914, pp. 43–52, March, 1915, p. 22; *Reach's Official Base Ball Guide*, 1913, p. 9, 1914, p. 9, 1915, pp. 360–65.

outlandish team names. Many Federal owners now believed that they had miscalculated the expanding public interest in baseball, and saw their cause as lost. It was bad enough that the Whales could not compete with the Cubs and White Sox, but it was downright disheartening that Baltimore could not hold its own against the International League Orioles. The gloom was deepened by the death of Ward, the man whose energy and bankroll had sustained the Federal League.

Although Ward's death was a staggering loss to Federal prestige, there were still formidable promoters like Sinclair, Ball, and Weeghman. Indeed, Sinclair managed to intimidate the defenders further by purchasing a stadium site in New York City for the apparent purpose of moving his Newark team into the major-league heartland. Sinclair even circulated blueprints describing an ultramodern ball park. Although Johnson favored calling the bluff, owners of the Yankees and Giants persuaded others that it was time to negotiate a peace.

Had they waited, major-league owners might have won a cheap victory, but by playing into the hands of Sinclair, Weeghman, and Ball, they settled for an expensive, negotiated peace. At the treaty table in Cincinnati, this Federal trio called the tune and demanded that each be given an opportunity to pick up available major-league franchises. In December an agreement was reached based on these conditions. Sinclair and Weeghman won the right to buy the Cubs from Charles Taft, while Ball was permitted to buy the Browns from Robert Hedges. After protracted negotiations, each won his prize; Weeghman and Sinclair paid $500,000 for the Cubs and moved them to the Whale grounds, later to become the site of Wrigley Field. In January, 1917, Ball got the Brown's franchise for $525,000. This classic settlement to a classic baseball war included the usual cynical disregard of the interests of poorer Federal owners. Under the agreement, the majors bought off the big powers, paying the Ward interests $20,000 a year for twenty years. Sinclair was paid $10,000 a year for ten years, and Pittsburgh owners received $10,000 a year for five years. Left in the cold were Baltimore, Kansas City, and Buffalo, whose owners won only the right to sell their players for what they could get. The players were protected from suspension or blacklisting, although pitcher Ford never again pitched in the majors.[4]

The Federal settlement cost the major leagues five million dollars as the price for preserving their baseball monopoly. Their expensive triumph was sweetened, however, by the knowledge that the invaders lost at least half a million.[5]

The warfare and its outcome haunted baseball for years. Certainly the cynical settlement left an undesirable implication that any line of action is acceptable, as long as it is backed by strong financial power. But mostly, the war's aftermath raised the specter of federal antitrust action against baseball. Suits were begun as a part of Federal League strategy during the war, but most of them were withdrawn as part of the peace settlement. Disgusted Baltimore promoters pressed on with theirs, however, eventually taking it to the United States Supreme Court. There, in 1922, Justice Oliver Wendell Holmes, Jr., speaking for the majority, upheld baseball's claim to being predominantly a sport, and judged it immune from antitrust prosecution. While this relieved many anxieties, the decision was by no means irrevocable, as later generations of owners would see.[6]

The war also raised anew the question of the reserve clause, and it helped give strength to the Players Fraternity in its efforts for collective bargaining. Also, by 1913 owners had almost persuaded fans to accept a base admission price of fifty cents, but the war revived the old quarter rate. This was a costly retreat for owners, since it came at a time of salary increases. To roll these back meant risking more ill will, and salaries never fell to former standards. Finally, the interleague war weakened the minor leagues and prevented their growth until the 1920's.

[4] *Reach's Official Base Ball Guide,* 1916, pp. 10–13, 31–69, 33–34; *Baseball Magazine*, October, 1915, pp. 81–82, November, 1915, p. 535, December, 1915, January, 1916, pp. 25–32.

[5] *The Sporting News,* December 30, 1915; *Baseball Magazine,* February, 1916, pp. 13–30.

[6] *The Sporting News,* July 30, 1913, December 30, 1915, April 6, 1916; *New York Times,* January 26, February 13, April 15, 1966; *Reach's Official Base Ball Guide,* 1915, pp. 360–65; Federal Base Ball Club of Baltimore, Inc. v. National League of

On the other hand, positive gains accompany wars, and this one brought bold new blood into the ranks of owners. Also, it brought new playing talent to the fore in the persons of men like Edd Roush and Ben Kauff. Above all, it increased attendance and kindled an interest in baseball in areas where major-league games were not to be seen.

Indeed, if baseball were not to be confronted by America's total involvement in a foreign war, this crisis might have been weathered easily. But baseball men had only one season to rest before the storm.[7]

2. The Guns of April 1917

Except for a brief experience with America's "splendid little war" of 1898, baseball owners knew nothing of promoting the sport in wartime. Indeed, only a few remembered the Spanish-American War and its impact on gate receipts, and there was little precedent to alert owners to the austerities and sacrifices demanded by total war.

The war came to America in April, 1917, at a time when owners were cheered by the prosperity of 1916. When the first alarms sounded, the season of 1917 was already under way, prompting owners to press on with business as usual. Until August, this seemed a wise course, as attendance ran high and players were untouched by the draft. Moreover, there was a high number of rejections of players for physical causes, so owners fully expected that their players would stay with them. Optimists hoped that baseball would be protected by the government for its morale-supporting potential. Hoping to plant this idea in the minds of officials, Clark Griffith established a bat and ball fund for the military services. Others showed their loyalty by admitting uniformed soldiers free and by drilling players in pre-game patriotic shows.[8]

By the end of 1917, however, baseball, like other American

Professional B. B. Clubs and American League of Professional B. B. Clubs, 259 U.S. 200, 42 Supreme Court 465.

[7] *The Sporting News,* March 26, 1947, May 30, 1964; *Spalding's Official Base Ball Guide,* 1914, pp. 17–26; *Spalding's Base Ball Record,* 1916, pp. 31, 68–69, 1917, p. 5.

[8] *The Sporting News,* August 16, 23, 30, 1917.

institutions, faced increasingly greater sacrifices. The society was moving to put five million men in uniform, with two million heading for France. At the same time, a vast propaganda machine proclaimed the no-nonsense "Work or Fight" slogan in support of the military effort. To survive, baseball had to convince war leaders that it was an adjunct of the war effort. This was a difficult task in that ballplayers were already being scored as "slackers."[9]

It mattered little that baseball men gave bats and balls, or drilled players, or sported flags on uniform sleeves; what hurt the game's image was the scarcity of voluntary enlistments, the reluctance of owners to accept a 10 per cent admissions tax, and the players' demand for higher salaries. For these reasons, baseball was accused of not sacrificing enough, and its status as an essential activity was much clouded.[10]

As the war drums beat, baseball men worried over scheduling, retention of players, travel restrictions, and rising costs of scarcer hotel space. At the winter meetings of 1917–18, bewilderment resulted in a decision to muddle along. Owners sent their teams south for training and ordered players to stay with the teams even if this made them easier to draft. Branch Rickey was the only one who understood the dangers of this policy clearly enough to sign draft-proof Cuban players as a hedge against the realities of military conscription.[11]

Sensing that baseball would never qualify as war work, many of the players sought more sheltered work. Some turned to war jobs, while others enlisted as physical training instructors or joined up hoping to play for service teams. Although shielded from bullets and shrapnel, these were caught in a verbal cross fire. On the one hand, club owners and sportswriters scored them as deserters from baseball and sought to list them on a "dishonor roll." On the other hand, outside critics attacked the government for allowing industries like Bethlehem Steel to use players in spurious "Patriotic Baseball Leagues." Among the players censured for joining these leagues were Joe Jackson, Jeff Tesreau, and briefly, Babe Ruth.

[9] *Ibid.*, November 15, 1917.

[10] *Ibid.*, October 4, 18, November 8, 1917.

[11] *Ibid.*, February 14, 1918.

Industrialist Charles Schwab was vilified for giving them the opportunity. Public feeling against players grew, and in September, 1918, workers at Philadelphia's Cramp Shipyard struck in protest of "do nothing" players who rode to work in cars and collected foremen's wages for playing baseball.[12]

Of course it was unfair to classify all players as opportunistic draft dodgers, since at least 550 present and future players saw service, and some like Eddie Grant and A. T. Burr died in action. Many were wounded or incurred disabilities like Mathewson, who was accidentally gassed in training with a chemical. The damage to his lungs led to his premature death from tuberculosis in 1925. The brunt of service naturally fell on the young, including those who came up to the majors in the period 1912–18 or those who played in the minors at this time. But older stars like Cobb, Sisler, and Alexander served too, as did administrators like Rickey and Huston.[13]

Despite such positive efforts, baseball's over-all war record was not enviable. Because theatrical and movie people had been declared essential to the war effort, baseball men expected the same treatment. But in May, 1918, the Provost Marshal, General Alvin Crowder, listed baseball along with other "games, sports, and amusements" as nonessential. A blow to baseball men, the decision was appealed to the President. In arguing their case, they pleaded possible financial ruin and waved the banner of the national game. But the appeal got nowhere. In July, Secretary of War Newton Baker backed Crowder and declared that after September 2, players would be drafted as nonessential. His only concession was to permit a two-week delay for the completion of the World Series.[14]

Baseball leaders complied, and the Series was completed by September 12 with the Red Sox winning and extending their unbeaten Series record to five. But there was little glory for anyone, and the Series drew poorly. Sensing a low payoff, the players threatened a strike for more money. Their rebellious mood caused an

[12] *Ibid.*, March 14, May 9, 23, June 20, July 4, September 26, 1918.

[13] Cobb and Stump, *op. cit.*, 189–91; *Reach's Official Base Ball Guide*, 1919, pp. 8–17; Lee Allen, "Statistical data on baseball players," 1919–20 entries.

[14] *Reach's Official Base Ball Guide*, 1919, pp. 8–17.

embarrassing delay before the last game, and only appeals to player patriotism headed off a real strike. Altogether, the combination of low attendance and a curtailed season made 1918 the worst financial year of the silver age. Because of ill will engendered, some writers suggested that baseball redeem its image by ceasing operations for 1919 and deeding the parks to the military for storage depots.[15]

During the same years, baseball's difficulties were compounded by charges of corruption. In August, 1918, Hal Chase of the Reds was suspended for betting and attempting to bribe an opposing pitcher to throw a game. When the story broke, others about Chase's earlier misadventures were recounted. One told how Chase was always hounded by jeers such as "What are the odds?" Since Chase was also a Federal turncoat, such charges led to his expulsion, but he went to the courts and forced officials to exonerate him for lack of evidence. Chase was eventually blacklisted, but his defiance and successful reinstatement encouraged imitators.[16]

Other complications were introduced as owners and managers tampered with each other's player contracts in the search for talent. In a famous case involving pitcher Scott Perry, the Athletics competed with the Braves. Under baseball regulations, Perry remained the property of the Braves even after he had taken a defense job in 1917. But the A's signed him for 1918, and, when challenged, went to court in defiance of the National Agreement. This attack on the Commissioner system was temporarily healed by Johnson's diplomacy, but the compromise so irritated President John Tener of the National League that he resigned in protest. It also suggested a new line of action for Yankee owner Ruppert who was busily buying players; in 1919 he too resorted to the courts when Johnson opposed his signing of Carl Mays.[17]

Under attack by hostile critics and suffering from wartime restrictions and financial losses, baseball men met in a gloomy session made more ominous by the influenza epidemic of the year

[15] *Ibid.; The Sporting News,* August 22, 1918.

[16] *Reach's Official Base Ball Guide,* 1919, pp. 147–48; *The Sporting News,* November 9, 1944.

[17] *Reach's Official Base Ball Guide,* 1919, pp. 1–17, 58–67, 1920, pp. 8–29.

1918. Although cheered by the Armistice, the magnates bearishly adopted a shortened schedule for 1919, since most assumed that war restrictions would be continued. But once again the players had a clearer grasp of reality. Already they were quitting defense jobs and resuming "usual off season loafing," confident that American fans would forget the war and the slacker talk and return to old-fashioned hero worship.[18]

3. The Black Sox Scandal, 1919–20

After the low point of 1918, baseball fortunes did a complete about-face in 1919. Trouble disappeared and war-weary fans returned in droves, bringing unprecedented profits. That year, even weak teams like the Phillies, Cardinals, Braves, and Senators made money. With Sunday baseball now legalized in New York, the city's three franchises swam in profits.

The season was also remarkable for the armies of youthful fans that editor John Foster of *Spalding's Guide* noticed at the games. In the National League, thousands cheered the Cincinnati Reds on to their first championship since 1882, which they won by nine games over McGraw's perennial champs. In the American League, even more turned out, braving late summer race riots to cheer "Kid" Gleason's Chicago White Sox as they drove to a hard-fought three-and-a-half game victory over Cleveland.

In October, excitement over the impending Series clash between the Red Sox and the White Sox gripped the nation and promised to topple all attendance records. Although the superbly balanced White Sox were favored, Cincinnati fans took heart as their team, playing at home, won the first two games, 9–1 and 4–2. Moving to Chicago, Manager Pat (Whiskey Face) Moran's team fell before Dickey Kerr 3–2 but rebounded to win the next two by scores of 2–0 and 5–0. Looking like a sure winner now, the Reds returned home to a delirious reception. Needing only one victory to clinch the Series, the Reds looked invincible, but Chicago fought back and won the next two games by scores of 5–4 and 4–1. The final two games were slated for Chicago, where Claude "Lefty" Wil-

[18] *Ibid.*, 1920, 8–29; *Spalding's Official Base Ball Guide*, 1920, pp. 5–29, 39–41.

liams seemed certain to win. However, Williams was hammered for five runs in the first two innings and the White Sox lost, 10–5.

The victory made the Reds World Champions, but there were "rumors of collusion" which Foster of *Spalding's Guide* dismissed as unfounded. As he saw it, the experts simply failed to appreciate Cincinnati's teamwork or the pitching of Dutch Reuther, "Slim" Sallee, and Jim Ring, or the lusty batting of Edd Roush.[19]

This version of the outcome of the 1919 Series might have prevailed and might have caused it to be ranked somewhere behind the victory of the "Miracle Braves" in the annals of underdog triumphs. No doubt it would have been dredged up from time to time to inspire the forlorn, or perhaps as filler material for unimaginative sportswriters. But it was not accepted, primarily because of persistent rumors telling of gamblers who corrupted some White Sox players and paid them to lose. The rumors were widespread and detailed. White Sox fans heard stories about Ray Schalk, the angry catcher, goading pitchers Cicotte and Williams with obscenities matched only by those of manager Gleason. Reds fans told of "Whiskey Face" Moran asking pitcher Hod Eller if gamblers had approached him. "Yep," replied Eller, who cheerfully admitted turning down a $5,000 bribe. Moran allowed Eller to pitch, but kept a close but unnecessary watch. Eller won easily.[20]

Had the rumors been confined to the playing field, it is probable that the players' code would have preserved the official version. But that year the rumors reached the pressbox where Hugh Fullerton toiled among a hundred other writers. To an inquisitive reporter like Fullerton, tracking down rumors was a joy of life. His tireless digging uncovered the tangled tale of corruption that made the 1919 World Series an American tragedy.

In lifting the lid on the Pandora's box, Fullerton was assisted by Christy Mathewson, who covered the Series for the *New York World*. Matty became Fullerton's expert witness, diagramming each questionable play during the Series. With these diagrams, plus his own findings, Fullerton wrote a sensational series of articles telling of the fix, the fixers, and all their spoils. Although Fullerton's

19 *Spalding's Official Base Ball Guide*, 1920, pp. 5–15.
20 Ritter, *op. cit.*, 201–14.

articles were widely read, they were discounted as improbable muckraking. One critic objected that Fullerton was "always scoffing at the honesty of an institution, no matter how sacred." Nevertheless, Fullerton's charges led to four independent investigations. Heydler, Johnson, Comiskey, and Bill Veeck of the Cubs each hired detectives to dig into the tale. Comiskey even offered a reward of $10,000 for any bona fide proof of corruption.[21]

At this point there was every chance that the episode might be eclipsed by other sensational news items. Americans in 1919 were daily reminded of threats posed by Bolsheviks, left-wing intellectuals, labor leaders, and sundry dissenters, all of whom were being pursued by patriotic witch hunters. Other stories told of looting in Boston in the wake of a police strike. The new year of 1920 brought lurid headlines about smuggling rings which provided bootleg liquor in defiance of national prohibition. And in August, 1920, came the exposure of Charles Ponzi, the former convict who swindled five million dollars out of investors with a sordid stock-jobbing scheme.[22]

Meanwhile, in the baseball world of 1920, Brooklyn coasted to an easy victory in the National League. The American League race was a lively fight between Cleveland, Chicago, and New York. Before the season ended, the public read much of Ruth's home runs and the tragic beaning of Ray Chapman. Chapman's death made Cleveland a sentimental favorite for the pennant, and the team beat the White Sox out by two games. This popular victory was cheapened, however, by late season revelations of new Chicago corruption.

An old campaigner like Comiskey should have known that unpunished corruption breeds more corruption. In 1919 he had debated for a long time whether to release the Series checks to the players suspected of throwing games, and he tarried longer before

[21] *Baseball Magazine*, December, 1919, pp. 59–60, February, 1920, p. 470, December, 1920, editorial; Hugh Fullerton, "Baseball on Trial," *New Republic*, October 20, 1920; *Reach's Official Base Ball Guide*, 1920, pp. 8–27; Eliot Asinoff, *Eight Men Out: The Black Sox and the 1919 World Series*, 133.

[22] Laurence Greene, *The Era of Wonderful Nonsense: A Casebook of the Twenties*, 52–53.

mailing them contracts for 1920. To his lasting regret he did not take decisive action, thus encouraging the men to do more game selling. Late in the 1920 season, new charges were made that some of his men had been paid off for losing key games, thus enabling Cleveland to take the pennant. By this time, game selling had spread beyond the White Sox, and before the season ended Lee Magee of the Cubs was fired for trying to fix a game with the Phils.[23]

By September a storm of publicity began to confirm these stories and to revive stories of previous misdeeds. In mid-September, baseball faced a grand jury investigation into the conduct of the 1919 Series. Soon after this announcement came James Isaminger's story in the *Philadelphia North American* based on an interview with gambler Bill Maharg, who supplied details of the fix and names of fixers. As this story broke, the White Sox were only a game and a half out of first place. At this point, pitcher Ed Cicotte and infielder Buck Weaver confessed their part in the conspiracy to Comiskey. Comiskey angrily told them to go to the Chicago grand jury. Only then did he suspend the eight whom he had long suspected of being guilty. The long-delayed action not only cost Comiskey the 1920 pennant and the services of the best players he ever had, but it revealed him as a man who put personal profits ahead of integrity and who had remained silent in the face of known corruption. The consequences of his dilatory action were far reaching; he undermined Johnson's prestige and the power of the three-man National Commission, and opened baseball to the rule of a single authoritarian commissioner.

The rest of the dismal story is well known. Eight men from Comiskey's team were implicated in the conspiracy and were branded as the "Black Sox," including Joe Jackson, owner of a .365 lifetime batting average, pitchers Cicotte and Williams, infielders Weaver, Swede Riseberg, and Chick Gandil (who had retired early in 1920), outfielder Oscar "Happy" Felsch, and utility man Fred McMullin.[24]

[23] Asinoff, *op. cit.,* 144–47.
[24] *New York Times,* September 29, 1920.

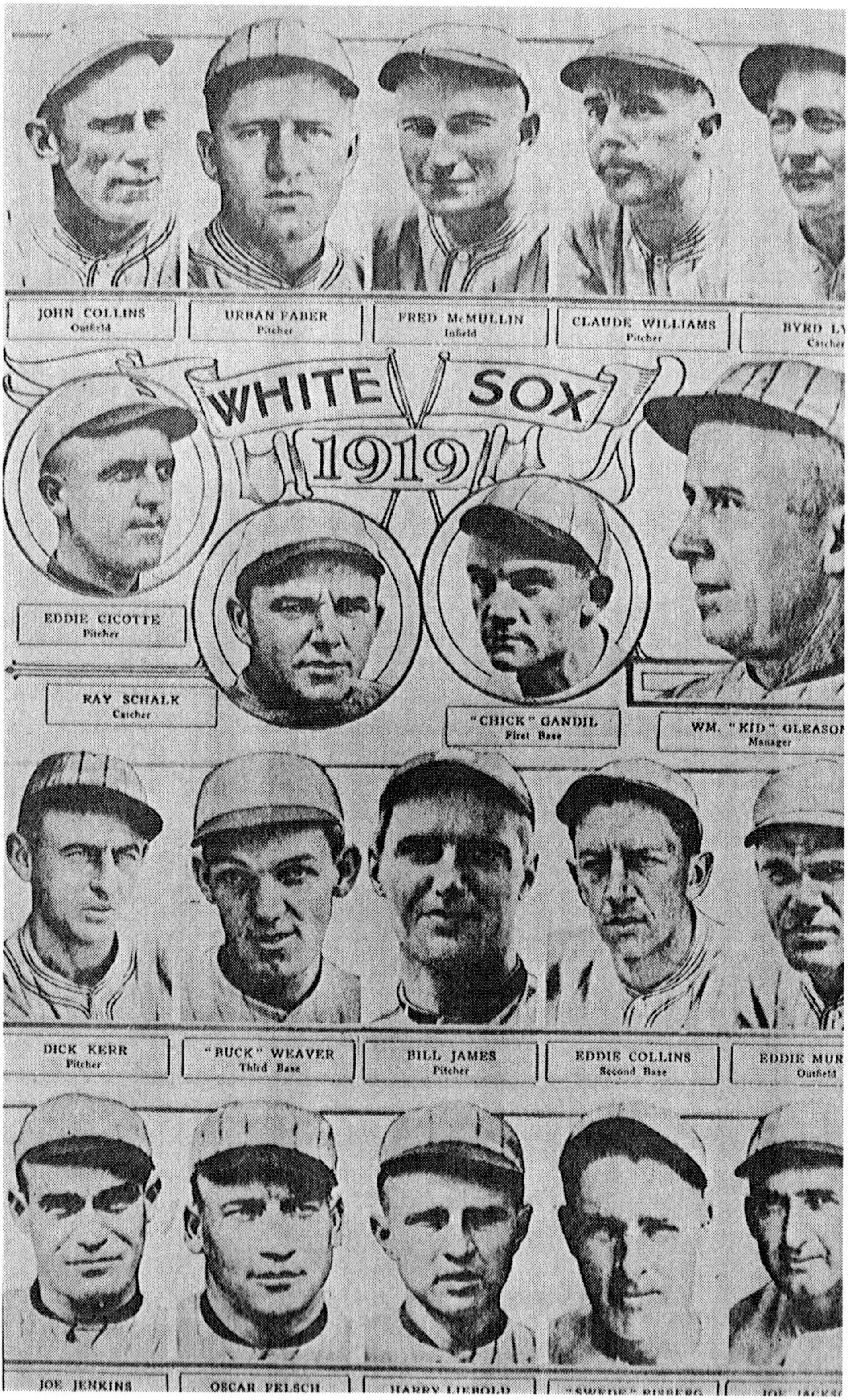

JOHN COLLINS
Outfield
URBAN FABER
Pitcher
FRED McMULLIN
Infield
CLAUDE WILLIAMS
Pitcher
BYRD LY
Catcher
WHITE SOX
1919
EDDIE CICOTTE
Pitcher
RAY SCHALK
Catcher
"CHICK" GANDIL
First Base
WM. "KID" GLEASON
Manager
DICK KERR
Pitcher
"BUCK" WEAVER
Third Base
BILL JAMES
Pitcher
EDDIE COLLINS
Second Base
EDDIE MUR
Outfield
JOE JENKINS
OSCAR FELSCH
HARRY LIEBOLD
"SWEDE" RISBERG

Facing the grand jury, Cicotte tearfully told of getting $10,000 which he used to pay for a farm mortgage, and Jackson said he got only $5,000 of a promised $20,000. Williams reported that gamblers threatened to kill his wife unless he let down in the final game. Several accounts agreed that Gandil, with $35,000, was the instigator and chief profiteer. Later testimony maintained that Cicotte had made extra money by betting on the Reds to win the fixed games. Only Weaver claimed to have gotten nothing, and he insisted that he had pulled out of the conspiracy but had agreed to shut up about the affair.

Of course the gamblers were the real winners. The grand jury summoned Arnold Rothstein, the "king of gamblers," but he appeared as a friendly witness and named Abe Attell as the chief conspirator, disclaiming any connection with the intrigue. Much later, in July, 1921, Ban Johnson, after spending $10,000 of league funds on his investigation, accused Rothstein of an active role. Even though the charge was libelous, Rothstein refused to sue, perhaps on the advice of a colleague who once told him, "Never sue. They might prove it."[25]

In June, 1921, a conspiracy trial was held in Chicago before Judge Hugo Friend, but it was a farce since the records of the grand jury and the confessions of Cicotte, Jackson, and Williams had mysteriously disappeared. This bizarre development made it possible for all eight of those accused to repudiate their confessions. The lack of evidence and a friendly jury turned the trial into a comedy. At one point, the eight were greeted by their "clean" teammates, who visited them in court. The trial ended on August

[25] *Ibid.*; Asinoff, *op. cit.*, 237–73; Lewis Thompson and Charles Boswell, "Say It Ain't So, Joe" *American Heritage,* June, 1960, pp. 24–27, 88–93; *Chicago Daily Tribune,* September 20, 21, 1920.

The Chicago White Sox of 1919 won the American League pennant but lost the World Series that year in what was to become American baseball's most notorious scandal. The eight "Black Sox" who accepted bribes for throwing the 1919 Series to the Cincinnati Reds were McMullin, Williams, Cicotte, Gandil, Weaver, Felsch, Risberg, and Jackson. All were barred from baseball for life by Commissioner K. M. Landis. (George Brace, photographer)

2, and the "not guilty" verdict was greeted by cheers from spectators, some of whom shouted, "Hooray for the clean Sox." Even though the men were found innocent in the world of civil law, they still faced judgment in the baseball world. The final arbiter was Commissioner Landis, and he summarily barred all eight for life.[26] For the rest of their lives they bore the stigma of "Black Sox." In spite of repeated appeals, Landis stubbornly refused to grant a single pardon.

To protest this arbitrary verdict on any grounds is probably fruitless. Yet the fact is that these scapegoats were denied their civil rights by the application of baseball regulations. Today, such a sentence would be preposterous; its imposition in 1921 rested on the moralistic consensus of baseball people and the support of a populace unaware of the undesirable effect on civil liberties and over-aware of moralistic strictures.

The harried later lives of these baseball Ishmaels underscore the complete subjection of players under the baseball regulations of the silver age. They were shunned by organized baseball, and any attempts to ply their trade were thwarted. Some managed to play with semipro or outlaw leagues under aliases, but exposure inevitably led to pressure which forced them out. Only Buck Weaver fought back. Suing in the courts, he won partial payment on his 1920 contract. He appealed six times to Landis for reinstatement, once with a petition bearing fourteen thousand signatures, but each time he was rebuffed. Jackson tried playing under an assumed name until he could no longer stand the pain of exposure, and the late Cicotte lived for years under an assumed name, proud of a relative whom he coached and who made the majors under the Cicotte name.[27]

One of the reasons why these eight so recklessly gambled their reputations on an ill-conceived intrigue is not hard to understand. They played on a clique-ridden team which pitted a sophisticated

[26] *New York Times*, May 2, 1966; *Chicago Daily Tribune*, August 3, 1921.

[27] Farrell, *op. cit.*, 177–78; Interview, Farrell with Voigt; Asinoff, *op. cit.*, 280–92; Thompson and Boswell, *loc. cit.;* Cicotte's death in May, 1969 renewed debate over the incident. See Charles Chamberlain, Associated Press article, August 10, 1969.

element, led by captain Eddie Collins, against a more earthy, less polished group, led by "Chick" Gandil. Jealousy and verbal abuse marked the infighting as the Gandil faction concentrated its attack on Collins's "dudish" manners and $15,000 salary. Since none of the Gandil faction made over $6,000, this clique continually groused about Comiskey's penny-pinching, and indeed his 1919 payroll was one of baseball's lowest.[28]

Although baseball legend continues to proclaim that there have been only three cases of proven dishonesty in the game's long history, the silver age was actually riddled with rumors of bribery and cheating. In the first modern World Series, catcher Lou Criger reportedly turned down a $12,000 bribe, and in the second Rube Waddell supposedly was offered $17,000 not to play. Whether by coincidence or not, he injured himself tripping over a suitcase and did not appear. There were rumors of fixed games in the 1918 World Series and recent evidence suggests that the Reds also had problems with fixers in 1919. Outfielder Edd Roush told of one suspected player who got on base accidentally. To score would threaten the fix, so he held back on Roush's long hit. Hot on his heels, Roush goaded him to score by shouting, "Get running, you crooked son of a bitch."[29]

There were other rumors of corruption in regular season games. In 1908, a group of Phillies threw a gambler down the clubhouse stairs at the Polo Grounds after he tried to bribe them to lose a game. That same season, after a pennant race that ended in a tie, umpires Klem and Johnson reported a bribe attempt in behalf of the Giants in the playoff. In 1916, the Giants were accused of malingering to help the Dodgers beat out the Phillies—a charge

28 Asinoff, *op. cit.*, 6–27; William Veeck, Jr., and Ed Linn, *Veeck As in Wreck*, 252–60; *Baseball Magazine*, March, 1916, pp. 53–67, made this prophecy concerning Jackson: "Wait five years or so. Then Joe will go through all he has made in baseball and be broke once more. What will he do? Why go back in the cotton mill . . . for $1.25."; In 1969 the octogenarian "Chick" Gandil hotly denied his guilt, stating that he'd go to his grave "with a clear conscience." He also warned that attorney Melvin Belli was exploring the possibility of suing organized baseball for defamation. *The Sporting News*, September 6, 1969.

29 William Veeck, Jr., and Ed Linn, *The Hustler's Handbook*, 252–99; Asinoff, *op. cit.*, 207; Lieb and Baumgartner, *op. cit.*, 138–45, 229; *Spalding's Official Base Ball Guide*, 1909, p. 29; *Baseball Magazine*, November, 1908, pp. 11–12.

that McGraw himself believed to be true. Persistent rumors of game selling centered around Hal Chase. Indeed, inquiry into the Black Sox fix turned up evidence that Chase and Joe Gedeon of the Browns made money betting on the Reds. And, by delaying the 1919 fix investigation, baseball men created a climate for more corruption in 1920. That year, detectives unearthed evidence linking two Giants and four Cubs with fix plots, and cast suspicion on some players for the Yankees, Braves, Red Sox, and Indians. That these were not mere rumors was testified to by the blacklisting of Magee and Hendrix of the Cubs.

Other questionable practices were openly sanctioned throughout the silver age. It was customary for contending ball clubs to offer a suit of clothes to a non-contending pitcher for defeating another contender. In 1917, the White Sox awarded suits to Detroit players for *losing* two doubleheaders.[30]

After two decades of maintaining that the game was incorruptible in the face of increasing evidence to the contrary, baseball men made scapegoats of the most brazen cheaters. But they did not purge Comiskey for sitting on evidence that could have cleaned house in 1919 and possibly headed off the scandals of 1920.[31] His colleagues avoided him after 1920, and his last years were lonely ones. His one consolation was that he kept his franchise. Apparently the fans could overlook even revealed corruption, for they kept coming, enabling the American League to exceed an attendance of five million in 1920. Moreover, in spite of banner headlines about the Black Sox scandal, the 1920 Series drew well.[32]

If owners had kept cool under the fire of publicity and probes they might have kept their power. But they panicked, and, led by President John Heydler of the National League, Albert D. Lasker, and William Wrigley, beleaguered owners called for an end to the National Commission and its replacement by an outsider such as Judge Landis. Johnson tried to prevent this, insisting

[30] *The Sporting News,* April 8, August 28, 1920.

[31] "Honesty in Baseball," *Literary Digest,* May 24, 1913; *The Sporting News,* November 4, 1920; Veeck and Linn, *Veeck as in Wreck.*

[32] U.S. House of Representatives, *Organized Baseball,* pp. 1617–18; *The Sporting News,* October 21, 1920.

that baseball should clean its own house and warning that Landis was a pompous fraud. Five American owners sided with Johnson, including those of Philadelphia, St. Louis, Cleveland, Detroit, and Washington, but the other three joined the solid National bloc in support of Landis. With eleven clubs arrayed against him, Johnson faced an ultimatum—submit to a new National Agreement naming Landis as commissioner or watch the eleven form a new major league. Johnson was unwillingly forced to let his power slip away while that of Landis rose.[33] Never again would a league president command anything like Johnson's power, nor, on the whole, use it so effectively. His passing from the scene in 1920, and the emergence of Landis, marked the end of the silver age.

[33] Veeck and Linn, *Veeck as in Wreck,* 252–99; *Baseball Magazine,* December, 1920, January, 1921; *The Sporting News,* October 7, 1920.

II. *Baseball's Second Golden Age*

6

A Trio of Demigods

1. A Man for the Guilty Season

North of the equator, the rhythm of natural processes decrees that October must be the month of withdrawal. This is most dramatically seen in the annual cessation of warm weather activities, including those of the baseball world. By 1920, three generations of fans had come to know that nature's autumn coloration meant the time of the dead season was at hand. But they also knew that baseball responded to the great rhythm, insuring a new season and the rebirth of hopes in the spring. Human intervention sometimes disturbed baseball's part in the natural order, but the essential rhythm had operated for sixty years. Then came the events of the 1920 season, especially the revelation of human fallibility, which threatened to destroy the ancient rhythm.

At the end of the 1920 season, the Black Sox scandal created a mood of doubt and anxiety. After seventeen peaceful years under the National Commission, the scandal struck at the very foundation of baseball, threatening the annihilation of the old pattern of order and offering no replacement.

In a struggle for survival, desperate owners banded together in search of a new equilibrium. Spurred by fear, they rejected the leadership of Johnson, and sought a new messiah, Federal Judge Kenesaw Mountain Landis. On November 12, 1920, a large delegation met in Chicago and voted unanimously to offer the judge the task of refurbishing the major-league image. Then, like the soldiers who saved Paris, they piled into taxis and headed for the Federal Building to anoint the chosen savior.

In their eagerness, it was understandable that they expected a cordial welcome, a fawning acceptance, and a pledge of loyalty to their interests. But the moment they entered the Federal Building, the owners abandoned such hopes. The atmosphere of the judicial temple overwhelmed them. They walked into the judge's courtroom and stood in the back where they contemplated their chosen leader. In the formidable setting of the court, Landis struck an awesome pose with black robes lending grandeur to a spare frame and a presence manifested by "a shock of gray hair, a piercing eye, a scowl and a rasping voice." These were great assets for any actor, and Landis was at his best that day.

The owners were ignored as Landis kept on with the case at hand. As the minutes ticked on, they shuffled their feet nervously. Landis then acknowledged them, but in a harsh voice which ordered them to stop the noise or be removed. Sheepishly, the owners accepted the rebuke and remained standing. At last Landis asked them to state their business. Although he had earlier indicated his willingness to take the job, the owners were obliged to restate their offer. Then came a ceremonial refusal as Landis said, "I am doing important work in the community and the nation." The owners quickly suggested he assume both positions, that of judge and baseball chieftain. Still playing cat and mouse, Landis demanded absolute control over baseball matters for a seven-year term. When this was meekly conceded, he agreed to a $50,000 annual salary from which $7,500, his salary as federal judge, would be de-

Shown in this Jovian pose is Judge Kenesaw Mountain Landis, seated in the Commissioner's box seat at a World Series game. Named sole commissioner of baseball in 1920 following the Black Sox scandal, Landis functioned for twenty-five years as the game's conscience. His presence was a part of every World Series contest until his death in 1944. (Spalding Collection, The New York Public Library)

ducted. Later, to the press, Landis pledged that neither "faults in the law, miscarriages in the courts, or complaisance of magnates would prevent him from taking action in every case where he felt there was wrongdoing." Thus the owners acquired a savior. From then until his death in 1944, he would be the symbol of their integrity, and his will would set a limit on their decision-making power.[1]

In January, 1921, the owners signed a new National Agreement binding them for twenty-five years to Landis's stern rule. In the event of his death, the agreement pledged to ask the American President to appoint a replacement. If this was highly speculative, Landis's powers were real enough. As written by John Heydler, the agreement bound players, umpires, and owners to Landis's decisions, because "Nothing is good enough for baseball that is not good enough for America." These were brave words, and to bring them to reality Landis was empowered to investigate "any act, transaction or practice charged, alleged or suspected to be detrimental to the best interests of the national game . . . with authority to summon persons and to order the production of documents, and . . . to impose such penalties as provided." Landis could thus fine,

[1] J. G. Taylor Spink, *Judge Landis and Twenty-Five Years of Baseball,* 64–73; *The Sporting News,* November 18, 1920, January 20, 1921; Frank Graham, "Kenesaw Mountain Landis," *Baseball Magazine,* February, 1945, pp. 291–92; *Reach's Official Base Ball Guide,* 1921, pp. 44–48.

suspend, or remove wrongdoers, levy fines as high as $5,000 on clubs or leagues, and issue public rebukes, all in the interest of maintaining baseball's honor and morale. In signing the new National Agreement, owners bound themselves to baseball regulations and waived their right to seek justice in civil courts.

In their mood of urgency, owners failed to set limits on just what behavior was "detrimental to the game," an oversight that haunted them after their "guilty season" was past and their confidence had been regained. There were a few checks on Landis's power, including the right of league presidents to handle internal troubles, and the creation of an advisory commission to work with Landis but subject to his overruling its decisions. The commission dealt with changes in playing rules, contracts, World Series promotion, the status of players, and the financing of Landis's office. Landis also won the right to name his own secretary-treasurer. His shrewd choice of Leslie O'Connor, a brilliant lawyer and trusted friend, enabled him to control baseball policy by drawing up the agenda for annual meetings.[2]

Landis quickly consolidated his power. His best weapon was his own image as the personification of baseball integrity. He used publicity masterfully and kept himself in the news along with the swashbuckling Babe Ruth. Each in his own style grabbed headlines, and together they epitomized the baseball revolution that produced the new golden age.

Ruth, of course, symbolized the nation's faith in skill and power, and his off-the-field antics represented the yearning for unrestricted pleasure. But because lingering Protestant values fed American guilt feelings, the incorruptible judge became the antidote to Ruthian excess. Baseball thus had two poles of attraction, each possessing great vitality and durability, with Landis holding an advantage inasmuch as his influence was less affected by declining bodily strength.

In retrospect, it seems incredible that the owners should have enthroned a man who they knew would seize the center of the

[2] Baseball Advisory Council, "Professional Baseball in America," 1–41; *Reach's Official Base Ball Guide,* 1921, pp. 40–42; *The Sporting News,* December 23, 1920.

stage. Certainly his potentialities were known. He was one of seven children of Civil War surgeon Abraham Landis who suffered a leg wound at the battle of Kennesaw Mountain, Georgia, during Sherman's campaign. When the future baseball czar was born in Millville, Ohio, in 1866, his father named him for the battle site, although for some reason an "n" was lost in the transferral. Slight in build and hot-tempered, the son bore the martial name well, gaining experience from frequent family moves and from a variety of jobs. The boy was interested in athletics and played some baseball, but did better as a bicycle racer and roller skater. Never a scholar, he had difficulty with high school algebra and did not earn a college degree. Yet by taking advantage of alternate routes to legal certification, later suspended, Landis qualified as a lawyer and passed the Illinois bar exam in 1891. Indeed, upon entering practice he even taught some courses at the Northwestern University Law School.[3]

His rise to ultimate fame began when his father's old friend, Federal Judge Walter Q. Gresham, became Secretary of State under Grover Cleveland and named Landis to be his private secretary. Landis worked hard in this post and made important contacts that lasted beyond his mentor's death in 1895. Returning to Chicago, he spent nine years building a practice while hobnobbing with rising politicians like Frank O. Lowden. This friendship, plus his horror of William Jennings Bryan, persuaded Landis to turn Republican. This, in turn, led to the opportunity to manage Lowden's campaign for the gubernatorial nomination. Although he lost the election, Lowden won the respect of President Theodore Roosevelt, who offered him a district judgeship, which Lowden declined. With a boost from Lowden and some pressure from Landis's two brothers, then occupying Congressional seats, Roosevelt was persuaded in 1905 to appoint Landis district judge for the northern Illinois district.[4]

3 Harvey Brougham, "America's Erratic Judge; How Judge Landis Entered Into Public Life," *Overland Monthly*, April, 1921, pp. 13–14.

4 William T. Hutchinson, *Lowden of Illinois: The Life of Frank O. Lowden*, I, 35, 45, 114–45, 166, 181; Matilda Gresham, *Life of Walter Quintin Gresham, 1832–1895*, II, 752, 760, 780–81.

The courtroom provided Landis with a fine stage for expressing himself and for sating his appetites for power and publicity. He made a reputation as a showman who ran a lively courtroom. In this he was helped by the rugged contours of his face, especially his jutting jaw, high forehead, and unruly shock of white hair. He resembled Andrew Jackson somewhat, and "Old Hickory" was one of his heroes. As an actor-judge, Landis combined tantrums and whimsical humor in badgering witnesses, lawyers, and reporters. His decisions reflected his personal beliefs, which generally followed the path of Rooseveltian liberalism. Ostensibly this meant hostility toward business corruption and dedication to the cause of the "little man."[5]

World War I, however, revealed the narrow limits of Landis's liberalism. Like Roosevelt, he showed a patriotic horror of pacifists, socialists, and labor leaders. Before the war, he made national news as a big business baiter when in 1907 he levied a $29,240,000 fine on the Standard Oil Company of Indiana in an antitrust suit. This impulsive decision was speedily overruled in 1908 by the Supreme Court.[6] However, if the decision showed an emotional disdain for legalities, it drew a popular response in America's "Age of Reform." It mattered little that he was overruled, or that he was castigated as theatrical by businessmen, because the public was enthralled by this "erratic judge." Nor did his super-patriotic wartime decisions hurt his image. By sentencing "Big Bill" Haywood of the Industrial Workers of the World and Socialist Congressman Victor Berger, he again appealed to popular prejudices. Even his ludicrous attempt to summon Kaiser Wilhelm II to his court to answer for the sinking of the *Lusitania* won the cheers of jingoists. Most important for his future career as baseball commissioner, his wartime decisions convinced businessmen that this supposed liberal was really an arch-conservative.[7]

During the years before the war, Landis was an ardent Chicago Cub fan—so much so that he was booed for his partisanship in the 1906 World Series. The first inkling of his future value to organ-

[5] Hutchinson, *op. cit.,* 166.

[6] "Standard Oil Co. of Indiana v. U.S.," 166 *Federal Reporter,* 376–96.

[7] Spink, *op. cit.,* 20–22; Brougham, *loc. cit.*

ized baseball came in 1915 when he presided over the Federal League antitrust suit. Instead of ruling on the case, he reserved judgment, giving the major leagues time to settle the case out of court. This did not prevent an antitrust suit, but Landis ingratiated himself with the owners by his pious statements in behalf of safeguarding the national game. And so he was marked as a man of baseball destiny and picked as the most suitable man from a host of national heroes including General Pershing, Leonard Wood, and William Howard Taft. Landis was to be the Moses who would lead his people back to the paths of righteousness. Will Rogers ridiculed the choice, but he echoed the public's approval by his quip: "Somebody said, 'Get that old guy who sits behind first base all the time. He's out there every day anyhow!' So they offered him a season pass and he jumped at it."[8]

Once he was installed, Landis flaunted his personally chosen title of "Commissioner." In filling the role, he projected the same puritanical, patriarchal, theatrical image that had served him so well as judge. Correctly perceiving his chief task as being a molder of public opinion, he posed as "fearless, impartial, and intolerant of crookedness." Despite the $50,000 salary, raised to $65,000 in the late 1920's, he chose to personify austerity with his "long, shaggy, unkempt hair . . . white as silver," his sloppy suits topped by a "faded fedora," his high starched collar that accented his "threateningly serious" face, and his heavy cane with the cluster of rubber bands wrapped around the knob. His Spartan headquarters in Chicago with the stark title "BASEBALL" lettered in black, completed the image of "Integrity Mountain."[9]

Landis's office handled $26 million in the years 1921–44, money that flowed from Series games, All Star games, city series contests, and fines. Of this sum, $3 million went for office expenses, which averaged $144,000 a year, with his salary and O'Connor's $25,000 salary as the big budgetary items.[10] His duties took him on nation-

[8] *The Sporting News,* December 30, 1915, November 30, 1944.

[9] "The First American Dictator," *The American Review of Reviews,* January, 1928, pp. 95–96; "Baseball's Integrity Mountain Signs Up," *Newsweek,* December 23, 1933, pp. 15–16; *ibid.,* October 26, 1944.

[10] *The Sporting News,* October 26, 1944.

wide tours, barking at owners in his determination to see the game "avoid even the appearance of evil." Observing his tireless performance, O'Connor early rejected any thought of succeeding him, saying, "I have a short life to live and I want none of that job. It's a killer."[11]

The pattern of the cases decided by Landis tells the story of baseball's adaptation to a fast-changing America. They can be sorted into five categories. The maintenance of the game's honest image was the most important of these. Beginning with the Black Sox, Landis constantly harried flagrant wrongdoers.

Throughout 1921, Landis acted as an avenging angel, ousting players accused of fixing and punishing others for general wrongdoing. First to be axed were the Black Sox, followed by Chase, Gedeon, Hendrix, Magee, and Zimmerman. Later, in spite of his acquittal in civil court, Ben Kauff was blacklisted for being linked with car thieves. Obviously, Landis was out to make players above reproach, but even those in management did not escape. Stoneham and McGraw of the Giants were ordered to divest themselves of racetrack investments. Later, Landis imposed a brief suspension on three Yankees, including Ruth, for violating the rule against postseason barnstorming.

By cracking down hard, Landis won a relaxed year in 1922, but the following year he ousted Phil Douglas, a Giant pitcher, after that player wrote a letter to a Cardinal player which revealed his intent to throw a game to spite McGraw. In 1924, Landis struck again, ousting Giants "Cozy" Dolan and Jim O'Connell for a fixing attempt.

As Ruth learned in 1925, Landis strongly supported disciplinary actions by club owners. When Ruth's misconduct prompted the club to impose an unprecedented $5,000 fine, Landis upheld it as proper. Likewise, in 1929, Art Shires was threatened with blacklisting unless he stopped his postseason boxing career, since it was hinted that his fights were fixed. Landis thus quieted baseball so that eventually he could afford to dispense some Christian charity. Thus, in the 1930's he condescended to allow two ex-convicts to

[11] *Ibid.*, November 30, 1944.

enter baseball on a trial basis. Nevertheless, he still had the power to punish and he wielded it for the last time in 1943, when he ousted owner William Cox of the Phillies for betting on games.

However, Landis was prudent enough to stay his hand when public support was not clearly with him. In 1927, an informant gave evidence linking Cobb and Speaker to game betting in 1920. Landis's decision on this was awaited with interest. He finally decided that the alleged infraction occurred before he took office. Thus he merely approved the transfer of both to other teams where they finished their careers.

This decision marked a change in Landis's tactics, a change dictated by the public's fading memories of past scandals. Sensing this, Landis pragmatically abandoned his punitive role and became the efficient priest. As priest-judge, he evolved an operational code that spelled out his notion of "conduct detrimental to baseball." By 1934, everyone knew that expulsion would result if one fixed games, attempted to fix games, or rewarded noncontenders for extra efforts. Then there were lesser crimes, punishable by temporary suspension, like fraternizing with fans. Such an act was forbidden after 1931, when Landis saw a photo of Gabby Hartnett chatting with Al Capone. Also tabooed were such acts as barnstorming after October 31, employment of an umpire as a scout, lending money to rivals or to umpires, any kind of open betting at a ball park, or racetrack betting by anyone in organized baseball.[12]

Landis used a corps of detectives in his investigations but no owner knew when he might personally appear. This same energy marked the conduct of the second of the five areas of his influence, which was the handling of the World Series. Because this annual affair had been the occasion of a great scandal, and since it was also the chief source of income for his office, Landis guarded it like a baby, supervising all games and collecting and disbursing the income personally.

Landis decided in 1921 that the Series was too long, and that

[12] Baseball Advisory Council, *op. cit.*, 1–80; *Baseball Digest*, April, 1951, pp. 13–14; *The Sporting News*, April 14, August 11, October 27, 1921, October 9, 1924, January 15, 1925, February 2, 1928, June 2, 1932, November 6, 1944; Spink, *op. cit.*, 74–79; *Baseball Magazine*, February, 1945, pp. 291–92.

seven games were enough. The seven-game pattern was quickly adopted and persists to this day. Throughout his regime there were on-the-spot decisions that shaped the Series to the judge's liking. He insisted that games begin on time and that players and umpires follow his orders. To dispute his will was to be hotly rebuked, as umpires learned in 1923 when they called a game on account of darkness. Infuriated, Landis ordered all receipts sent to charity, and from then on umpires were obliged to consult with him on any similar decision. Nor would the judge permit the expulsion of a player or manager from a Series game without his permission. As a result, such ousters were so rare as to make headlines, as in 1934 when Landis ordered the removal of Cardinal outfielder "Ducky" Medwick for his own protection. Angered at Medwick's aggressiveness on the bases, Detroit fans pelted him with refuse and bottles, thus causing Landis to issue his order.

The awesome presence of Landis was usually enough to make a Series run smoothly, so that such direct interventions were rare. His last such act came in 1943 when he decreed that all receipts after the players' shares go to the war effort. This patriotic move was also political, as Landis wanted the government to favor baseball during the war.[13]

The challenge of World War II was the third major area in which Landis's influence was exerted, and the aging commissioner handled it with *élan*. America's task was more formidable during this two-front war than in 1917. Knowing this, Landis wrote President Franklin D. Roosevelt in 1942, asking for a clarification of baseball's status. The answer came back the next day, and while it gave the game a "green light," it offered no special consideration. Baseball was regarded as useful to national morale, but would have to utilize its older players. Pleased at the response, Landis worked with Paul V. McNutt of the defense transportation office, and got enough railroad transportation to keep the teams moving.[14]

A fourth area of challenge for Landis was the impact of the

[13] Baseball Advisory Council, *loc. cit.*; *The Sporting News,* October 20, 1921, October 21, December 6, 1923, September 16, October 13, 1943.

[14] *The Sporting News,* January 22, 1942, January 7, 1943.

revolution in communication. By the early 1920's, radio broadcasts were making serious inroads into attendance, but it was 1934 before Landis belatedly made radio corporations pay for the privilege of broadcasting Series games. Annually thereafter his office negotiated contracts which swelled Series income. This precedent paved the way for his successors to secure large profits from television rights.[15]

During Landis's tenure, the stability of the minors was the fifth area of his concern but was the one he handled least successfully. Landis never really understood how urban growth processes were making it impossible to maintain small-town baseball organizations. Furthermore, the automobile and the development of new leisure interests were eroding the minors. Yet Landis stubbornly battled the farm systems as the outstanding evil. Under this system, clubs like the Cardinals scouted and signed young players and assigned them to minor-league teams that were controlled or owned by the major-league team. By the 1930's, the Cardinals controlled a vast empire extending into all minor-league levels. Inevitably, protests arose, and Landis and O'Connor vainly tried to stop the practice. On the advice of O'Connor, Landis favored a common draft of players, hoping this would give each major club equal access to promising talent. But owners like Sam Breadon of the Cardinals resisted this suggestion as "socialistic," and in 1930 Phil Ball of the Browns defended his right to operate farm teams in a federal court case. Landis thereafter fought a rearguard action using baseball regulations that limited the number of players a club might control. With this device he struck at the farm system in 1938, declaring seventy-three players free agents, and again in 1939 by freeing ninety. As a free agent, each player could negotiate a new contract, and some won bonuses. Soon afterwards Landis fined Cleveland $5,000 for violating a player acquisition rule.[16]

Dramatic and well publicized though these actions were, they did little to halt the spread of the farm system, since owners re-

15 *Ibid.,* December 21, 1933.

16 *Ibid.,* November 10, 1921, December 20, 1928, March 21, 1929, December 18, 1930, April 1, 1943, November 30, 1944.

garded the device as an efficient and inexpensive means of developing talent. Not only did Landis fail to appreciate this, but he missed the chief reason for the decline of the minors, namely the shift from a small-town to an urban-centered society.

Landis's fight against the farms was a conservative effort. Neither a deep thinker nor an innovator, he leaned heavily on advice from O'Connor and owner Navin of Detroit. Indeed, O'Connor investigated 90 per cent of the problems and wrote most of Landis's decisions while routinely handling contract records, transfers, and options covering every player in organized baseball. By 1944, an estimated fifty thousand such records were on file. It was O'Connor who wrote the "Landis Plan" calling for an unrestricted player draft to replace the farms. His loyalty was unstinting, and it is significant that this great baseball legalist should content himself with being the power behind the throne.[17]

With the passing of time after Landis's appointment, owners and writers began to criticize his sanctimonious posture. Foremost of the critics was J. G. Taylor Spink, editor of *Sporting News*, who allowed Landis a two-year honeymoon before attacking him. Then, sneering at "Landis the First," Spink reminded the judge that he was not God and that baseball could exist without an "erratic and irresponsible despot." In conclusion, Spink urged the judge to earn his salary by forcing out incompetent owners, stamping out gamblers, improving the minors, and eliminating the rampant commercialism that seemed to be stifling baseball.[18] Late in 1923, writer Frank Menke rapped Landis for taking the credit for the Black Sox purge and for stubbornly clinging to his judicial post in spite of the Congressional disapproval which ultimately forced his resignation. Menke also objected to Landis's Kauff decision as partisan, and asked why he allowed Stoneham to stay on in spite of his legal difficulties.[19]

Landis peevishly called Spink a "swine" and denounced other critics in highly emotional terms. His outbursts gave some credence to Johnson's prophecy that Landis would be a costly liability to

[17] *Ibid.*, April 5, 1934; *Baseball Magazine*, March, 1945, pp. 331–32.

[18] *The Sporting News*, March 29, October 11, 1923.

[19] *Ibid.*, December 6, 1923; *Literary Digest*, March 27, 1926, May 31, 1930.

baseball. But with his enormous public support, Landis rode out the storm and watched as his old enemy Johnson was eased out of office in 1927. Added prestige came to Landis in 1927 when Hollywood imitated baseball by naming Will Hays its "Czar." Landis was also favorably compared with President Coolidge. Buoyed by this emotional support, Landis won a second term, but his popularity reached its highest point in the late 1920's and dropped briefly during the Depression. He had unwisely invested surplus baseball funds in Samuel Insull's utility stock which collapsed completely with the fall of that empire. Although he repaid the loss from his own pocket, this incident exposed him to criticism and opposition in his second term.

His closest call came in 1931 when Phil Ball's successful legal action opened the possibility of a new antitrust suit against baseball. To forestall this, Ball dropped his case, but Landis's wings were clipped. In 1932, he took a "voluntary" salary cut of $25,000 officially for depression austerities, but if he had not chosen to do so he might not have won a third term in 1933.[20]

As the judge grew older, he limited himself to occasional swipes at the farm system and at wrongdoers, and his handling of the war crisis served to redeem a hectic third term. After Landis's reelection his declining health astonished even those who had suggested he retire. Hospitalized after the 1944 Series, the seventy-eight-year-old commissioner sank rapidly, and he died of coronary thrombosis on November 25, 1944.

Judge Landis dominated the headlines for the last time as expressions of sympathy, tributes to his honesty, and recollections of his mannerisms combined to secure his place in American folklore. Within a month, his name and battered leather chair went to Cooperstown as part of his canonization in the Hall of Fame which he had dedicated in 1939. The speed of this act probably emphasized the eagerness of owners to close this episode in baseball history. His death marked the end of the autocratic commission rule, an expedient born of guilt engendered by the scandals of

20 *The Sporting News*, January 7, 1931, October 13, December 21, 1932, July 21, 1945.

1919 and 1920. In choosing Landis, the owners had not counted on the possibility of his influence extending far beyond that period. He left behind a legend of the incorruptible judge who purged the game. To this day, the living legend explains why major-league owners cling to the façade of a single commissioner in spite of the obvious impotence of the office.

2. The "Big Bang" in Baseball

In 1920, Ty Cobb was made painfully aware of the decline of his style of play. At the time he was the supreme hero of the silver age, had won nine straight batting titles, and had captured twelve batting titles in thirteen years. With such credentials, and a $30,000 annual salary in 1920, Cobb had every right to feel secure. Moreover, he was soon to be named playing manager of the Tigers, a recognition that could only add to his stature. When Cobb fell ill in the summer of 1921, he confidently expected his public to be awaiting him eagerly. But on his return, he was dismayed to find that everywhere his own popularity had been overwhelmed by the acclaim for Babe Ruth. The switch in affection signalled the passing of Cobb's style of play and the rise of a new style.

Today some cosmologists use the "big bang" theory to explain the explosive processes that mark the beginning and ending of universes. Its baseball equivalent occurred in 1920, when the home-run style of offense exploded in the baseball galaxy. As Yankee manager Miller Huggins put it, the fans love the guy "who carries the wallop." Citing men of muscle who were powering their way to success in boxing, golf, and football, Huggins forecast Cobb's eclipse. Cobb was too deliberate and too studied, and his style of "inside baseball" was too slow for a keyed-up generation that liked the explosive, decisive, "big bang" of the home run.[21]

Huggins's prophecy was made in 1920 when the Yanks paid Boston $125,000 for the man whose twenty-nine homers had broken Ed Williamson's record set in 1884. Derided for extravagant

[21] *Ibid.*, August 12, 1920; Frederick Lewis Allen, *Only Yesterday*, 45–71; *Spalding's Official Base Ball Guide*, 1921, pp. 3–5.

folly, the Yankees proceeded to pay their new chattel $20,000 for the 1920 season. Obviously, 1920 was to be a moment of truth, with glory or reproach hinging on Ruth's performance. But Ruth responded magnificently, hitting an unprecedented fifty-four homers. The twenty-five-year-old star bestrode the baseball firmament, serving notice to all that his "big bang" style was to be the strategy of the new golden age.

In many ways, George Herman Ruth was an unlikely hero. One of two surviving children of eight born to a Baltimore saloonkeeper, he was branded incorrigible at the age of seven. His distraught parents placed the swearing, stealing, tobacco-chewing child in the St. Mary's Industrial Home for Boys in Baltimore, where it was hoped that the Xaverian Brothers might show him the path to righteousness. Except for occasional leaves prompted by maternal guilt feelings, there he stayed, learning the tailoring trade and gratifying his huge appetite for baseball under the coaching of Brother Mathias. This tall, 250-pound priest became a surrogate father to the love-starved lad, and the boy even imitated his mentor's habit of running with toes pointed inward. He grew to become a hulking, unsophisticated teen-ager, filled with desire for worldly pleasures but mostly interested in a baseball career. Baseball was his only solid achievement at St. Mary's, and he was so good as a pitcher and hitter that at nineteen he was sought by the Baltimore Orioles of the International League.

The owner and manager of the Orioles, Jack Dunn, was one of the best of the minor-league promoters and a shrewd judge of talent. So certain was he of Ruth's worth that in order to get him out of the home he signed as his legal guardian. Their relationship was brief, however. The Federal League war hurt Dunn financially and forced him to sell Ruth to the Red Sox for $2,900. Dunn knew the real worth of his "babe," as shown by the pay raises he gave him, but 1914 was a desperate year for Dunn. His pressing need for cash forced him to take what he could get.

As a Red Sox pitcher, Ruth was an immediate success, winning eighteen in 1915 and twenty-three the next year. He was a player of rare grace and co-ordination, but he was loudmouthed and arrogant about his ability. Ridiculed by his mates for bragging about his batting, Ruth silenced them by establishing himself as the team's best pinch hitter. When the war created a serious player shortage, he did double duty as pitcher and outfielder. By 1918 he was playing every day, and the following year his record-shattering twenty-nine homers shifted him forever from a promising pitching career. Young, willing, and talented, he made the switch with ease, and it brought him undreamed-of wealth. He went from a salary of $4,000 in 1914 to $10,000 in 1919, and on to a dazzling $20,000 in 1920.[22]

The rapid acquisition of money only revealed Ruth's lack of sophistication. Ignorant of middle-class values of thrift and prudence, he spent his fortune recklessly, wasting huge sums at race tracks and on dissipation. Such behavior quickly branded the giant as an unmanageable troublemaker, and his wartime reputation as a "draft dodger" was another blemish to his name.[23]

However, Ruth's ability to deliver the big hit overrode all character deficiencies and made him the darling of fans and the hero of American youth of the golden age. How the "Babe Ruth mania" could have occurred at the very moment of the Black Sox scandal merits an examination of the changes that made the "roaring twenties" a watershed in American ethics and values. Only a decade before, America had still been solidly committed to rural-Protestant values of thrift, godliness, and honesty, restimulated by the idealism of a reformist age and the call to action of the social gospel movement. But the upheaval of war and increasing industrialism and urbanism drastically modified views on the brotherhood of man, the solidarity of workers, and the righteousness of thrift and hard work. New values gained acceptance including increasing reliance on personal success and material comforts. As a result of an unprecedented output of consumer goods, America of 1920 was becoming a society of mass consumption and instant gratification. Increasingly tempted by a dynamic advertising in-

[22] Allen, *American League Story,* 101–10, 136, 147; *The Sporting News,* August 12, 1920; *Baseball Magazine,* April, 1920.

[23] Edward Barrow, *My 50 Years in Baseball,* 89–121.

dustry, America was already becoming a mass culture where the spending habits of a newly affluent majority dictated standards of propriety and set behavioral trends.[24] With the "fun morality" one of the most important of the new standards, Americans of the age found themselves acting in a national marketplace where entertainment cues were packaged and sold through movies, radio, and popular literature. Fun seekers were increasingly becoming celebrity watchers, deriving their pleasure from the performances of outstanding personalities whose prowess in "public dramas" took mass audiences "vicariously out of everyday roles into a new kind of 'reality' " with a magic of its own, but always dependent on the willingness of mass audiences to identify with the new celebrity heroes.[25]

During the 1920's, adoring publics made celebrities out of many different kinds of performers. The movies and radio gathered huge audiences for the public dramas that made national heroes out of actors like Rudolph Valentino, popular comics out of the radio team of "Amos and Andy," and a powerful hero-villain out of boxer Jack Dempsey. As celebrities of the 1920's, these personalities, along with many others in diverse fields, found their every movement zealously reported and avidly followed by admiring throngs who identified with them. To receive such attention meant fabulous wealth and an intoxicating sense of power for the new elites, but it cost them their personal freedom. A strange dialectical process operated to make each hero a prisoner of an adoring public, whose expectations forced the hero into a straitjacketed "public image." Often the hero was obliged to permit the invasion of the most intimate areas of his life, to serve at times as a scapegoat, and to shoulder doubts about his ability to sustain his heroic performance. Many celebrities rocketed to fame only to burn out quickly as public attention shifted to new idols. Only a matchless few, whose lives became living legends, succeeded at the beginning of the electronic age.[26]

24 George W. Mowry (ed.), *The Twenties: Fords, Flappers and Fanatics,* 1–3; F. L. Allen, *op. cit.,* 71–73, *passim.*

25 Orrin E. Klapp, *Symbolic Leaders: Public Dramas and Public Men,* 7, 13–14, 250, 257.

26 *Ibid.,* 13–25.

Only in retrospect in a particular case can we explain how celebrity building works. To this day, the making of a celebrity is completely unpredictable; the process has baffled and bankrupted many a press agent who tried to bend it to his will. In its own mysterious way, the public chooses its heroes and does so in response to many hidden factors. A combination of war weariness, new values glorifying power and fun, new publicity techniques such as action photography, sprightly feature stories, ghost-written articles, and the additional exposure provided by radio and movies, all combined to promote Ruth to stardom. Yet in the end this would not have been possible without the consent of the public.

Babe Ruth's most obvious assets were his size and muscular power. Year after year he won the home-run title. In 1927 he hit a record 60, and by his retirement in 1935 he had clouted 714 in the majors. Like Cy Young's 511 wins, or Cobb's .367 lifetime batting average, this record is sacrosanct. Ruth hit the ball hard; according to one physicist he developed 44 horsepower at the peak of his swing. He also hit often, as his .342 average attests, and his versatility included defensive ability and fleetness of foot. But above all, he radiated a personal magnetism on and off the field, never failing to inspire cheers and jeers. During his long career he autographed thousands of balls, caught balls dropped from buildings and airplanes, and once, in the Series of 1932, reputedly signalled his intent to hit a homer on the next pitch and then did it. He had ordinary days and off days, of course, but his cocky swaggering style made even his strikeouts memorable.[27]

In an age of changing values, Ruth's naïvely comic ability to deflate the egos of traditional heroes only made him more appealing. Many Americans of the 1920's may have wanted to say to President Coolidge, "Hot as hell, ain't it 'Pres'?" Or, on meeting Gen-

[27] *The Sporting News,* December 8, 1921, March 23, 1944; Greene, *op. cit.*, 267–74.

George Herman "Babe" Ruth smacked 714 home runs and posted a lifetime batting average of .342 in twenty-two years of play. The towering hero of baseball fans of the 1920's, Ruth is still familiar as baseball's most celebrated hero. (Courtesy New York Yankees, American League) eralissimo Ferdinand Foch, "Hey, 'Gen', they tell me you were in the war." But only Ruth did this, and for worshiping fans it was as if he did it for all of them.[28]

From his early days in the majors to the day he left, he demonstrated a voracious appetite. As a rookie with the Red Sox, he horrified veteran Harry Hooper by gulping six hot dogs and six bottles of soda pop, after which he belched loudly and bellowed, "Let's go."[29] As his fortunes increased, so did his spending. Even with an unheard-of $52,000 in 1925, he was mired in financial troubles, which prompted his employers to dole out payments in the vain hope that he would learn thrift. Far from accepting advice, the undisciplined Ruth defied managers, owners, and league presidents.

Not until 1925, when Ruth's defiance of authority forced Manager Huggins to take extraordinary action, was he humbled. In the spring of that year his excesses undermined his health. In April, while en route from the South, he was felled by a combination of flu and acute indigestion and was carried from the train to a hospital. This was widely reported in the papers, one account erroneously reporting his death. He was operated on for an intestinal abcess, and as he recovered writers speculated on how much he had cost the team. One estimate said $500,000. The sick star was scolded for setting a bad example for youth. At the same time, *Sporting News* blamed the nation's "Rutho-mania" for making him bigger than baseball. "You will never be Ty Cobb," wrote editor Spink, who reported that Ruth had fallen from "king to jester." But even this publicized "big bellyache" failed to break Ruth's spirit. His continuing breach of rules finally led to a $5,000 fine. At last he realized that he must follow team rules or leave baseball. And so he shaped up a little, but the legends of his gargantuan appetite and reprimand hardly hurt his image; indeed, mingled with his later triumphs they enhanced it.[30]

[28] Branch Rickey, *The American Diamond: A Documentary of the Game of Baseball,* 40.

[29] Ritter, *op. cit.,* 136–38.

[30] *The Sporting News,* January 13, December 8, 1921, March 19, April 16, September 3, 1925.

Placed on a strict diet administered by a doctor, Ruth in 1926 led the Yankees to the first of a string of three consecutive flags. In subsequent years he maintained a high level of performance that lasted until he was overtaken by age in 1934. Although he never became a model of middle-class behavior, he at least invested some money in annuities, thanks to the influence of his second wife and his ghost writer, Christy Walsh. If the press celebrated this change as a moral transformation, Ruth remained a free spirit. His annual salary battles fascinated the public. Some critics protested the absurdity of paying a "subnormal giant" more than the American President, but Ruth's reply made the protest laughable. "Why not more than Hoover? After all I had a better year."[31]

In his fifteen years with the Yankees, Ruth netted well over one million dollars, and who could say he was not worth all of it? Surely major-league baseball profited by his presence, and because of him the Yankees became baseball's outstanding team. Before Ruth, the team's best draw was six hundred thousand fans a year; with him the team averaged over one million each year. Before Ruth, the Giants consistently outdrew their tenants, but after Ruth began to attract larger Sunday crowds, the Giants canceled the Yankee lease at the Polo Grounds. Ruppert then decided to build the Yankee Stadium, and when this baseball mecca opened in 1923, writers justly celebrated it as the house that Ruth built. Indeed, he baptized it with a homer in the first game played there, and in the fall led the Yankees to their first Series triumph. From then on, the Yankees were the number one team in New York and subsequently in baseball.[32]

Throughout his career, Ruth did the most to lead the American League to clear-cut dominance over the National. And always he was the public hero who captured the headlines and the subject of the feature stories that kept baseball ahead of rival sports spec-

31 *Ibid.*, December 29, 1927, October 22, 1931; "What Babe Ruth Does With his Money," *Literary Digest*, October 5, 1929; "Babe Ruth's $210,000 for Three Years of Swat," *ibid.*, March 19, 1927; "What is Babe Ruth Worth to the Yankees," *ibid.*, March 29, 1930.

32 U.S. House of Representatives, *Organized Baseball*, pp. 1617–18; *The Sporting News*, October 22, 1931.

tacles. Everything he did made copy, including his obvious heroics and his stupid utterances. For laughs, fans read about his "big belly," his intention of shooting "peasants" on a projected hunting trip, and his inability to patent a Babe Ruth chocolate bar. He was unable to do so because a "Baby Ruth" candy bar, named for the daughter of President Grover Cleveland, had long been on the market. However, most fans still think that the "Baby Ruth" bar was named for him.[33]

Notwithstanding Ruth's magnetism, baseball executives saw him as too erratic and shallow to lead men. In his last years with the Yankees, he resented Manager Joe McCarthy's presence, because he felt he should have had the job. This led to petty quarrels, and Ruth's leadership of an anti-McCarthy faction hurt the team. Nevertheless, he could have stayed with the Yankees if only he had learned, in Ed Barrow's words, "to manage himself." But when in 1935 Barrow offered the fortyish, fading star a job as manager of the Yankees' Newark farm club, Ruth spurned the offer as "bush league." He failed to see that this was his only choice, and that his usefulness had otherwise ended. Barrow surprised everyone by handing him an unconditional release. Shocked by the rejection, Ruth landed a job managing the lowly Braves, but soon learned that the club merely wanted to exploit his publicity value. His last year in baseball was a bitter one, and he left the majors in 1935 to begin a long wait for the big-league offer that never came. He had many offers to manage minor-league teams, and there was a suggestion that he be sent on a grand tour of the minors so fans could see him in the flesh. But for various reasons these offers did not materialize, and Ruth worked at odd jobs, once serving as a wrestling referee. At least his resentment in these years was lessened somewhat by continuing public adulation. He remained good copy, was elected to the Hall of Fame, and was often invited to serve briefly as batting instructor to big-league clubs.[34]

[33] *The Sporting News,* March 6, 1930.

[34] *Baseball Digest,* February, 1951, p. 5; *The Sporting News,* April 30, 1934, April 12, November 15, 1945, June 12, 1946.

He lived thirteen years after retiring in 1935, undoubtedly dull years for the man who once inspired a boy to tell President Hoover that he'd rather be "Babe Ruth than President." He was slowly dying of cancer by 1946, but he kept busy with a part-time job with the Ford Motor Company's "Junior League Program." Hollywood also gave him belated recognition by filming "The Babe Ruth Story." In 1948, Ruth briefly left his hospital bed to see the film that was later criticized as "low grade fiction."[35] He died in August, 1948, bewildered by the illness he never understood.

In life, Ruth never doubted his importance, and it would have gladdened him to know that his passing was marked by practically all Americans. For weeks before the end, newsmen mounted a death watch, some openly hoping he would die for morning, rather than afternoon editions. When death came, newsmen vied with each other in recalling his past glories. The Yankees gave him the baseball equivalent of a state funeral, resting his body in the Stadium rotunda so that one hundred thousand people could pass by his bier, and furnishing fifty-seven honorary pallbearers to carry him to his final resting place.[36] Thus ended Babe Ruth's physical existence, but his legend never died, and to this day major-league baseball employs the "big bang" style of play that he personified.

3. Baseball's Vulcan

In Greek and Roman mythology the god Vulcan made the weapons for the other gods. He was ugly and unloved, but none of the other Olympians could have done without him. His baseball equivalent was Wesley Branch Rickey, born in Ohio in 1881 of Methodist parents who had him sign the "pledge" and who insisted that he seek an education to rise above his rural poverty. He fought his way through Ohio Wesleyan University and on to a law degree from the University of Michigan. But while he was getting an education, he also put his physical talents to work as football and baseball coach at both schools. A passable catcher, he came to the majors in 1904. Veteran players derided him for refusing to play

35 *The Sporting News*, August 4, 1948.

36 *Ibid.*, August 25, 1948.

ball on Sundays and mocked him with the phrase, "He promised his old lady."

Rickey played his first major-league game in 1905 as a member of the Browns, but weak hitting and a bout with tuberculosis ended his playing career. When owner Robert Hedges took over the club in 1912, he signed the thirty-year-old Rickey for $7,500, charging him to scout and develop new talent. This decision took account of Rickey's reputation for recognizing promising talent. As a student-coach in his college days, Rickey knew many other coaches and kept a line on hundreds of players. He conceived the idea that such young players could be nurtured and developed at low cost through working agreements with minor-league teams. Rickey was a born teacher of baseball, and he developed all kinds of teaching aids including sliding pits, batting cages, web outlines of the strike zone to teach control to pitchers, and, later, pitching machines to facilitate batting. He also used a blackboard to inspire, and sometimes bore, players with chalk talks on tactics and strategy.

When Rickey was given a chance to manage the Browns in 1914–15, he did well, in spite of the opposition his methods evoked. However, he was forced to shift to the moribund Cardinals in 1917, after Phil Ball took over the Browns in 1916 and excluded Rickey from his plans. With Rickey as manager and president in the early 1920's, the Cardinals rose from inferiority to become one of the most prosperous franchises.

The key to his success was his development of the modern farm system. Indeed, after the Cardinals paid $10,000 for pitcher Jess Haines in 1919, it was more than twenty-five years before they purchased another established star. All of the great Cardinal players during the intervening period came from minor-league farms where they learned their trade under Rickey's advanced scouting and development system. In building the great network of minor-league teams, some of which were owned by the Cardinals, Rickey used his personal diplomacy to clear the way with minor-league officials and a shrewd knowledge of coaching and teaching talent to staff the teams with good men. The best players were moved from the minors upward to the Cardinal team. Nobody knew better than Rickey who the most promising players were, where they were, and even facts about their habits and temperaments. This information he kept with him in a famous black book, which he frequently consulted to fill the club's needs.[37]

Although the farm system was ridiculed by McGraw and denounced by Landis and some independent minor-league operators, it was a much-needed remedy for the chronic difficulties of the minors. Under the old system of buying talent, wealthy clubs like the Giants and Yankees could win easily by outbidding poorer rivals. The system also promoted a constant dog-eat-dog competition between scouts which sometimes led mercenary minor owners to set one against another. Rickey knew the frustration of trying to compete in such a market and often watched in helpless rage as one of his carefully selected minor-league players was sold by an avaricious owner who had pledged that player to Rickey.

To compete successfully, Rickey elected to train his own players. His scouts were sent to high schools and colleges to look over prospects and to sign the most promising. Rickey himself often took over their initial lessons beginning in the spring. The spectacle of droves of youngsters in Cardinal tryout camps was often ridiculed, but taunts meant little to a man like Rickey. He had lived with them much of his life, and he patiently labored at the task of screening the youngsters. The best were retained and sent to Cardinal-owned minor-league teams which by 1921 were planted in the three highest classified minor leagues.

In retrospect, Rickey's experimentation was more than a mere revival of a discarded nineteenth-century practice, or a cheap way of gaining talent. More than anyone else at the time, Rickey had caught a vision of an America that was growing increasingly interdependent in outlook and tastes. In this developing society people looked beyond the small town and its activities; their sights were trained on the doings of national heroes like Ruth and the Yankees. Radio and other mass media were responsible for the change, something that Rickey sensed more keenly than his colleagues. In

[37] Arthur Mann, *Branch Rickey: American in Action,* 4–13, 31–33, 42–47, 65, 69, 74–76, 100–116.

assessing this trend in American life, Rickey foresaw the eventual eclipse of independent minors and the coming of a day when minor leagues must be subsidized by major-league teams. He ascribed the coming changes to relentless and impersonal forces and consequently disclaimed being the villain he was called by disgruntled minor-league promoters.

When Rickey attempted to revive the outlawed farm system, he was vilified by many, including Judge Landis. However, something had to be done to prevent further attrition, and Landis could come up with no other solution than a vague universal draft. This was unacceptable to most major-league owners, some of whom branded it "communistic." Ironically, organized baseball would come to this solution one day, although not in the manner that Landis had envisioned.

With the support of other owners, Rickey succeeded in having the old ban on farming rescinded, thus denying Landis a legal weapon. Landis then blustered and tried to maintain his position by decrees. In defending his course of action, Rickey pointed to the failure of many minor-league teams during and after the First World War. When the Depression struck heavy blows at minor-league stability, officials pleaded for major-league support, thus vindicating Rickey. During the 1930's, most major-league clubs took on farm affiliates, and by 1939 the minors were largely under the control of the majors.

In the race to establish minor-league dominions, Rickey led all rivals both in organizing and administering them. Years later, Rickey admitted to a Congressional investigating committee that the greatest benefit of the farm system to the majors was in providing them with cheaper talent, yet he insisted that his brainchild also stabilized the minors and gave greater satisfaction to minor-league fans.

Opponents like Landis and O'Connor were not the only ones who attacked Rickey. One vindictive New York writer hung the nickname "El Cheapo" on him, and this epithet was shouted at him by fans in Brooklyn where he had gone as general manager in 1942. But wherever he went, either to Brooklyn or later to Pittsburgh, he planted ideas of efficient recruiting and successful promotion. One of his last acts before he died in 1965 was to promote a "Continental League," designed to bring major-league baseball into the new urban regions of America. Although he was unable to implement the idea, the suggestion prompted owners to expand the majors into these areas, lest Rickey do it for them.

Rickey was unquestionably a fashioner of tools, human and mechanical, that did much to advance the sport. Paradoxically, this Bible-reading Calvinist was branded as a sort of unholy experimenter and thus denied a heroic rank in his lifetime. After his death, however, he was awarded a place in the Hall of Fame, and as baseball catches up to his suggestions, it becomes clear that Rickey belongs in the company of baseball's immortals.[38]

[38] U.S. House of Representatives, *Organized Baseball,* pp. 1018–23; *New York Times,* December 12, 1965; *The Sporting News,* March 9, 1907, November 9, 1916, February 8, 1923, December 1, 1932, May 25, 1960; Mann, *op. cit.,* 158, 248–53; Veeck and Linn, *The Hustler's Handbook,* chapter 5; Allen, *National League Story,* 178–91; *Baseball Digest*, June, 1948, pp. 9–10, February, 1951, pp. 29–31, November, 1954, pp. 9–10; Rickey, *op. cit., passim.*

7

The Age of the New York Yankees

Ever since the mid-1920's Yankee domination of baseball has been a subject that divides fans into hostile camps, allowing for no neutrality. This is primarily because the Yankee reputation has been built upon a record of relentless crushing of the opposition. After 1921, each successive decade carries the brand of Yankee efficiency. To this day, Yankee domination is the outstanding fact of twentieth-century baseball history, and its imprint extends far beyond the year of 1943, when full-scale war mobilization brought an end to baseball's second golden age.

In the decade ending in 1931 the Yankees had won their way to six pennants and three world championships to establish themselves as the most potent team in baseball. In the succeeding decade they expanded their control, winning six more pennants and six world championships, including an unprecedented four straight

Series titles in the years 1936–39. A world war interrupted but did not stop the march of these seemingly invincible warriors. By 1951, another six pennants flew over Yankee Stadium, along with five more Series banners. By then all previous team records were theirs, yet they plunged on, extending their position by setting still more records up to 1961. In the decade 1951–61 they captured eight pennants and six world titles, including a skein of five straight Series victories ending in 1953. Even if, as it now appears, these conquerors have at last been put to rout, the decade ending in 1971 will show at least another three pennants and a Series triumph.

Perhaps the most devastating result of this single team's record of success was that it overshadowed other efforts for most baseball fans and explains why so many have difficulty recalling the achievements of other great teams like Anson's Colts, Hanlon's Orioles, Selee's Beaneaters, Chance's Cubs, Mack's Athletics, or McGraw's Giants. Even though Yankee might overrides all and deprives all rivals of past glories, this has not been done without cost. The Yankees have paid a price in a hatred which has deepened over the years until it has become a part of American folklore. Like most national hates, this passionate Yankee phobia serves mostly as an emotional catharsis and obscures the reason why this single team became so powerful.

Not that Yankee haters are without answers to the question; indeed there are a great variety of answers. Some explanations rely on a "great man theory" and blame Ruth, general manager Ed Barrow, farm director George Weiss, or one of three brilliant Yankee managers. A reversal of this theory is the "devil theory" which attacks Harry Frazee, the Boston owner, for selling Ruth to the Yankees. Another popular theory cities the wealth of owner Jacob Ruppert as cause. Some argue that superior bureaucratic organization is the key to Yankee success. There is also a theory that the club's strategic location in greater New York is the key. Still another explanation states that the Yankees are really a propaganda creation of the mass media centered in New York.

Finally, let us look at a social psychological theory, proffered tongue-in-cheek by Douglas Wallop, who wrote the best-selling book, *The Year the Yankees Lost the Pennant.* Wallop's theory uses the magical concept of *mana* to account for the Yankees' strength, which he claimed resided in their pin-striped uniforms. According to him, if their suits were taken away they might become mere mortals. All together, these several explanations may help to account for Yankee successes, but they raise as many questions as they give answers. After all, other teams have had great players, charismatic managers, courageous campaigns, wealthy owners, and the like, but it was the Yankees alone who dominated American baseball in the golden age. Any study of causes ultimately forces the baffled researcher to burrow into past history, hoping to find in the records and campaigns answers to what made the golden age "The Age of the New York Yankees."[1]

1. The Conquest of Gotham City, 1921–31

The Yankee empire grew out of a power struggle between a lackluster American League club and the powerful Giants. At stake were the rich profits coming from a growing army of baseball fans. The struggle grew more intense with the advent of Sunday baseball in New York in 1919, a development that promised to swell the army of fans further. McGraw was in a position to learn this quickly, for he, along with Charles Stoneham and Judge McQuade, formed the triumvirate that controlled the Giant empire. Giant preeminence in New York City seemed to be guaranteed, but in 1919 McGraw became concerned by the vigorous rebuilding efforts of his American tenants. At the time, the Yankees were about to buy pitcher Mays from Boston, and there were rumors of more purchases in the offing. To meet the challenge, McGraw summoned Branch Rickey, the Cardinal president, to New York for trade negotiations, hoping to get the superstar who was needed to replace

[1] "I Hate the Yankees," *Life,* April 17, 1950; "Love Those Yanks," *ibid.,* October 9, 1950; Arthur Daley, "Fabulous Yankees Through Fifty Years," *New York Times Magazine,* March 9, 1952; "Why the Yankees Win," *Nation,* September 17, 1938; "Break Up the Yankees," *Colliers,* February 25, 1939; "Stop Squawking—in Defense of the Yankees," *ibid.,* March 4, 1939; "The Yankees," *Fortune,* July, 1946; Douglas Wallop, *The Year the Yankees Lost the Pennant.*

Christy Mathewson. McGraw had singled out the Cardinal second baseman, Rogers Hornsby, as the most likely prospect, since he was a hitter of remarkable promise.

Stoneham was at hand and ready to spend money, and McGraw quickly got down to serious bidding. Before long, Stoneham had offered an amazing $250,000 for Hornsby. Although Rickey was tempted by the sum, which he knew would solve the Cardinals' financial ills, he asked that the Giants throw in Frank Frisch. Angrily McGraw refused, but Rickey stuck to the demand until McGraw in disgust broke off negotiations.[2] If McGraw's plan had succeeded, the Giants would have obtained a player whose lifetime batting average stood second only to Cobb's, and who also hit homers. Instead, Rickey kept Hornsby and used him to help build a dynasty which in eight years rivaled that of the Giants.

Shrugging off this failure, McGraw turned to other clubs for the men who could lift the Giants back into contention for the pennant. With Stoneham's cash available, the logical solution was to bargain with the have-not owners of the Braves and Phillies. As usual, both were tractable, and in 1919 the Braves released Art Nehf, a fine lefthanded pitcher. In 1920, the Phillies sold star shortstop Dave Bancroft to McGraw and in 1921 gave up Emil "Irish" Meusel and the veteran Casey Stengel. These players and third baseman "Heinie" Groh, purchased in 1922 from Cincinnati, provided the nucleus for a potential winning team. McGraw then set to work welding the newcomers to his youthful crew—outfielder Ross (Pep) Youngs, first baseman George Kelly, second baseman Frisch, and catcher Earl Smith. With the help of a veteran pitching staff, McGraw urged this team on to four consecutive flags, a managerial feat unequalled since Comiskey did it back in the 1880's.

The Giants machine was a typical McGraw creation, with McGraw himself as the master mechanic and programmer. McGraw fully justified his reputation as a "Napoleonic genius," as his team won by four games in 1921, breezed home with a comfortable seven-game lead in 1922, gained a four and a half game victory over the rising Reds in 1923, and finally wrested a cliff-hanging game and

[2] Mrs. John McGraw, *op. cit.*, 271–73; Mann, *op. cit.*, 101–104.

a half victory from Robinson's Dodgers in 1924.[3] This brutally successful formula seemed certain to insure the support of Gotham fans. Nevertheless, the Giants were outdrawn by the Yankees.

McGraw's strategy failed primarily because he lacked a superstar to match Ruth's appeal. If McGraw had sensed the coming new style of play, he might have outbid the Yankee owners for Ruth, although it is doubtful that he could have tolerated so unmanageable a star. Because the Yankees made the effort and gave rein to Ruth's talents and energies, they won the support of fans who came to see this colorful figure in action. McGraw must have realized the extent of his miscalculation when in 1921 the corps of newsmen usually assigned to cover the Giants were reassigned to the Yankees.

In the early years, there was a strong possibility that the Yankees might not succeed in getting established. For one thing, relations between the club's owners, Colonels Ruppert and Huston, were becoming increasingly discordant. The formation of their partnership in 1913 had been a marriage of convenience, since each had independently sought to acquire a major-league club in New York. They had been introduced by Johnson, who persuaded the American League owners to vote them into the fellowship for having agreed to take over the floundering New York club. For a time the partnership worked well, and the two owners spent lavishly to build a contender. At first they sought Johnson's advice before making purchases. But after five years they had only two solid stars, Wally Pipp and Bunny High, to show for $200,000 they had spent. This meager return convinced the businesslike Ruppert that he should seek no more "help" from colleagues.[4]

Determined to run the team with something like the efficiency of his brewery, Ruppert sought the services of experts who would be responsible to him alone. But this was difficult, at least until the war sent Huston to France. Ruppert then hired Miller Huggins, an experienced player and manager. Huston cabled his objections, declaring that Robinson of the Dodgers should have been named.

[3] Mrs. John McGraw, *op. cit.*, 274–75; Tom Meany, *Baseball's Greatest Teams*, 181–93; Frank Graham, *The New York Giants*, 121–29.

[4] Mrs. John McGraw, *op. cit.*, 272–73.

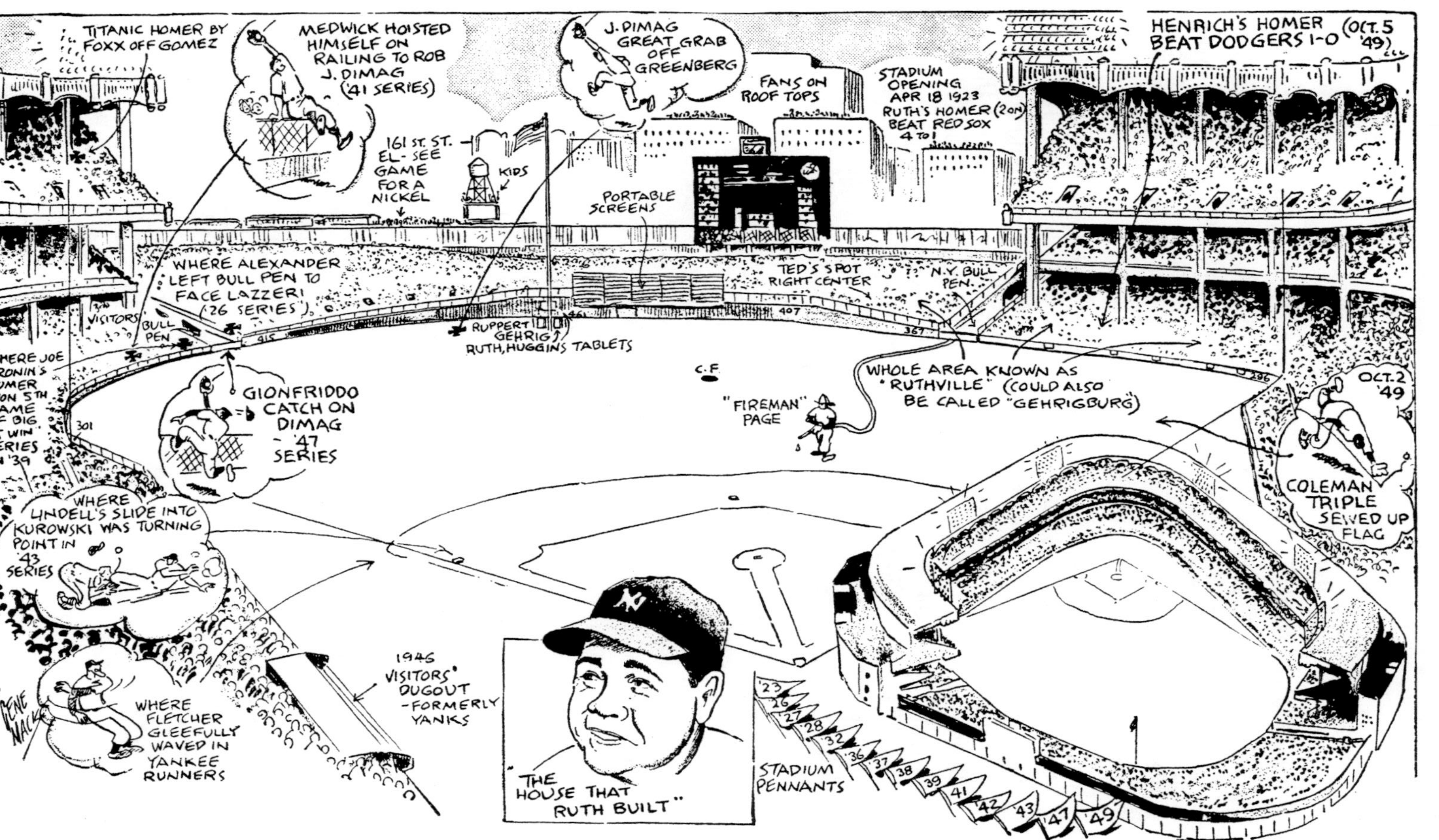

Yankee Stadium, New York. Gene Mack's Hall of Fame Cartoons, Major

Later, when Huston came home, he undercut Huggins by siding with the players against the manager. By 1920, the frail, pipe-smoking Huggins was in the middle of a growing rift between the owners, bridged only momentarily when Johnson's veto of the Mays purchase united them in a successful court battle.[5]

After a brief respite, the bickering was renewed, this time over Ruppert's decision to hire Red Sox manager Edward G. Barrow as general manager of the Yankees. The two colonels quarreled loudly even in public, and neither Huggins nor Barrow could operate in the climate of controversy. By now it was 1921, and the Giants told the partners to find new quarters away from the Polo Grounds. But Ruppert had already acquired a tract of land across the Harlem River in full view of the Polo Grounds as a site for a new stadium. Although Huston first reacted against the plan, he finally co-operated and gave valuable engineering advice on construction. By 1923, the mammoth structure was ready for occupancy. This magnificent $2 million citadel soon symbolized the concentrated power and mastery of the Yankee organization.

The hopes of envious rivals for a disastrous outcome to the internal dissension were dashed when Ruppert bought out his partner for an estimated $1.5 million. Huston was well compensated considering that his original investment had only been $225,000. Ruppert was now in full control, and he gave free rein to his lieutenants Huggins and Barrow. At the same time, this aristocratic millionaire, who never called an employee by his first name, made it clear that championship results were expected.[6]

One can forgive Ruppert for impatience in 1923, since up to that point his team's performance was nowhere near his hopes. In the eight years before the arrival of Mays and Ruth, Ruppert's spending had produced only two winning seasons. In 1919, Huggins's first winning team had drawn an encouraging 619,000 fans. Hopes were high for 1920, and with Ruth crashing fifty-four homers

[5] *Baseball Magazine*, June, 1918, interview with Jacob Ruppert; *The Sporting News*, December 2, 1920; Barrow, *op. cit.*, 127–55.

[6] *The Sporting News*, December 2, 1920, January 4, October 25, 1923; Fitzgerald (ed.), *The American League*, 3–36; "The Yankees," *Fortune*, *loc. cit.*

attendance zoomed to 1,289,000, an awesome total unprecedented in baseball history.[7]

The Yankees were still unable to acquire their first pennant, however, and in 1921 the future careers of Huggins and Barrow hung on the successful attainment of that goal. Working together, Huggins listed team weaknesses and Barrow, drawing on Ruppert's money and his own friendship with Frazee, went after the key men needed to secure the 1921 flag. Early that year, Barrow gave Frazee four average players and a large sum of money for pitcher Waite Hoyt, catcher Wally Schang, and a utility man. The key figure was Hoyt, a young righthander about to embark on a long career in the majors. In 1921, his nineteen victories strengthened the pitching staff whose only dependables had been ex-Red Sox Mays and Bob Shawkey. The infield consisted of Pipp at first, Aaron Ward at second, Roger Peckinpaugh at short, and veteran Frank Baker at third. Ruth and Bob Meusel strengthened the outfield flanks, but center remained a problem. Nevertheless, Huggins knew this to be the best team he had ever managed. By babying it, by overlooking Ruth's infractions, and by tolerating Huston's slights, Huggins prodded it to first place, and kept it there to win by four and one-half games over Cleveland.

That fall, the Yankees met the Giants in the Series, the first of many subway series for New York fans. Both managers saw the 1921 encounter as a crucial one. To McGraw's consternation, the first two games went to the Yankees by shutouts, but then Ruth injured his leg and sat out the remaining games and the Giants went on to win the first test of strength, five games to three.

Huggins and Barrow faced the 1922 season with mingled hope and concern. Their biggest problems were Ruth and Meusel, who defied Landis's orders against postseason barnstorming and were suspended from play for the first two months. To solve this problem, Barrow turned again to Frazee, and this time the Ruppert check bought shortstop Everett Scott, third baseman Joe Dugan, and pitchers Leslie Ambrose "Bullet Joe" Bush and "Sad" Sam Jones. Next, Barrow shored up center field by getting Whitey Witt

[7] U.S. House of Representatives, *Organized Baseball,* pp. 1617–18.

from the Athletics. All were established players, and they kept the team in contention until Ruth and Meusel returned. Rejuvenated, the Yankees plunged into a seasonlong struggle, barely beating the Browns after a close race.

Meanwhile, the Giants, on the second leg of their record-breaking four straight championships, won easily. Confronting their American tenants, the Giants were embarrassed because they had drawn fewer fans in their own park. The Yankees had been given notice to depart, both sides were vengeful, and the rivalry ran high. The Yanks were hopeful, but Giant pitchers Nehf and George McQuillan limited Yankee sluggers to a team average of .200. Ruth was completely ineffective. He was held to a .118 average and no homers. McGraw upset him by calling every pitch from the bench. For the Yankees, it was a bitter humiliation and only a tie game saved them from a complete blanking.[8]

Ruth, however, was determined to regain the esteem of the fans. To a lesser extent, this was also true of Huggins and Barrow, who were now freed from the meddling Huston. If Yankee fans were disappointed, at least the opening of the great stadium offered symbolic promise of success in another Giant duel. On opening day, Ruth rekindled all hopes when he baptized the citadel with a game-winning homer before sixty thousand.

Huggins and Barrow continued to merge their ideas and skills to improve the team, and another Red Sox deal brought pitchers Herb Pennock, a veteran lefthander of unfulfilled promise, and the talented rookie George Pipgras into camp. To Huggins's delight, Pennock joined with Hoyt and Jones to make an effective trio, and added joy came from Ruth's resolute attitude. Observers noted that he was working harder and carousing less. His 1923 effort was prodigious. His .393 batting average was his lifetime best, although second that year to Heilmann's .403. But Ruth led everyone else with 41 home runs, 130 runs batted in, and 151 runs scored. This output won him the league's most-valuable-player

[8] Graham, *The New York Giants*, 130–42; *The Sporting News*, November 3, 1921, March 2, 1922.

award and powered the Yankees to a fifteen and one-half game victory over the Tigers.

In the National League, McGraw drove his disciplined team to victory, thus setting the stage for a third subway Series. Just before the opening game, Ruppert gave his manager a vote of confidence, saying, "Huggins has managed the team faultlessly and Barrow has looked after the business details so well that I no longer have things to worry about. As the sole owner . . . I have been able to adjust matters in a most satisfactory manner."[9] This tribute boosted Huggins's morale even though the Giants, paced by Stengel's homers, won the first two games. Twice beaten and shut out once, the Yankees came back strongly. Ruth blasted three homers and compiled a .368 Series average, and the Yankees drubbed the Giants four straight times to take the Series, thus initiating the new stadium as the home of world champions. Anyone who wondered why a millionaire like Ruppert dallied with a baseball club found the answer in his boyish enthusiasm over the victory.[10]

This defeat by the Yankees was the beginning of the end for McGraw, even though he pushed his club to a 1924 flag with the help of a new star, first baseman Bill Terry. The Dodgers pressed hard, however, and the Giants won by the narrowest of margins. Instead of headlines to celebrate McGraw's fourth straight pennant, news stories told of a bribe attempt by Giant players Dolan and O'Connell. Because of the doubt this revelation cast on the Giant victory, Landis threatened to cancel the Series, but the Giants played and took far worse punishment.[11]

The Yankees lost the 1924 American League pennant to the Senators in a close race, and with it went the opportunity to vanquish the unpopular Giants. It was up to Washington to do so. The club had long been financially insecure and pathetically dependent on the drawing power of star pitcher Walter Johnson. In 1920, the Senators had come under the ownership of their dedicated

[9] Graham, *The New York Giants,* 140–50; *The Sporting News,* May 31, October 11, 25, 1923.

[10] Frank Graham, *The New York Yankees: An Informal History,* 95–96; Graham, *The New York Giants,* 143–58; *The Sporting News,* October 25, November 6, 1923.

[11] Fitzgerald (ed.), *The National League,* 217-44.

manager, Clark Griffith. Seizing a chance to buy 80 per cent of the club's stock for $145,000, Griffith borrowed heavily to realize his dream. For the rest of his life his fortunes were tied to this luckless team, and he struggled for years to win the pennant that would help repay his indebtedness.

Griffith relinquished his post as field manager in 1921 to concentrate on recruiting. He sent scouts on the trail of youngsters who might revive the team. Up to 1923, his efforts brought little success; the Senators trailed the Yankees by twenty-three and one-half games that year. Yet Griffith managed to secure outfielders Leon "Goose" Goslin, a future Hall of Famer, and Earl McNeely. Third baseman Ossie Bluege joined shortstop Roger Peckinpaugh, Joe Judge at first base, and Stanley "Bucky" Harris at second. This skilled infield supported veteran pitchers Johnson, George Mogridge, and Tom Zachary. Muddy Ruel did a superb job of catching.

Griffith chose "Bucky" Harris as the playing manager in 1924. Called the "boy manager" by the press, the twenty-seven-year-old Harris toughened himself by playing basketball in the off-season. At first his performance did little to justify Griffith's confidence; mid-May found the team buried in seventh place. Meanwhile, the Yankee rush was stalled by pitchers with sore arms and Ruth's "swell-headed" defiance of authority. At this point, Harris and the Senators began to move slowly upward. By midseason they were in full stride. The rejuvenated Johnson delivered twenty victories, and Goslin's .344 batting made him the runs-batted-in leader. Struggling all the way, the team won sixteen of their last twenty-one to capture the flag by two games.

This victory was a popular one. It brought Johnson the most-valuable-player award and Harris acclaim as a "boy wonder." A California congresswoman introduced a bill to make Walter Johnson's birthday a legal holiday, but the bill failed to reach the floor of the House.

In October, America's "Senator mania" reached its peak as the underdogs went into action against the Giants, perhaps the most unpopular team to enter a World Series. What followed was a see-saw battle, with the Giants winning three times and the Senators thrice rallying to square the struggle. In the seventh and decisive game, Johnson, who had yet to win a game, came in as a relief pitcher. With defeat threatening, Johnson prevented further scoring and his mates rallied to tie the game with the help of a ground ball which took an erratic bounce away from Giant third baseman Fred Lindstrom. There followed three more scoreless innings and the game moved into extra innings. As the Senators batted in the last of the twelfth, the Giant catcher missed a pop foul, giving the batter another chance which he used for a double. The next batter hit a grounder to Lindstrom and this also bounced crazily off a clod of dirt, enabling the winning run to score. The victory gave the Senators their first world championship, Johnson got his first Series victory, and McGraw made his last appearance in a Series.[12]

Nobody needed to tell the veteran Griffith of the transient quality of baseball glory, or the freakish aspect of his 1924 win. Over the winter he worked hard to bolster his team, especially its pitching staff. Unable to secure young replacements, he obtained old Dutch Reuther on waivers and traded a younger man for Stan Coveleskie, one of a handful of legal spitballers. These and other older pitchers gave Griffith an experienced but creaky staff. Since other replacements like Everett Scott and Joe Harris were equally old, Griffith knew that if he failed to win the 1925 flag he would not soon get another chance.

His biggest worry was the Yankee colossus which almost stole his 1924 glory. This was a misplaced fear, for the Yankees were mired in troubles. Early in 1925, rumors were prevalent about lax discipline and widespread dissipation on the part of team members. Ruth was reported to be the chief carouser, and at the very time Huggins was predicting a victory, his star player fell deathly sick from overindulgence in food and drink. Hospitalized until June, he returned, but slumped badly. He continued to head a cabal of veterans in attempting to undermine Huggins's power. At last

[12] *The Sporting News*, September 1, 22, 1924; *New York Times*, October 10, 1924; Fitzgerald (ed.), *The American League*, 58–87; Meany, *op. cit.*, 209–23; Shirley Povich, *The Washington Senators*, 97–132; *Reach's Official Base Ball Guide*, 1925, pp. 12–13, 36–65.

Huggins suspended him and fined him $5,000 for insubordination. Irritated by the size of the fine, Ruth turned first to Barrow and Ruppert, then to Landis for redress. All spurned Ruth, and Huggins, agonizing over his second-division team, won a badly needed vote of confidence from Ruppert. Given a free hand to clean house, he cut the dissidents from his team, replacing them with youngsters like hard-hitting Lou Gehrig at first, Mark Koenig at short, and Tony Lazzeri at second. Huggins's action laid a foundation for future success, but in 1925 his young players languished in seventh.

With the Yankees out of contention, manager Harris faced a challenge from Mack's Athletics, coming on strong with stars like first baseman Jimmy Foxx, catcher Mickey Cochrane, and outfielder Max Bishop. But in August, Athletic pitching wilted, the team lost twelve straight, and the Senators coasted to an easy eight and one-half game victory.[13]

That year, the Giants also collapsed, although less dramatically. McGraw's health was failing and he grew increasingly testy and quarrelsome with his veterans, some of whom were shipped to other teams. McGraw's worries were heightened by sicknesses that struck down friends like Matty, who died of tuberculosis, and coach Hugh Jennings, who retired with a lingering illness. Most painful was the loss of Ross Youngs, the key to the Giants batting attack, who was felled by an illness that would soon take his life. McGraw was further embittered by a Landis decision that allowed the Cubs to appropriate Lewis "Hack" Wilson, a promising slugger from a Giants farm, and grew increasingly unequal to the task of rebuilding.[14]

While the Giants faltered, Bill McKechnie's Pirates came on to win the pennant with the help of three future Hall of Fame players, third baseman Harold "Pie" Traynor and outfielders Max Carey and Hazen "Ki-Ki" Cuyler. Like the Yankees, this team suffered from player cliques that would soon cost McKechnie his post. But in 1925 he held it together, enabling the Pirates to win by eight and one-half games.

[13] Povich, *op. cit.*, 132–48; *Reach's Official Base Ball Guide*, 1926, pp. 12–15, 61–72; *The Sporting News*, June 18, 25, September 3, 1925.

[14] Mrs. John McGraw, *op. cit.*, 296–303; *The Sporting News*, August 1, 1929.

In the Series that fall, Walter Johnson won two games to give Washington a three game to one lead. Needing only a single victory to clinch the Series, the Senators lost the next two. Badly shaken by the Pirate comeback, the Senators collapsed. Johnson took the loss in a 9–7 game that was marred by Peckinpaugh's three errors at short. To the tune of jeers from fans and an angry telegram from league president Johnson, Harris and Griffith saw themselves transformed from champs to chumps, a humiliation compounded by the knowledge that their overage team was finished.[15]

With the Senators aging and the Pirates feuding, hopes of outsiders soared in 1926. Most experts picked the Athletics or the Indians, with one veteran writer, Fred Lieb, naming the Yankees. Good Yankee pitching and hitting appeared to be offset by the inexperience of youngsters like Gehrig, Lazzeri, Koenig, and Combs. Much depended on young Lazzeri, who bore the brunt of the pressure, although it was well known that he was an epileptic. Lazzeri had the approval of Barrow's chief scout, Paul Krichell, who demanded poise under fire and determination, along with orthodox talents in running, throwing, and hitting. A tireless traveler, Krichell followed his choices everywhere and competed skillfully with other scouts for top talent. Backed by Huggins and Barrow, his approval carried weight and his growing reputation as baseball's top scout rested on these 1926 rookies. Ruth, the key to the Yankee attack, was determined to get in stride again. Not that he ever would abandon his love of night life, but never again would he sink to the depths of 1925.[16]

In 1926, Pennock, Hoyt, and Urban Shocker provided the pitching and Ben Bengough and Pat Collins the catching. Ruth, Meusel, and Earl Combs made up the outfield, and the infield consisted of Gehrig, Lazzeri, Koenig, and Dugan. The Yankees started slowly, then reeled off eight straight victories. By August they held a comfortable lead, but in September they almost cracked under pressure from Tris Speaker's Indians. They hung on, however, to win

15 Povich, *op. cit.*, 132–48; Fitzgerald (ed.), *The National League*, 50–67; Allen, *American League Story*, 113–17; *Spalding's Official Base Ball Guide*, 1926, pp. 67–109.

16 Dave Camerer, "36 Years a Yankee," *Baseball Digest*, July, 1957, pp. 27–39; Barrow, *op. cit.*, 100–55.

by three games, clinching the pennant in St. Louis, where the Cardinals had won the National pennant.

In winning the National flag by two games over the Reds, the Cardinals brought St. Louis its first pennant since the Von der Ahe era, and began a dynasty that would rank second to that of the great Yankees. The win vindicated president Rickey's controversial farm plan and proved that young players could be nurtured by imaginative teaching of playing techniques. By 1926 his system had developed stars like first baseman Jim Bottomley, shortstop Tom Thevenow, and outfielders Taylor Douthit and Chick Hafey. This home-grown quartet blended with veterans like pitchers Grover Alexander, Jess Haines, and Bill Sherdel. Above all, the team had Rogers Hornsby, the superstar second baseman, who succeeded Rickey as manager in 1925 and drove the team to victory in 1926.

Hornsby was a blunt, outspoken perfectionist who was intolerant of mediocrity and outside criticism. Because he said what he thought in aggressive and obscene language, he alienated both Rickey and Breadon. With such adversaries, his St. Louis days were numbered. Nevertheless, he goaded the team to a dramatic victory over the Yankees in a seven-game Series, during which the veteran Alexander struck out Lazzeri for the third out in a tension-packed seventh inning of the last game. Hornsby was cherished by St. Louis fans, who were outraged when Breadon traded him to the Giants for Frisch that winter. Because Rickey helped to trade Hornsby he was denied his share in the glory for making the Cardinals a contender. The bitterness continued as the Cardinals dropped a close 1927 race to the Pirates, and lingered on even when the team scored victories in 1928 and 1930–31. Nevertheless, Rickey was able to weather the storm and to help garner two more pennants before a quarrel with Breadon sent him on to further triumphs in Brooklyn and Pittsburgh.[17]

Although experts in 1927 emphasized Hornsby's value in their

[17] *New York Times,* December 11, 1965, January 30, 1967; "The Mahatma," *Time,* December 17, 1965; *The Sporting News,* February 18, 1967; *Reach's Official Base Ball Guide,* 1927, pp. 15–43, 89–117.

A perfectionist at the bat, Rogers Hornsby is ranked as the greatest right-handed batter in baseball history. During his twenty-three-year career in the National League, he thrice topped the .400 batting mark and in 1924 set the modern record of .424 while playing with the St. Louis Cardinals. Hornsby was also a standout at second base, and his play gave National League fans something to brag about in the age of Babe Ruth. (George Brace, photographer)

Lloyd Waner, junior member of one of baseball's most famous brother combinations, poses in this photograph. For fourteen seasons, beginning in 1927, the Waner brothers teamed together in the Pittsburgh Pirates outfield, and their timely hits helped land the 1927 pennant. Recently, both brothers were elected to baseball's Hall of Fame at Cooperstown, New York. (George Brace, photographer)

forecasts, the Giants managed only a third-place finish with this superstar. Predictably, the blunt Hornsby clashed with McGraw. Once again he was traded, this time to Boston. The experts were correct, however, in forecasting a Cardinal defeat, although manager Bob O'Farrell missed by only a game and a half. To the surprise of most, victory fell to the Pirates, now managed by Donie Bush and buttressed by the brothers Paul and Lloyd Waner, a pair of heavy-hitting outfielders.

This well-balanced team was fated to grapple with the Yankees in the World Series. In their 1926 Series defeat, Huggins's youthful team had passed through a difficult trial that left them battlewise and vengeful. In mustering them for 1927, Huggins saw little need for replacements beyond recalling Pipgras and adding Wilcy Moore, a great relief specialist, to the pitching staff. Once under way, the team used pitchers Pennock and Hoyt to hold enemy batters back, while Ruth and Gehrig pounded out a joint output of 107 homers. The race really ended on the Fourth of July, when the challenging Senators were beaten in a doubleheader, 12–1 and 21–1. After that, all rivals submitted meekly as the Yankees, hailed as the greatest team in baseball history, went on to win by nineteen games. But even with the race a foregone conclusion, the drama of a record-shattering home-run duel between Gehrig and Ruth held the interest of fans all the way. At the end of the season, Ruth had set a modern record of 60 home runs.[18]

The Yankees used the "big bang" to dominate the Series, and if the games were closely fought, Yankee homers usually decided the outcome. The "window breakers" swept four Series games in a row from the Pirates.

In 1928, except for Ruth and Gehrig, the team was less frightening. For one thing, a flood of injuries swamped the team, and Shocker's death from heart disease was a serious loss. Moreover, the Athletics made a powerful bid, but were downed in decisive battles in September, as the Yanks won by a mere two and one-half games. Meanwhile, Rickey's Cardinals, with crafty Bill McKech-

[18] *Reach's Official Base Ball Guide*, 1928, pp. 3–62, 100; Meany, *op. cit.*, 17–30; *New York Times,* October 3, 1927; Graham, *The New York Yankees,* 127–37.

nie at the helm, rebounded to the top, edging the Giants by two games. But in the Series the Cardinals suffered the same fate as the 1927 Pirates and were cut down in four straight games. Seven homers from the bats of Ruth and Gehrig sparked the crippled Yankees.[19]

That winter, shouts of "break up the Yankees" were an understandable reaction to Huggins's monopoly. Not since Wright's Reds ruled the National Association in the 1870's had fans witnessed such overwhelming domination by a single team. Nor did the future hold hope of a Yankee decline, since Huggins was grooming brilliant new finds like catcher Bill Dickey. Nevertheless, as rivals groaned, circumstances were about to end this phase of Yankee tyranny.[20]

Injuries and illnesses dogged the 1928 team, especially the pitchers and catchers. The club also suffered from complacency, which a concerned Huggins attributed to overpay, oversuccess, and overconfidence. Meanwhile, Mack's Athletics, a team cast in the Yankee mold, became a real threat. Eight years in the making, this team had the powerful outfield of Bing Miller, Mule Haas, and Al Simmons and an infield of slugging Jim Foxx at first, Max Bishop, Joe Boley, and Jim Dykes. Up to 1929, pitching was its weakness, but apparently hot-tempered "Lefty" Bob Grove had at last conquered the wildness that kept him from achieving greatness. Joining Grove as a starter was another Oriole purchase, the aristocratic collegian George Earnshaw, who gave fine balance to the pitching staff.

From the start, the 1929 American race was a battle of titans. The A's moved at a fantastic .735 clip through July, widening a lead over the Yankees who played above .600. Huggins pressed his men hard, but by August he could foresee the gloomy outcome. Worry and strain led to his physical impairment, and he was hospitalized in September with an infection. Four days before the season ended, he died, knowing at the end that his demoralized

[19] *The Sporting News,* September 9, 16, October 7, 1928; *Spalding's Official Base Ball Guide,* 1929, pp. 29–46, 85–86; *Reach's Official Base Ball Guide,* 1929, pp. 25–31, 140.

[20] Graham, *The New York Giants,* 157–59.

team would lose by a wide margin. The first phase of the Age of the Yankees had come to a halt.[21]

Although the 1929 pennant belonged to the A's, the man who would command the Yankee revival was near at hand. That year the Cubs won the right to test the A's in the Series. Their manager was Joseph V. McCarthy, former minor-league infielder and manager, noted for his objective way of appraising talent and his sensible manner of coaxing the best out of his men. Called to the Cubs in 1926, he took a badly mauled team and brought it into contention in one season. After three years of chasing Cardinals and Pirates, his team of right-handed power hitters finally captured first place. Included were superstars Hornsby and Cuyler, along with Hack Wilson and Riggs Stephenson. With such hitters and sound pitching from Charley Root, Guy Bush, Sheriff Blake, and Pat Malone, the Cubs won easily and hungered for the world title.

October, 1929, was a bad month for championship dreams. Before the month ended, the stock market collapsed, exploding the get-rich-quick visions of the late 1920's, including those of many players. Connie Mack started the veteran Howard Ehmke, who had not pitched in six weeks, against the Cubs. So superbly did he throttle Cub power, that his 3–1 win included a Series strikeout record. Earnshaw won the next game 9–3, after which Bush scored the first Cub victory. With rising hopes, McCarthy watched Root take an 8–0 lead into the seventh inning of the fourth game. But in the bottom of that inning the A's unleashed the most remarkable batting volley in Series history, scoring ten runs to wrench the game away. Crushed by this, the Cubs fell 4–3 in the finale. The beating erased memories of McCarthy's good work during the year and lost him the confidence of the owners. Before the 1930 season was out, he was replaced by the ever-available Hornsby.[22]

For American fans, the Athletic triumph provided a glittering end to a lush baseball era. But as the year 1929 ended, the shock

21 *Reach's Official Base Ball Guide*, 1931, pp. 13–22, 45–65; *The Sporting News*, February 21, July 25, October 3, 1929; For sketches of Foxx, Grove and Simmons, see *Baseball Digest*, April, 1951, June, August, 1956.

22 Meany, *op. cit.*, 45–59; Fitzgerald (ed.), *The American League*, 130–52; Fitzgerald (ed.), *The National League*, 101–27; Warren Brown, *The Chicago Cubs*, 111–28; *Spalding's Official Base Ball Guide*, 1930, pp. 39–57, 97–98.

of the Wall Street failure quickly cut away incomes, jobs, and purchasing power throughout the land. It was no time to launch a baseball dynasty, and this hard fact became Mack's agony. With a successful and highly priced team on his hands, he felt the squeeze of high salary demands and decreasing attendance. His team was too good (winning by eight over Washington in 1930 and thirteen and one-half over the Yankees in 1931), so that bored fans stayed away, leaving Mack with little profit. It was small comfort to him that the same fate befell Rickey's Cardinals, piloted now by former catcher Charles "Gabby" Street. After a close two-game win over the Cubs in 1930, the Cardinals won by thirteen in 1931 over the Giants. It was McGraw's last full year as the manager of the Giants.

In the Series struggles between these titans, the A's won the 1930 meeting four games to two. But the next year, an unshaven, disheveled third baseman, "Pepper" Martin, whose unkempt appearance symbolized the national mood of deprivation, ran wild on the bases. Batting .500 and stealing bases with daring, Martin led his mates to victory in seven games. Although the 1931 victory ranks as one of the memorable Series encounters, declining profits distressed Rickey, who was also finding that this was no time for dynasties.[23]

2. The Depression Era, 1931–41

During the depths of the Depression in 1932, an estimated thirteen million American workers were jobless. With the exception of the National League's Cincinnati and Pittsburgh, every major-league team suffered attendance losses, and these two merely recovered slightly from losses of the year before. In Philadelphia, Connie Mack watched with dismay as his team drew only four hundred thousand—the third straight year of serious decline. Desperate for cash, Mack began selling his stars after 1933, and, as ever, there were buyers. By 1936 practically all of his best players

[23] *New York Times,* October 8, 1931, March 6, 1965 (Martin's obituary); Allen, *National League Story,* 178–91; *Baseball Magazine,* December, 1931; *The Sporting News,* October 15, 22, 1931; *Spalding's Official Baseball Guide,* 1931, pp. 35–93, 1932, pp. 17–29, 31–57, 61–87.

were gone except for Jimmy Foxx, and soon he wore the uniform of the Red Sox. And so for a third time Mack dismantled a superb team, voluntarily sentencing the A's to years of second-division finishes. As before, he counted on rebuilding once prosperity returned, but this time he was wrong. For the rest of his life, ending in the 1950's, Mack tried unsuccessfully to reassemble a winning combination.[24]

The depletion of the Athletics brought about a shift in the balance of power in the American League. In 1932, the Yankees returned to power under Joe McCarthy. Still powering his team were Ruth, Gehrig, Combs, and Lazzeri, while Pennock and Pipgras steadied the pitching. New faces included Dickey, a tall, powerful catcher, hailed as the Yankees' greatest. His careful handling made first-string pitchers of Red Ruffing, a castoff from the Red Sox, and of Vernon "Lefty" Gomez. Paced by these stars, the explosive Yankees won 107 games. This personal triumph for McCarthy was crowned with a four-game sweep over the Cubs in the Series. Baseball legend has it that in the third game Ruth responded to Cub jeers by gesturing in the direction of the bleachers, then blasting a homer in that area. Notwithstanding the mythology surrounding the feat, it made Ruth's last Series his most memorable.[25]

In regaining their dominance, the Yankees showed no such timidity as characterized the Athletics. Instead, Ruppert abruptly announced the purchase of the Newark team in the International League. In this manner, the Yankees joined the farm movement, and as soon as the surprised Barrow regained his composure he named George M. Weiss, a veteran minor-league official, to head the operation. Weiss proved to be a gifted administrator. The Newark outpost quickly became the staging area for quality Yankee replacements. The foundations were thus laid for the second era of Yankee domination.[26]

[24] *Literary Digest,* December 23, 1933, August 8, 1934.

[25] *The Sporting News,* May 26, July 14, October 6, 13, 20, 1932; *Reach's Official Base Ball Guide,* 1933, pp. 11–12, 21–59, 101–17; *Spalding's Official Baseball Guide,* 1933, pp. 19–34, 38–41; Graham, *The New York Giants,* 174–86.

[26] For a sketch of Weiss, see *New York Times,* June 14, 1966.

No one expected the Yankees to falter in 1933, but several misfortunes hobbled the team. For one, McCarthy, like Huggins, was plagued by Ruth's unruly moods. Because he coveted the managerial post, Ruth resented McCarthy and put himself at the head of a clique that refused to speak to McCarthy or to those players who did. On top of this, slumps hit men like Combs, Sewell, and Frank Crosetti. Ruth was aging, but his popularity and still deadly power kept him in the lineup.

With their attack dulled, the Yankees won only ninety-one games, good for second in 1933. As the Yankees faltered, the Senators rushed ahead with a pennant-winning spurt similar to that of their first breakthrough in 1924. Once again, a young manager led the team. This time it was shortstop Joe Cronin, at the peak of his career as hitter and fielder. Behind him were hitters like Goslin, Heinie Manush, and Bluege, while "General" Al Crowder led pitchers with twenty-four wins, two more than Earl Whitehill. Their balanced attack accounted for ninety-nine victories, and a comfortable seven and one-half game lead over the Yankees, who fought back savagely, often using their fists against their conquerors.[27]

Despite his league victory, it was a profitless season for Griffith. He also saw his team fall before the Giants in the Series. The New York team was piloted now by playing manager Bill Terry. In winning the pennant by five games over the Pirates, Terry depended on a superior pitching staff made up of knuckle-balling Fred Fitzsimmons, fast-balling Roy Parmalee, curve-balling "Prince" Hal Schumacher, and the king of the staff, Carl Hubbell. Among Hubbell's varied deliveries was a mystifying "screwball," which he used to win twenty-three victories. With Hubbell winning twice and home-run king Mel Ott supplying the power, the Giants brushed by the Senators four games to one. Defeated in the Series and at the turnstiles, Griffith now chose to retrench along with other American League owners.[28]

[27] Povich, *op. cit.*, 174–90; Allen, *American League Story*, 139–41; *The Sporting News*, September 14, 1933; *Reach's Official Baseball Guide*, 1934, pp. 11–13, 25–48.

[28] *The Sporting News*, November 2, 1933; Graham, *The New York Giants*, 202–209; *New York Times*, October 7, 1933.

In this 1935 photograph, Boston Red Sox' newly appointed playing manager, Joe Cronin (left), talks with his star left-handed pitcher, Robert "Lefty" Grove. In spending heavily for the services of such established performers as Cronin and Grove, Red Sox owner Tom Yawkey hoped vainly to wrest the American League pennant from rivals such as Detroit and the Yankees. (Courtesy Boston Red Sox, American League)

Because Goslin had quarreled with Cronin, Griffith shipped him to Detroit. While this weakened the Senators, nothing prepared Griffith for the shock of a seventh-place finish in 1934. Faced now with worse financial woes, Griffith listened to a $250,000 offer by millionaire Tom Yawkey of the Red Sox for the services of Cronin. Although he was somewhat constrained by the fact that Cronin had become his nephew by marriage, Griffith accepted.

In spite of Yawkey's lavish spending, his teams finished no better than fourth in 1934 and 1935. Instead, Navin of Detroit reaped a bountiful harvest as his Tigers hung up two consecutive pennants. For Navin, the key trade came late in 1933 with the purchase of catcher Cochrane from Mack for $100,000. By installing the fiery Cochrane as playing manager, Navin had the answer to his perennial pitching problem. Overnight, Cochrane made stars out of Tommy Bridges and Lynwood "Schoolboy" Rowe. With slugger Hank Greenberg vying for the homer title, and Goslin and Charles Gehringer rattling base hits, "Black Mike" Cochrane's Tigers mounted the best attack in the league. As usual, the Yankees were the chief contenders, but in 1934 Ruth slumped to .288 and appeared in only 125 games. Without his punch, the Yankees fell behind, and at the finish the Tigers led by 7 games. During the fight to bring Detroit its first flag in twenty-five years, 919,000 fans jammed Navin Field, the best attendance mark in baseball that year, and triple the Tiger mark of 1933.[29]

Meanwhile, under manager Frank Frisch, the Cardinals regained their winning touch, although they drew a discouraging attendance of only 325,000. This happened in spite of the presence of the flamboyant pitching duo of Jerome "Dizzy" Dean and his brother Paul, an infield of Rip Collins, Leo Durocher, Martin, and Frisch, and an outfield with stars like Joe Medwick and Ernie Orsatti. This colorful crew, fittingly called the "gashouse gang," fought out a red hot race with Terry's Giants, winning by two games. According to popular baseball legend, Terry's flippant preseason remark, "Is Brooklyn still in the league?" rallied the

[29] Fitzgerald (ed.), *The American League*, 76–87; *New York Times*, April 20, 1968, for a sketch of Bridges.

Trick photography shows Lynwood "Schoolboy" Rowe of the Detroit Tigers sitting on top of the baseball world. The year was 1934 when Rowe won sixteen straight games and posted a 24–8 pitching record. Sadly enough, the "gashouse gang" of the St. Louis Cardinals took the measure of Rowe and his mates in the World Series that year. (Courtesy Detroit Tigers, American League)

Dodgers to defeat the Giants in late season games, thus insuring the Cardinal victory.

The Cardinals showed championship mettle in the Series. Led by the Dean brothers, who together won more than fifty games during the regular season and four in the Series, the Cards outlasted the tough Tigers. Still, it took seven games before Dizzy Dean won the clincher, 11–0. Victory came at Detroit, where angry

fans showered Cardinal outfielder Medwick with garbage for his part in an earlier brawl. For Medwick's safety, Landis ordered him removed. Although he was widely criticized for the move, Landis at least gained something of value from the Series. Watching Pepper Martin, he later admitted, had taught him how to spit tobacco juice between his teeth.[30]

The defeat evoked memories in Detroit fans of the old jinx that kept the Tigers from winning a Series during the Cobb era. Yet back they came, over a million strong in 1935. This was a gesture of support unmatched anywhere in the Depression decade. Responding to this, the Tigers outlasted the Yankees as Greenberg hit 36 homers and drove in 170 runs. Pitchers Rowe and Bridges were slightly off from the previous year, mainly because of tough opposition. In the end the Tigers won by only three games over the Yankees.

While the Tigers were battling the Yankees in the American League, the Cardinals seemed to be well on the way to winning in the National. But in September the picture changed. By winning twenty-one consecutive games in that month, often by climactic rallies, the Chicago Cubs snatched the pennant from the Cardinals by two games. The decisive win came in St. Louis, when the young Cub first baseman, Phil Cavaretta, hit the homer that brought down the "gashouse gang."

Tempered hard in that race, and with two twenty-game winners in Bill Lee and Lon Warneke and the best infield since its Tinker-to-Evers-to-Chance era, the Cubs confronted the Tigers. Like their rivals, the Cubs had lost four consecutive Series battles and were determined to win.

The Cubs began well, beating the Tigers 3–0 in the opener behind

[30] *New York Times*, October 10, 1934; Reach's *Official Baseball Guide*, 1935, pp. 11–12, 46–49, 117.

Five years out for military service in World War II kept Henry "Hank" Greenberg of Detroit from assaulting Ruth's records as baseball's prima *slugger. Nevertheless, the Tiger first baseman's record of fifty-eight homers in 1938 is high for a right-handed batter.* (Courtesy Detroit Tigers, American League)

His nineteen years of quiet efficiency as star second baseman for the Detroit Tigers earned Charley Gehringer the nickname of "the Mechanical Man." Shown here, the stylish, left-handed batter connects in batting practice at Navin Field in the early 1930's. When he retired in 1942, Gehringer's lifetime average of .320 earned him his place in the Hall of Fame. (Courtesy Detroit Tigers, American League)

Warneke. But in the second game, Detroit won 8–3, although losing Greenberg when he was injured sliding into Cub catcher Hartnett. This incident caused tempers to flare and again Landis faced a riot threat. None developed, but in all the games players purpled the atmosphere with curses and obscenities. Landis later confessed, "I learned from these young men some variations of the language even I didn't know existed." Of course, they also played all-out, especially curve-baller Tom Bridges whose two victories helped bring the Tigers their first Series victory.[31]

It was a joyous winter for Detroit fans, warmed as they were by hopes of future conquests. Instead, they were to learn that the Yankees must be added to the list of inevitables, along with death and taxes. In 1936 it was time for another Yankee surge.

Following McCarthy's victory of 1932, his teams finished second for the next three years. In the view of Ruppert and Barrow, this was barely acceptable, but it was totally unacceptable to McCarthy. A compulsive perfectionist, this pudgy, long-jawed Irishman longed for the pennants that would prove him the equal of Huggins. He tinkered endlessly, looking for the combination to do the job. Gone now was Ruth, along with Pennock and Sewell, while Combs had been moved to the coaching staff. Many new prospects, dredged up by the scouting staff, were studied by McCarthy and usually farmed out.[32]

A chosen few reported for duty in 1936, but none were so favored as Joseph Paul DiMaggio. Early in the decade, this young Californian had been considered by many scouts, but the fact that he had suffered a knee injury discouraged all but a few. Acting on inside advice, Bill Essick, Yankee scout, signed the outfielder, who continued to lead the Pacific Coast League in hitting. During 1935, DiMaggio had a .398 average with the San Francisco Seals. Next year he was ready, and when he joined the Yankees in the spring, Crosetti and Lazzeri watched over him with brotherly solicitude. With DiMaggio in center, flanked by George Selkirk in right

31 Brown, *op. cit.*, 145–46; *New York Times*, October 8, 1935; *Reach's Official Baseball Guide*, 1936, pp. 34–51, 55–97, 101–41.

32 "The Yankees," *Fortune, loc. cit.*

and Ben Chapman in left, McCarthy had a strong outfield. But Chapman was too emotional for McCarthy, who traded him for another southerner, Jake Powell. In the infield, captain Gehrig gave stability at first; he had already set a record for most consecutive games played. With him were Lazzeri, Crosetti, and the young Dartmouth star, Robert "Red" Rolfe, at third. Ruffing and Gomez were the mainstays of the pitching staff, but John Allen, Monte Pearson, and Irving "Bump" Hadley were dependable regulars, and curve-balling John Murphy was a star relief man. Backing this staff, of course, was Dickey, challenged only by Cochrane as the best catcher in the league.

The devastating victory scored by this team might be compared to President Roosevelt's landslide victory over Governor Alf Landon in the fall. Both wins were equally awe-inspiring. The Yankees scored theirs first, ripping the league apart and clinching the flag earlier than anyone before, winning by nineteen and one-half games. That year, five Yankee regulars topped .300. Dickey led all with a .363 average, and Gehrig led in homers with forty-nine. But most encouraging was DiMaggio's performance; he compiled a .323 average and hit twenty-nine homers, enough for fans to acclaim him as a worthy successor to Ruth.[33]

McCarthy's task resembled Huggins's 1921 task. Again, the Yanks had to face the Giants in the Series. Manager Terry had little of McGraw's appeal, but he had a fighting ball club that had taken the flag from the Cubs by five games. As in 1933, pitching was the team's forte, with Hubbell, Schumacher, and Fitzsimmons as masters. With them were other veterans of 1933 like Ott, Joe Moore, Hank Lieber, Gus Mancuso, and Henry Danning. Terry quit active play and replaced himself with Sam Leslie at first.

Terry got off to a good start against the Yanks at the Polo Grounds, where Hubbell opened with a masterly 6–1 victory. But the next day the Yankees set a Series record, scoring eighteen runs to rout the Giants and dash Terry's hopes. This was followed by two close games in which Yankee pitching prevailed. Then the Giants won again, 5–4, behind Schumacher, but in the sixth game

[33] Graham, *The New York Yankees,* 221–40.

the "Bronx Bombers" closed the Series out, beating Fitzsimmons 13–5.[34]

The two teams met again the following year, with essentially the same cast of characters, except for newcomers like outfielder Tom Henrich of the Yanks and pitcher Cliff Melton of the Giants. Even their pennant-winning efforts were like those of 1936, the Giants winning by three over the Cubs, the Yankees by thirteen over the Tigers. During the regular season, Yankee pitcher Hadley accidentally beaned Cochrane of the Tigers, ending his playing career and hastening his departure as Tiger chief. The accident stirred memories of Chapman's death, but the Yankees rode it out and capped their pennant win with an authoritative 4–1 Series victory. The triumph was decisive enough to stir renewed cries of "break up the Yankees."

But the Yankees were still far from a breakup. In a tough age which called for tough men in baseball, the Yankees were toughest. They were managed by a perfectionist, bossed by a president who

[34] *New York Times,* October 3, 1936.

Manager Joseph V. McCarthy crouches in the dugout at Yankee Stadium, New York City. McCarthy managed the Yankees to eight pennants and seven World Championships in the years 1931 to 1946. From 1936 to 1939 his teams won four consecutive World Championships. (Courtesy New York Yankees, American League)

hated second place, and owned by a man who could say, even with a seventeen-game lead in 1936, "I can't stand this suspense. When are we going to clinch it?" If this were not enough, Weiss was quietly building a compact Yankee farm empire, and was co-ordinating all scouting activity. By 1938, this policy was paying dividends. In the spring, Weiss sent up brilliant rookies like second baseman Joe Gordon, pitchers Atley Donald and Spurgeon Chandler, and catcher Buddy Rosar, each ready for a frontline job. Indeed, in these years the Yankees' Newark farm team was so good that some observers said it belonged in the majors.

And yet, because Yankee veterans were so durable, talented young players often had to wait on the bench for a walk-on part. A notable exception was Gordon, who replaced Lazzeri and with Crosetti gave the Yankees their best double-play combination. This defensive duo supplemented the Yankee hitting attack, in 1938 helped to deflect a pennant challenge from the Red Sox, and sparked a win by eight and one-half games.[35]

Facing them in the Series were the Cubs, a team that somehow managed to win a pennant every three years. They surprised experts by beating the Pirates, whose management had been so sure of victory that they sent out gaudy press buttons for the Series. But the Cubs were managed by hard-driving catcher Hartnett, a tough martinet. His pitching staff was led by veterans Bill Lee and Warneke and supported by Dizzy Dean who had been purchased from the Cardinals for $125,000 despite his lame arm. Given Dean's character, it was a fair bargain. To a reporter's question about his arm he drawled, "It ain't what it was . . . but then, what the hell is?" That year his tired arm was good enough for a 7–1 record, including a key win over the Pirates in the stretch drive. In the third game of that crucial series, Hartnett broke a 5–5 tie by hitting a homer in the gathering darkness. The win put the Cubs on top for the first time, and the next day they romped over the Pirates, 10–1, ending the race in a melodramatic style.

[35] Graham, *The New York Yankees,* 221–40; Graham, *The New York Giants,* 220–32; Barrow, *op. cit.,* 155–75; *Reach's Official Baseball Guide,* 1938, pp. 25–34, 39–79, 1939, pp. 49–59, 67–106, 111–50.

But it took more than a storybook plot to beat the Yankees. The Cubs fell in four games, and they fell hard as the Yankees outhit, outpitched, and outfielded them. A highlight was Dean's performance as he held the Yanks at bay for eight innings with his pitching skill, but he finally succumbed and his mates had to be satisfied with a record high loser's share of $4,674 each.[36]

Next year, it was the Yankees' turn for a lesson in baseball reality. Ever since 1925, the Yankees had counted on durable Gehrig at first. Always available, this handsome slugger was a model of quiet efficiency. By the spring of 1939, he had played 2,122 consecutive games, a fantastic testimony to his drive and conditioning. In 1938, however, he slumped to a .295 batting average and was ineffective in the Series. In the spring of 1939 he had become painfully inept. He was only thirty-six, however, and because he had done so well in the past, McCarthy stayed with his captain, but after eight games Gehrig benched himself. Soon the reason was evident; Gehrig had multiple sclerosis, a progressive paralysis, usually fatal.[37]

Weiss's farm system was unequal to the task of providing a man of Gehrig's ability for first base. Only a passable successor was available. Nevertheless, the Newark farm did produce Charley Keller, a slugger whose dark features won him the nickname "King Kong." With Keller in left, Henrich in right, and DiMaggio in center, the Yankees had one of the great outfields in history. That year, DiMaggio won the batting title and the team won 106 games, finishing 17 games ahead of Boston.

Against this Olympian team stood the Cincinnati Reds, a dark-horse team in the winner's circle for the first time since the scandals of 1919. Managed by Bill McKechnie, the team presented a balanced attack built around the tight infield of Frank McCormick, Lon Frey, Bill Meyer, and Bill Werber, and a pitching staff headed by Bucky Walters, Paul Derringer, and John Vander Meer. That year, the left-handed Vander Meer astounded the baseball

[36] Brown, *op. cit.*, 169–78; Fitzgerald (ed.), *The National League*, 117–27; Rice, *op. cit.*, 57.

[37] George Bulkley, "See You Later, Lou," *Baseball Magazine*, June, 1939; *New York Times*, May 3, 1939.

world by pitching two consecutive no-hit games. With such pitching, and a hitting attack built around McCormick, outfielder Ival Goodman, and catcher Ernie Lombardi, the Reds beat the Cardinals by four and a one-half games.

In the Series, after suffering two close losses in the first two games, the Reds collapsed completely under the vaunted Yankee power. This victory enabled the Yankees to set a new record, four straight championships followed by four straight Series victories. Comparisons with past performances were common, since major-league baseball was celebrating its spurious centennial for a history-minded fandom. Only Wright's old Association teams stood comparison with McCarthy's team, and few remembered Harry Wright. McCarthy was now acknowledged to be the greatest of the Yankee managers. But the team no longer had the owner who had made all things possible, for Ruppert died that year, and although this bachelor sportsman allowed for the club in his will, his passing made the future of the empire uncertain.[38]

Meanwhile, anti-Yankee sentiment had grown and now dominated league councils. Early in 1940, a rule was passed barring a pennant winner from making trades. This ruling, however, did not stop the Yankees from using their farms. Furthermore, the team was young and their most recent conquest justified optimism.[39]

Nevertheless, rivals were stirring. The Tigers, managed now by Del Baker, were aging but formidable. In 1940, Baker picked up the seasoned Louis "Bobo" Newsome, a flashy right-handed pitcher already noted for many changes of his baseball address. Baker next persuaded superstar Greenberg to switch to the outfield so that slugging Rudy York, a poor fielder, could take over the less crucial first-base post. With George Tebbets developing into a first-class catcher, the Tigers were ready to challenge the Yankees.

The Cleveland Indians, long silent since winning in 1920, were also ready. They now had baseball's fastest pitcher, Bob Feller, a first-rate infield, and a good batting attack. Directing them was

[38] "The Yankees," *Fortune, loc. cit.*

[39] Graham, *The New York Yankees,* 231–57; Allen, *American League Story,* 152–59; *New York Times,* June 17, 1938, for Vander Meer's second no-hitter; *Spalding-Reach Official Baseball Guide,* 1940, pp. 29–73, 129–45.

Oscar Vitt, formerly the manager of the Yankees' great Newark team.

Boston, with its young slugger, Ted Williams, was also a contender, and American League fans were treated to a closely fought four-cornered race. Suffering from weak pitching, the Yankees faltered until Weiss sent Ernie Bonham up late in the season. Meanwhile, the Tigers took the lead, pursued by Cleveland. At that stage, a serious morale problem hit Cleveland, and players circulated a petition calling for Vitt's ouster. This action was widely publicized and stamped the Indians as baseball's "crybabies." Yet they went down fighting. In a last crucial game with Detroit, Tiger rookie Floyd Giebell outpitched the great Feller and helped to secure the pennant with a 2–0 win. With ninety victories, the Tigers won by a single game over Cleveland. The Yankees finished two games back.

In contrast, Cincinnati's twelve-game victory over the rising Dodgers was decisive, and the team was well rested for the Series. Still, the contest went seven hard-fought games, ending when Paul Derringer scored a 2–1 victory over Newsome. The win brought the National League its first world championship in five years.[40]

The reign of the Yankees was far from over, however. Amidst gathering war clouds, McCarthy's men bounced back with a decisive win in 1941. That year, pitchers Bonham, Chandler, and Marius Russo provided youthful strength to complement the aging Gomez and Ruffing. As usual, DiMaggio provided the batting heroics by setting a record of fifty-six straight games in which he made at least one hit. Halted in Cleveland, he quickly went on another sixteen-game hitting streak. He finished with a .356 average, but this was far overshadowed by Ted Williams's .406 effort, an achievement unmatched since by any major-league regular. Williams's effort boosted the Red Sox to second place, but they were still seventeen games behind the Yankees.[41]

40 Graham, *The New York Yankees,* 257–60; Allen, *American League Story,* 159–63.

41 Allen, *American League Story,* 159–63; Graham, *The New York Yankees,* 260–65; Barrow, *op. cit.,* 174–85; *New York Times,* July 18, 1941; *Baseball Digest,* September, 1956, p. 40.

The race was much closer in the National League. Victory went to the Dodgers after a hard fight with the Cardinals, now managed by Billy Southworth and supported by a brilliant crop of Rickey farm hands, including superstar Stan Musial. The Dodgers were managed by Leo Durocher, a former Yankee and Cardinal infielder, whose team had been assembled by judicious trades, including some with Rickey. Headed by Kirby Higbe, Whitlow Wyatt, Curt Davis, and Fred Fitzsimmons, the pitching was strong, and the team was powered by outfielder Pete Rieser, who had come up from the Cardinal farms. In the infield was Dolph Camilli, a first baseman from the Phillies; third baseman Cookie Lavagetto, and second baseman Bill Herman, a former Cub. Nor was Harold Reese, the tiny shortstop destined for all-time greatness, a Dodger farm product.

Once again it was a subway Series, and the Yankees, taking advantage of breaks, won it four games to one. The decisive break came in the fourth game when Dodger catcher Mickey Owen dropped a third strike, enabling Henrich to take first base. Had Owen held the ball, the Series would have been tied. Instead, the Yankees exploded for four runs and a 7–4 victory which broke the hearts of the Dodgers. The next day, the Yankees settled the issue, and vocal Dodger fans who had supported the team a million strong sounded the hopeful cry of losers ever since: "Wait till next year."[42]

Two months later, the nation was unexpectedly plunged into total war. Full-scale mobilization took time, and the Yankees were still able to win wartime pennants in 1942 and 1943. The Cardinals, though playing without their wizard Rickey, also retained enough good youngsters to keep on winning. By 1944, however, the Yankees had lost most of their stars, and so, for the time being, another phase of Yankee domination ended. But it took a world war to break their grip. When that war was won, the Yankees returned to their triumphal ways.[43]

[42] Graham, *The New York Yankees*, 265–67; *New York Times*, October 7, 1941.
[43] *New York Times*, October 7, 1942.

8

Heroes and Hero-Worshipers

1. The Golden Age Style

Whenever abrupt changes seemed about to upset baseball's traditions, some critics stood ready to write the game's obituary. And so it was in the 1920's when the big bang style of play arrived. Instead of celebrating the new era, John Sheridan of *The Sporting News* described a ghastly deathbed scene. Unimpressed by rising salaries, ticket prices, and attendance, all of which he dismissed as symptoms of decline, Sheridan concentrated on other defects like the grotesque park architecture and the wretched caretaking inside each "brickyard." He predicted that the public would not continue to put up with cramped seats and primitive restrooms just to watch shabbily clad players perform on burnt yellow grass. This was larceny enough, he continued, but outside each park urchins took advantage of inadequate parking to cadge dimes and quarters from drivers with intimidating offers to "watch their cars."

Sheridan conceded that attendance was up 25 to 40 per cent over silver age standards and that the fans were enraptured with Ruth's slugging style, but he was sure that the mania would quickly pass away, exposing the insecure foundation of the new age. And when it did, baseball would have to do a costly about-face, damaging to its image.[1]

This reaction was typical of the attitudes of conservative critics. They were most contemptuous of tricks like moving in the fences in order to glean more homers. To listen to these Cassandras was to get the impression that baseball had no slugging past at all, a myth neatly dispelled by Al Reach, who recalled the booming 1860's. But history lessons were not to decide the matter; in the end profits did. Because fans willingly paid to see the new style, even diehards like McGraw converted to it. Indeed, his short right-field fence became the scandal of the league with its opportunity for "Chinese" home runs.

Since no rules barred the tactic, fence-moving went on everywhere, the main consideration being whether a club's power batters were right-or left-handed. Clubs like the White Sox who lacked hitters kept their fences back to favor their pitchers. Meanwhile, players were learning the cash value of a slugging reputation. Because long-ball hitters were the darlings of fans, smart players chose light bats, thick at the barrel and tapering sharply at the handle. Designed for slugging, these bats powered the lively ball, shooting it hard at infielders who in turn armed themselves with more efficient gloves that made for dazzling fielding plays. Most marvelous from the fan's viewpoint was the infield double play, now becoming a standard defensive tactic. By the late 1930's several celebrated double-play combinations had appeared, among them the talented Yankee pair of Crosetti and Gordon. The flashy double play added drama to the golden age game, and went far to balance defense with offense.[2]

The chief sufferers of the new age were pitchers. After years of

[1] *The Sporting News,* January 26, February 9, 1922.

[2] "Base Stealing's Sensational Decline," *Literary Digest,* April 29, 1922; "Baseball Shudders at the Home Run Menace," *ibid.,* January 5, 1924; *ibid.,* July 23, 1931; *Baseball Digest,* June, 1955, pp. 33–34.

superiority, their power waned when rules banned artificially aided pitches. The lively ball also made it easier for a batter to ruin a pitcher's performance. Naturally, pitchers complained, and statistics of 1924 showed that they had every right to do so. Shutouts were rarer; forty-and even thirty-game winners were nonexistent. Yet good pitchers adapted. Not that any ever fully adjusted to the crushed feeling that comes when one's Sunday pitch is hammered into the stands, but by learning legal trick deliveries like sliders, sinkers, knucklers, screwballs, and occasionally smuggling in an illegal spitter, good pitchers still managed to baffle batters.

Best of the golden age pitchers were such left-handers as Grove, Nehf, Pennock, Hubbell, and Gomez, and right-handers like Dean, Vance, Ruffing, Bridges, and the perennially able Walter Johnson. But after Grove and Dean exceeded thirty wins in the early 1930's, nobody managed the feat until 1968. Thus, twenty-game winners now became super heroes, and anyone winning more than nine laid claim to a successful season. Salary scales followed the new norms, and pitching staffs were enlarged to include relief specialists whose task was to rescue shell-shocked starters. Pitchers enjoyed, if not a happy lot, at least a tolerable one.[3]

It was fortunate that baseball adopted the "big bang" style when it did. Certainly the new power game made it possible to compete successfully in a fast-moving, action-oriented society and vitalized the game enough to keep the roving eyes of fans from turning too much to rivals like boxing, football, and basketball. Tournament golf and tennis were also becoming summer rivals, but happily for baseball neither of these came off very well on radio.[4]

Yet the threat of other sports was real enough for baseball publicists to take a close look at the shape of the game and the tastes of its fans. And what they saw convinced them that the game

[3] "The Passing of the Super Pitcher," *Literary Digest*, February 16, 1924; "Doctored Baseballs," *ibid.*, September 22, 1923; "The Passing of Trick Pitching," *ibid.*, October 6, 1928; Allen, *The Hot Stove League*, 158-68; *The Sporting News*, February 12, October 23, 1931, December 21, 1933.

[4] James A. Michener, "Is the American Boy Quitting Baseball?" *Literary Digest*, July 12, 1930; "Football or Baseball the National Game?" *ibid.*, December 6, 1924; "The Rise of Basketball," *ibid.*, December 19, 1936; U.S. House of Representatives, *Organized Baseball*, p. 963.

had outgrown its time-honored two dimensions. The new frontier was in radio, and in the 1920's advertisers eyed baseball as a means of promoting their products. By the 1930's, the rights to broadcast baseball's World Series were being sold, thus bringing in an extra $100,000 to the total receipts.[5]

Also in the 1930's, depression-wracked minor-league promoters discovered night baseball, that rejected and half-forgotten child of the 1880's. With brighter lights and dependable power sources, the night spectacle proved an efficient and exciting variation on the traditional baseball setting, and fans quickly supported it. Owners with courage enough to risk the gamble were often saved from bankruptcy. After watching their successes from the sidelines, major-league owners jumped in. In 1935, Cincinnati's general manager Larry MacPhail, won grudging approval to try a seven-game schedule of night contests. The experiment worked and the public's response was "What took you so long?" The answer, of course, was that major-league baseball was burdened with tradition which made such a move seem blasphemous to purists, including writers, fans, owners, and players. Players blamed night games for ruining eyes and disrupting body metabolism; fans blamed it for attracting thrill-seeking dilettantes to the parks; owners, like Wrigley and Ruppert, opposed on personal grounds; and general manager Barrow of the Yankees added it to his other phobia—steadfast hostility to cigarette-smoking female fans! But when night games began to draw as well as Sunday doubleheaders, the majority climbed aboard, leaving the purists isolated in stubborn opposition.[6]

There is a homely adage which says, "When it gets dark enough, you can see the stars." Certainly night baseball verified this maxim, for it brought an attendance upturn that helped to banish memories of Depression years. Since its inception in 1936, except for two wartime seasons, baseball promoters have never known seasons in which attendance has fallen below the four million mark in either league.[7]

[5] "A Million Dollar World Series," *The Digest,* October 9, 1939.
[6] *The Sporting News,* April 9, 1931.
[7] U.S. House of Representatives, *Organized Baseball,* pp. 1617–18.

2. The Fans

Long before night games came to baseball, each league viewed a total annual attendance of four million as an ultimate objective. This seemingly unsurpassable mark was shattered with dramatic suddenness in 1920, when American attendance topped five million. This auspicious omen signalled the opening of a new age of prosperity. By the mid-1920's, most owners accepted five million as a new mark of perfection. Up to 1942, this total was exceeded six times, four times by the Americans and twice by the Nationals. Four million now spelled ordinary success, and until the Depression drove down attendance both leagues regularly surpassed that figure.[8]

Of course, attendance was never divided equally; usually the American League bested the National, and some clubs within each league did better or worse than others. Although a super hero like Babe Ruth accounted for much of the disparity, the size of parks also played a part. Because the American League, by 1932, had two parks capable of seating more than 70,000, this gave the junior circuit a decided advantage. Only the Polo Grounds in the National League could house as many as 56,000, so the potential daily capacity in that league was about 300,000, some 96,000 less than the American's. Moreover, until the mid-1930's, the National park inventory included the ludicrous Baker Bowl with its seating capacity of 18,000.[9]

Along with diversity in seating capacities, there were other differences between parks. Some parks, like Wrigley Field or Yankee Stadium, were satisfying both physically and aesthetically. Although most owners recognized the popular wish for comfort, only a few cared enough to supply it. Of those who did, Cub owner William Wrigley and his son Philip enjoyed the support of loyal, if critical, fans. Even today, Wrigley Field, with its ivy-covered walls, sanitary rest rooms, and meticulously tailored grounds, remains a mecca for Chicago fans. Most satisfying to the owners was the

[8] *Ibid.*

[9] The two big American parks were Yankee Stadium and Municipal Stadium in Cleveland; *The Sporting News,* August 11, 1932, June 5, 1933.

team's perennially respectable attendance, which continued in spite of the owner's adamant refusal to install night lighting.[10]

Because good attendance accompanied comfortable parks, it seems strange that some owners chose to continue with outdated ones. After all, rising attendance sparked the great building boom between 1910 and 1920. No such boom followed the attendance revolution of the 1920's primarily because of worrisome factors like the rising cost of city real estate, rising construction costs, and a conservative fear that the boom was only temporary. When the Depression struck, and total war followed, most owners were even less able to refurbish old parks. Then when postwar real estate prices soared ever higher and owners were confronted with problems of auto parking, baseball construction was priced well beyond the reach of private capital. Perhaps as early as 1930 this was already true. Never again would an owner erect an edifice like Yankee Stadium with his own capital; the future called for municipally financed parks. Of these, Cleveland's Municipal Stadium was first. Available to the Indians in the 1930's, it was seldom used until after the war because the club wanted more favorable terms than it was offered.[11]

Just why so many fans should have thronged to these diverse sites in search of thrills is a question still unanswered. To be sure, many writers tried to explain why, but at best their efforts are impressionistic. Indeed, they cover many theories of human behavior, including psychological notions of man's need to identify with national celebrities to escape the boredom of urban-industrial life. Answers based on economic factors also abound and include the notion that thrill-seekers had more money to burn for leisure. Of course there were sociological explanations embracing one that held baseball to be a lower-class outlet and another that saw lonely Americans choosing baseball as a means of finding social interaction at the park. While all of these are plausible, even probable, no single one offers a complete explanation.

10 *Ibid.*, October 24, 1929; Veeck and Linn, *Veeck as in Wreck*, 28–36.

11 Gene Mack, "Hall of Fame Cartoons, Major League Ball Parks"; Hy Turkin and S. C. Thompson, *The Official Encyclopedia of Baseball*, 48–55; *The Sporting News*, January 28, 1932.

In deriding the idea that baseball fans were lower class, Edgar F. Wolfe, a Philadelphia sports columnist writing under the pseudonym Jim Nasium, insisted that far from being rabble, fans came from all social strata. In Wolfe's opinion, no more than 20 per cent were working class; the rest were "moneyed classes," including Americans from business, the professions, and public life.[12]

In one sense, Wolfe was right, for certainly American Presidents and political dignitaries found it politic to lend their presence to key games. President Taft began the custom of throwing out the first ball on opening day in Washington, and during the golden age all Presidents followed his lead. Some, like Harding, who once owned a club, were baseball zealots. However, his puritanical successor, Coolidge, was more restrained and visibly annoyed at Ruth's familiarities. Hoover, a sincere fan, was displeased when greeted by derisive chants of "We want beer" at Shibe Park in the Series of 1929, and crushed when roundly booed at Yankee Stadium in the Depression Series of 1932.[13] Hoover lived long enough to transcend his unpopularity, and because he continued to attend games he was later cheered as an honored President emeritus. Because succeeding Presidents have continued to preside over key games, baseball still enjoys the position of being the national game. With such prestige, even ministers who once were convinced of the game's sinfulness either kept silent or mouthed platitudes, as did Billy Sunday, who said, "Every time I see a grandstand of a Base Ball diamond, the blood surges through my veins like water pressure through a fire hose."[14]

If fans were no longer regarded as reprobates, they were often blamed for being mere thrill-seekers. Usually such criticism disregarded the fact that the "big bang" style was making the game an entertainment device. In 1923, Richter of *Spalding's Guide* expressed this point of view, complaining that fans were like the breed "that flock to the movies." Not that Richter was overly dis-

12 Edgar F. Wolfe, "The Benevolent Brotherhood of Baseball Bugs," *Literary Digest,* July 7, 1923.

13 Rickey, *op. cit.,* 40; Meany, *op. cit.,* 58; *The Sporting News,* August 9, 1923; "President Hoover's Trials at the World Series," *Literary Digest,* November 12, 1929; "Some Presidential Ball Fans," *ibid.,* May 19, 1920.

14 *Spalding's Official Base Ball Guide,* 1925, p. 7.

turbed; rather, with his usual insight, he wondered if baseball's profitable future called for promoting the game as an amusement.[15] Yet when Harry Frazee of Boston tried to do so at about that time, Boston fans were incensed at his blatant commercialism. Loud rejoicing greeted his 1923 resignation, but his uninspired successor brought little cheer. Not until the 1930's, when millionaire Tom Yawkey took the team and promoted it in the classic style of a gentleman-sportsman, did attendance pick up. Still, this single incident did not prove much, since the hustling style of men like MacPhail was equally successful in luring fans.[16]

Attracting fans by means of gimmicks was an old trick, well developed by Von der Ahe in the 1880's. In the later era, new touches were applied including musical acts, baseball vaudeville shows featuring the clowning of Al Schacht and Nick Altrock, lotteries, and fireworks. Strategies varied greatly, ranging from Cincinnati's famous free German lunch on opening day to Chicago's formula of aesthetic beauty. But always promoters leaned on hard-core fundamentals. For one, there was no substitute for a winning team; for another, fans like quick service at concession stands, an important item since these sales now rivaled ticket sales as a source of income; and, finally, promotion gimmicks served best to relax fans and put them in a spending mood. The biggest problem was to get them to the park in the first place.[17]

In the golden age, promoters did a good job of luring fans to the park, even in Depression days. A helpful device was the use of uniform numbers for easy identification of players. Introduced by the Yankees of 1929, the practice soon spread to all clubs and proved a sound psychological lure. But more fundamental was the hard legwork, routinely done by club representatives who spoke before all kinds of civic groups. Many clubs even used star players for this kind of work. And by the mid-1930's, both leagues were making well-constructed films freely available to civic groups. This tactic owed much to a hobby of Lew Fonseca, a former American League batting champion. While some owners were mourning the

[15] *The Sporting News,* January 4, 1923. [16] *Ibid.,* June 7, 1923.
[17] Veeck and Linn, *Veeck as in Wreck,* 14–42.

competition from movies, manager Fonseca was using action films to instruct his White Sox players. After his retirement in 1934, Fonseca organized his films into illustrated lectures which became so popular that the American League hired him as their film representative. By the 1940's, Fonseca was filming training camp life, All-Star games, and World Series matches. The films were freely available to any interested groups and did much to popularize American baseball.[18]

However, getting fans into the parks did not mean that owners would like what they got. Most of the spectators behaved in orderly, civil fashion. Yet every gathering had its abusive types, whose epithets were heard in spite of the increased distance between fans and players. Harried players frequently chased and fought their tormentors. One of the chief victims of abuse, Babe Ruth, eventually overcame his own bad reputation and lectured a high school assembly on the wisdom of refraining from cursing at ball parks.[19]

In 1932, both leagues made a determined effort to separate players and fans by adopting a rule forbidding all conversations with fans. But the rule proved so ridiculous and unenforceable that it was rescinded later in the year.[20]

Players came to expect heckling, booing, and obscenities as part of the game. Until owners hired enough police to cordon off the field after a game, players were regularly surrounded by jostling throngs, some bent on stealing hats, gloves, and clothing. Spectators also continued to insist on keeping balls hit into the stands. Apparently this was the price fans demanded for otherwise submitting to greater restrictions. At any rate, they kept on scrambling and scuffling for all loose balls, at times jumping on the field to snatch a rolling foul ball. By 1930 the battle ended with victory conceded to the fans, and owners shouldered a new cost, sometimes amounting to 150 baseballs in a doubleheader.[21]

[18] *The Sporting News,* January 31, 1929, January 4, August 23, 1934.

[19] *Ibid.,* July 17, 1924, May 28, 1925, January 7, 1928, May 30, 1929.

[20] *Ibid.,* June 2, 1932.

[21] Clifford Bloodgood, "After the Game is Over," *Baseball Magazine,* January, 1946, pp. 267–68; *The Sporting News,* May 17, November 29, 1928, July 16, 1931.

One note of comfort in the struggle to cope with increasing numbers of fans was the reduced number of ball-park riots. Although nobody understood why this was so, explanations were plentiful. They included theories of increasing public conformity and the idea that more lady fans acted as a restraining influence. Many games featured angry protests from fans and missiles were often hurled, but crowds seldom surged onto the field in a riotous mood. Effective policing kept most gatherings orderly, but Brooklyn fans gained a reputation for critical hubbub, especially from the mouths of individual critics like the voluble Hilda Chester.[22] In the opinion of most observers, the new breed of fans were celebrity watchers, dazzled by the home-run mania and willing to put up with ever longer games, more doubleheaders, and more night games, in hopes of satisfying their appetites.[23]

3. The New Heroes

Fans of the golden age were lavish with their money, especially in 1929, an early peak year in baseball history when receipts totalled $17 million. After that, the impact of Depression brought a steady decline to a low point of $10.8 million in 1933. Then came a slow upturn toward a new peak of $21.5 million in 1939. This was followed by wartime decline, after which receipts hit a new high, a stupendous $68.1 million in 1948.[24]

Certainly these figures indicate a voracious public appetite for baseball, a passion that was fed by a plenitude of superstars whose daily feats fired public imagination. In skills and personalities, the stars came in variety enough to gratify the most varied tastes of fans. The most memorable of the stars of the golden age are commemorated at the Hall of Fame at Cooperstown, New York. For a player to be enshrined in that pantheon, his life and performance had to withstand the severe scrutiny of sportswriter

22 Tom Meany and Bill McCullough, "Once a Dodger . . . " Quoted in B. A. Botkin (ed.), *Sidewalks of America,* 402–404.

23 A. Demaree, "Grandstand Girls—Women and Baseball Don't Mix," *Colliers,* June 2, 1928; *The Sporting News,* January 18, 1923, July 10, 1925, March 22, 1928; Mowry, *op. cit.,* 82–85.

24 U.S. House of Representatives, *Organized Baseball,* 960.

judges. Among many nominees, few were chosen. Nevertheless, nearly forty were selected from those who played in the golden age.

When this array of talent is appraised for patterns in public tastes, the overwhelming number of sluggers furnishes proof of the popularity of the big bang style. Far ahead of all such competitors of the golden age looms the towering figure of Ruth, the most magnetic player in history. As the outstanding slugger with a lifetime total of 714 home runs, Ruth also held the seasonal record of 60 and the runner-up mark of 59. After him, with a 534 total, came Jimmy Foxx, whose feat of hitting 30 or more homers for thirteen straight years was unmatched even by Ruth. Foxx's feat of once hitting 58 in a season was equalled by Hank Greenberg, the Detroit slugger. Right behind Foxx was Ruth's teammate, Gehrig, whose total of 493 homers was cut short by the ravages of disease. But his passing from the scene coincided with the rise of DiMaggio, whose 361 surpassed the 307 wrought by Al Simmons of the Athletics.

Superiority in homer production was established by the American League by the 1930s. Nevertheless, Mel Ott of the Giants, a powerful left-handed slugger, compiled a lifetime total of 511 homers for the National high. And Lewis "Hack" Wilson, a good hitter but a poor fielder, hit 56 homers in 1930 for the National's seasonal high of the era. Over-all Wilson's lifetime total was surpassed by the 300-plus efforts of Rogers Hornsby and Chuck Klein.

Although home runs were the *leitmotiv* of the golden age, fans relished all-round batting feats. Indeed, all of the great sluggers consistently hit for high averages, but it was Hornsby who best kept alive the Cobb tradition. Easily the best right-handed batter of his time, Hornsby strung together six consecutive batting titles and a lifetime average of .358 to rank second to the great Cobb.[25] Not that reminders were needed, for both Cobb and Speaker played through the first half of the golden age, and Cobb himself tutored teammate Harry Heilmann, who became a four-time American batting champ. In addition to these top-flight sluggers, there were

[25] *New York Times*, June 14, 1966; *Literary Digest*, January 13, 1923, May 15, 1926; *Baseball Digest*, January, 1951, July, 1959; Rogers Hornsby, "Why Good Pitchers are Easy to Hit," *Baseball Magazine*, April, 1919.

Joe DiMaggio, star outfielder of the New York Yankees from 1936 to 1951, shows his classic batting stance in this spring-training photograph. A powerful right-handed batter who hit safely in fifty-six consecutive games in 1941, DiMaggio succeeded Ruth as the object of hero-worshiping fans. (Courtesy New York Yankees, American League)

a host of solid batters destined for Hall of Fame memberships. Among American leaguers were Henie Manush, Goose Goslin, Sam Rice, Luke Appling, Joe Cronin, Bill Dickey, Mickey Cochrane, and Charley Gehringer. National leaguers included Bill Terry, Max Carey, Zack Wheat, Edd Roush, Joe Medwick, the Waners, Frank Frisch, Harold Traynor, and Charles "Gabby" Hartnett.

Superiority in everyday, unadorned solid hitting went to the National League, whose hitters in 1930 *averaged* .302, an amazing achievement. Observers credited this record to the new lively ball, but this was a high-water mark in batting. After 1932, hitting fell off steadily. Even though homers continued to dominate the game, pitchers slowly caught up with their tormentors.

That the golden age was not the best era for pitchers is evident from Hall of Fame admissions. In the twenty-year span, only eleven joined the immortals. The National League sent stars like Grover Alexander, the flamboyant Dizzy Dean, Eppa Rixey of the Reds, spitballing Burleigh Grimes, fireballing "Dazzy" Vance, and the left-handed master, Carl Hubbell. In the American League, where pitchers fared worse, honors went to Ted Lyons of the White Sox, Ruffing and Pennock of the Yankees, Grove of the Athletics, and Bob Feller, the Cleveland speed king.[26] In general, National League pitching was superior, as evidenced by the number of times pitchers won most-valuable-player awards. Grove won the American League award in 1931 with his great 31–4 record, but this was the only time a pitcher won. In the National, however, pitchers won the award four times—Hubbell scoring twice in 1933 and 1936, Dean in 1934, and Mort Cooper of the Cardinals in 1942.[27]

Babe Ruth was, of course, the favorite of the fans. For one reason, he personified the rampant individualism and hedonism that continued to gain in American lifeways. Ruth's flamboyant style inspired many imitators. Perhaps the most successful was

26 Robert Smith, *Baseball's Hall of Fame,* 112–22; *The Sporting News,* January 9, 1930; "Lively Controversy Over the Lively Ball," *Literary Digest,* October 5, 1929.

27 *National League Green Book,* 1964; *American League Red Book,* 1962; Jack Kofoed and Max Carey, "20 Greatest Players," *Esquire,* October, 1955.

Dizzy Dean, the pitching ace of the Cardinals, whose matchless skill combined with rural wit and wisdom to make him the legitimate heir to Ruth. In off-season antics and defiance of discipline, he aped Ruth. In later life, he continued to appeal to fans, but in the role of an overweight sportscaster who fractured the American language. And even on arriving at Cooperstown for his enshrinement, the old *élan* burst through and the middle-aged hero told his attractive female escort, "I'm sure glad they didn't send one of them-thar old-timers to fetch me."[28]

Among sluggers of the golden age, Ruth's closest imitators were men like Foxx, Greenberg, and Ott. But there were many lesser ones, men like Zeke Bonura and Babe Herman, who swung with Ruthian authority but whose inept fielding halted further comparison.

For many, Lou Gehrig of the Yankees came close to being the Galahad of the era. Incredibly durable and efficient and terribly determined to better himself, Gehrig personified the Protestant ethic in baseball. Such diligence was rewarded, and he was celebrated in three popular biographies. When his disease closed his career, his admirers participated in one of baseball's most poignant dramas. Some sixty thousand fans gathered at a 1939 game to honor Gehrig and heard his modest acceptance of their tribute as he told them, "Today I consider myself the luckiest man on the face of this earth. . . ."[29] Even today, his memory, and his uniform number "4," serve as reminders to aspiring sports-minded youths.

Gehrig headed a host of efficient heroes, including Grove, Everett Scott, Charlie Gehringer, Luke Appling, and Wes and Rick Ferrell.

[28] Interview, Lee Allen with D. Voigt.

[29] *Baseball Magazine,* June, 1939, p. 29; Paul Gallico, *Lou Gehrig: Pride of the Yankees;* Frank Graham, *Lou Gehrig, A Quiet Hero;* Richard Hubler, *Lou Gehrig: Iron Horse of Baseball.*

Once described as "the guy who hit all those homers the year Ruth broke the record," muscular Lou Gehrig was overshadowed for years by his superstar teammate. Nevertheless, Gehrig was a hero in his own right; a durable performer whose record of playing in 2,130 consecutive big league games stands as the major endurance feat in baseball history. (Courtesy New York Yankees, American League)

YORK

For sheer durability among pitchers, there was forty-seven-year-old Jack Quinn, who still threw his legal spitball in 1932 after twenty-six years in the majors. But most of these men lacked the drive which would have enabled them to share the Galahad legend with Gehrig. Yet they remained heroes in spite of quirks of temper or living habits. Indeed, the 1920's favored independence of spirit, especially if backed by brilliant play. Thus Edd Roush, a consistent hitter and superb fielder, habitually avoided spring training, claiming it was useless and that he could condition himself. In defying McGraw in 1930, he refused to play without more pay. As a result, he was returned to Cincinnati where he spent his last year as the idol of fans who long admired his "style."[30]

As fans learned to accept heroes as human beings with the weaknesses of ordinary mortals, the golden age produced an ever greater variety of hero types. For rural-minded fans,[31] there were the Deans; for sophisticated urbanites, there was Earnshaw of the Athletics; for sectionalists, there were players from every corner of the nation and its territories; for the sons of immigrants, there were Italian-American stars like DiMaggio, Polish-Americans like Stan Musial, Czech-Americans like Elmer Valo, Russian-Americans like Lou Novikoff, and a host of others. And for religious groups there were Jewish stars like Harry Danning and enough organized Christian athletes to gladden the hearts of Sunday school superintendents.[32]

Fans did not attend for the love of the game alone; indeed, some came to spew out pent-up resentment and hatred. For them, the slightest letdown of a hero was enough to evoke jeers, and they loved to taunt star players on enemy teams. For most fans, some villains were needed, and in this age Carl Mays was the supreme example for his beaning of Chapman. But others also gained the reputation of the beanballers. Pitcher Hadley of the Yankees was reviled for striking down Cochrane, and Walter Mails carried the

[30] *New York Times,* January 27, 28, 1967.

[31] "Country Boys in the Big Leagues," *Literary Digest,* April 18, 1925.

[32] *New York Times,* March 6, 7, September 2, 1965, June 9, July 16, 1967; *The Sporting News,* October 16, 1930 (Earnshaw), June 7, 1934 (DiMaggio), December 11, 1930 (Lazzeri), February 18, 1967.

hated nickname of "Duster" for his close pitching. Even more despised as villains were those who were regarded as crooks, including, of course, the Black Sox and such successors as Douglas of the Giants.

Then there was a type of villain-fool, usually some notorious "goat" whose misplay at a critical moment cost the club an important victory. Mickey Owen of the Dodgers, for example, saw years of creditable service forgotten because he dropped a third strike in a 1941 Series game, thus opening the gates for a winning Yankee rally.[33] Finally, for those fans who found comfort in hating symbols of social evils, there was Jake Powell of the Yankees, a southerner who once admitted anti-Negro prejudice on a New York radio show.

As might be expected, baseball has always provided a goodly measure of fools. One needs only to mention the Dodgers of this era to conjure up a legend of ineptitude. Out of the frustration of repeated defeat, the Dodgers often chose buffoonery as a compensation, as, for example, manager Casey Stengel, who once ribbed an umpire in full view of Brooklyn fans by doffing his cap and permitting a bird to escape! When combined with repeated failures on the field, these antics led fans to dub the team, "The Bums." Legend has it that in the mind of one fan, called "The Spirit of Brooklyn" by writers, Dodger performance reached such a low point in the 1930's that one day he shouted, "Youse bums, youse," and never returned again.[34]

An outstanding example of a superfool of the era was Art Shires, a brawling, loudmouthed Texan who came to the White Sox in 1928. When Shires joined the team, he immediately typed himself as a character by saying, "So this is the great American League . . . I'll hit .400." For a while he did hit well, but his self-styled name of "Arthur the Great" drew jeers, as did his spending on clothing and cars and his off-season boxing career. As a scrapper, he did succeed in blacking the eye of his manager, but when his

33 *Baseball Digest*, June 12, 1957, pp. 9–11; "Batter Up, Batter Down—Beanball," *Literary Digest*, June 12, 1937; *The Sporting News*, October 18, 1923; *Reading Eagle*, July 17, 1966, has feature article on Owen.

34 Meany and McCullough, *loc. cit.*

professional boxing career led to charges of fixed fights, Commissioner Landis ordered him to quit the ring or be banned from the diamond. Shires complied, but soon after, while on his honeymoon, he was involved in a fracas with Hollywood police which kept him out of the majors in 1931. Drafted by the luckless Braves in 1932, Shires accepted by telegram, signing it, "Your latest sensation." But by then his batting eye was gone, and after a .238 season this boisterous character dropped out of sight.[35]

The passing of baseball's fools corresponded with the onset of the Depression which also sobered the flappers and faddists of the 1920's. In the 1930's, holding one's job was a serious business, and players, fearful of pink slips, extended themselves mightily. Nevertheless, a few characters enlivened the grim times, but mostly there was a pervasive mood of tough-minded professionalism. A writer in 1931 wondered if the trend might be due to the "craze for college players" and noted that scouts seemed eager to sign polished collegians rather than sandlotters. This interesting observation anticipated today's practices in recruitment. But at the time it was only Mack, Rickey, and Weiss who sought college men while others watched and waited. If the practice made for better-behaved, more professional players, it also made for dullness, prompting at least one noted general manager to cry, "Where are the drunks of yesteryear?[36]

Another new trend was a geographical shift in recruiting. Ever since 1900, most players came from the Northeast, and during the golden age this continued to be a favorite hunting ground. However, in the 1920's, hungry Southern boys, especially Texans, came to outnumber those from the Midwest as the secondary source of supply. And by the 1930's, California became a new mother lode of ballplaying talent.[37]

Meanwhile, this age gave birth to the myth that immigrant sons were displacing "native" Americans in baseball. Many children of immigrants did enter baseball, including those of Italian and Polish

[35] David Q. Voigt, "Arthur 'the Great' Shires."

[36] *The Sporting News,* July 23, 1931; Veeck and Linn, *The Hustler's Handbook,* 152–73.

[37] Allen, "Statistical data on baseball players."

parents. But these never amounted to more than a fraction of any year's crop of rookies. What made it appear so was the great noticeability of their surnames. To careless observers, a few foreign-sounding names in a lineup seemed like an invasion. One writer even predicted an Italian takeover since they "take to baseball quicker than they take to spaghetti. These Tonies walk right into baseball. . . ."[38]

However, no evidence supports any ethnic takeover past or present. Nor does evidence support the idea of superior baseball aptitude in any group's genetic makeup. On the contrary, American baseball provided an open avenue leading to middle-class status for any youngsters eager enough to work and learn the skills. As other avenues to middle-class life were opened to hyphenated-Americans, baseball lost some of its appeal and thus the baseball avenue was opened for still more deprived groups. After World War II, the way was finally opened for caste-bound groups like Negroes and Puerto Ricans, traditionally barred by baseball's Jim Crow practices. But the greatest number of major-league ball players was, and continues to be, white and native born.[39]

In other ways, players reflected dominant American characteristics. Indeed, ball players carry the ten most common surnames in America, with a generous dash of Irish names like Sullivan, Moore, and Murphy. Amongst such company, those with Italian, German, or Polish surnames stood out as easy targets of jokes and jibes, so typical of the "immigrant humor" of this era. To escape ridicule, some adopted Anglicized surnames; Syzmanski of the A's became Simmons, Casimir Kwietniewski of the White Sox became Cass Michaels, Schultenreich of the Cubs became Schulte, Pizzola of the Yanks became Bodie, and Petrosky of the Senators became Clark. Others went partway, changing unwieldy first names as in the case of Fiero Rizzuto, a longshoreman's son, who became first a Yankee shortstop, then a Republican party committeeman, and finally a sportscaster, all under the name of "Phil" Rizzuto.

Of course, players were eternally subjected to a wide range of

[38] "How Tony Gives a Latin Tone to Our National Game," *Literary Digest*, July 2, 1932.

[39] Allen, "Statistical data on baseball players."

nicknames by teammates. Some stressed nationality as Ruth did in labeling Lazzeri "dago" and "wop"; others emphasized stature as in the case of "Rabbit" Maranville, temperament as for "Sad Sam" Jones, physical attributes as for "Moose" McCormick or "Lefty" Gomez, and whimsical as in the case of Ruth, who was called "Gidge," a corruption of George. Unprintable epithets and obscenities were always used in bench jockeying, and in addition phony, romanticized nicknames were coined by sportswriters.[40]

Gradually, the tendency for players to seek middle-class respectability cramped the style of profane old-timers.[41] Under pressure from Landis, foul language was curbed so that needlers became circumspect about using "magic words." Not that they ever stopped swearing, but at least they found it expensive to do so publicly. These restraints put bench-jockeys on their mettle, but now they learned more subtle ways to infuriate rivals. These worked as well as obscenities for experts like Leo Durocher who had few equals in the art of imaginative name-calling.

By the late 1930's, the diminishing number of baseball brawls signalled the end of the old hard-nosed style.[42] Still, every season had its trouble cases, including free-for-alls and beanball vendettas, but these were becoming rarer.[43] Rules and fines helped keep the peace, but the significant change was in the players themselves. By the end of the era, successful leaders like McCarthy and Rickey openly demanded well-dressed, well-behaved, cool-tempered players. In the Yankee organization, evaluations of such requirements were part of scouting reports, and new men were judged on their ability to fit the Yankee image of professionalism. Under Weiss, the farms speedily weeded out nonconformists, and as McCarthy tightened his control, hotheads like Ben Chapman, Johnny Allen, and Jake Powell were released. McCarthy's prej-

40 Allen, *The Hot Stove League,* 1–23.

41 "Joshing is Business in Baseball," *Literary Digest,* April 28, 1923; "What Ballplayers Read," *ibid.,* May 31, 1930; "Rosy Twilight of the Vanished Ball-player," *ibid.,* April 21, 1928.

42 Baseball brawls are reviewed in *Baseball Digest,* September, 1950, pp. 59–62.

43 Allen, *The Hot Stove League,* 135–37; *The Sporting News,* January, 1930, July 23, 1931; "Batter Up, Batter Down—Beanball," *loc. cit.; New York Times,* October 10, 1967.

udice against Southern players, because of their alleged lack of sophistication was well understood.[44]

As father of the farm system, Rickey furthered the trend toward co-operative personalities. Aside from a preference for collegiate types, he demanded above all that a player be teachable. In a real sense, he was baseball's schoolmaster, who demanded that players be graded not only on skills but on attitude and character as well.[45] Above all, he sought specialists, and he tended to stockpiie relief pitchers, pinch hitters, and defense specialists to fit his strategy of "playing the percentages." A winning technique, it also shaped players in the assembly-line mold that was dominating American work life.[46]

Perhaps the ultimate concession to middle-class ways came as players tried to combine marriage with their playing careers. Although the trend was slowed by Depression and war, America was fast becoming the most married society on earth, and one where people married young. As early as 1929, one observer complained about wifely cliques whose incessant gossip and domestic demands sapped player energies and divided their loyalties. By now, single men posed a problem, and the same observer damned the "baseball Daisys," as diamond camp followers were called, for impeding pennant races.[47]

Apparently women were now replacing drink as the chief means of comforting frustrated players. Indeed, national prohibition in the 1920's supposedly put an end to drinking, but like confirmed American drinkers in general, tippling players managed to keep supplied until the faucets turned on again in 1933. By then, players needed all the comfort they could get, for the Depression magnified the usual fears of injury, failure, dismissal, and aging.[48] In the 1930's, all four conditions could result in joblessness, and because it was difficult to find work outside, the prevailing attitude

[44] Graham, *The New York Yankees*, 177–78, 187–93, 255–56; For the Cubs' attempt to halt hazing of rookies, see *The Sporting News*, March 29, 1934.

[45] *New York Times*, November 17, 1965.

[46] *Baseball Digest*, February, 1959, p. 71; *New York Times*, March 3, 1968.

[47] *The Sporting News*, January 3, 1929.

[48] "When the Clock Strikes Forty," *Literary Digest*, March 10, 1934.

John D. Rigney pitched for the Chicago White Sox from 1937 to 1947. He won sixty-four games and lost the same number, but married a granddaughter of Charles A. Comiskey, founder and owner of the club. (Courtesy Chicago White Sox, American League)

was one of sober seriousness. To overcome the threat of discharge because of age, players continued to lop off at least two years from their true age.[49] Because old-timers hung on, opportunities for newcomers dwindled for a time. Even those who stayed on were often unsure of regular pay, especially members of the Boston Braves. Players everywhere took Depression salary cuts.

New Deal welfare measures stimulated union activity in the industrial world, but in baseball it was still every man for himself. The only hint of unionization came with the formation of the "Association of Professional Baseball Players of America," a welfare organization aimed at helping indigent ex-players and umpires. Under its bylaws, major and minor players could join, and dues were scaled according to salary. By 1933, 150 men drew financial assistance and 45 got monthly allotments. For years the organization had a precarious existence and was supported mainly by the proceeds from the annual All-Star game, a contest instituted in 1933 and thereafter played annually in July between teams of National and American stars. The game attracted big crowds, and most of the revenue went to the Association. At first, receipts averaged $50,000 a year, but later shares from radio and television,

[49] Interview, D. Voigt and Lee Allen. Allen has two cases of players cutting seven years off their true ages.

along with a portion of the World Series revenue, added to the fund. From this financial base came the modern retirement and pension funds which today guarantee a lifetime income to any player with as much as five years of major-league service. Beyond this, the Association served as a launching pad for present-day collective bargaining.[50]

Meanwhile, some alleviation of the old fears of injury and illness came as clubs hired more skilled trainers and offered expert medical care. In time, these services were expanded to include even free psychiatric help.[51] Better equipment, including such items as the plastic helmets developed by Rickey in Pittsburgh after the War, also helped to provide better playing conditions.

But the most welcome benefit of the golden age was the steady rise in pay, always the best palliative for the rigors of the playing life. With Babe Ruth setting the pace, old salary records fell resoundingly. In 1925, Ruth made $52,000 plus $15,000 extra in endorsements; in 1929 he drew $70,000, and in 1930 he set the golden age record with $80,000.[52] Such achievements, always dramatized by newsmen, added to his magnetism. But because Ruth got his way, the star became baseball's example of the so-called "Shorenstein effect" in politics. This consists of naming a popular candidate on a ticket with a bunch of lightweights. At election time, the effect is likened to that of a docking garbage scow, dragging in its wake floating garbage and debris. In baseball, Ruth was the leader who pulled the salaries of lesser men upward. In 1923, the average salary was about $5,000; in 1924 it was close to $6,000; and in 1929–30 it came close to $7,000. Depression economies dropped averages to $5,000 in 1933 and then down to $4,500 in 1936.[53] Then came an upward trend, so that the end of the era saw average salaries approaching those of 1924.

[50] *The Sporting News,* February 23, 1933; "Future Interleague Baseball Games," *Literary Digest,* July 22, 1930.

[51] *The Sporting News,* February 12, 1925.

[52] "What Babe Ruth Does With His Money," *Literary Digest,* October 5, 1929; "What is Babe Ruth worth to the Yankees," *ibid.*, March 29, 1930.

[53] *The Sporting News,* March 21, 1929; U.S. House of Representatives, *Organized Baseball,* pp. 1392, 1610; "Big League Baseball," *Fortune,* August, 1937, pp. 37–45, 112–16; "Play Ball," *Literary Digest,* April 17, 1937.

As the spearhead in the movement toward higher salaries in the golden age, Ruth made it possible for other stars to get more pay. Not all clubs could afford the practice, since the trend was tied to attendance and favored rich clubs like the Yankees, Cubs, Dodgers, and Giants. But to be a teammate of Ruth's was a lucky break, as Ruppert admitted in 1924 when he announced that his regulars had averaged $12,000 in salaries since 1920.[54] Even in the Depression year of 1937, the Yankee payroll came close to $275,000, with Gehrig's salary of $36,000 said to be the highest in baseball.

Although salary information remained a jealously guarded secret, it was generally true that salaries amounted to one half of a club's gross operating expenses. In 1937, gross operating expenses of rich clubs like the Yankees and Cubs exceeded $600,000, while poorer clubs spent considerably less. Among the latter, such teams as the Browns were unable to attract a hundred thousand fans during one Depression season. Such disparity in 1925 made for a Yankee payroll of $370,000 at the lush end of a scale and placed the Pirates and Dodgers each with $200,000 in the middle. Poorer clubs like the Browns dragged along somewhere above $100,000.[55]

Outside the Yankee kingdom, stars also won higher wages during the golden age. In 1921, Edd Roush of the Reds drew $15,000 for his outfielding. In 1923, Ty Cobb made $30,000 as Detroit's playing manager, and in his last two seasons with the Athletics he made $40,000 a year. Meanwhile, Hornsby became the highest paid National leaguer with $42,000 as a playing manager. Altogether, the great Rajah was paid $565,000 in salary for twenty-three years' service in the National League. Great pitchers like Grove, Hubbell, Dean, and Vance commanded salaries of better than $25,000. If Gehrig's $36,000 was the best in baseball in 1936, the end of the decade saw DiMaggio touch the $50,000 mark.[56]

[54] *The Sporting News,* March 6, 1924.

[55] *Ibid.,* June 9, 1930. With the Phillies, Lefty O'Doul's $8,000 was the most ever paid a player by President Baker. O'Doul wanted $17,000 for winning the 1929 batting championship; U.S. House of Representatives, *Organized Baseball,* p. 1529.

Although owners were often reluctant to pay higher salaries, players now learned to apply pressure by threatening to withhold services. These cat-and-mouse tactics were publicized in news stories on "holdouts" that often mobilized the opinion of fans against owners, but sometimes worked in reverse.[57]

Over-all, the striking fact was that players had achieved a salary revolution of sweeping proportions without the aid of unions. Indeed, players of the golden age were stubbornly individualistic, and in negotiations each man defended his own interests. That so many succeeded with only their past record as an asset was undoubtedly because of the great public support for the spectacle. Bolstered by public adulation, many players bargained skillfully, knowing that owners must concede in time. With the stars leading the way to higher salaries, *Sporting News* could say in 1925 that ballplaying was as lucrative as any profession, and that even the ordinary player did better financially than his industrial counterpart.[58] Moreover, players managed to maintain this edge even during the Depression.

It was also possible for players to acquire additional rewards. Potential sources included World Series checks of as much as $6,000 for a winner's share. Extra money also flowed from endorsements, literary efforts (usually ghosted), and from personal appearances in theaters or on radio. These new outlets mingled with traditional sources of extra money, such as bonuses for signing, for outstanding performances, and for appearances at winter banquets.[59]

Even average salaries spelled big money to Americans of the "aspirin age," so that a baseball career at this time was highly desirable. In time, postwar prosperity opened up higher salary opportunities in other career fields for middle-class youths, but for minority groups a baseball career still offered talented aspirants an opportunity for success and status.

[56] *The Sporting News,* February 28, 1924, February 25, 1925, January 19, October 18, 1928, August 22, 1929, December 25, 1941 (for Hornsby's revelation).

[57] *Ibid.,* August 23, 1934.

[58] *Ibid.,* March 12, 1925.

[59] *Ibid.,* December 25, 1930. In 1930. In 1930 Grove chose a straight salary of $20,000 instead of a bonus offer of $1,000 per winning game. Had he chosen the latter, he would have earned $26,000.

4. Baseball's Once and Future Villains

In the golden age, almost everyone accepted the presence of baseball umpires. This is not to say they were beloved, but only that they were regarded as necessary. Even though fans saw players as being of varied character types, they still classed umpires as villains, the difference being that some were bigger villains than others. And yet the same processes that were easing player careers also helped umpires.

Umpiring was gradually becoming a respectable professional career. There were still echoes of old mob scenes, and sometimes umpires were bombarded by bottles, but under the double umpire system, soon to become a three-man system,[60] umpires worked as a team. Each man had his special area to cover, and a smooth-working unit operated like a combat team, using signals to alert one another to a possible missed call. To Americans in an age of expertise, umpires were acknowledged to be expert enough. With this recognition, mobbings virtually disappeared, leaving only curses and boos, once considered too trivial to mention, as major hazards.

Although fans tended to lump all umpires together, some distinctive personalities came in for special attention. One was the martinet Klem, an institution now, but unbeloved. Booed for his self-righteousness, he was often petulant; in Paul Gallico's words, Klem was "like a naughty, obstinate child who knows he is wrong but is going to be nasty about it." When Klem was present, fans and players feared to provoke him, and even Landis feared to bruise his ego.[61] But at the end of the age, this painfully honest puritan was enshrined in the Hall of Fame along with other standouts like Tom Connolly, Bill Evans, and Hank O'Day, whose careers extended over from the silver age. They joined eight others from baseball's frontier days in a special umpiring niche reserved in the Hall of Fame.[62]

With the passing of the old guard, new personalities emerged,

[60] *The Sporting News,* April 24, 1930.
[61] *Ibid.,* December 6, 1928, October 13, 1932.
[62] Allen, *The Hot Stove League*, 148–50.

including ex-players like Babe Pinelli, Bill Stewart, Jocko Conlan, George Pipgras, and Ed Rommell, and former football stars Charley Mann and Cal Hubbard. Because the profession was becoming respectable and safe, hundreds of applicants vied for each opening, so both leagues appointed senior umpires to act as recruiting scouts. Usually, these scouts scoured the minor leagues for material. If acceptable prospects were found, their contracts were purchased. To meet the demands of anxious candidates, umpiring schools were established. Graduates moved into the minor leagues and up the ladder from there.[63]

Like most professionals, umpires were most impressed by monetary rewards. By 1937 the salary scale of big-league umpires ranged from $4,000 to $10,000, with good prospects of an extra $2,500 every five years as payment for Series duty. Moreover, working conditions were improving. With Klem carrying the fight, umpires enjoyed private dressing rooms and bigger expense accounts. In the 1930's, virtuosos determined to be the very best were offered an umpire-of-the-year award, which automatically meant extra pay and endorsement income. In 1934–35, Albert "Dolly" Stark, a onetime urchin from New York's East Side, won the award. He took it seriously, too, staging a year-long sit-down strike in 1936 for higher pay, which came to him in 1937.[64]

In spite of their material gains, umpires continued to suffer as professional villains. As always, the job was nerve-wracking, especially for plate umpires. At that post, a man had to make at least 250 calls, some of which were highly debatable and liable to evoke insults. Umpire Bill McGowan went so far to say that defining balls and strikes was largely guesswork, something Klem would never have admitted. If so, other decisions were equally problematical, like determining when a pitch was an intentional beanball, what constituted interference, or how to define a balk. When obliged to make such rulings, most umpires shuddered, for any decision made enemies.[65]

[63] Kahn, *op. cit.*, 156–60; *Baseball Digest,* March, 1951, pp. 17–20.

[64] "Kill Him," *Literary Digest,* May 22, 1937.

[65] *Baseball Digest,* May, 1947, pp. 3–5, 45–49, May, 1955, pp. 43–51; Kahn, *op. cit.*, 143.

As ever, umpires lived monklike lives on the road. Sometimes they were comforted by the presence of a wife, but more often they were confined like celibates in the loneliness of hotel rooms. When games were under way, umpires were almost always booed. If they were cheered, it was usually because they were writhing in pain after being hit by a foul tip. Add the inevitable curses and obscenities, the crude jockeying from benches, and the frequent practical jokes visited upon them, and no one could deny that they earned their money.

Under such pressures, good men continued to break, including Stark, who quit in a huff in 1931, tired of serving as everyman's scapegoat, and who complained: "I'm fed up on being ragged by the fans and abused by four-flushing ballplayers who try to use umpires as alibis." Yet after a month of idleness, he appealed for reinstatement, and President Heydler, himself a former umpire, took him back.[66] From this and other incidents it is clear that being a baseball umpire still took a special kind of courage. Perhaps this is why so many were former athletes—strong men well able to acquit themselves in confrontations.

Happily for golden age umpires, brawn was becoming less imperative. No longer did each man function as a lonely tower of strength, as did O'Day in the famous Merkle case. For the rest of his career, which ended in the 1920's, fans hounded him for that call. But O'Day was tempered in the frontier days and neither fans nor players frightened him. In his last year, however, when he was rushed to the hospital critically ill with appendicitis, he knew fear. En route to the operating room, he told a doctor, "I'm not afraid of you," but to a priest he said, "I guess I am afraid of you."[67]

The golden age saw the passing of such war-horses. Newcomers expected and received a life of greater comfort and security. And along with players, umpires were attaining such goals. It is true

[66] *The Sporting News,* October 8, 1931; *Baseball Digest,* July, 1947, pp. 8–10, May, 1955, pp. 35–39; Arthur Daley, "Jocko Called 'Em," *New York Times,* September 12, 1967; Herbert Simons, "Life of an Ump," *Baseball Magazine,* April, 1942, pp. 156–62.

[67] *The Sporting News,* January 1, 1931.

that they continued as lonely untouchables. Yet on the whole, umpiring in the 1930's offered an easier life and a safer career. Even grizzled Bill Stewart, one of the toughest, probably realized this although he said in 1955, "Nuthin's new in baseball."[68]

[68] *Baseball Digest,* June, 1955, pp. 39–45.

9

New Frontiers in Baseball Promotion

1. Baseball's "Third Dimension"

Fortunately for baseball operators, the new "big bang" style of play came at the very moment when radio was revolutionizing American leisure habits. By 1925 the new medium offered hours of free entertainment, which was eagerly devoured by millions. Businessmen saw the profit potential in this mass audience and paid to sponsor shows in return for the right to hawk their wares during breaks in the programs. For the greatest return on their advertising dollar, sponsors naturally wanted to buy programs that would command the biggest audiences. In their search for likely offerings, especially during the summertime, advertisers soon realized that baseball posed a good possibility. Major-league owners were at first unwilling to face the risks in this arrangement. Yet time would show that this union was to bring a third dimension to the American game.

New Frontiers in Baseball Promotion

Ever since the establishment of the first major league, baseball had presented itself to the public in two dimensions. Of these, the most important in the minds of owners was always the game itself, as played in the parks before paying fans. Less important, but regarded as quite valuable, was the extensive coverage freely given by newspapers. This coverage helped to sell papers, which pleased publishers, and since it provided free advertising and whetted appetites for baseball, owners were pleased. Thus, for half a century up to 1920, baseball and newspapers presented a traditional pattern of promotion that was upset by radio's sudden appearance.

By the mid-1920's, there was no ignoring radio's immense presence. From experimental origins early in the century to its strategic value in World War I, the commercial possibilities of the medium were obvious. The boom came after the war, when armies of purchasers lined up to buy receivers. By 1925 most families owned sets. By 1929 the infant industry had grown to a billion-dollar enterprise. Radio thus took its place alongside the movies and automobiles as one of the three great innovations that revolutionized American leisure in the 1920's.[1]

Because these giant new enterprises towered above baseball in wealth and popularity, owners regarded them all with hostility. Such a reaction was human enough, since as the ancient Greek playwright has reminded us, "Nothing that is vast enters the life of mortals without a curse." Owners cursed radio because they saw the medium as a threat to live attendance. Few attempted to understand radio, and most likened it to the telegraph tickers that had been used at ball parks since the 1880's to transmit accounts of games to saloons and other rallying points. In the past, most owners had looked at the telegraph ticker as an evil that hurt gate receipts. Nevertheless, most tolerated the practice because of its advertising value and because it was too clumsy and dull a medium to hinder live attendance.[2]

But this was a bad comparison, because glib announcers made baseball games on radio sound lively, interesting, and suspenseful.

[1] Mowry, *op. cit.*, 43, 59–65.

[2] *The Sporting News,* May 31, 1928.

Here we see the key to radio's appeal, for it is a "hot" medium, highly capable of firing the imagination of listeners.[3] Stirred by the words of eloquent announcers, the radio audience entered an imaginary world where players performed heroically, accomplishing deeds that never happened. To sustain and magnify this mental drama was the job of a new expert, the "sportscaster." Among the first to emerge was Graham McNamee, who gained fame as a World Series sportscaster early in the 1920's. With a rich voice and fertile imagination, he shaped the game for millions of listeners, in spite of his lack of knowledge of the game. In the opinion of Ring Lardner, who listened in disgust from his pressbox perch, McNamee's dramatization was completely out of touch with reality. Of course, the same might be said of newspaper accounts or of any eyewitness account. Nevertheless, the radio broadcasts captivated audiences, who made gods out of the sportscasters.

Ever since McNamee broke the ground, every sportscaster has been faulted by newsmen for lack of expert knowledge, for bad puns as in the case of Mel Allen, or for bad grammar as in the case of Dizzy Dean. When he began his new career as a baseball announcer, Dean's butchery of the language prompted the Missouri Teachers' Association to demand his ouster. Among many affronts to pure diction, Dean was accused of using the nonverb "slud" in place of "slid." Dean replied, "What do they expect me to say, 'slidded?' " The teachers' attack boomeranged, triggering instead a wave of anti-intellectual hostility toward a profession sadly lacking in power and influence. Meanwhile, other ballplayers turned sportscasters, and men like Dean, Waite Hoyt, Harry Heilmann, and Walter Johnson provided the missing expertise. Their success enabled them to cash bigger checks than they did as players.[4]

For a while it seemed as if sportscasters would have to describe other sports, since many owners opposed the free broadcast of Series games. Fearful that baseball would become a free show, the most outspoken opponents demanded that radio pay for the

[3] Marshall McLuhan, *Understanding Media: The Extensions of Man,* v–x, 122–32.

[4] *The Sporting News,* August 7, October 23, 1946; Sam J. Slate and Joe Cook, *It Sounds Impossible,* 49–58; Mel Allen and Ed Fitzgerald, *You Can't Beat the Hours,* 1–12; Jerome H. (Dizzy) Dean, *Dizzy Baseball, passim.*

privilege of broadcasting the games. Others, echoing disgruntled newsmen, blamed radio for hurting sales of "sports extras," and demanded a curb on broadcasts lest the game lose its important second dimension.[5]

The popularity of radio continued to grow, and its consumer market expanded to include 250,000 auto radios by 1932. By then radio's overwhelming appeal crushed its opposition. Certainly owners welcomed the offer of networks to pay for the privilege of broadcasting games. Late in 1933, owners let bids for the exclusive rights to broadcast Series games. Landis represented baseball at the annual bargaining sessions, and in 1936 he signed a $100,000 contract for exclusive broadcasting rights. Nor did he usually have to bargain hard. In 1941, the Gillette Safety Razor Company gladly paid a large sum for the privilege of peddling blades to presumed hordes of bewhiskered sports fans.[6]

During the same period, individual owners were free to negotiate cash deals for their home game broadcasts. In 1933, the Boston club of the National League made a modest $5,000 from radio, and within six years all clubs were profiting. In 1939, the lowest sum any club received was the $33,000 paid to the Cardinals, while the Giants led all with $110,000. Altogether, some $410,000 in radio money flowed to National League treasuries that year. American League radio income climbed from $11,000 in 1933 to $420,000 in 1939, with the Yankees banking a quarter of the 1939 total.[7] This flow of revenue came from diverse masculine products like gasoline, cigarettes, and beer, while breakfast food manufacturers and the Whelan Drug Store made a pitch for the family dollar.[8]

Income from radio was, of course, most welcome during the Depression. Nor did radio show signs of hurting live attendance or newspaper sales. Indeed, newspaper sales actually gained as listeners bought more papers in order to follow game statistics. The broadcasts did not hurt live attendance, although a flood of

5 *The Sporting News,* June 7, 1923, October 10, 1929.

6 "The Radio in the Auto," *Literary Digest,* July 9, 1932; *ibid.,* October 13, 1932, September 28, 1933, June 18, 1934.

7 U.S. House of Representatives, *Organized Baseball,* pp. 1602–1603, 1606–1607.

8 *The Sporting News,* May 27, 1943.

post–World War II regional broadcasts of major-league games struck another blow at the already crippled minor leagues. But by then the task of subsidizing the minors was viewed as a necessary major-league commitment.[9]

In sum, baseball's hesitant union with radio proved to be a useful adjustment to the new wonderworld of electronic leisure. As for night baseball, the acceptance of the new radio dimension was most difficult for conservative owners. Yet hardly had they readjusted their thinking about radio than they found themselves confronted by a fourth dimension—television. The medium was technically feasible in the 1920's, and its commercial future was clear to many who saw it for the first time at the New York World's Fair of 1939–40.[10] Had the war not halted its commercial development, conservative owners might have been confronted with another problem earlier. And yet television seemed less novel than radio. After all, the medium resembled movies, another bogeyman from the recent past which had proved to be more helpful than harmful.

2. Baseball's Stolid Second Dimension

In the golden age, nothing in the familiar second dimension of newspaper baseball reportage rivaled the drama of radio. Indeed, newspaper reporting of baseball, with a few exceptions, could easily be written off as a baroque continuation of the styles of the silver age. Newspaper publishers were largely responsible for this conservative state of affairs. Ever since World War I, there had been a decrease in the number of big city papers, with morning dailies heading the decline. In the years between 1910 and 1930, the number of morning dailies dropped from 500 to 388, and by 1933 most cities of over one hundred thousand people had only a single morning paper. One effect of this conservative trend was to stifle journalistic enterprise. As the chief powers in American journalism, the heads of giant chains like Hearst and Scripps-Howard tried to create the illusion of a journalistic revolution by devices like the tabloid form with many headlines and photos. Yet there was little that was new in the writing. Indeed, since advertising

[9] *Ibid.*, October 9, 1941; *Baseball Digest*, February, 1951, pp. 81–82.

[10] *The Sporting News,* June 24, 1943, September 25, 1946.

had grown in quantity so as to become the main source of newspaper revenue, the amount of hard news, including sports, actually shrank. What remained had a quality of "gray sameness" that contrasted starkly with the vigorous personal journalism of earlier eras.[11]

In the golden age, this "gray sameness" characterized baseball reporting. There were more reporters covering big-league teams and reporting on special events like All-Star games and World Series matches. And they did a workmanlike job with action photos, box scores, and features, all bound up in stylized prose. Moreover, fans greedily gobbled this fare, thereby banishing fears that radio would eclipse the working baseball writer.

But over-all there was a fixed quality to baseball writing that failed to keep pace with the growing sophistication of American readers. Only a handful of reporters of this period rose above this baroque style, including men like Red Smith of the *New York Herald-Tribune* and John Kiernan and Paul Gallico of the *New York Times*. Otherwise, the same leading writers of the silver age, men like Rice, Lieb, Vila, and H. G. Salsinger, served fans of the new age. But if most were content to follow the mold of "gray sameness," a few first-rate talents emerged, using sportswriting as a stepping-stone to higher literary callings. Thus, after fourteen years as an ace sportswriter, Paul Gallico bade "farewell to sport," choosing a literary career which would establish him as a solid novelist. Nevertheless, he credited his sportswriting career for sharpening his powers of description and expression. Certainly, few writers ever wrote so graphically of baseball as he did. The following description of a double play typified Gallico's enthusiastic love for the game:

> How much faster, then, and more beautiful in speed and execution is the double play when three men handle the ball in the same length of time and retire two runners on the one play, the man speeding to second . . . and the batter heading for first. Three seconds flat or better, and yet the shortstop fields the batted ball, or rather scoops it over to the second baseman, who sends it on to first. It would take

[11] John Tebbel, *The Compact History of American Newspapers*, 209–48.

> a delicate timing instrument to measure the fraction of a second that the shortstop actually has possession of the ball. Crack! goes the bat. Step, and flip, goes the shortstop. The second baseman in that time has run from his position perhaps five or six yards from the bag as the ball is started towards him by the shortstop. Ball and man meet on the base, and likewise with the same motion, in which there is no check or hesitation, the second baseman whirls and lines the ball down to first. He can whip the ball the ninety feet from second to first in three-fifths of a second. And he is lucky to have that much time left.[12]

Others, like Gallico, recognized that sportswriting was basically an immature literary calling, bade farewell, and marched on to other literary fields. Ring Lardner and Damon Runyon chose short stories, Lloyd Lewis, history, Ralph McGill, a distinguished editing career, and Westbrook Pegler became a vitriolic political columnist. Still others, like John Kiernan, took up careers in radio or television. Of those who stayed, some were, in the blunt words of H. L. Mencken, "keen-witted and clever boys who make the stuff entertaining, but the grade of their copy has not advanced since 1892."[13]

Happily, some like Tom Meany, Arthur Daley, Shirley Povich, Lee Allen, Fred Lieb, Frank Graham, and H. G. Salsinger undertook the necessary task of chronicling the history of the game and its teams. Their popularly written, informal efforts serve as background material for students interested in the impact of baseball on American life and of America's impact upon the game.

These men were exceptional, however. Most baseball writers seemed content to limit their literary efforts to routine writing. Such reporters often ran in packs, drinking much, writing much, and satisfying their creative urge by varying old clichés. Changing political currents sometimes furnished leads. Thus, in 1920, as America suffered under the witch-hunting mania of Bolshevik-baiters, some baseball writers took cues from this paranoid rhetoric and referred to player arguments as "outbreaks of Bolshevism," while others laced accounts with new scare words like "anarchy," "commissars," and "socialism."[14]

[12] Paul Gallico, *Farewell to Sport,* 126.
[13] H. L. Mencken, *The American Language,* 562.
[14] *The Sporting News,* June 4, 1920.

Some reporters found escape from boredom by feuding with players or owners. Baiting Ruth made good copy all over the nation; in Detroit, second-guessing manager Cobb was a pastime; and in Chicago, writers found relief in harassing the Cubs. Now and then a victim might strike back, as did manager Bill Terry of the Giants when he wrote that he was not impressed "with a craft that could violate a public trust by misinforming millions of fans intentionally or otherwise." Terry paid for this outburst as writers bombarded him with volleys of abuse.[15]

Baseball men learned to shrug off attacks, choosing the safer course of giving cliché-ridden interviews in the interest of free publicity. No harm was done to either side, but readers suffered by being fed a steady diet of escapist literature. Of course, writing such pap routinized writers' lives, but at least they could look forward to the annual chapter dinners of the Baseball Writers' Association.[16]

Writers sometimes earned extra money ghostwriting books and articles for leading baseball stars. From 1921 to 1937, Christy Walsh headed a syndicate of some thirty-four baseball writers who were paid to write for and about player heroes. At one time, four ghosts were assigned to Babe Ruth, including Ford Frick, a future baseball commissioner. Frick reportedly made $10,000 ghosting for Ruth. Bozeman Bulger was said to have received even more for ghosting McGraw's autobiography, entitled *My 30 Years in Baseball.* Altogether, Walsh's writers received $100,000 over the period 1921–36. In 1929, the peak year, seven writers grossed $43,000 for their covert labors.[17]

Even though sportswriters of the golden age were better paid than ever before, many carped about getting less than players. Some of this ill will was undoubtedly because of conflict between

15 "A Baseball Manager Gives Sportswriters a Lecture," *Literary Digest*, February 19, 1938; *ibid.*, January 23, 1921, November 3, 1921, March 30, 1930; Brown, *op. cit.*, 166.

16 Baseball Writers Association of America, *Constitution, 1967*; Interview, Lee Allen with D. Voigt; Gary Cartwright, "Confessions of a Washed-Up Sportswriter," *Harper's Magazine*, April, 1968.

17 Christy Walsh, "Adios to Ghosts!" *Cleveland News*, September 21, 1937. To read this is to credit Walsh with wisdom enough to hire other writers.

owners and those writers assigned to work as official scorers. Scoring games was traditionally a writer's job, done by them to insure accurate baseball records. But it was essentially a thankless job, paying as little as $1.50 a game. Because the scorer decided hits and errors, he was often subject to recriminations from players. Most writers felt the compensation was unequal to the drawbacks. The Writers Association fought for and won better pay, and in time owners began paying expenses of writers at spring training.[18] This last concession brought charges of intellectual prostitution. Yet such possibilities were so remote as to suggest this modification of a famous rhyme:

You cannot hope to bribe or twist,
Thank God, the [baseball] journalist,
For seeing what unbribed he'll do,
There's really no occasion to!

Probably the really solid contribution of baseball writers of the golden age came in the field of statistics. The word alone is enough to frighten most Americans, but baseball statistics are meat and drink to dyed-in-the-wool fans. Although most writers did not deny their importance, few liked the job of working with statistics. In the past, it had been a dedicated few like Chadwick, Morse, or Ernie Lanigan who carried on, and since all were heavy-handed writers, it is possible that they were compensating for literary shortcomings. Of this trio, Lanigan lasted through the golden age and beyond. Named as historian to the Hall of Fame in 1939, Lanigan kept the post until he was eighty. At last he yielded, and Lee Allen took over, giving baseball writing a man who could write facilely and who liked to compile statistical data.

During his early career as a writer covering the Reds, Allen spent much time tabulating and recording general baseball records. In this same period, he was in touch with two amateur statisticians, Sherley C. Thompson and Frank Marcellus. Just what motivated this pair is difficult to specify; Thompson was a professional musician and Marcellus a veritable recluse. Marcellus's dedication re-

18 *The Sporting News,* January 4, 1923, October 30, 1930.

calls the labors of monks of the Middle Ages who kept learning alive by copying books. Born of a middle-aged mother who was widowed early, Marcellus grew up under the sheltering influence of his mother and an aunt. Although he never played baseball, he loved the game and its records. During his young manhood, while waiting for his inheritance from a snuff-manufacturing relative, Marcellus did little but gather baseball statistics. Supported by family income, he held no job and lived a recluse's life in hotels, all the time collecting box scores and compiling the facts in them. Until he was past sixty, Marcellus pursued this life of a statistical pack rat until love suddenly entered his life. He was still "going steady" twenty years later, but the girl (who was then sixty-two) accepted her lot. This was a blow to the cause of baseball statistics, since Marcellus took to keeping records of courtship activities rather than baseball. At one point, he had detailed records covering three thousand dates and dinners. Finally, the aging Marcellus sold his baseball records to Thompson, who with reporter Hy Turkin published the *Encyclopedia of Baseball*, the most accurate and complete register of statistics to date.

This tale of dedicated "figure filberts" still continues. After purchasing the Thompson-Marcellus data, the late Lee Allen combined them with his own exhaustive collection of data and published a computerized overhaul of all baseball records since 1876. Under the title of *The Baseball Encyclopedia,* this brought to fruition the most revolutionary updating of baseball records since Chadwick's time.[19]

League officials belatedly moved to insure accurate compilation of records. Hitherto, their maintenance had been left to the editors of the various baseball guides, but the Howe News Bureau of Chicago was now designated official compiler of American League records and the Al Munro Elias Bureau of New York was selected for the National. Beginning in the 1930's, the Howe bureau published the American League's official *Green Book* and Elias the

[19] Interview, Lee Allen with D. Voigt; *New York Times*, March 23, 1967. Thompson's obituary; Thompson and Turkin, *op. cit.*, *passim*; See Leonard Koppett's discussion of the *Encyclopedia, New York Times*, August 31, 1969.

National's *Red Book*.[20] With these handy works at their sides, reporters and sportscasters were insured a stock of accurate figures with which to leaven their extravagant prose.

Meanwhile, better novels and accounts of the game were becoming available. Up to 1930, the baseball fiction of Gerald Beaumont, Charles E. Van Loan, Heywood Broun, and Ring Lardner set new standards in realism and technical accuracy. First-rate novelists like James T. Farrell and Thomas Wolfe also included generous descriptions of baseball in their novels on American life.[21] Above all, Farrell acknowledged a debt to baseball for sharpening his outlook on life. He once wrote about sportswriting: "There is tragedy, joy, and fulfillment in sports, the realization that man is master of his destiny no matter the obstacles, that faith must be based on reason and self-confidence . . . and there is intense emotion after labor and sweat, the salty pleasure of the white moment."[22]

Finally, golden age baseball inspired students to make serious studies of this long-lasting institution. In 1937, Edward J. Nichols wrote his dissertation on "A Historical Dictionary of Baseball Terminology." This student of literature was impressed by the widespread impact of baseball jargon on the American language, especially since 1920. In his dictionary, Nichols traced the origins of baseball expressions and their entry into the language, taking care to distinguish between terms arising naturally and those coined by sportswriters. In all, Nichols explored the origins of twenty-five hundred words which moved from the diamond to enliven American speech.[23] This pioneer work served to convince academicians of the value of studying a "frivolous" institution like baseball for insights into the American character. After World War II, many more such scholarly studies were produced. No greater justification for their pursuit is needed than the words of humanist Jacques Barzun: "Whoever wants to know the heart and mind of America had better learn baseball, the rules and realities of the game."

[20] *Spalding-Reach Official Baseball Guide*, 1940, p. 14.

[21] Ralph S. Graber, "Baseball in American Fiction," *The English Journal*, November, 1967, pp. 1107–14.

[22] Interview, James Farrell with D. Voigt.

3. Stirrings on the Financial Frontier

One of the popular myths of the 1920's was that owners of the golden age were wallowing in profits. Newspaper and magazine stories of soaring attendance and salary figures led fans to believe that baseball was no longer a sport, but an immensely popular business venture. According to one hardbitten sportswriter, any fan who believed otherwise was hopelessly naïve:

> Baseball very frankly is a professional game. Ball players are in it for all the money they can get out of it. Once in awhile a magnate gets Pecksniffian and insists that he is promoting the sport for the upbuilding of sturdy Americanism, but the general run of them admit it is a business.[24]

Like many a myth, this one has a ring of truth to it. Franchise values certainly climbed to new heights. Even the least valuable were now worth half a million dollars or so, while those of the Yankees and Cubs were valued at three million.[25] By 1930, baseball admissions for both major leagues amounted to $17 million a year, putting baseball ahead of competing professional sports such as hockey, basketball, and football. It is true that baseball always involved less total income than other spectacles like college football, movies, and legitimate theaters,[26] but the breadth and diversity of these operations made comparison unfair.

On the other hand, baseball has always had a high degree of internal diversity, and there have always been huge differences between have and have-not clubs. Indeed, when the differences in character of owners, fans, parks, promotion tactics, and profits are compared, it is clear that no such thing as a typical major-league club ever existed.

Perhaps the key to the diversity is to be found in the personalities

[23] Edward J. Nichols, "An Historical Dictionary of Baseball Terminology."

[24] *The Sporting News*, July 12, 1928; Hugh Fullerton, "Baseball the Business and the Sport," *Review of Reviews*, April, 1921; "Is Professional Baseball A Sport?" *Literary Digest*, September 17, 1921; "Baseball Business From the Inside," *Colliers*, March 25, 1922; John Kiernan, "Big League Business," *Saturday Evening Post*, May 31, 1930.

[25] Gerald R. Curtis, "Factors that Affect the Attendance of a Major League Baseball Club," 3.

[26] U.S. House of Representatives, *Organized Baseball*, p. 963.

and life styles of the owners. All clubs had owners, but any similarities vanish at this point. Yet fans often lumped all of them together, depicting them as fat and craven Shylocks. Such an image was a survival from the robber baron era and the silver age, but it was a bad fit for the golden age.

To begin with, banks and trust companies took a dim view of baseball promotion. One anonymous owner complained that a serious investor could do better in almost any other legitimate enterprise. He informed sportswriter Bozeman Bulger that most fans are convinced that they are smarter than any owner. But he insisted that the owner's task was incredibly difficult. While he admitted that he made money in baseball, he argued that profits came slowly and only after strenuous years of learning the tricks of running a club. He gave his ten commandments of baseball promotion. First of all, go in with enthusiasm and spend freely. Then get a good field manager, give him free rein, and never abuse him for loss of games. Next, he supplied a set of rules for dealing with fans. One must work hard to get their support, make good on every promise, get them a star to worship at any price, and continually take fans into your confidence. Next, cultivate the press by talking freely and positively.

Having urged all this, the owner warned that almost no one makes a fortune at baseball. Most become owners out of love for the game and its lusty life. Indeed, he knew only three who set out to make fortunes, and of this trio only Comiskey succeeded, primarily because he grew up in the game.[27]

This appraisal presents a brief, but, on the whole, an accurate portrayal of owners of the golden age. Besides Comiskey, Frank Navin of Detroit, who died a few months before his team won its first World Series in 1935, was the only one who grew rich from baseball alone. Both he and Comiskey used knowledge gained from years in the game as their formula for success, a recipe that also worked well for Mack and Griffith. However, the latter pair merely managed to earn a good living from the game and both were at the mercy of economic fluctuations.[28]

27 " 'Inside' Baseball From an Owner's View-Point," *Literary Digest*, April 8, 1922.

Others, like Ruppert, Yawkey, Ball, Walter "Spike" Briggs of Detroit (who succeeded Navin), and Alva Bradley of Cleveland, were well-to-do men before entering baseball. Ruppert of the Yankees personified the public image of the successful owner. He always spent lavishly, and as a gentleman-sportsman he never regarded his baseball club as a profit-making venture. To Ruppert, his brewery and real estate enterprise spelled business, and he always kept separate accounts for baseball.[29] Yawkey was also a millionaire gentleman-sportsman who undertook the restoration of the moribund Red Sox. This formidable task took $3 million over the first decade of his tenure, yet like Ruppert, Yawkey was able to absorb monetary losses. To a lesser extent, this was true of Ball of the Browns, who tolerated losses of $300,000 to field a fighting team in St. Louis.[30]

By the close of the golden age, men like these were a vanishing species. After Ball's death in 1933, his club fell into less capable hands and mounting losses quickly made it the sick man of the league.[31] By 1941, plans were afoot to move the club to the West Coast, but this move was prevented by wartime restrictions. Meanwhile, Ruppert's death and succession spelled the end of the gentleman-sportsman breed.

At this time, the National League presented a more complicated pattern of ownership. As the older league, it was more tradition bound. Owners like Ebbets, Dreyfuss, and Herrmann were holdovers from the grim years of the 1890's. These were gentlemen-sportsmen in the classic mold, which meant that none was rich enough to escape the lessons learned during the ups and downs of baseball's silver age. For these men, the profit revolution of the 1920's was bewildering. Ebbets died in 1925, just as his franchise was returning undreamed-of profits. Ironically, his end came just after he had announced that his Dodgers were worth $3 million. Soon after, in 1927, Herrmann ended his long career of service to

28 *The Sporting News*, September 28, 1933; Povich, *op. cit.*, 243–44; John Ford, "The End of an Era," *Baseball Magazine*, March, 1955.

29 *The Sporting News*, November 10, 1932, January 11, 1934.

30 "Yawkey of the Red Sox," *Literary Digest*, December 21, 1935; Fitzgerald, (ed.), *The American League*, 37–63, 109–30, 157–62, 190–247.

31 *The Sporting News*, October 20, 1932, December 28, 1933.

the National League at the very time when he too looked forward to less pennypinching. Dreyfuss held on until 1931, when his death ended the longest tenure of any owner. His record of success made him rich and gave him years to enjoy his wealth, but the death of the son he wanted to succeed him broke his spirit at the end.

The passing of these titans paralyzed their clubs. In Brooklyn, the crisis was worsened when Ebbets's longtime partner, Ed McKeever, joined him in death.[32] Eventually, the heirs chose Steve McKeever to head an ineffective directorate which quickly alienated fans by firing the popular Wilbert Robinson. After that, beset by conservatism and falling attendance, Brooklyn entered a dark age that lasted from 1931 to 1937. The pall was lifted only by Larry MacPhail's appointment as general manager in 1938.

After Dreyfuss's death, the Pittsburgh club passed into the reluctant hands of a son-in-law, William Benswanger, who managed to keep the club in the black for a time. But wartime reverses persuaded him in 1946 to sell to a syndicate headed by John W. Galbreath and popular singer Bing Crosby.

Cincinnati was spared an interregnum of reluctant family management. After Herrmann's death, the club was sold to Sid Weil, an auto tycoon and Wall Street plunger. As a baseball financier, he was willing and daring, but the Depression drove him to the wall. In 1934, the club passed into the hands of a rich radio entrepreneur, Powell Crosby. Crosby wisely chose MacPhail as general manager and allowed him to pioneer in night ball.[33]

Although no National League owner matched the dazzling successes of Ruppert, he had a close rival in the chewing-gum king, William Wrigley. As head of a lucrative, Depression-proof business, Wrigley was a baseball zealot. In his scheme of things, victory and contented fans came first, and both goals were met by his loyal general manager, William Veeck, Sr. Under Veeck, Wrigley Field became the most beautiful park in the majors. The walls were kept free of advertising posters, except for an unobtrusive pair of elves, the trademark of Wrigley's gum empire. After the death

[32] *Ibid.*, January 3, 1929.

[33] *Ibid.*, February 23, December 7, 1933, February 8, 1934.

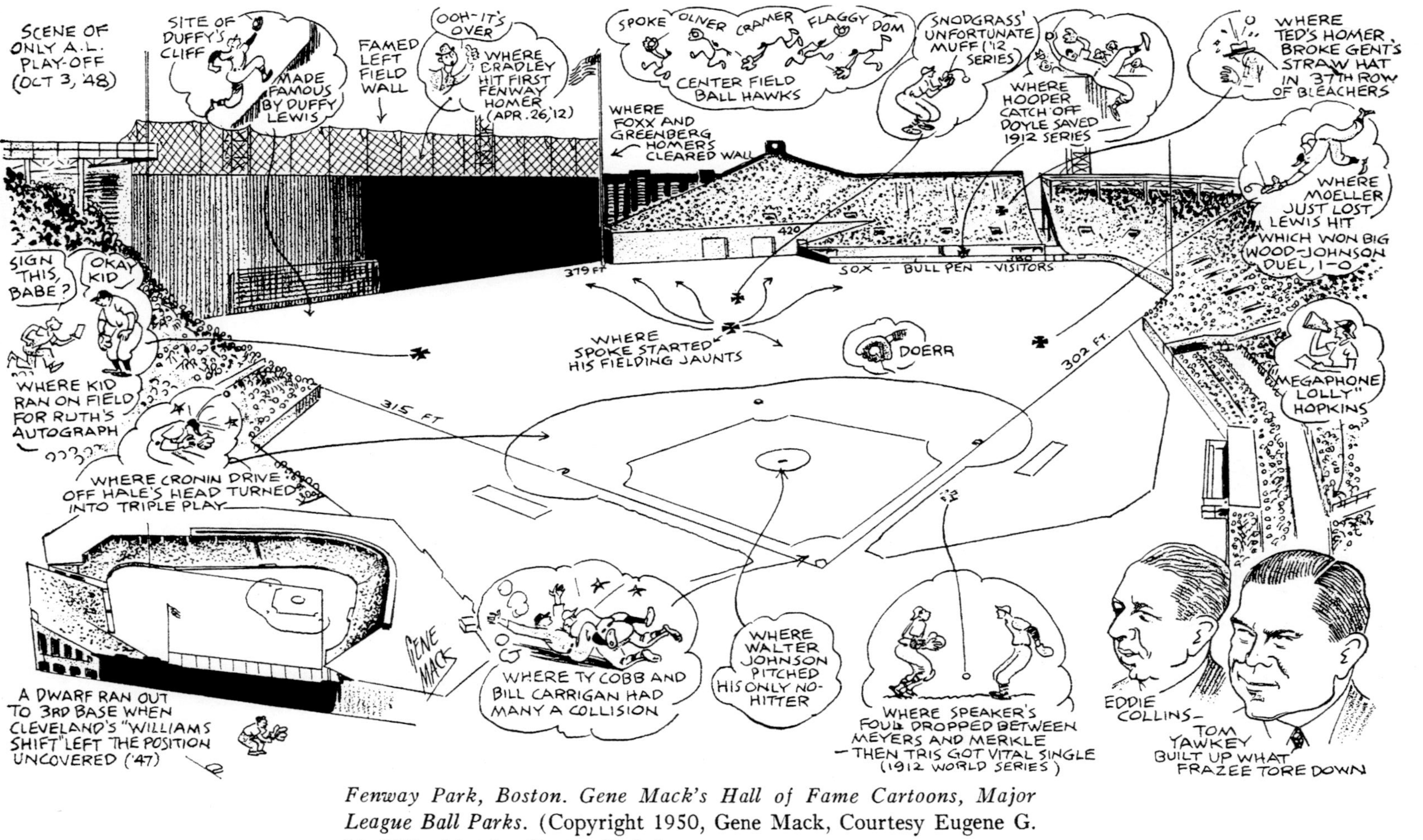

Fenway Park, Boston. Gene Mack's Hall of Fame Cartoons, Major League Ball Parks. (Copyright 1950, Gene Mack, Courtesy Eugene G. McGillicuddy, Jr., Boston Globe)

of Wrigley and that of his general manager, his son Philip faithfully carried on, even to the point of employing the teen-age son of Veeck. Although this was done out of filial loyalty, the hiring of Veeck in the 1930's set the young man on a course that was to make him a famous general manager.[34]

The third member of baseball's elite, Giants owner Charles Stoneham, was far less notable than Ruppert or Wrigley. A broker and race horse owner who reputedly consorted with gamblers and ticket scalpers,[35] he headed a triumvirate which included McGraw and McQuade. In spite of formidable competition from the Yankees, Giants stockholders collected 400 per cent profit in the period 1919–29, and the club carried a $3 million price tag.[36] But bitter disagreements divided the three owners and led first to McQuade's ouster and then to McGraw's. Stoneham, who was left in full charge, died in 1936 and passed the Giants on to his "dumpy, chubby, apple-cheeked son," Horace. The son loved profits as much as his father and fought hard for a share of the Gotham market.

[34] *Ibid.*, January 28, 1932; Brown, *op. cit.*, 161–226; Veeck and Linn, *Veeck as in Wreck*, 14–30; Veeck and Linn, *The Hustler's Handbook*, 313.

[35] Veeck and Linn, *The Hustler's Handbook*, 96–102.

[36] *The Sporting News*, February 5, 1925, November 21, 1929; Graham, *The New York Giants*, 103–108.

Horace Stoneham succeeded his father, Charles Stoneham, as owner of the Giants in 1936. One of the oldest names among major-league owners, the Stoneham family first gained control of the National League Giants in the early 1920's. (George Brace, photographer)

But when the Yankees continued to outdraw his team, he was ready to pull up stakes and move elsewhere.[37]

The industrialist Sam Breadon, who took over the Cardinals from Mrs. Britton, was perhaps representative of a new breed of owner. Breadon watched the formerly moribund club grow into a consistent pennant winner under Branch Rickey. But when the Depression drove down attendance, Breadon adopted close-fisted practices which eventually provoked Rickey's resignation. By the end of the war, Breadon was aging and tired, but he found energy enough to hold out for a $4 million selling price, a tenfold return on his original investment.[38]

Meanwhile, the Braves and Phillies continued as the National's most abject clubs. Both were notorious for their owners' niggardly practices. Until he sold out in 1923, George Grant of the Braves often chased foul balls hit into the stands in attempts to snatch them away from fans. His successor, Judge Emil Fuchs, was an able man but lacked the funds to build the club. The Philadelphia story was worse. Under the Baker regime, which lasted until 1933, the highest-paid player got less than $300 a month, and the club's player expense account was the league's lowest. Baker's successor, Gerry Nugent, was even more miserly. He depended on baseball income for a living and used such expedients as selling promising players to earn money, After years of suffering these leeches, their colleagues managed to ease in more resolute owners during the War. Bolder expenditures rekindled pennant hopes in the hearts of fans, a tribute to the eternal optimism of baseball enthusiasts.[39]

Although vast differences in approach separated owners in the golden age, the success or failure of an individual depended mightily on the location of his franchise. It was easy to be bold with a team located in a key population center. The Yankees, Tigers, White Sox, Giants, Dodgers, and Cubs were each located in a center of better than two million people. As a result, these clubs regularly exceeded 12 per cent of the total annual attendance.

37 Veeck and Linn, *The Hustler's Handbook*, 96–108.

38 Allen, *The Hot Stove League*, 191.

39 Fitzgerald, (ed.), *The National League*, 3–43, 68–100, 128–49, 182–249.

If two clubs competed within the same locale, as did the Cardinals and Browns, Phillies and Athletics, or the Red Sox and Braves, the success of one often spelled failure for the other. Thus, the superior drawing power of the Athletics and Cardinals drove the owners of the Browns and Phillies into deeper conservatism. And in the 1930's, Yawkey's free spending policies with the Red Sox almost finished the Braves.

As always, large crowds spelled high profits, and in the golden age, teams from the big population centers regularly exceeded $100,000 in profits. In the National League, the Dodgers, Giants, Cardinals, and Pirates each bettered this mark at least eleven times, with the Giants doing it fifteen times. Only the Cubs scored annual profits of $500,000, and they did it twice, a feat that placed them in a special category of success.[40] The poor showing of the Braves and Phillies ranked them as the *lumpenproletariat* of the league. In the golden age, the Braves lost money eighteen seasons, the Phillies twelve. Only once did the Phillies better the $100,000 mark in profits, and the Braves never did. Certainly this dismal record helps to explain the timidity of the owners, the low player salaries, and the scandalous accommodations. At least their timidity kept losses down so that they seldom dropped as much as $100,000 in a season. This was not true of the elite teams, whose high salaries and operating costs made losing years memorable. Every club had at least five losing seasons, the Giants and Cubs setting the seasonal high mark of losses of better than $247,000 in a single season.[41]

However, the biggest gap between rich and poor teams was to be found in the American League. There, two teams, the Tigers and the Yankees, comprised the elite. In the twenty-six years between 1920 and 1945, Navin's Tigers topped the $100,000 profit mark eighteen times, one less than Ruppert's Yanks. The Tigers twice bettered the $500,000 mark. The Yankees managed this once, but were compensated by three seasons when profits exceeded

[40] U.S. House of Representatives, *Organized Baseball*, pp. 1591–94.

[41] *Ibid.*, p. 1600; "Them Phillies—How to Make Failure Pay," *Saturday Evening Post*, October 4, 1941.

$450,000. Among the other clubs, only the White Sox and Indians surpassed $100,000 as many as seven times, and only the Senators topped $400,000, and only once. There were more American losers than Nationals. No National League team lost as often as the Red Sox with their record nineteen losing years.

During the period beginning in 1933, while Yawkey was rebuilding the Red Sox, there were seven consecutive years when annual losses exceeded $100,000. In 1933, the club lost $537,000 to set an all-time record. No other club matched the Red Sox in suffering, but the Athletics and Browns underwent twelve losing seasons, partly redeemed by five years in which profits topped $100,000.[42]

Experience and statistical evidence showed that weak teams almost never captured more than 8 per cent of the league's annual attendance. Obviously, fans preferred winners, and statistics showed that a fighting team, playing close to .600 ball, could count on at least 14 per cent of the league's annual attendance. On the other hand, statistics showed that those clubs that stormed along at a .700 gait lost attendance. A .600 race was apparently close enough to be interesting, while a .700 clip was apt to be dull.[43] Of course, there were exceptions to the rule. In the Depression year of 1934, the Cards battled to victory in a tight race, but snared only 7 per cent of the attendance. In contrast, the Yanks of 1927, in a devastating runaway race, captured 25 per cent of the league's attendance! Such exceptions underscored the uncertainty of baseball and emphasized the importance of "style" and "class," factors guaranteed to frustrate those who would make a science out of baseball promotion.[44]

In fact, making a profit in baseball was increasingly acknowledged to be a complicated art, since it was almost impossible to know the whims of the fans whose dollars were sought. Perceptive owners sensed that more than victory was needed and that fans came for a variety of reasons. Some were sons of immigrants who came to identify with players of their own nationality; smart own-

42 U.S. House of Representatives, *Organized Baseball*, p. 1599.

43 *Ibid.*, p. 1593.

44 *Ibid.*, pp. 1997, 2520; *Baseball Digest*, May, 1968, pp. 77–87.

A crowd of 20,422 turned out to watch the first championship game played under the lights in the major leagues. The game took place May 24, 1935, at Cincinnati's Crosley Field with the Philadelphia Phillies opposing the Reds. (Courtesy Cincinnati Baseball Club, National League)

ers gratified their wishes by hiring such players.[45] Others came for sheer amusement, lured by night baseball, by food and beer, or by the extras such as comedy shows or fireworks. To understand the variety of motivations and to exploit them has remained the great challenge of baseball promotion.[46]

However, even the smartest promoters guessed wrong at times, and every club lost money at some point in the golden age. Even the glamorous Yankees were three-time losers, and during the

Depression losers outnumbered winners. The poorer teams suffered most. During the Depression, these teams banded together in support of a profit-sharing plan, but the plan was voted down. For better or worse, the baseball enterprise would continue in an untrammeled fashion, and the Devil take the losers. Ruppert put the case for rugged individualism eloquently: "I found out a long time ago that there is no charity in baseball, and that every club owner must make his own fight for existence." This spokesman for free enterprise opposed anything that threatened to make a free show of baseball, including radio broadcasts and night baseball.[47]

Although his words helped to defeat the profit-sharing plan, Ruppert failed to halt radio broadcasts or night baseball. Indeed, proponents of both flung his words back in his face, insisting on their freedom to tap these profits. Of the two innovations, night ball faced the most stubborn opposition, but it enabled minor-league clubs to hold on in the Depression. Backed to the wall by 1930, eleven minor-league owners installed lighting systems. To their delight, fans accepted the novelty, thus encouraging other owners. Soon critics like *The Sporting News* had to eat crow for damning the night game as bad for digestion, sleep, and morale. In a pragmatic reversal in 1934, that paper now argued that night games were "natural," no more corrupting than movies, and a potential stimulus to daytime crowds. Major-league owners did an about-face soon after and lifted the rule against night ball. The technical problems were formidable, however, as MacPhail learned when he promoted seven games in Cincinnati in 1935. But the experiment worked, and when MacPhail moved to Brooklyn in 1938 he installed lights there. After that, the rush was on, and by 1940 every National club but Boston and Chicago had turned on the lights. By 1941, in the American League only the wealthy Red Sox, Yankees, and Tigers held out.[48] A final push came in 1942, when

[45] Curtis, *loc. cit.*, 36–39, 52–53.

[46] Veeck and Linn, *Veeck as in Wreck*, 28–42.

[47] U.S. House of Representatives, *Organized Baseball*, pp. 1599–1600; *The Sporting News*, July 21, 1932, November 10, 1933.

[48] U.S. House of Representatives, *Organized Baseball*, p. 1594; *The Sporting News*, May 8, July 16, 1930, April 9, 1931, August 23, 1934; "Thumbs Down on Night Baseball," *Literary Digest*, June 8, 1935.

President Roosevelt urged more night games to meet the leisure needs of war workers, a plea that Washington's Griffith heeded by staging twenty-one night games.[49]

In an age of sweeping change in the baseball world, some flexibility was required. Some of the owners resisted change, but they were counterbalanced by the Rickeys and MacPhails. By the end of this age, hardly an owner dared run his baseball operation singlehandedly. Success favored the dynamic element of "managerial enterprise." As practiced by MacPhail and Rickey, professional expertise proved profitable, and the role of general manager took on great importance.

Weiss of the Yankees had to overcome the conservatism of Barrow in order to put his streamlined farm system into effect. Otherwise, the Yankees followed the lead of free-wheeling innovators like Rickey and MacPhail, who outran others so far that they became controversial figures. Indeed, Rickey was forced out of St. Louis in the early 1940's, but he turned up in Brooklyn and Pittsburg where he was able to apply his ideas. As for the volatile, red-headed MacPhail, he quickly outgrew Cincinnati and moved on to Brooklyn. After war service, he stunned the baseball world in 1946 by heading a combine that purchased the Yankees from conservative bankers for the bargain price of $3 million.[50]

Although this energetic pair were thought to typify the hustling general manager, it was an inaccurate stereotype. Others were much more representative, including Eddie Collins, the former star, who served as Yawkey's steward; Bill Evans, the umpire, who became Cleveland's general manager; Bill Veeck, Sr., of the Cubs; or Eddie Brannick of the Giants. It was the elder Veeck who designed the much-admired Cub bureaucracy, with experts in charge of concessions, ticket sales, ground-keeping, and police. Altogether, Veeck headed an army of 350 workers in a streamlined operation that won high praise from the conservative journal,

[49] *The Sporting News*, January 29, 1942, February 12, 1942.

[50] "The Yankees," *loc. cit.*; "Baseball Business From the Inside," *Colliers*, March 25, 1922; "Amazing Mr. MacPhail," *Newsweek*, June 24, 1940; "Fall of the House of MacPhail," *Saturday Evening Post*, April 17, 1943.

Factory and Industrial Management.[51] Men of this caliber were hard-working, smart enough not to rush to lay the old aside, but bold enough to adopt proven new ways.

General managers were mainly responsible for many successful practices that cultivated the loyalties of armies of fans. In this age, the familiar team names and symbols were adopted, although weak clubs like the Phillies and Braves struggled to find identity in labels like "Blue Jays," "Quakers," and "Bees" before accepting natural labels of "Phillies" and "Braves" hung on them by long-suffering fans. Fans came to expect managed news stories and familiar rituals such as the playing of the National Anthem before each game.[52] If players suspected general managers of being cold, heartless, and willing to trade anybody if the price was right, at least they welcomed the good offices of traveling secretaries who took care of bodily comforts and the services of skilled medics and trainers, like Dr. Robert Hyland of the Cardinals, who tended all kinds of baseball injuries.

But this was as far as most general managers went in meeting player needs. Not until the postwar era did any club care enough to keep records on retired players or to show any interest in their adjustment to life outside baseball. First to do so were the Phillies under Robert Carpenter, but the move came a bit late. By the late 1940's, players were banding together to wrest concessions through collective power. Their success forced managers to adopt new practices in dealing with militant player groups.[53]

If owners and general managers had been more sensitive to signs of player unrest, they might have headed off the coming union

[51] *The Sporting News*, December 8, 1932; "The Cubs: Baseball's Contribution to Successful Management," *Factory and Industrial Management*, October, 1929; William Wrigley, Jr., "Owning a Big League Team," *Literary Digest*, September 13, 1930; "Yawkey of the Red Sox," *loc. cit.*; Quentin Reynolds, "Eddie Brannick, Secretary of the Giants," *Colliers*, May 1, 1937.

[52] *The Sporting News*, November 17, 1910, July 28, 1912, October 29, 1931; "Doctoring Our National Anthem," *Literary Digest*, February 19, 1938; *Baseball Digest*, March, 1947, pp. 51–61.

[53] Veeck and Linn, *Hustler's Handbook*, 51–53, 119–45; *The Sporting News*, December 12, 1929, June 19, 1930, December 17, 1931.

movement. Certainly by 1930, players were chafing under old-fashioned dictatorial field managers like Hornsby and McGraw. Gone were the days when McGraw could curse players with impunity or tell a third baseman to block a ball with his chest, because, in his words, "Young man, that is what your chest is for." Not that firmness or discipline were gone, but players were demanding consideration and understanding. This new mood owed much to Rickey's patient tactics; their general acceptance in the postwar era called for a new breed of teaching field managers.[54]

Like other institutions of American society, major-league baseball was buffeted by winds of change. New methods in management, technological innovation, and the application of human relations were dynamic responses to the changing world outside of baseball. The 1920's raised hopes of affluence in all Americans; the 1930's called attention to the needs of deprived Americans. Both periods saw wrenching changes in baseball. And as the golden age ended amidst the drums of another total war, baseball in the 1940's faced changes even more sweeping.

[54] For changing field management practices, see *The Sporting News*, June 4, 1925, March 28, 1930; *Baseball Digest*, November, 1945, p. 12, November, 1946, p. 42, January, 1949, pp. 13–14; Barrow, *op. cit.*, 155–71; Allen, *Hot Stove League*, 135, 215–24, 234–40.

10

The End of an Era

1. World War II

Something like "normal" prosperity returned to major-league baseball in 1941, but for such a tantalizingly brief stay that it was utterly frustrating. It was as if after eight years of struggling to escape from a cave, one finally saw daylight, only to be forced to enter another cave. For baseball men, the caves were the limitations imposed by the years of depression and war. Ironically, just as the optimism of 1941 was banishing the gloom of eight years of financial reverses for the baseball world, the nation faced the prospect of war with the Axis powers. There had been warnings; the military draft of 1940, for example, had taken several players, including superstar Hank Greenberg. Nevertheless, promoters hoped that the draft was only a temporary expedient. But in December, 1941, the attack on Pearl Harbor brought on an all-out war with Japan and Germany.[1]

[1] *The Sporting News*, October 30, November 18, 1941.

For most Americans, the rapid course of events caused bewilderment, fear, and electrifying excitement. Although they trembled at the prospect of induction for themselves or their sons, Americans sensed that the war would create new jobs in new industries. But baseball operators used young men in a nonessential industry. Memories of events during World War I reminded them of what might lay in store, and it looked like a grim struggle for survival with the future of the game hinging on decisions made in Washington.

However, the government now seemed more sympathetic toward baseball than it had been in the days of General Crowder. Early in 1942, at the low ebb of our military cause, Commissioner Landis wrote President Roosevelt about baseball's immediate future. To his delight, Roosevelt promptly responded with a "green light" for the game's continuance, for Roosevelt viewed the game as an important means for sustaining morale. Baseball would not get special concessions in draft deferments or transportation allocations. Instead, promoters would have to use their own resources and make do with overage, underage, or rejected players and adjust their schedules to limited transportation and hotel accommodations. Along with the rest of America, baseball people came to know the biting humor in the phrase, "There's a war on, you know." To survive was to follow the letter and spirit of Roosevelt's advice: "Carry on to the fullest extent consistent with the primary purpose of winning the war."[2]

Amidst the preparation of arms, men, and morale for warfare, baseball executives gathered for their annual meetings in 1941 and voted $25,000 to pay for bats and balls for military use. This voluntary contribution marked the beginning of four years of sacrifices and austerities during which money from All-Star games and the World Series would be donated to the war effort. Fans, too, were enlisted in the effort, for foul balls hit into the stands were to be thrown back for collection and shipment to the camps. If any fan took more than a short, wistful look at his catch, boos

[2] *Ibid.*, Janu'ray 1, 1942; James Gould, "The President Says, 'Play Ball,'" *Baseball Magazine*, January, 1942.

from others, including uniformed servicemen who were admitted free to all parks during the war, quickly evoked the desired patriotic response.

The greatest sacrifice was the loss of playing years suffered by promising players who entered military service. With them went dreams of championships, and owners who watched them go found comfort only in the knowledge that other clubs were also losing men. More than a thousand major leaguers exchanged baseball uniforms for military garb in these years, half from those who came to the majors since 1931 and half from those who came up in the years 1941–46.

Because it took time to mobilize an army of twelve million men, clubs were able to retain the services of key men long enough to get through the campaigns of 1942–43. During those years, at least, the quality of play was respectable, but thereafter the steady drain of talent lowered standards.

2. "Coming in on a Wing and a Prayer"

Although they were not of the highest quality, the baseball campaigns of 1942–45 provided thrills enough to sustain public interest in the game. Owners also sought to bolster the game by offering free admission to servicemen, by increasing the number of night games, and by broadcasting through the Armed Forces Network. Of course, none of these moves were profitable, but as investments in goodwill they promised future dividends.

With stars drifting off to war and attendance falling, the low quality of play came in for increasing criticism. But in the years 1942 and 1943 there was some measure of excitement in the continuing vendetta between the Yankees and the Cardinals. Because these clubs had extensive farm systems, they were better able than their rivals to fill the gaps left by the departed players. American League owners thus still found themselves at the mercy of Yankee tyranny. In 1942, despite the loss of key men like John Sturm and Tom Henrich, the Yankees were able to win easily, clinching the pennant in mid-September.

The Cardinals, meanwhile, were struggling to overtake the

Dodgers. Until August, the Brooklyn team enjoyed a big lead and looked like a certain winner. With Durocher driving them hard, the Dodgers won 104 games, 4 more than in 1941, but this was not enough to offset the final push of the Cardinals. Managed by Billy Southworth, the Cardinals got sturdy pitching from Mort Cooper, John Beazley, and Ernie White, and hard and timely hitting from outfielders Enos Slaughter, Terry Moore, and the young superstar, Stan Musial. Not only did the Cardinals beat out the Dodgers by 2 games, but they went on to rout the Yankees in the Series 4 games to 1. For the Yankees, it was their first Series defeat since 1926, when another Cardinal team had done the job; for America's host of Yankee haters, it was a bright moment in the gloomy war era.

But 1943 was another story. Determined to avenge the setback, McCarthy and Barrow worked to plug the holes left by departing stars like DiMaggio, Rizzuto, and Ruffing. By now, wartime austerities demanded that clubs train in the North, so McCarthy assembled his men at Asbury Park, New Jersey. He re-shaped his team with patience and care, using Joe Gordon to anchor a new infield of young Bill Johnson at third, George Stirnweiss at short, and Nick Etten at first. In the outfield, Keller was the mainstay, while Chandler and Bonham held down the pitching staff and Dickey carried the burden of the catching. This patchwork team bore little resemblance to past "Bronx Bombers," but it played steady ball, mowing down rivals in a record string of seasonal triumphs and going on to win the pennant by thirteen games. Then, to the great delight of Barrow, who watched his last Series as a Yankee president, the team avenged the previous year's humiliation and clipped the Cardinals four games to one.

By the end of 1943, most of the superstars of the 1930's were off to war, leaving a mixture of recruits, rejects, and overage vets behind. At its best, the kind of baseball they played was "triple A" ball, but amusement-hungry fans came anyway. Perhaps the chief attraction of 1944 was a new outcome in the American League. For the first time since the days of Von der Ahe, the Browns came up with a winner. Veteran catcher Luke Sewell headed a team of ancient pitchers and draft rejects who outfought both the Tigers and Yankees. Needing a sweep of their last four games, the Browns responded magnificently by crushing the Yankees at their own stadium. In winning, the team drew more than half a million fans, double the attendance of 1943. But then came the Series test with their hometown rivals, and the Browns failed miserably. This dismal anticlimax only underscored the ineffectiveness of this outpost in war or in peace.

Meanwhile, the war was drawing to a close. In spite of the German breakthrough in the Ardennes in December, 1944, the Axis powers were being harried everywhere. This provided some encouragement to baseball men who had been preparing themselves for the possible loss of physical rejects to the draft. In the spring, Germany's surrender aroused the hope that some first-class players might be discharged from the services in time for play. Of course, Japan remained to be conquered, but in August news of the atom bombings of two Japanese cities, was soon followed by Japan's capitulation. The prospect of a return to normal conditions was reflected in rising attendance as the American League topped the five million mark for the first time since 1940.

With the victory of the Allied powers in 1945, the pennant chase took on new color. For much of the season, the Detroit Tigers, on the strength of excellent pitching by Paul "Dizzy" Trout and Hal Newhouser, battled the Senators, a team fortified by draftproof Latin-American players and overage knuckleball pitchers. It looked like a Senator year until slugger Hank Greenberg rejoined the Tigers after five years of military service. Although he was unable to condition himself properly, Greenberg bludgeoned some key homers and managed a .311 average in seventy-eight games, enough to lift the Tigers to a slim game-and-a-half victory. Then came the Series, which the Tigers won from the Cubs four games to three, but which one writer said was really a test to see who could lose first![3] But fans enjoying the exhilaration of peace supported this ugly duckling of a Series, and it set a new record for attendance and profits.

[3] John Drebinger, "Who Was the Hero of the '45 Series?" *Baseball Magazine*, December, 1945; Brown, *op. cit.*, 229.

3. The Caretaking Era

To play major-league baseball during the war years required a quality of dedication bordering on fanaticism. Fans and reporters sneered at the *ersatz* quality of play, and much of the glamour was lost. Seasoned observers called this an age without heroes, a caretaking era that awaited the return of the real heroes. Those who served on the playing fields did so with the certain knowledge that after the war they would be cast off with little or no recourse.

Conditions for baseball grew steadily worse after 1942. Because of transportation problems, spring training for all teams was conducted in the North above the so-called Landis-Eastman line, named for its chief negotiators. The cold weather made training difficult, and matters were worsened by daily shortages of railroad sleepers, rooms, equipment, and nourishing food. Players complained of lack of sleep and blamed extra night games for upsetting their physiological equilibrium.[4]

Had players been compensated by extra cash, such conditions might have been tolerable, but players were bereft of cash or glory. America's political leaders conceded the morale-boosting importance of the game, but baseball was nevertheless classed as nonessential to the war effort.[5] In 1943, Manpower Commissioner Paul V. McNutt refused to list baseball among thirty-five essential occupations, an action that threatened to drive players to essential war jobs. Owners relaxed when McNutt clarified his stand and allowed players to leave winter factory jobs to play ball. Of course, those players who did so lost their draftproof status. However, McNutt was no Crowder, and he demonstrated his friendliness to baseball by throwing out the first ball of the 1943 season as a substitute for the President.[6]

With defense work booming, workers' incomes rose sharply,

[4] *The Sporting News*, February 5, 1942, March 1, 1945; The wartime ball was made of balata or "bastard rubber," and observers claimed it was deader than any of the thirities. *Ibid.*, March 18, 1943, April 29, 1943; *Baseball Digest*, November, 1945, p. 4.

[5] *The Sporting News*, March 11, 1943; baseball's closest call came in 1945 when the green light on transportation allotments was delayed until March. At last, on March 21, owners were told to proceed. *Ibid.*, March 29, 1945.

[6] *Ibid.*, April 15, 1943.

narrowing the gap between a worker's wage and a player's salary. But rising incomes and spiraling prices led to a federal salary freeze in 1942. This rule hit players hard, for it ignored baseball's record of paying in relation to quality of performance. Players protested in vain and by 1945 the situation was so bad that Barrow of the Yankees had difficulty signing his men. A serious revolt took place in the Cardinal camp, where players of the three-time championship team protested the owner's rigid salary policy. In 1945, stars like the Cooper brothers and Marty Marion got no more than $12,000, and owner Breadon was accused of exploiting the salary freeze order. Embittered by Breadon's "no-raise" policy, the Cooper brothers held out for $15,000. In retaliation, Breadon traded Morton Cooper to the Braves, a petulant gesture that cost his club the 1945 pennant.[7]

Players certainly deserved sympathetic consideration during this difficult time. Because wartime inflation boosted prices, they lost much of their purchasing power. By 1945 even Greenberg's 1941 salary of $55,000, baseball's highest since Gehrig's day, seemed small; Dickey's $22,500, baseball's highest in 1944, seemed niggardly. Fully aware of the losses they were taking, players were seething by the end of the war, and returning veterans who shared their sentiments helped push a unionization movement in 1946. Under the "G. I. Bill of Rights" for returning servicemen, players were to be paid at the same salaries as before. Legally, owners were bound to accept this rule, but they were hardly prepared for new demands for collective bargaining, tenure, and pensions.[8]

Of course, the chief beneficiaries of this new militancy were the regular players, not the much-ridiculed band who held the fort in wartime. This motley crew looked pathetic when compared with the golden age warriors. By the end of 1942, the glamorous stars were gone, including the great DiMaggio and the brilliant young Ted Williams, owner of baseball's last .400-plus batting average.[9] By 1943 only a few good players remained, like young Stan Musial

7 *Ibid.*, February 18, 25, 1943, November 9, 1944, May 31, 1945.

8 *Ibid.*, February 4, 1943, April 25, 1946.

9 Dwight Freeburg, "Batter Number One," *Baseball Magazine*, January, 1942.

of the Cardinals whose offspring gave him a 3-A draft status until 1944.

In 1944, desperate owners were using players classified 4-F, those whose physical defects rendered them unfit for service. But even such a classification did not always prevent induction, as Red Ruffing discovered. Although four of his toes were missing, this thirty-eight-year-old pitching great was judged fit and was inducted in 1943. However, a host of players with all kinds of ailments remained, and the Browns' victory in 1944 was owing to the presence of eighteen 4-F's on the team. On other teams, an amazing variety of ailments kept men out of service uniforms. In Cincinnati, two infield positions were held by epileptics, and Cleveland hired a player with size 17 shoes which kept him out of the armed forces. Howie Schultz of the Dodgers was rejected as too tall; a heart murmur allowed Detroit's Hal Newhouser to become the outstanding pitcher of the era. The Yankees were able to retain infielder Stirnweiss because of ulcers which defied Army chow, while the Cardinals kept Whitey Kurowski because of his badly mangled throwing arm. Another notable 4-F'er was Pete Gray, the one-armed outfielder of the 1945 Browns. Gray batted only .218, but amazed fans with his one-handed hitting and his ability to field and throw in spite of his handicap.[10]

The Browns and Giants seemed to have a corner on the 4-F market, so other teams sought overage stars. Among the host of elderly players were such greats as the Waner brothers, Mel Harder, Al Simmons, Debs Garms, Charley Root, Pepper Martin, Hod Lisenbee, and Paul Schreiber. The latter pair of pitchers were good examples of how far back a club might reach for personnel. Lisenbee had yielded homers to Ruth in his record-breaking year of

10 *The Sporting News*, July 1, September 16, 1943, April 6, 1944.

Theodore Samuel "Ted" Williams of the Boston Red Sox ranks as one of the greatest batters in baseball history. In 1941, the twenty-three-year-old Williams batted .406 to lead the American League. To this day, no major leaguer has since topped the .400 mark in seasonal hitting. (Courtesy Boston Red Sox, American League)

1927, while Schreiber, the longtime Yankee batting-practice pitcher, found himself throwing in earnest in 1945.[11]

Meanwhile, Clark Griffith discovered a better source of talent. By combing Latin-American countries where baseball was becoming popular he discovered some good men, thus making others aware of this scarcely tapped source. The language barrier often posed a problem for these men. One of them, Roberto Estallela, developed a strange rash which resisted treatment until it was discovered that he had been eating ham and eggs three times a day for a month. Nobody had bothered to check his diet or to notice his ignorance of English that drove him to order this fare with the only words he knew.[12]

Still another source of players was found in those too young to be drafted. Usually they proved inadequate to the test of big-league baseball. Nevertheless, clubs kept trying. The Reds tried Joe Nuxhall, a fifteen-year-old fastball pitcher, who was bombed in his only start. Nuxhall later came back to the majors for a long career extending into the 1960's. Two other youngsters were slightly more successful than Nuxhall, including Rex Barney, a fast but wild pitcher, and Rogers Hornsby McKee, better known for his milk-drinking than his pitching prowess with the Athletics.[13]

By 1944 there had been a 60 per cent personnel turnover in the major leagues, and owners were forced take whatever they could get. Not surprisingly, discipline fell off. Toward the end of the war, there were ugly salary wrangles off the field and brawls and beanball battles on the field. By 1945 even patient Connie Mack complained that players were talking back to him, and Sig Jakucki, an effective pitcher for the Browns, was so unmanageable that he was dropped for his part in a memorable brawl.[14]

At this low point, owners joyfully watched the return of real players from the services. Of course, some never returned, and others like Lou Brissie bore grievous wounds from battle. Yet

[11] *Ibid.*, July 1, 1943, April 6, 1944.

[12] Interview, Lee Allen with D. Voigt.

[13] *The Sporting News*, November 6, 1942, September 16, 1943; Sketches on Nuxhall may be read in the *New York Times*, April 12, 17, 1967.

[14] *The Sporting News*, April 6, 1944, June 28, 1945.

many found an opportunity to sharpen their baseball skills in the services, including a number of stars who made the Great Lakes Naval Training Station team a powerhouse. When major-league teams played this service team, they often faced fireballing Bob Feller.[15] Naturally, such assignments drew complaints from citizens with sons on the firing lines, but *Sporting News* insisted that the ballplaying was done on off-duty time. Charges of favoritism echoed similar ones from World War I, but while they were sometimes justified, baseball did not lose face because of them. After all, in a war of modern technology, twelve million servicemen had to be fitted into many specialized assignments and only one in twelve actually saw combat action. Obviously, baseball players were not given special privileges. Most fans accepted their service records without question and welcomed them joyously when they began to trickle back in 1945.[16]

Umpires returning from service were greeted with much less enthusiasm. Apparently, few fans realized they had served too, and, if reminded of this, some seemed to assume that they had fought for the *Wehrmacht*. But the war was equally tough on umpires, and so many were drafted that baseball had to return to two-man teams. This added to the discipline problem, and led to one disgraceful incident known as the "battle of the runway," which saw a troop of White Sox battle Umpire George Moriarty.[17]

Moriarty narrowly missed being expelled for inciting this debacle.[18] But umpires were hard to come by, and the supply dried up early in the war. In 1942, higher wages in defense plants cut enrollments in umpiring schools, proof enough that umpires' salaries barely topped industrial wages. By 1945 umpires were demanding more pay. When he was asked to air complaints before Commissioner A. B. Chandler, Ernie Stewart told of frozen salaries and expense accounts that were unrealistic in wartime inflation. Stewart was fired by American League president William Harridge for

15 *Ibid.*, July 15, 1943.

16 Arthur Mann, "Baseball Reconverts," *Baseball Magazine*, June, 1946, pp. 222–23.

17 *The Sporting News*, July 29, November 4, December 30, 1943.

18 "George Moriarty," article in "Landis File," office of Baseball Commissioner.

"disloyalty," and that tired phrase so favored by petty despots, "for the best interests" of the league.[19] Because Commissioner Chandler lacked Landis's powers, Stewart's dismissal stood. The war's end found umpires in no position to use collective action against owners. And yet, like cabooses tagging after modern diesel engines, umpires drew strength from military player organizations.

Accustomed to wartime substitutes, baseball fans accepted baseball in much the same way. Because live entertainment was scarce, baseball games looked good in spite of the low caliber of the players. Moreover, extra night games proved attractive, and if the field play was dull, the byplay was not. In Brooklyn in 1945, the irrepressible Leo Durocher slugged a fan for calling him by a most uncomplimentary name. But the fan was a war vet and the ensuing legal tussle added another blemish to Durocher's reputation and led to a year's suspension for him.[20]

Some of the characters frequenting ball parks were every bit as exciting as wartime players. In Brooklyn, Hilda Chester with her cowbell reigned as queen of the bleachers. When interviewed, this loquacious middle-aged fan proved strangely tight-lipped, saying "skip it" to most personal questions, although she admitted to having played once on a bloomer girl team. In St. Louis, a woman named Mary Ott owned such a terrifying yawp that owner Breadon gave her a free pass to Cardinal games, hoping to enlist her vocal support against rivals.[21]

There was almost always gaiety at the parks, especially in Milwaukee, where the younger Veeck was completing a minor-league apprenticeship that would establish him as the foremost huckster of the postwar era. In accord with his motto, "Give 'em a gag as well as a game," Milwaukee fans were treated to free shows, including morning games with free milk and cereal, quiz games with prizes, tightrope acts, and, above all, hard-to-buy beer. In most parks, news of Allied victories was piped over loudspeakers with highlights coming in August, 1943, when Italy surrendered, and in

[19] *The Sporting News,* March 26, 1942, August 23, 1945.
[20] *Ibid.,* June 21, 1945; *Baseball Digest,* October, 1945.
[21] *The Sporting News,* April 22, June 3, 1943.

Ebbets Field, Brooklyn. Gene Mack's Hall of Fame Cartoons, Major League Ball Parks. (Copyright 1950, Gene Mack, Courtesy Eugene G. McGillicuddy, Jr., Boston Globe)

1945 with the news of Hitler's defeat and the subsequent collapse of Japan.[22]

Often, gaiety was mingled with little acts of wartime courage. At Wrigley Field in 1945, a reporter noted the brave humor of crippled soldiers who shouted, "No foul balls this way." Such sights and sounds were sobering, but were balanced by opportunities for the "innocent flirting" of soldiers and young ladies. In providing diversions to counteract the grimness of war, baseball proved its worth as a morale booster. Some observers noted less yelling, but one reporter insisted that ladies made up for it by learning to whistle male-style with their fingers in their mouths.[23]

Since violent former fans found themselves in military uniform alongside players, it was inevitable that some time some player would confront a former heckler. This happened on a New Guinea battlefield when player Morrie Arnovich met the fan who once had hit him in the face with a hot dog complete with mustard and relish. Although Arnovich had vowed to maim his tormentor, their common plight made them friends instead.[24]

Pressed for an opinion of American baseball in wartime, George Bernard Shaw, after scanning a copy of *The Sporting News,* snorted that the game was still "the great American tragedy."[25] Perhaps so, but fans of this era gave no sign of deserting the game. After attendance had slumped badly in 1942–43, it picked up sharply in 1944–45, topping all records since 1930 and rekindling hopes for a bright postwar future. That future, however, might not be much different from the past. When given a chance to air their views on the game, Browns fans urged the return of the nickel scorecard, the fifteen-cent hot dog, and the installation of more comfortable park facilities, it was hoped with glass posts and radios built into the seats. Elsewhere, broad-beamed fans requested wider seats, a request the Yankees met as soon as wartime restrictions were lifted.[26]

22 *Ibid.*, August 5, 1943.
23 *Baseball Digest*, October, 1945, p. 30.
24 *Ibid.*, April, 1951, p. 40.
25 *The Sporting News*, May 27, 1943.
26 *Ibid.*, August 5, 1943, November 23, 1944; *Baseball Digest*, April, 1946, p. 21.

Meanwhile, radio continued to indoctrinate new fans. In 1943, millions at home and overseas listened to the voice of sportscaster Red Barber describing the World Series. Although wartime radio broadcasts exaggerated the drama of the games, this was exactly what baseball needed at the time. All clubs but the Yankees stepped up radio broadcasting, thus further tying the game to the electronic age of the future. That television was soon to be a part of this future was apparent in the popularity of Dennis James's "Sports Parade" show among the handful of television set owners of this era.[27]

4. The Rise of the Hustlers

The frustrating task of promoting their clubs through a long Depression followed by four war years took the heart out of some owners. After battling falling profits, rising expenses, and discouraging conditions for so long, several bowed out. In 1939, overall profits had finally amounted to 6.9 per cent of the average gross income, the best profit-taking in a decade. But the war brought new reverses, and in 1942–43 average losses of 2.2 per cent of gross income were sustained. After that, even with an upward trend in the offing,[28] some owners were so baffled by the uncertainties of wartime promotion that they were unwilling to take a chance on the future.

A major problem of 1943 was the greatly inflated cost of equipment and services. An impoverished club like the Athletics had to spend $600 a day merely to keep the club on the road. On top of falling attendance, owners now faced a 20 per cent admission tax on each ticket along with their self-imposed duty of admitting servicemen free. Rising costs of recruitment and of ball park staffs only added to the plight of the owner. To press on under such conditions required the utmost dedication, and most owners were realists first and zealots second. Even though attendance rose in 1944, problems still seemed to outweigh opportunities.[29]

27 *The Sporting News*, May 27, June 24, October 7, 1943, October 23, 1946.

28 *Ibid.*, May 28, 1952; U.S. House of Representatives, *Organized Baseball*, pp. 1599–1600.

29 U.S. House of Representatives, *Organized Baseball*, p. 1618; *The Sporting News*, May 27, 1943, March 9, October 19, 1944, October 18, 1945; "Batter (if still there) Up!" *Newsweek*, May 3, 1943.

To meet the challenge new approaches to problems were needed, but could hardly be expected from elderly owners. Moreover, old age and death were taking their toll. By the war's end, many familiar faces were missing. Among the fallen was Ruppert, whose death left management in the hands of Barrow, with ultimate control in the hands of bank executors. Although Ruppert wanted the team to carry on in his name, this was not to be the decision of his executors. Taking note of 1945 earnings, (less than 5 per cent of total assets), they declared the club a bad investment and elected to sell. Bids were asked in 1945, at a time when the book value of the Yankees was $7,000,000. Bidders were few, however, and the club went to a syndicate headed by Del Webb, Dan Topping, and Larry MacPhail for $3,000,000. In the light of future events, this was a tremendous bargain. Although this trio laid claim to being sportsmen, they were of a far different breed from Ruppert. Rather than represent their kind of hustling enterprise, Barrow retired in 1945. Midway in 1946, McCarthy also quit. With them went the old tradition; the new owners were free to lead the club into a new era of championships and profits.[30]

Soon after this startling announcement came news of the sale of the Dodgers to a syndicate headed by Walter O'Malley. Part owner with him was Rickey, who had served since 1942 as the club's general manager. Rickey was already signing promising youths from schools and colleges and planning an extensive farm system. He also did not hesitate to trade local favorites even though he angered diehard fans. The confidence of this "baseball Merlin" was fully justified. "Wait till 1947," was his promise, and such was his efficiency that he made good. Nevertheless, he was soon to leave Brooklyn for a last stop at Pittsburgh, a club that Bill Benswanger had sold to a syndicate headed by Galbreath and Bing Crosby in 1945.[31]

While Rickey was keeping his promise to Dodger fans, his old boss Sam Breadon was selling the Cardinals to Fred Saigh and Robert Hannegan. Breadon was able to ask for and get $4,000,000

[30] "The Yankees," *loc. cit.*; U.S. House of Representatives, *Organized Baseball*, pp. 872–73; *The Sporting News*, February 1, 8, 1945.

[31] *The Sporting News*, December 30, 1943, September 19, 1944, August 16, 23, 1945.

for the club that Rickey had built. Yet when Breadon and Rickey had parted, Breadon had charged angrily that Rickey was a mere figurehead. But after the players Rickey had recruited won the 1946 pennant for the Cardinals, the team collapsed, and it took fifteen years to rebuild what Rickey had wrought.[32]

Lesser figures among the old guard were quietly slipping into oblivion. After their success of 1944, the Browns fell into their old rut and acquired a new part owner in Richard Muckerman. The health of this club was so bad that there were persistent rumors the franchise would be shifted to another city. The move was postponed until 1952, and became the first break in the solid ranks of the American League. Other clubs soon followed the example.[33]

Sick as the Browns were, in the early war years they looked healthier than the Braves or Phillies. Both teams had been badly promoted by men who made money in developing and selling players and by cutting expenses to the bone. These tactics had long been resented by other owners, and there were cheers when new owners took over. Relief for the Braves was accomplished under promoter Lou Perini. He quickly built the team into a solid contender that captured the pennant in 1948. However, Perini was a hustler who scorned tradition. When attendance sagged in the following years, he moved the team to Milwaukee in 1953, blazing a trail for other National League teams to follow.

Reform of the Phillies was achieved only after a great deal of difficulty. Mismanaged by Baker until his death in 1930, the club passed to Mr. and Mrs. Gerald Nugent, who continued Baker's practice of selling players for profit. Nugent fell into bankruptcy early in the war, and the league bought control of the club for less than $50,000, an incredibly low price. In his anxiety to put the club in firm hands, President Ford Frick acted hastily in selling to lumberman William Cox. The impetuous Cox succeeded in alienating players, fans, and fellow owners in only three months. His habit of betting on games antagonized Landis, who banished him. His successor, Robert Carpenter, a wealthy Du Pont executive, hired Herb Pennock as general manager and financed an expensive program of

32 *Ibid.*, December 28, 1949, December 27, 1950.

33 *Ibid.*, August 16, 1945.

One of the new generation of owners, William C. Bartholomay is chairman and president of the Atlanta Braves of the National League. A thrice-removed franchise, the Braves show how American baseball adjusts to meet the changing population distribution of the country. A charter member of the National League in 1876, the club was located in Boston, then shifted to Milwaukee in the 1950's and more recently located in Atlanta. (Courtesy Atlanta Braves, National League)

Robert M. Carpenter, Jr., present owner of the Philadelphia Phillies of the National League and son of a Du Pont executive, acquired the moribund franchise in the late 1940's and built a respectable contender out of what was for years the laughing-stock team of the National League. (Courtesy Philadelphia Phillies, National League)

Like Carpenter, Lou Perini rebuilt the Boston Braves into a contender and pennant winner in 1948. Prior to Perini's accession, the Braves rivaled the Phillies in futility. In the early 1950's, Perini shifted the club to Milwaukee, where the Braves landed two more pennants. More recently, Perini sold out, allowing the shift to Atlanta. (Courtesy Atlanta Braves, National League)

The late Lou Comiskey, son of the famous Charles A. Comiskey, inherited the Chicago White Sox upon the death of "The Old Roman" in the 1930's. Since the turn of the century, the Comiskey name was associated with American League baseball, but today the family no longer controls the White Sox. (Courtesy Chicago White Sox, American League)

recruiting young players that led to a pennant in 1950. Dazzled by Carpenter's enterprise, Philadelphia fans deserted the lackluster Athletics. In 1954, the franchise Mack had fostered was transferred to Kansas City.[34] By then, the nonagenarian manager had retired, but he lived long enough to see the collapse of the baseball world he and Griffith had built. At least Griffith was spared the pain of watching his lifework evaporate. In just a few years after his death, his club was uprooted and transferred to the twin cities of Minneapolis and St. Paul.[35]

This ruthless willingness to uproot traditional franchises and transplant them in more promising sites was a hallmark of the hustling new promoter. But this was only one of many characteristics. Usually, the newcomer shared ownership with others in a syndicate. Like his associates, he knew about tax loopholes and regarded his baseball investment as a device for "writing off" profits gained from other business ventures. He willingly spent to build the club, because he recognized the profit potentials in such sidelines as night baseball and sale of television rights. Like all owners since 1871, the newcomer loved money, but he was likely to admit the fact. Because he did so openly, fans and players began to look on the game as a commercialized entertainment industry first, and a sport second. This was by no means a new point of view, but its nonchalant acceptance was. The spread of the attitude led Congress, in 1951 and 1957, to reopen the question of baseball's status under antitrust laws.

It would be presumptuous to judge the hustling new breed of owners as bad for baseball. Certainly, they were not robber barons or money-grubbing opportunists. They were, instead, the modern version of the old gentlemen-owners, products of new shaping forces such as changing tax laws and management and advertising techniques. Each in his own way was interested in baseball and its growth as a commercial spectacle, but their methods often irked tradition-bound fans.[36]

[34] *Ibid.*, February 18, 25, July 15, December 2, 1943; *Baseball Digest*, November, 1950, pp. 93–94, August, 1956, p. 22; Lieb and Baumgartner, *op. cit.*, 182–200.

[35] *The Sporting News*, October 18, 1950. Mack "retired" in 1950.

Of course, fans seldom met the new entrepreneurs, for most of them remained aloof and delegated authority to experts. Bill Veeck, Jr., was an exception. While working for Wrigley as a youth, Veeck had learned much about baseball promotion. When a serious leg wound sent him home from the war unfit for further service with the Marines, Veeck acquired the minor-league Milwaukee Brewers. The club prospered under his leadership, earning him a clear $250,000 when he sold out in 1945.

Veeck was eager for a try with the majors, and in 1946 he scouted available franchises. After trying unsuccessfully to acquire the White Sox or the Pirates, he moved on Cleveland, a sleepy franchise ostensibly owned by Alva Bradley. After some investigation, Veeck learned that Bradley was only a minor stockholder and that the majority were receptive to a good offer. Veeck moved swiftly to use the favorable credit rating and the goodwill that had accrued to him from his father's friends and his Milwaukee venture. In a short time, he fashioned a syndicate of two bank presidents and two meat packing heirs. He persuaded his backers to invest in what he called a "debenture common stock grouping." This was admittedly a means of avoiding taxes in that it allowed investors to claim their investments as a loan rather than as stock holdings although each kept his rights as a stockholder. As organizer of the scheme, the hustling Veeck invested $250,000, and acquired 30 per cent of the stock, enough to control the club. With a thirty-day option to buy, Veeck's syndicate narrowly beat the deadline and wrested the club from an angry Bradley.

Now came the tough job of winning new fans and stimulating the old ones accustomed to years of pinchpenny operations who were still denied radio broadcasts of games. It was a challenge Veeck welcomed, and to read his two books is to sense how much this hustler loved every minute of it. In his own words: "Most of all, we showed the fans that we weren't just out for the money, that we cared about them and wanted them to have a good time." Veeck backed up the words with deeds. Convinced that most fans were working-class entertainment-seekers with unsophisticated

[36] *Ibid.*, November 25, 1943, January 20, November 23, 1944, January 11, February 8, December 6, 1945, January 10 1946.

tastes, Veeck offered a variety of amusing gimmicks. A typical Veeck offering was a night ball game with plenty of beer for sale and many free attractions like fireworks, prize nights, giveaways, and such extras as a red jeep for delivering relief pitchers to the mound. He saw women as potential baseball zealots, and catered to them shamelessly, using nylons, orchids, and a free baby-sitting service as lures.

Such gimmicks added to his costs, but Veeck expected to make more money from volume attendance. That he did was evidenced by his attendance records. Under Veeck, Cleveland in 1948 set a new attendance record for a single game and a new seasonal attendance record. Concession sales of food and drink figured in his scheme, and his careful attention to such details swelled profits.

Perhaps Veeck was too much of a hustler. At any rate, he made enemies among other owners who charged him with debasing the game. Indeed, some of his devices, like moving the fences and landscaping the field to suit his team, made their charges reasonable. But before Veeck's time, few owners ever personally checked toilets or wandered about talking leisurely with fans, ever alert for new ideas. Nor did any attend so many civic affairs or support more local charities and causes. But because his methods and personality offended many and because he lacked the fortune to maintain his control, he was obliged to sell out at the peak of his success in 1948. According to him, a divorce settlement was the real cause. After that, his career took him on to a brief stint with the Browns and to a pennant with the Chicago White Sox. On both occasions, however, opposition to his policies forced him out. Yet his opponents did him honor by imitating many of his tactics, thereby acclaiming this appealing huckster as a modern pioneer in present-day methods of promotion. A living legend today, Veeck may well be waiting to strike again by seizing control of a club and hustling it to fame and profit. Meanwhile, he serves as a model of the hustling style of managerial enterprise.[37]

[37] "Bill Veeck and the Cleveland Indians" *Business Week*, October 2, 1948; Veeck and Linn, *Veeck as in Wreck*, 76–93, 116–31; Veeck and Linn, *Hustler's Handbook*, 1–33; *The Sporting News*, November 21, 1941, July 3, 1946.

III. *The Dawn of the Plastic Age*

1

Mid-century Upheaval

1. In Search of a New Equilibrium

After four long years of groping through the maze of war, baseball men suddenly found themselves in a new era signalled by the two atomic bombs detonated over the Japanese cities of Hiroshima and Nagasaki. So unfamiliar seem its landmarks, so challenging its opportunities and perils, that it baffles our understanding to this day.

To know its patterns and demands are the tasks of a host of physical and social scientists. By our common consent, these scientists serve as our guides to this new age. Americans have long idolized scientists, but never before did we honor them so much or expect so much from them.

Because scientific training demands the discipline and knowledge of higher education, Americans in unprecedented numbers entered colleges and graduate schools in search of scientific credentials, and, it was hoped, knowledge. The *leitmotiv* of American life in the new age is a passionate faith in higher education, especially scientific training. In a real sense, our people now believe that civilization is man's own show and that with the proper scientific expertise any problem is solvable.

Nobody would deny that postwar America offered plenty of unsolved problems. Probably this very mania for knowledge makes us look for problems. At any rate, it barred us from celebrating for long the triumph of our arms in World War II. Rather, we took our new position as a big power seriously, spending huge sums of money trying to revitalize allies, neutralize conquered enemies, and thwart what we defined as the evil designs of our recent cobelligerent, Soviet Russia.

Although no nation in history ever succeeded in keeping the world's peace for long, we thought we could. But our utopian dreams have evaporated under the realities of practical diplomacy. Perhaps hardest to take was the loss of feelings of innocence, for the era of the "cold war" thrust us into global rivalry with Soviet Russia for prestige and power. Since 1945, no year has passed without some saber-rattling incident, and sometimes, as in Korea and Viet Nam, there were hot brushfire wars, maddening to Americans because they offered no victory in the traditional sense.

A major outcome of our great global involvement was the ongoing centralization of our government. Not that this was new, for depression and war only accelerated trends which had been afoot since the Civil War and earlier. Nor were its consequences necessarily frightening. Indeed, if we had been less concerned with problems, we might have taken smug pride in the fact that no nation ever went through such a costly war and emerged so prosperous. Since 1943, the specter of mass unemployment has seemingly all but vanished, and except for brief recessions no longer poses a threat to national morale. In place of the old depression psychology was a new spirit of optimism, a faith in continuing growth for our new industrial state. This optimism had some foundation, since statistics showed that only eighteen million families in 1945 had incomes of less than $3,000 a year. This meant that an overwhelming majority had incomes that guaranteed a comfortable life. In 1947, 62 per cent had incomes above $4,000, a healthy majority that increased to 77 per cent by 1960.[1] For this unprecedented improvement in human comfort, the central government was much responsible, as it continued to pour money into projects that expanded industrial and commercial opportunities.

A student of world economic conditions once said that there is nothing harder to take than a reversal of a people's standard of living.[2] Certainly, Americans believe this, for we seem to have made a fetish of the annual increase in our Gross National Product. Each year this figure must advance lest we fail to keep faith with our national religion of dynamic abundance and material progress. To insure this "progress," we expect the national government to stimulate the economy. The distribution of federal tax money for scientific and technological research, for education, for civic betterment, and a variety of other projects has elevated the national government to the position of economic arbiter of our lives.

From this has come a revolution in the expectations of all Americans, with no sizable group willing to take less than a fair share of the fruits of affluence. For each group to get its share requires organization, and people have learned to band together to pressure lawmakers. In 1946, labor groups, after gaining strength and recognition under New Deal policies, tested their power in a series of strikes which won sizable pay increases. These in turn triggered rising prices which led to more pay demands. The continuing round worked to maintain spiraling prosperity while convincing other groups that the "union ethic" was a sure way to affluence. By now, pressure groups were everywhere and were learning tactics from labor, farmers, professionals, retailers, and industrialists. The wielding of power became a fact of life in this age. As sociologist Robert S. Lynd put it: "We live in an era in which only organization counts; values and causes with unorganized or only vaguely organized backing were never so impotent."[3]

1 Murray Gendell and Hans L. Zetterberg, *A Sociological Almanac for the United States*, 70; Frederick Lewis Allen, *The Big Change*, 150–55.

2 Melville J. Herskovits, *Economic Anthropology*, Ch. 1.

3 Gendell and Zetterberg, *op. cit.*, 9.

It was a lesson that downtrodden minorities were learning well. This was especially true of American Negroes. During the Depression and war, their leaders learned to wield the "union ethic" to advantage. After gaining the rights of other jobless during the New Deal, they persuaded President Roosevelt to insure equal access to defense jobs during the war. Such concessions hastened the barring of discrimination from the military service, the U.S. Civil Service, and federally sponsored work projects. The taste of victories led to new aspirations and demands, including equal participation in education, housing, and consumer goods, and the right to share in decision-making. By the mid-1950's, the words "black power" were heard for the first time, and soon they became a rallying cry for twenty million deprived Americans and a challenge of awesome implication to American unity. Not without reason did Professor Baltzell judge the confrontation between the white and colored peoples of our land as the most significant problem of the time.[4]

Of course, other social critics had their candidates for the worst problem of the day. A leading headliner was the cold war confrontation with Communist powers that forced the continuation of the military draft. Other contenders included the spread of big government, the influence of gigantic business corporations, the changing American "city," the character of affluence, the decline of traditional religion, and our polluted environment.

For baseball promoters, as for all Americans, the challenge was to grab the rewards while warding off the dangers. Baseball men were especially concerned with a relative newcomer to the American list of problems. Given the optimistic title of "America's Leisure Revolution," this one took note of the changing nature of American work. Under new techniques of applied science and technology such as automation and cybernetics, work underwent drastic modification in this age. If in the past Americans accepted long hours of work as necessary for livelihood and heavenly grace, work was now regarded as necessary to earn money for fun. A dangerous attitude perhaps, but it should be remembered that in no age has

[4] E. Digby Baltzell, *The Protestant Establishment*, Preface.

work been fun for most. And in this age of specialization and machinofacture it is possible that work becomes more boring. True, there were now more "maximizers," as the late Jules Henry called those whose work gives a deep sense of fulfillment.[5] But most American workers were not maximizers.

For the majority of nonmaximizers, fulfillment came from spending money earned at work in one's "free time." And while much of this time was tied up with home and family, there was plenty left for fun. New commercial outlets sprang up to sell fun to Americans. Most popular was television, that stepchild of the radio age, which grew so fast that by 1950 most Americans were ogling its offerings. Like the bicycle, auto, movie, and radio crazes of past eras, this one frightened baseball men. But so did the rise of other leisure attractions. Indeed, by 1950 Americans were tempted by the greatest variety of participant and spectator leisure offerings in human history. For active participants there was a proliferation of golf courses, bowling alleys, and many other activities that threatened to tempt leisure worshipers away from baseball. The new outdoor spectacles were even more menacing. Horse racing towered above all, but professional football, basketball, hockey, and soccer, all organized after baseball's pattern of American and National leagues, posed greater threats to baseball's pre-eminence. Today, all of these overlap the baseball season, and soccer and professional golf pose direct confrontations.[6]

Fortunately for baseball, many of its owners were pragmatic and tough-minded men of action. It was a time when commitment to past traditions might have been fatal to successful competition. Yet, given a sense of history, any promoter should have smelled opportunity in this age. After all, the aftermath of past American wars always provided lucrative opportunities for baseball. The post–Civil War era first opened up commercial opportunities for the game, and the end of the Spanish-American War saw the creation of the two-league system which provided half a century of

[5] Jules Henry, *Culture Against Man, passim.*

[6] Sebastian de Grazia, *Of Time, Work, and Leisure*, 56–182; "The Golden Age of Sport," *Time*, June 2, 1967; "Working More, Sleeping Less," *ibid.*, September 8, 1967.

equilibrium. And who can forget how the post–World War I era kindled such a great revival in the game? While it is foolish to assume history must repeat itself, it was reasonable enough to assume that commercial baseball would be flexible enough to claim a large share of the affluence of this age. Time would show that baseball would share the rewards of affluence, and also the defeats and frustrations that went with the problems of this age.

2. New Opportunities for Baseball

Like most Americans in 1946, baseball operators were unaware that they were entering a new era. They can be forgiven for this, since their world looked much the same as it had before the war. That spring, the training camps were crowded with familiar faces newly separated from the services. So swollen were rosters that most clubs had sixty or more proven performers to choose from. Some were overflowing with talent, like the Phillies with thirty pitchers and sixteen infielders or the Tigers with nineteen outfielders.[7] As managers pored over past records of these prospects, pennant hopes mounted. Some players had been badly shot up and were limping, but many seemed hale and eager to show their stuff. As one prewar slugger put it: "The desire to play baseball is an indestructible thing. . . . It's a form of hunger. . . . The ex-servicemen are so hungry to get back into a lineup that they'll try to give far beyond their normal ability. . . . Because of this, big-league lineups, I think, will be essentially prewar stuff."[8]

These were brave words, but unfortunately too many returnees were unequal to them. As the season wore on, it became clear that many could not regain big-league form. In general, youngsters on the way up did better than old-timers who found the ordeal of relearning most difficult.[9] The great surpluses of players vanished as many called it quits; some retired, some went to the minors, and a few chanced the outlawed Mexican League. Such losses worried some owners, but few despaired, since newly revived farm systems

[7] *Baseball Digest*, April, 1946, pp. 25–40.

[8] Arthur Mann, "Baseball Reconverts," *loc. cit.*; *The Sporting News*, October 25, 1945.

[9] Mann, "Baseball Reconverts," *loc. cit.*

THE WHITE SOX
All Time All Star Team
as selected by Chicago baseball fans
August 10, 1954
Joe Kuhel
Eddie Collins
Second baseman (1915-'26)
Luke Appling
Shortstop (1930-'50)
Willie Kamm
Third baseman (1923-'31)
Johnny Mostil
Outfielder (1918-'29)
"Red" Faber
Pitcher (1914-'33)
Al Simmons
Outfielder (1933-'35)
Ted Lyons
Pitcher (1923-'46)
Orestes Minoso
Outfielder (1951-)

were counted on for furnishing young talent. With youth at a premium now, owners were determined to prevent Rickey from cornering the market, and many of them began paying high bonuses for promising high school and college talent.

Some of the veterans performed brilliantly, however. In 1946, Ted Williams led the Red Sox to a twelve-game victory over the Tigers. The Cardinals, paced by Stan Musial, outlasted the Dodgers in a thrilling playoff duel after the two clubs tied for the regular season. Boston lost the World Series, but American League fans drew comfort from the apparent eclipse of the Yankees. Their 1946 season was disappointing; poor performances from veterans were compounded by front-office tensions between owners and the field manager. In midseason, McCarthy quit, and when Bill Dickey failed to spark the team, he was replaced. The season's end found the club foundering, allowing rivals to assume that the Yankee tyranny was ended.[10]

It did not end and was one of the few prewar baseball patterns to survive this age of change. In 1947, under manager Bucky Harris, the Yankee veterans came to life and tore the league apart, then crushed the Dodgers in the Series. That year, the only loser was President MacPhail, McCarthy's nemesis, whose indiscretions led to his ouster. But the next year Harris was fired for losing to the Cleveland Indians. He was replaced by Casey Stengel, who drove the club to a dramatic victory over the Red Sox in 1949, then to a Series triumph over the Dodgers. Thus began the new age of the Yankees, an unprecedented tyranny that produced five consecutive league and Series championships by 1953. After losing to Cleveland in 1954, Stengel led another four-year rampage before bowing to Chicago in 1959. Not until 1965 did the Yankee terror end; then, like the wonderful one-hoss shay, it fell apart, "all at once and nothing first."[11]

Altogether, the Yankee tyranny paralyzed American League

[10] *The Sporting News*, June 5, 1946.

[11] *Baseball Digest*, September, 1947, pp. 25–26, March, 1951, pp. 62–63, March, 1954, pp. 11–13, February, 1957, p. 54, February, 1959, p. 30; Leonard Koppett, "A Yankee Dynasty Can Never Come Back," *New York Times Magazine*, October 2, 1966.

Charles D. "Casey" Stengel directed his Yankee platoons from his command post in the home dugout at Yankee Stadium. The most victorious manager in major league history, Stengel led his Yankee teams to five consecutive pennants and five World Championships in the years 1949–53. (Courtesy New York Yankees, American League)

rivals for two decades. All challengers looked impotent, and the annual submission made the whole league seem inferior. In the National League the Dodgers also posed a dynastic threat, but rivals crashed through often enough to keep fans interested. Even though the Yankees usually won the Series, the other test of inter-league strength, the All-Star game, more often went to the Nationals. For this reason, and because the National had a better distribution of stars, the National League by 1956 was touted as superior to the American. Certainly this was a departure from the golden age, when the Cardinals alone upheld the National shield.[12]

Superstars like DiMaggio, Williams, Musial, Mickey Mantle, Willie Mays, and Sandy Koufax drew salaries of over $100,000, and their batting, fielding, and pitching matched or surpassed golden age performances. Nevertheless, for several reasons, old qualities were missing in the new heroes. For one, there were so few of them that the breed seemed on the verge of extinction. For another, their personalities were rather dull, and none had the radiance of a Cobb or a Ruth. Third, Negro stars like Mays labored under the public's unwillingness to identify with them. Finally, the new superstars saw themselves as professionals doing a job, and the lucrative investment of their earnings ranked high in their scheme of things.[13]

Of course there were colorful moments. Before retiring, the great DiMaggio married the movie sex goddess, Marilyn Monroe. Asked for his impressions, the groom quipped, "It beats rooming with Joe Page!" But this was a peak for this taciturn star. Williams feuded with reporters and fans and several times spat in the general direction of the stands.[14] Decorum aside, it was an honest expression of disdain for the limelight and of Williams's unwillingness to play the public demigod. Like organized American religion, baseball also faced the death of its gods. One of them, Babe Ruth, passed on in 1948 leaving no successor.

[12] *Baseball Digest*, September, 1956, pp. 49–50, May, 1947, pp. 15–16.

[13] *Ibid.*, April, 1951, pp. 15–16 (DiMaggio); *ibid.*, November, 1946, pp. 17–22, October, 1952, pp. 35–39 (Musial); *ibid.*, July, 1958, pp. 5–10 (Warren Spahn); *ibid.*, October, 1956, p. 41 (Mantle); *The Sporting News*, October 29, 1958 (Williams); *New York Times*, August 21, 1966 (Mays).

The same dullness also characterized lesser stars, and some critics wondered if baseball was reflecting the general trend of the times toward nonheroes. Some blamed television for exposing promising heroes too quickly, then discarding them as the next promising candidate came along. But the main reason baseball heroes shone so briefly on television was that the medium drew on an enormous reservoir of competent celebrities from the entertainment world. There were also changes in playing style that worked against the establishment of heroes. The shuffling of players in and out of lineups as strategy dictated in the platoon system completed the trend of making part-time specialists out of players. Not that this trend necessarily hurt playing careers, for a pinch-hitting specialist like Forrest "Smoky" Burgess extended his career through twenty years by his timely services.[15] Pitching was also highly specialized, with "long men" like Jim Brosnan summoned from the bullpen for several innings of work, and "short men" like Joe Page summoned for a few innings of blazing speed. Pitchers mastered new deliveries like the slider and knuckle ball or smuggled in the tabooed "spitter," and batting fell off sharply. Homers still dominated, however, although the whiplike bats now used also made for easier outs, enabling pitchers to regain their old mastery over batters.[16]

Many players now saw themselves as workers and seemed more interested in money and pensions. Some observers worried about the lack of color, wondering if a return to "the drunks of yesteryear" would help. Implicit was the idea that players ought not to be interested in respectability, college, marriage, or romping with their children. But most players wanted all of these, and one of the most literate, Brosnan, defended their attitudes, saying, "ballplayers resent being scapegoats, symbols, and story-material rather than normal men with a little extra athletic talent. Some even claim that ballplayers are human."[17]

[14] Ted Williams and John Underwood, "Hitting Was My Life," *Sports Illustrated*, June 24, 1968.

[15] William Furlong, "How Specialized Can You Get?" *New York Times Magazine*, August 14, 1966.

[16] *New York Times*, December 1, 1967, March 21, 1968; On the "slider," see *Baseball Digest*, June, 1956, pp. 71–72, July, 1959, p. 18.

[17] Jim Brosnan, *The Long Season*, 160.

Not many of the fans complained about the game's dullness or the bourgeois habits of its players. Perhaps they were becoming accustomed to a new type of American hero who minded his business, did his job, and took his share of victories and defeats. The type was everywhere—in literature, television, magazines, and movies. A new type was also emerging, the modern antihero whose ludicrous failures in crucial situations evoked a certain black humor. Baseball had its share of these, including a whole team of New York Mets. This product of baseball's expansion program titillated fans with the variety and extent of its ineptitude and produced that symbol of futility, "Marvelous Marvin" Throneberry.[18]

For seven long years of baseball famine, Mets fans turned out in record numbers, cheerfully enduring each losing campaign. Then came 1969, and the suddenly successful Mets won the league pennant, following it with a dazzling victory over the favored American League Orioles in the World Series. In their outburst of joy, the fans tore up the sod of Shea Stadium field on two occasions, and later drowned New York in the greatest blizzard of ticker tape since the end of World War II.

The same forces that made specialist-heroes out of players made specialist-villains out of umpires. By the late 1950's, most of the fiery individualists had retired, replaced now by graduates of umpire schools.[19] Apprenticed in the minors and carefully groomed, they worked on four-man teams in the majors, with six on hand at a World Series. Their very numbers made individuals less visible, and since each man shifted daily from one vantage point to another, there was less likelihood that he would be singled out as

[18] "On the Difficulty of Being a Contemporary Hero," *Time*, June 24, 1966; "The Vulnerable Star," *New York Times*, April 14, 1965; Veeck and Linn, *Hustler's Handbook*, ch. 6; *Baseball Digest*, October, 1953, pp. 73–74.

[19] *The Sporting News*, May 11, 1949; Jocko Conlan and Robert Creamer, "Nobody Loves an Umpire," *Sports Illustrated*, June 26, 1965.

Mickey Mantle, star outfielder of the New York Yankees, retired in 1969 after hitting 536 home runs in eighteen seasons. A superstar in the Yankee tradition of Ruth and DiMaggio, he wrote the last glorious chapter in the forty years of Yankee dominance. (Courtesy New York Yankees, American League)

a scapegoat. Their existence was still far from utopian, however, for they still heard curses, ritualized boos, and exasperating comments on their judgments. Television added a new problem, since viewers sometimes called in their protests on decisions.

Nevertheless, under rising salaries, pension rights, and Series checks amounting to $5,000 by the 1960's, working conditions improved handsomely.[20] By any standard, umpiring was now a choice profession. Jobs were eagerly sought by aspirants, including those who had been traditionally barred by discriminatory practices. As Negro-Americans gained rights under antidiscrimination laws, baseball leaders were forced to include them as candidates. Negro fans and players were now so much a part of the baseball scene that the first Negro umpire joined the big leagues in the 1960's with little fanfare. The prospect of female umpires brought anguish to otherwise hardened officials. Although the cry of "play ball" has yet to be sounded in soprano, a suit now pending against organized baseball suggests that the day is not far off. The suit is being brought by a comely aspirant, a *magna cum laude* graduate of an umpiring school, who seeks to prove her mettle and admits only to the tricky problem of finding an adequate chest protector.[21]

In the years after the war, baseball crowds became predominantly family gatherings, united by the ethic of "togetherness" in their fun-seeking. Television pushed the trend by bombarding families with ball games in the summertime. Molded by television and bound by togetherness, the new breed of fans demanded and won comforts and pleasures from promoters. To meet their demands, a variety of extras were provided, including neatly packaged food, canned music, and giveaways. Food and drink sales now rivaled ticket sales in revenue production. Concessionaires no longer shoved an uncovered hot dog down rows of sweaty hands to an intended receiver. This classic lunch joined with a variety of popular foods, all prewrapped in plastic, at a much higher price. Music also became a packaged part of the scene as songs blared forth at

[20] Hy Gittlitz, *Don't Kill the Umpire*, 6–28, 78–159.

[21] *Reading Eagle*, April 17, 1968; Joseph Durso, "Emmet the Great," *New York Times*, August 21, 1966.

every break, with fans being asked to sing along. Most popular of the "giveaways" were the free bats, balls, caps, and helmets given to youngsters on special days, provided they were accompanied by a paying adult.

An added stimulus to this family outing atmosphere was provided by trick scoreboards which spelled out birthday announcements and other folksy greetings. These could lead to occasional embarrassment, however, as a Dodger staff member learned. When the engagement of a young lady was announced at her request, her parents and the intended groom were shocked. As a Dodger official sadly summed up the incident, "How did we know that she was pregnant?"[22]

The carnival atmosphere evoked outcries from purists who claimed that the game was being prostituted. It did seem at times that the game had been lost amidst the sideshows. Occasionally, writers sought to measure the effects of the changes on fans. Their questions, however, had little relevance in the cheaper seats or "bleachers," now the last preserve of traditional male fans who passed the day sunning, betting, and debating the fine points of the game in traditional Anglo-Saxon speech.[23]

All indications suggested that this sector was a vanishing part of the baseball scene. Hustling owners were devoting practically all their efforts to family fans and their pocketbooks. If such fans liked night games, doubleheaders, or air-conditioned domed stadia, promoters began thinking about some publicly financed scheme of getting such accommodations. A 1967 survey sponsored by the Commissioner revealed that fans like all these and that they did not care if games dragged on for two and one-half hours.[24]

Before 1946, a combined major-league annual attendance of 10 million paying fans was considered marvelous. But in 1946 18.5 million fans jammed the parks. This fantastic upsurge dwarfed all

[22] Charles Einstein, "The New Breed of Baseball Fan," *Harper's*, July, 1967.

[23] William Furlong, "Out in the Bleachers Where the Action Is," *New York Times Magazine*, July, 1967; Larry Merchant, "The Bleachers," *New York Post*, August 1, 1967.

[24] *New York Times*, January 22, 1967; The more scientific Lou Harris poll reaches roughly the same conclusion. See *New York Post*, July 11, 1967.

previous records. Moreover, the trend was to continue. The 1946 record was followed by five years of soaring attendance as 19.8 million came in 1947, 20.8 million in 1948, 20.2 million in 1949, 17 million in 1950, and 16 million in 1951. Although these were followed by five years when attendance was less than 16 million, the increase was enough to convert most club owners to the hustling ethic. Even during the so-called "famine" years, television contracts brought extra income into every club treasury.[25]

As usual, profits were unequally distributed among the teams, but no longer did a have-not club have to endure this status indefinitely. Owners won the right to move a lackluster franchise to a more promising urban area. Among the first to decamp were the Browns, Braves, and Athletics, and when each of these banked unprecedented profits, others followed. Naturally, these moves shocked traditionalists, but the loudest outcry came from New York when the Dodgers and Giants departed for Los Angeles and San Francisco in the late 1950's. The owners of both clubs defended their actions by arguing that the game must go national to keep up with population trends and to convince Congressional probers that the game was no monopoly. At the same time, they made it clear that profit was the key motive. They pointed out that each new site offered a capacious, publicly financed stadium, vitally important for comfort-seeking fans and quite beyond the resources of private capital in an age of skyrocketing prices.

Such candor only increased the complaints of some outraged fans and writers, but they failed to stir up any organized opposition. On the contrary, the ease with which all moves were accomplished and the resulting profits convinced owners that the time was ripe for a more dramatic break with the past. In the 1960's, each league added two new franchises, an expansion that made major-league baseball for the first time a truly national structure, with teams located in every section of the mainland United States. In 1969, both leagues began to operate with twelve clubs sub-

[25] *The Sporting News*, April 25, June 12, 1946; U.S. House of Representatives, *Organized Baseball*, pp. 1617–18; U.S. House of Representatives, *Organized Professional Team Sports*, p. 2442.

divided into two six-team sections in each league.[26] Serious consideration is also being given to locating teams in Hawaii and Japan.

Not the least of the postwar changes in baseball was the passing of conservative leadership in league councils. Landis's death in 1944 paved the way for more flexible leadership, for it is certain that his policies would have stalled the hustlers. His death relieved owners of what they felt were unwarranted intrusions, and they now took steps to insure that no successor would wield comparable power. When Landis's immediate successor, Senator A. B. Chandler, showed signs of assuming dictatorial powers, his contract was allowed to lapse. After a brief interregnum with no commissioner, Ford Frick, a supporter of expansion, was given the job. The post became a ceremonial one, with Frick limiting himself to administrative tasks and providing baseball with a respectable image in the press and mass media.

The league presidencies had long been rendered ineffectual, and no one since the time of Johnson or Heydler had any hope of opposing the owners. With full power and decision-making in the hands of hustling owners, changes came rapidly. Although damned as carpetbaggers and robber-barons, the new owners were not to be compared with their counterparts of baseball's feudal age. Instead, they worked together as an effective board of directors, treating American baseball as if it were an interstate corporation. In general, their actions have been circumspect and successful in tailoring the game to fit a fast-changing society.[27]

3. New Problems for Baseball

Hard-bitten pragmatists that they were, baseball men could have profited from reading a two-thousand-year-old injunction by Sophocles: "And ever shall this law hold good, nothing that is vast enters the life of mortals without a curse." Owners who knew this would have expected their opportunties to be matched by a fair

[26] *New York Times*, June 9, 1957, 12E, August 11, 1963, December 3, 1967, April 28, 1968; On the high cost of stadia, see *Sports Illustrated*, May 20, 1968; *Baseball Digest*, July, 1958, pp. 64–68; Vincent X. Flaherty, "Miracle Move of the Dodgers—From Flatbush to Fantasia," *Baseball Register*, 1960, pp. 3–21.

[27] Red Smith, "The Fabulous Invalid," *Baseball Digest*, January-February, 1957, p. 29–30.

share of problems and tribulations. They would know that they had to cope with the problems of the knowledge revolution, of cold war, of big government, of economic growth, of rising expectations of players, of threats to America's internal security, and of the leisure revolution. To describe in detail the impact of all these problems on baseball would take another book. They can only be sketched here.

All of these problems are linked in complicated functional relationships. The knowledge revolution, for example, is tied in with many related problems, all stemming from the great American mania for formal learning and certified wisdom.[28] A logical development of our faith in science, this revolution was fostered by the G. I. Bill of Rights, which sent millions of men to colleges and graduate schools in search of the certificates that would qualify them for professional careers. Since former servicemen were getting college degrees in great numbers, American youth began to take for granted the idea of four more years of study, thereby making the knowledge industry the nation's most viable new enterprise.

This new trend played havoc with baseball recruitment. More than any other factor, the rush to colleges reduced baseball's huge talent surplus of 1946.[29] And this was only the short-term result. Because college graduates won good jobs in expanding fields, interest in baseball careers flagged. By the 1950's, promoters had to offer lavish bonuses and scholarships to lure promising high school and college players into the majors. By the 1960's, all clubs participated in a common draft of scholastic stars, making Landis's old dream come true in a way he could never have foreseen. Once drafted, interested youths usually claimed bonuses and were assigned to minor-league teams for seasoning.[30]

The American mania for higher education also struck a new blow at the minor leagues, long regarded as the sick man of the baseball world. Ravaged by depression and war, the minors rallied in 1946, then relapsed under the onslaughts of television, radio,

[28] Christopher Jencks and David Riesman, *The Academic Revolution*, *passim.*

[29] Alfred Andreano, *No Joy in Mudville*, 126–30.

[30] *New York Times*, February 28, June 9, 1965; *Baseball Digest*, March, 1951, p. 46, August, 1967, pp. 67–74; *The Sporting News*, November 5, 1931.

and the knowledge revolution. By bringing broadcasts of major-league games into smaller towns, the media had already killed much of the local interest in minor-league teams. In the words of one sports editor, "Let's face it, the fans are tuned to the majors these days, not the minors."[31]

Nevertheless, the minors were needed as training centers and so they were kept alive in spite of annual losses and skimpy public interest. The major leagues now paid the minors' bills and shouldered their losses, which was only just, since it was the majors' greed for radio and television revenue that had deepened their problems.

However, one man's misery is often another's opportunity. While baseball owners were cursing the minors as a profitless wasteland, a new breed of baseball aspirants was using them as a gateway to the promised land of the majors. These were American Negro players. Traditionally barred from the majors by a long-standing "gentleman's agreement" of incredible solidarity, Negro players had been forced to play in segregated leagues. Even outstanding stars like LeRoy "Satchel" Paige were barred by the Jim Crow policy of the majors.[32]

After almost one hundred years of exclusion, the thaw came in 1946. It was partly a product of growing knowledge which exploded myths of Negro ineptitude and inferiority, and partly a product of rising Negro demands. Like most Americans, Negroes wanted an equal share of the benefits of the new industrial society and asked for the unimpeded right to get and spend their dollars. Now, more Negroes than ever had dollars to spend as they chose, and hustling baseball promoters determined to tap them. As early as 1943, Bill Veeck, Jr., tried to purchase the moribund Phillies and to build the team with men like Paige, but he was warned off by Landis and Frick.[33]

Something more than avarice or altruism was behind baseball's decision to swing open its doors to black players in 1946. Not to

[31] J. Anthony Lukas, "Down and Out in the Minor Leagues," *Harper's* June, 1968, p. 74.

[32] Leroy (Satchel) Paige and David Lipman, *Maybe I'll Pitch Forever*, 1–13, 57–77, 243–45.

[33] Veeck and Linn, *Veeck As in Wreck*, 174–96.

LeRoy "Satchel" Paige, one of the greatest pitchers in baseball history, warms up for the 1968 Atlanta Braves of the National League. In that year, Atlanta reactivated the sixty-year-old (some say seventy) Paige in order to qualify him for a league pension.

have done so at that time would have violated antidiscrimination laws, soon to be backed by federal court decisions. Furthermore, with middle-class white youth spurning baseball careers, Negro players represented a valuable source of replenishment for the game. Nonetheless, owners feared to use too many black players lest prejudiced fans accused them of selling out to Negroes. This racist rationale prompted owners to disperse black players lightly around the majors; there were just enough to make baseball appeal to urbanized Negro fans without offending white sensitivities.

In effect, baseball operators were still demanding that Negro aspirants "prove" their fitness for equality by running a gauntlet of suspicious fans and players. In 1946, Rickey chose Jackie Robinson, a college graduate and brilliant infielder, as a test case. After being counseled by Rickey about the necessity of turning both cheeks to insult or injury, Robinson spent a year at Montreal and then joined the Dodgers in 1947. He was an immediate success, vindicating Rickey's judgment and blazing the trail for other "selected" Negroes to follow. Rickey was hailed as an "emancipator," while other baseball men accepted plaudits for granting what had always been a legal and moral right. Even with the patronizing condescension that marked their entry into the majors, Negro

Barred by "gentleman's agreement," Paige waited until 1948 for a chance to play in the majors. Prior to that time, beginning in 1929, he played year-long baseball with black teams, once pitching 153 games in a single year. (Courtesy, Atlanta Braves, National League)

players welcomed the chance for a share of major-league cash and glory.[34]

Hard after Robinson came others. Veeck brought in Satchel Paige, Larry Doby, and Luke Easter, and other promoters followed his example. It was not easy going at first. Robinson had to endure several years of vicious insults from both fans and players. Indeed, the Dodgers were obliged to move their spring training camp from the American south to Cuba, but eventually the presence of Negro players on most teams, together with more antidiscrimination laws, forced southern cities to comply with the trend.[35]

By the 1960's, more than one hundred Negro players had joined the majors, but subtle discriminatory practices hung on. Although black players are no longer screened as Robinson was, existing quota systems paradoxically demand that to be equal to a white player a black player must be better.

A recent sociological study has shown that Negro pitchers maintain consistently better averages than white ones and that Negro batters generally hit harder and for higher averages than do whites.

[34] *The Sporting News*, April 12 (Ives-Quinn Act, New York State antidiscrimination law), October 14, 1945, March 28, October 30, 1946; For the Powell incident, see *The Nation*, September 17, 1938.

[35] *Baseball Digest*, August, 1950, p. 84, November-December, 1954, pp. 45–46, July, 1957, pp. 60–63; Richard Bardolph, *The Negro Vanguard*, 451–58.

Obviously, a Negro cannot be merely a journeyman player to make the majors; he must instead be a very good player. Data for 1967 show that twenty-three National League Negroes and seventeen American League Negroes accounted for well over half of the base hits made in the majors that year. Nevertheless, black players usually get less cash for their performances and are more quickly shelved when their effectiveness declines. Although Robinson has made the Hall of Fame and some blacks now draw over $100,000 a year in baseball, no Negro has yet been named a manager of a big-league team. Finally, peripheral rewards like lavish publicity and lucrative endorsement opportunities go mainly to whites.[36]

Obviously, American baseball continues to offer problems for the Negro to solve. Consider the frustrating problem of the unwillingness of white fans to identify with Negro stars in the manner with which they took Cobb, Ruth, or even Zeke Bonura to heart. Sam Smith, president of the Southern League, once said, "There are folks down here who just don't want their kids growing up to admire a Negro ballplayer even if he's Willie Mays or Hank Aaron." Who can deny that this kind of discrimination is present in every major-league park?[37]

Those owners who feared the consequences of employing "too many" Negroes turned elsewhere in their search for talent. By the 1950's, the hunt centered in Latin America, including the American territory of Puerto Rico and such outposts as Cuba, Panama, the Dominican Republic, Venezuela, the Virgin Islands, and the Bahamas. For a long time, these areas had been hotbeds of baseball interest, and during the war some recruiters discovered first-rate manpower there. In 1950, recruiting began in earnest, since by then the Korean War made it clear that the military draft would continue to drain off promising American talent.

Cuba was the most promising site, since Havana was an International League outpost until the Cuban revolution of 1959. Although Fidel Castro's triumph severed Cuba's connection with

[36] Aaron Rosenblatt, "Negroes in Baseball: The Failure of Success," *Transaction Magazine*, September, 1967, pp. 51–53; *New York Times*, September 8, 1964, November 25, 1967.

[37] J. Anthony Lukas, *loc. cit.*

American baseball, twenty-four Cuban players held major-league positions in the 1960's, and Puerto Rico and the Dominican Republic sent almost as many. By 1965 more than seventy Latin-American players wore major-league uniforms and provided the new blood so necessary to vitalize America's game. Like Negroes, Latin-American players found prejudice here, but their own long experience in racial amalgamation softened the impact. Fans and sportswriters have found it difficult to ascribe traditional color categories to these players. Nevertheless, some were viewed with racist disdain and the same subtle discrimination barred their acceptance. Like Negroes, they had to be better than good, and they generally drew less compensation than did white stars.[38] Nevertheless, the future of American baseball promises a greater influx of Latin-American stars, perhaps along with others from Japan. Indeed, with commercial air travel so highly developed, it seems likely that Japan will provide its own franchises in a global major league in the near future.

The growing involvement with foreign players has forced owners to consider some of the realities of American foreign policy. Both Tokyo and Mexico City have been considered as possible major-league sites for future expansion. Their admission would, of course, raise difficult problems of control and administration. Some of the difficulties were foreshadowed in 1946, when the Pasquel brothers of Mexico City promoted a rival major league and lured several American stars with high salaries. American owners responded by blacklisting the players and outlawing the league, a hostile act that angered Mexico and infuriated American players. Although American stars soon learned that the Mexican League was a jerry-built structure hardly to their liking, one of them, Dan Gardella, took the matter of his blacklisting to the courts. Fearful of the weakness of their position, baseball executives rescinded their blacklists and issued amnesties to all fugitive players. Gardella won an out-of-court settlement in return for dropping his suit. The experience was a sobering one for baseball men. They learned

[38] *Reading Eagle*, April 4, 1965; *New York Times*, September 9, 1964, December 15, 1966, January 17, 1967.

that baseball regulations were not only limited, but subject to review in federal courts when they involved international matters or issues of personal rights.[39]

Indeed, baseball regulations have their domestic limitations. As we have seen, baseball's "gentleman's agreement" against Negroes did not stand against national antidiscrimination laws. Likewise, the assumed arbitrary right of owners to hand out franchises was called into question in the postwar era. On two occasions—in 1951 and again in 1957—Emmanuel Celler's Congressional subcommittee, inquiring into monopolistic practices, summoned baseball officials and players to testify on their policies. At issue were proposed laws seeking to restrict baseball regulation of franchise allocations, player contracts, and minor-league involvements. Although no repressive legislation followed these inquiries, baseball men were put on the defensive and forced to give voluminous testimony on their practices. Even though baseball's special status under the anti-trust laws was reaffirmed in the 1960's, baseball operators had cause to fear Congressman Celler's subcommittee. They became much more circumspect in their treatment of players and in their allocation of new franchises.[40]

Although owners came to hate and fear governmental interference, players looked upon big government as an ally of sorts. In 1946, baseball was obliged to follow federal laws in dealing with returning war veterans, which meant that a player had to be guaranteed a fair trial at his prewar salary. The letter of the law failed to help those whose skills had been lost, but the spirit helped bring about major contract reforms. Players won a "magna charta" contract revision which set the minimum major-league salary at $5,000, placed a 25 per cent limit on salary cuts, and provided free medical benefits and an allowance for spring training. The wording of the reserve clause was also changed to "a right to renew" the contract, a necessary phrase for convincing critics that ballplayers were not peons.[41]

[39] *The Sporting News*, February 28, 1946, August 31, September 28, October 19, 1949; *Reading Eagle*, January 22, 1967.

[40] For a list of proposed laws aimed at regulating baseball, see U.S. House of

If the owners had not yielded on the contract matter, it would probably have been crammed down their throats. For early in 1946, another players' organization, The American Baseball Guild, arrayed itself against owners. It was headed by Robert Murphy, a Harvard law graduate and a onetime examiner for the National Labor Relations Board. Owners came to fear the power of the organization and its leaders. Besides, at this very time waves of strikes for labor recognition were taking place throughout the land. When the Guild's Pittsburgh chapter almost struck against the Pirate owners in June, owners determined to yield. Commissioner Chandler opened channels of communication, and players were allowed to send delegates to discuss grievances. Although Murphy and the Guild were kept out of the discussion, the price of outflanking the union was high. Its immediate cost was the new "magna charta"; its long-term cost was that players found that union "clout" would work against owners. The incident led directly to the establishment of the powerful Major League Baseball Players Association of today. Under the leadership of Marvin Miller, a lawyer, 97 per cent of major-league players now contribute toward its $150,000 annual budget.[42]

The ability of organized players to pry lucrative concessions from owners certainly owed much to the riches that television brought to baseball. Beginning in 1946, when most video fans had to view ball games from bars, television baseball grew steadily more popular and accounted for the purchase of many family sets. In 1951, an estimated three million family set owners watched the climactic playoff between the Dodgers and Giants, while perhaps an equal number viewed it in bars and grills which used television as a lure. One can only speculate how proud a confirmed drinker like Phil Douglas would have been to know that he could, by television, enter a million bars at once! It is understandable that promoters wasted no time in siphoning profits from the medium.

Representatives, *Organized Professional Team Sports*, p. 6; *New York Times*, April 15, December 13, 1966.

41 *Sporting News*, November 15, 1945, November 13, 1946.

42 *New York Times*, January 21, 1968; *ibid.*, April 25, June 19, August 7, 1946; U.S. House of Representatives, *Organized Professional Team Sports*, p. 1309–31; Interview, Curtis Simmons with D. Voigt.

There was continuing public clamor for sports programs of all kinds, and by 1967 sports televising accounted for 796 hours of program time.[43] Because summertime was the slack season in television programming, baseball faced little competition from rival shows. Hence, as one of the few live shows of the hot season, its share of the profit melon was assured. No wonder that television contracts and the television marketplace became major concerns in decisions to relocate a franchise or expand a major league. In 1966, baseball's television income amounted to $27.5 million.[44]

Of course, this popular fourth dimension of baseball also had its problems. For one, the cameras could only focus on part of the action at a time, which gave the impression of dullness to those who knew the game only from having seen it on television. For another, the mass televising of games undoubtedly cut down on live attendance locally. Another problem came from attempts by the television networks to influence the timing of games in order to suit their programming interests.

Television has increasingly threatened to reshape the game and perhaps work it into an entertainment format that might cause public revulsion. Certain observers have expressed the fear that wealthy networks might try to buy and control baseball franchises. Thus, when the Yankees were purchased by the Columbia Broadcasting System in the 1960's, the baseball world, along with the United States Congress, kept a watchful eye on further developments in this unfinished drama.[45]

Television has also caused concern among the peripheral people of baseball. Dispossessed sportswriters, whose status sank lower as that of television sportscasters rose, accused the new medium of prostituting the sport by tailoring the descriptions of games. In rebuttal, spokesmen for television accused writers of jealousy born out of a frustrating knowledge that newspapers were growing obsolete.[46] Minor-league promoters, who saw the "big eye" as the evil

[43] Graham, *The New York Giants*, 306; *The Sporting News*, September 25, 1946; "A Locker in the Living Room," *Time*, October 20, 1967.

[44] *New York Times*, February 28, 1966.

[45] *Ibid.*, January 21, 1968; Veeck and Linn, *The Hustler's Handbook*, 69–93; Stanley Frank, "Corrupts! Debases! Exploits!" *T.V. Guide*, February 4, 1967, pp. 6–11.

eye, also complained about the new medium as the leading cause of all their troubles. And finally, the controversy over television must include the attitudes of countless housewives who found themselves in conflict with the new masculine world of television baseball and canned beers.

Television represents an enormous segment of America's new leisure revolution. The revolution itself is a many-sided phenomenon with many promises and pitfalls brought into being by millions of Americans with more time, more money, and more inclination to have fun. They meet the challenge of fun in varying ways, with responses following their values and goals. Some have sought fun in work, others in family life, still others in learning or aesthetics, and countless other possibilities are still to be found. For many people, commercialized activities are the primary outlet, and postwar merchants of leisure have used every skill to promote them. In this period, under advertising stimuli, hordes of Americans have taken up bowling, golf, and tennis along with other participant activities. At the same time, spectator sports have undergone a major explosion. Stimulated by television, professional football, hockey, and basketball have now joined baseball as public favorites. Soccer may become a rival of the future.

Understandably, baseball men have been disturbed by the popularity of rival sports even though affluent America obviously has room for all. If the spectator sports overlap the baseball season, most of them are fall and winter attractions, leaving baseball in command of the summer.[47] What has hurt most is the knowledge that no sport, not even baseball, can now lay claim to being the national game. American tastes are now much too diverse, and far too fickle, to linger exclusively over one dish. Even if pragmatic owners could take this loss of glory in stride, it is far more difficult to take the loss of promising talent to other sports. This threat is real and is compounded by high bonus offers from football and basketball promoters. Offers of up to $400,000 were made to stars in the late 1960's. Moreover, the rival spectacles used short-term

[46] Melvin Durslag, "When Will Sportscasters Be Allowed to Speak Up?" *T.V. Guide*, June 24, 1967; *New York Times*, June 22, 1967.

[47] Andreano, *op. cit.*, 79–100.

option contracts that posed a serious threat to the sanctity of baseball's reserve clause.[48]

On the other hand, the threats have been tempered by the knowledge that baseball's fast-growing rivals all had growing pains of their own and that they were just as vulnerable to the fickle whims of armies of fun-seekers. Baseball men could take some comfort in the knowledge that each spectacle has its season, and as each passes in review it whets popular tastes for the next. Indeed, even the organization of its chief rivals apes baseball's ancient design of "American" and "National" divisions—an imitation that has brought all rivals closer together inasmuch as they share common problems.

Finally, hope arises from the fact that the four rivals are wrestling with common problems in technology, recruitment, and television coverage. As each has grappled for solutions, sometimes the knowledge gained by one has proved useful to others.

All things considered, baseball has a favorable outlook in the 1970's, provided its leaders keep their adventurous spirit of energetic optimism tempered by constant concern for public feelings. Certainly, history lends comfort by showing some paths to avoid and some to traverse, for major-league baseball has behind it a century of experience, having navigated prosperous and catastrophic periods in American life. If there is a lesson to be learned from the turbulent history of the twentieth century, it is the absolute importance of avoiding rigid approaches to problems. At its prosperous best, baseball was always flexible enough to adapt to changing public tastes. The same dynamism will be equally necessary as the game adapts to a new era. Unquestionably, our fast-moving society demands bold application of new techniques, even in the teeth of outraged protests. This is a vital message, but it can be made simple enough and earthy enough for all owners to comprehend. Let them heed the advice of Satchel Paige, a man who waited thirty years for his chance to pitch in the majors. Said Paige, ". . . Don't look back. Something might be gaining on you."[49]

[48] "The Golden Age of Sport," *Time*, June 2, 1967; U.S. House of Representatives, *Organized Professional Team Sports*, p. 2446; *New York Times*, February 13, 1966, June 21, 1967.

[49] Paige, *op. cit.*, 227.

Appendices

Appendix 1. Pre-1900 National League Standings and Statistics

PRE-1900 NATIONAL LEAGUE PENNANT WINNERS

Year	*Club*	*Manager*	*W.*	*L.*	*Pct.*
1876	Chicago	Albert Spalding	52	14	.788
1877	Boston	Harry Wright	31	17	.646
1878	Boston	Harry Wright	41	19	.683
1879	Providence	George Wright	55	23	.705
1880	Chicago	Adrian Anson	67	17	.798
1881	Chicago	Adrian Anson	56	28	.667
1882	Chicago	Adrian Anson	55	29	.655
1883	Boston	John Morrill	63	35	.643
1884	Providence	Frank Bancroft	84	28	.750
1885	Chicago	Adrian Anson	87	25	.777
1886	Chicago	Adrian Anson	90	34	.726
1887	Detroit	William Watkins	79	45	.637
1888	New York	James Mutrie	84	47	.641
1889	New York	James Mutrie	83	43	.659
1890	Brooklyn	William McGunnigle	86	43	.667
1891	Boston	Frank Selee	87	51	.630
1892	Boston	Frank Selee	102	48	.680
1893	Boston	Frank Selee	86	44	.662
1894	Baltimore	Edward Hanlon	89	39	.695
1895	Baltimore	Edward Hanlon	87	43	.669
1896	Baltimore	Edward Hanlon	90	39	.698
1897	Boston	Frank Selee	93	39	.705
1898	Boston	Frank Selee	102	47	.685
1899	Brooklyn	Edward Hanlon	88	42	.677

PRE-1900 NATIONAL LEAGUE YEARLY FINISHES

Year	*Bos.*	*Bkn.*	*Chi.*	*Cin.*	*N.Y.*	*Phil.*	*Pit.*	*St.L.*	*Bal.*	*Buf.*	*Cle.*
1876	4	..	1	8	6	7	..	3	..	..	..
1877	1	..	5	..	..	..	..	4	..	..	..
1878	1	..	4	2	..	..	..	..	..	..	..
1879	2	..	*3	5	..	..	..	..	..	*3	6
1880	6	..	1	8	..	..	..	..	..	7	3
1881	6	..	1	..	..	..	..	..	..	3	7
1882	*3	..	1	..	..	..	..	..	..	*3	5
1883	1	..	2	..	6	8	..	..	..	5	4
1884	2	..	*4	..	*4	6	..	..	..	3	7
1885	5	..	1	..	2	3	..	8	..	7	..
1886	5	..	1	..	3	4	..	6	..	..	..
1887	5	..	3	..	4	2	6	..	..	..	..
1888	4	..	2	..	1	3	6	..	..	..	..
1889	2	..	3	..	1	4	5	..	..	..	6
1890	5	1	2	4	6	3	8	..	..	..	7
1891	1	6	2	7	3	4	8	..	..	..	5
1892	1	3	7	5	8	4	6	11	12	..	2
1893	1	*6	9	*6	5	4	2	10	8	..	3
1894	3	5	8	10	2	4	7	9	1	..	6
1895	*5	*5	4	8	9	3	7	11	1	..	2
1896	4	*9	5	3	7	8	6	11	1	..	2
1897	1	*6	9	4	3	10	8	12	2	..	5
1898	1	10	4	3	7	6	8	12	2	..	5
1899	2	1	8	6	10	3	7	5	4	..	12
Year	*Det.*	*Hart.*	*Ind.*	*K.C.*	*Lou.*	*Mil.*	*Prov.*	*Syr.*	*Troy*	*Was.*	*Wor.*
1876	..	2	..	..	5	..	..	..	..	..	..
1877	..	3	..	..	2	..	..	..	..	..	..
1878	..	..	5	..	..	6	3	..	..	..	..
1879	..	..	..	..	..	..	1	8	7	..	..
1880	..	..	..	..	..	..	2	..	4	..	5
1881	4	..	..	..	..	..	2	..	5	..	8
1882	6	..	..	..	..	..	2	..	7	..	8
1883	7	..	..	..	..	..	3	..	..	..	..
1884	8	..	..	..	..	..	1	..	..	..	..
1885	6	..	..	..	..	..	4	..	..	..	..
1886	2	..	..	7	..	..	..	..	..	8	..
1887	1	..	8	..	..	..	..	..	..	7	..
1888	5	..	7	..	..	..	..	..	..	8	..
1889	..	..	7	..	..	..	..	..	..	8	..
1890	..	..	..	..	..	..	..	..	..	..	..
1891	..	..	..	..	..	..	..	..	..	..	..
1892	..	..	..	..	9	..	..	..	..	10	..
1893	..	..	..	..	11	..	..	..	..	12	..
1894	..	..	..	..	12	..	..	..	..	11	..
1895	..	..	..	..	12	..	..	..	..	10	..
1896	..	..	..	..	12	..	..	..	..	*9	..
1897	..	..	..	..	11	..	..	..	..	*6	..
1898	..	..	..	..	9	..	..	..	..	11	..
1899	..	..	..	..	9	..	..	..	..	11	..

* Tied for position.

Appendix 2. Annual Club Standings and Statistics: The National League

BRAVES†

Yr.	Pos.	W	L	Pct.
1900	4	66	72	.478
1901	5	69	69	.500
1902	3	73	64	.533
1903	6	58	80	.420
1904	7	55	98	.359
1905	7	51	103	.331
1906	8	49	102	.325
1907	7	58	90	.392
1908	6	63	91	.409
1909	8	45	108	.294
1910	8	53	100	.346
1911	8	44	107	.291
1912	8	52	101	.340
1913	5	69	82	.457
1914	1*	94	59	.614
1915	2	83	69	.546
1916	3	89	63	.586
1917	6	72	81	.471
1918	7	53	71	.427
1919	6	57	82	.410
1920	7	62	90	.408
1921	4	79	74	.516
1922	8	53	100	.346
1923	7	54	100	.351
1924	8	53	100	.346
1925	5	70	83	.458
1926	7	66	86	.434
1927	7	60	94	.390
1928	7	50	103	.327
1929	8	56	98	.364
1930	6	70	84	.455
1931	7	64	90	.416
1932	5	77	77	.500
1933	4	83	71	.539
1934	4	78	73	.517
1935	8	38	115	.248
1936	6	71	83	.461
1937	5	79	73	.520
1938	5	77	75	.507
1939	7	63	88	.417
1940	7	65	87	.428
1941	7	62	92	.403
1942	7	59	89	.399
1943	6	68	85	.444
1944	6	65	89	.422
1945	6	67	85	.441
1946	4	81	72	.529
1947	3	86	68	.558

* World Champions

† Boston, 1900–52, incl. Milwaukee, 1953–65, incl. Atlanta, 1966–.

1948	1	91	62	.595
1949	4	75	79	.487
1950	4	83	71	.539
1951	4	76	78	.494
1952	7	64	89	.418
1953	2	92	62	.597
1954	3	89	65	.578
1955	2	85	69	.552
1956	2	92	62	.597
1957	1*	95	59	.617
1958	1	92	62	.597
1959	2	86	70	.551
1960	2	88	66	.571
1961	4	83	71	.539
1962	5	86	76	.531
1963	6	84	78	.519
1964	5	88	74	.543
1965	5	86	76	.531
1966	5	85	77	.525
1967	7	77	85	.475
1968	5	81	80	.500
Total		4887	5627	.465

CUBS

Yr.	Pos.	W	L	Pct.
1900	5	65	75	.464
1901	6	53	86	.381
1902	5	68	69	.496
1903	3	82	56	.594
1904	2	93	60	.608
1905	3	92	61	.601
1906	1	116	36	.763
1907	1*	107	45	.704
1908	1*	99	55	.643
1909	2	104	49	.680
1910	1	104	50	.675
1911	2	92	62	.597
1912	3	91	59	.607
1913	3	88	65	.575
1914	4	78	76	.506
1915	4	73	80	.477
1916	5	67	86	.438
1917	5	74	80	.481
1918	1	84	45	.651
1919	3	75	65	.536
1920	5	75	79	.487
1921	7	64	89	.418
1922	5	80	74	.519
1923	4	83	71	.539
1924	5	81	72	.529
1925	8	68	86	.442
1926	4	82	72	.532
1927	4	85	68	.556
1928	3	91	63	.591
1929	1	98	54	.645
1930	2	90	64	.584
1931	3	84	70	.545
1932	1	90	64	.584
1933	3	86	68	.558
1934	3	86	65	.570
1935	1	100	54	.649
1936	2	87	67	.565
1937	2	93	61	.604
1938	1	89	63	.586
1939	4	84	70	.545
1940	5	75	79	.487
1941	6	70	84	.455
1942	6	68	86	.442
1943	5	74	79	.484
1944	4	75	79	.487
1945	1	98	56	.636
1946	3	82	71	.536
1947	6	69	85	.448
1948	8	64	90	.416
1949	8	61	93	.396
1950	7	64	89	.418
1951	8	62	92	.403
1952	5	77	77	.500
1953	7	65	89	.422
1954	7	64	90	.416
1955	6	72	81	.471
1956	8	60	94	.390
1957	7	62	92	.403
1958	5	72	82	.468
1959	5	74	80	.481
1960	7	60	94	.390
1961	7	64	90	.416
1962	9	59	103	.364
1963	7	82	80	.506
1964	8	76	86	.469
1965	8	72	90	.444
1966	10	59	103	.364
1967	3	87	74	.540
1968	3	84	78	.519
Total		5452	5100	.517

REDS

Yr.	Pos.	W	L	Pct.
1900	7	62	77	.446
1901	8	52	87	.374

1902	4	70	70	.500
1903	4	74	65	.532
1904	3	88	65	.575
1905	5	79	74	.516
1906	6	64	87	.424
1907	6	66	87	.431
1908	5	73	81	.474
1909	4	77	76	.503
1910	5	75	79	.487
1911	6	70	83	.458
1912	4	75	78	.490
1913	7	64	89	.418
1914	8	60	94	.390
1915	7	71	83	.461
1916	7	60	93	.392
1917	4	78	76	.506
1918	3	68	60	.531
1919	1*	96	44	.686
1920	3	82	71	.536
1921	6	70	83	.458
1922	2	86	68	.558
1923	2	91	63	.591
1924	4	83	70	.542
1925	3	80	73	.523
1926	2	87	67	.565
1927	5	75	78	.490
1928	5	78	74	.513
1929	7	66	88	.429
1930	7	59	95	.383
1931	8	58	96	.377
1932	8	60	94	.390
1933	8	58	94	.382
1934	8	52	99	.344
1935	6	68	85	.444
1936	5	74	80	.481
1937	8	56	98	.364
1938	4	82	68	.547
1939	1	97	57	.630
1940	1*	100	53	.654
1941	3	88	66	.571
1942	4	76	76	.500
1943	2	87	67	.565
1944	3	89	65	.578
1945	7	61	93	.396
1946	6	67	87	.435
1947	5	73	81	.474
1948	7	64	89	.418
1949	7	62	92	.403
1950	6	66	87	.431
1951	6	68	86	.442
1952	6	69	85	.448
1953	6	68	86	.442
1954	5	74	80	.481
1955	5	75	79	.487
1956	3	91	63	.591
1957	4	80	74	.519
1958	4	76	78	.494
1959	5	74	80	.481
1960	6	67	87	.435
1961	1	93	61	.604
1962	3	98	64	.605
1963	5	86	76	.531
1964	2	92	70	.568
1965	4	89	73	.549
1966	7	76	84	.475
1967	4	87	75	.537
1968	4	83	79	.512
Total		5163	5385	.489

ASTROS

Yr.	Pos.	W	L	Pct.
1962	8	64	96	.400
1963	9	66	96	.407
1964	9	66	96	.407
1965	9	65	97	.401
1966	8	72	90	.444
1967	9	69	93	.426
1968	10	72	90	.444
Total		474	658	.419

DODGERS‡

Yr.	Pos.	W	L	Pct.
1900	1	82	54	.603
1901	3	79	57	.581
1902	2	75	63	.543
1903	5	70	66	.515
1904	6	56	97	.366
1905	8	48	104	.316
1906	5	66	86	.434
1907	5	65	83	.439
1908	7	53	101	.344
1909	6	55	98	.359
1910	6	64	90	.416
1911	7	64	86	.427
1912	7	58	95	.379
1913	6	65	84	.436
1914	5	75	79	.487
1915	3	80	72	.526

‡ Brooklyn, 1900–57, incl. Los Angeles, 1958–.

1916	1	94	60	.610
1917	7	70	81	.464
1918	5	57	69	.452
1919	5	69	71	.493
1920	1	93	61	.604
1921	5	77	75	.507
1922	6	76	78	.494
1923	6	76	78	.494
1924	2	92	62	.597
1925	6	68	85	.444
1926	6	71	82	.464
1927	6	65	88	.425
1928	6	77	76	.503
1929	6	70	83	.458
1930	4	86	68	.558
1931	4	79	73	.520
1932	3	81	73	.526
1933	6	65	88	.425
1934	6	71	81	.467
1935	5	70	83	.458
1936	7	67	87	.435
1937	6	62	91	.405
1938	7	69	80	.463
1939	3	84	69	.549
1940	2	88	65	.575
1941	1	100	54	.649
1942	2	104	50	.675
1943	3	81	72	.529
1944	7	63	91	.409
1945	3	87	67	.565
1946	2	96	60	.615
1947	1	94	60	.610
1948	3	84	70	.545
1949	1	97	57	.630
1950	2	89	65	.578
1951	2	97	60	.618
1952	1	96	57	.627
1953	1	105	49	.682
1954	2	92	62	.597
1955	1*	98	55	.641
1956	1	93	61	.604
1957	3	84	70	.545
1958	7	71	83	.461
1959	1*	88	68	.564
1960	4	82	72	.532
1961	2	89	65	.578
1962	2	102	63	.618
1963	1*	99	63	.611
1964	6	80	82	.494
1965	1*	97	65	.599
1966	1	95	67	.586
1967	8	73	89	.451
1968	7	76	86	.469
Total		5444	5085	.517

METS

Yr.	Pos.	W	L	Pct.
1962	10	40	120	.250
1963	10	51	111	.315
1964	10	53	109	.327
1965	10	50	112	.309
1966	9	66	95	.410
1967	10	61	101	.377
1968	9	73	89	.451
Total		394	737	.348

PHILLIES

Yr.	Pos.	W	L	Pct.
1900	3	75	63	.543
1901	2	83	57	.593
1902	7	56	81	.409
1903	7	49	86	.363
1904	8	52	100	.342
1905	4	83	69	.546
1906	4	71	82	.464
1907	3	83	64	.565
1908	4	83	71	.539
1909	5	74	79	.484
1910	4	78	75	.510
1911	4	79	73	.520
1912	5	73	79	.480
1913	2	88	63	.583
1914	6	74	80	.481
1915	1	90	62	.592
1916	2	91	62	.595
1917	2	87	65	.572
1918	6	55	68	.447
1919	8	47	90	.343
1920	8	62	91	.405
1921	8	51	103	.331
1922	7	57	96	.373
1923	8	50	104	.325
1924	7	55	96	.364
1925	6	68	85	.444
1926	8	58	93	.384
1927	8	51	103	.331
1928	8	43	109	.283
1929	5	71	82	.464
1930	8	52	102	.338
1931	6	66	88	.429
1932	4	78	76	.506

1933	7	60	92	.395
1934	7	56	93	.376
1935	7	64	89	.418
1936	8	54	100	.351
1937	7	61	92	.399
1938	8	45	105	.300
1939	8	45	106	.298
1940	8	50	103	.327
1941	8	43	111	.279
1942	8	42	109	.278
1943	7	64	90	.416
1944	8	61	92	.399
1945	8	46	108	.299
1946	5	69	85	.448
1947	7	62	92	.403
1948	6	66	88	.429
1949	3	81	73	.526
1950	1	91	63	.591
1951	5	73	81	.474
1952	4	87	67	.565
1953	3	83	71	.539
1954	4	75	79	.487
1955	4	77	77	.500
1956	5	71	83	.461
1957	5	77	77	.500
1958	8	69	85	.448
1959	8	64	90	.416
1960	8	59	95	.383
1961	8	47	107	.305
1962	7	81	80	.503
1963	4	87	75	.537
1964	2	92	70	.568
1965	6	85	76	.528
1966	4	87	75	.537
1967	5	82	80	.506
1968	7	76	86	.469
Total		4665	5842	.444

PIRATES

Yr.	Pos.	W	L	Pct.
1900	2	79	60	.568
1901	1	90	49	.647
1902	1	103	36	.741
1903	1	91	49	.650
1904	4	87	66	.569
1905	2	96	57	.627
1906	3	93	60	.608
1907	2	91	63	.591
1908	2	98	56	.636
1909	1*	110	42	.724
1910	3	86	67	.562
1911	3	85	69	.552
1912	2	93	58	.616
1913	4	78	71	.523
1914	7	69	85	.448
1915	5	73	81	.474
1916	6	65	89	.422
1917	8	51	103	.331
1918	4	65	60	.520
1919	4	71	68	.511
1920	4	79	75	.513
1921	2	90	63	.588
1922	3	85	69	.552
1923	3	87	67	.565
1924	3	90	63	.588
1925	1*	95	58	.621
1926	3	84	69	.549
1927	1	94	60	.610
1928	4	85	67	.559
1929	2	88	65	.575
1930	5	80	74	.519
1931	5	75	79	.487
1932	2	86	68	.558
1933	2	87	67	.565
1934	5	74	76	.493
1935	4	86	67	.562
1936	4	84	70	.545
1937	3	86	68	.558
1938	2	86	64	.573
1939	6	68	85	.444
1940	4	78	76	.506
1941	4	81	73	.526
1942	5	66	81	.449
1943	4	80	74	.519
1944	2	90	63	.588
1945	4	82	72	.532
1946	7	63	91	.409
1947	7	62	92	.403
1948	4	83	71	.539
1949	6	71	83	.461
1950	8	57	96	.373
1951	7	64	90	.416
1952	8	42	112	.273
1953	8	50	104	.325
1954	8	53	101	.344
1955	8	60	94	.390
1956	7	66	88	.429
1957	7	62	92	.403
1958	2	84	70	.545
1959	4	78	76	.506

1960	1*	95	59	.617
1961	6	75	79	.487
1962	4	93	68	.578
1963	8	74	88	.457
1964	6	80	82	.494
1965	3	90	72	.556
1966	3	92	70	.568
1967	6	81	81	.500
1968	6	80	82	.494
Total		5495	5043	.521

CARDINALS

Yr.	Pos.	W	L	Pct.
1900	5	65	75	.464
1901	4	76	64	.543
1902	6	56	78	.418
1903	8	43	94	.314
1904	5	75	79	.487
1905	6	58	96	.377
1906	7	52	98	.347
1907	8	52	101	.340
1908	8	49	105	.318
1909	7	54	98	.355
1910	7	63	90	.412
1911	5	75	74	.503
1912	6	63	90	.412
1913	8	51	99	.340
1914	3	81	72	.529
1915	6	72	81	.471
1916	7	60	93	.392
1917	3	82	70	.539
1918	8	51	78	.395
1919	7	54	83	.394
1920	5	75	79	.487
1921	3	87	66	.569
1922	3	85	69	.552
1923	5	79	74	.516
1924	6	65	89	.422
1925	4	77	76	.503
1926	1*	89	65	.578
1927	2	92	61	.601
1928	1	95	59	.617
1929	4	78	74	.513
1930	1	92	62	.597
1931	1*	101	53	.656
1932	6	72	82	.468
1933	5	82	71	.536
1934	1*	95	58	.621
1935	2	96	58	.623
1936	2	87	67	.565
1937	4	81	73	.526
1938	6	71	80	.470
1939	2	92	61	.601
1940	3	84	69	.549
1941	2	97	56	.634
1942	1*	106	48	.688
1943	1	105	49	.682
1944	1*	105	49	.682
1945	2	95	59	.617
1946	1*	98	58	.628
1947	2	89	65	.578
1948	2	85	69	.552
1949	2	96	58	.623
1950	5	78	75	.510
1951	3	81	73	.526
1952	3	88	66	.571
1953	3	83	71	.539
1954	6	72	82	.468
1955	7	68	86	.442
1956	4	76	78	.494
1957	2	87	67	.565
1958	5	72	82	.468
1959	7	71	83	.461
1960	3	86	68	.558
1961	5	80	74	.519
1962	6	84	78	.519
1963	2	93	69	.574
1964	1*	93	69	.574
1965	7	80	81	.497
1966	6	83	79	.512
1967	1*	101	60	.627
1968	1	97	65	.599
Total		5456	5081	.518

GIANTS§

Yr.	Pos.	W	L	Pct.
1900	8	60	78	.435
1901	7	52	85	.380
1902	8	48	88	.353
1903	2	84	55	.604
1904	1	106	47	.693
1905	1*	105	48	.686
1906	2	96	56	.632
1907	4	82	71	.536
1908	2	98	56	.636
1909	3	92	61	.601
1910	2	91	63	.591
1911	1	99	54	.647

§ New York, 1900–57, incl. San Francisco, 1958–.

1912	1	103	48	.682
1913	1	101	51	.664
1914	2	84	70	.545
1915	8	69	83	.454
1916	4	86	66	.566
1917	1	98	56	.636
1918	2	71	53	.573
1919	2	87	53	.621
1920	2	86	68	.558
1921	1*	94	59	.614
1922	1*	93	61	.604
1923	1	95	58	.621
1924	1	93	60	.608
1925	2	86	66	.566
1926	5	74	77	.490
1927	3	92	62	.597
1928	2	93	61	.604
1929	3	84	67	.556
1930	3	87	67	.565
1931	2	87	65	.572
1932	6	72	82	.468
1933	1*	91	61	.599
1934	2	93	60	.608
1935	3	91	62	.595
1936	1	92	62	.597
1937	1	95	57	.625
1938	3	83	67	.553
1939	5	77	74	.510
1940	6	72	80	.474
1941	5	74	79	.484
1942	3	85	67	.559
1943	8	55	98	.359
1944	5	67	87	.435
1945	5	78	74	.513
1946	8	61	93	.396
1947	4	81	73	.526
1948	5	78	76	.506
1949	5	73	81	.474
1950	3	86	68	.558
1951	1	98	59	.624
1952	2	92	62	.597
1953	5	70	84	.455
1954	1*	97	57	.630
1955	3	80	74	.519
1956	6	67	87	.435
1957	6	69	85	.448
1958	3	80	74	.519
1959	3	83	71	.539
1960	5	79	75	.513
1961	3	85	69	.552
1962	1	103	62	.624
1963	3	88	74	.543
1964	4	90	72	.556
1965	2	95	67	.586
1966	2	93	68	.578
1967	2	91	71	.562
1968	2	88	74	.543
Total		5828	4699	.554

Appendix 3. Annual Club Standings and Statistics: The American League

ORIOLES

Yr.	Pos.	W	L	Pct.
1954	7	54	100	.351
1955	7	57	97	.370
1956	6	69	85	.448
1957	5	76	76	.500
1958	6	74	79	.484
1959	6	74	80	.481
1960	2	89	65	.578
1961	3	95	67	.586
1962	7	77	85	.475
1963	4	86	76	.531
1964	3	97	65	.599
1965	3	94	68	.580
1966	1*	97	63	.606
1967	6	76	85	.472
1968	2	91	71	.562
Total		1206	1162	.509

RED SOX

Yr.	Pos.	W	L	Pct.
1901	2	79	57	.581
1902	3	77	60	.562
1903	1*	91	47	.659
1904	1	95	59	.617
1905	4	78	74	.513
1906	8	49	105	.318
1907	7	59	90	.396
1908	5	74	79	.484
1909	3	88	63	.583
1910	4	81	72	.529
1911	5	78	75	.510
1912	1*	105	47	.691
1913	4	79	71	.527
1914	2	91	62	.595
1915	1*	101	50	.669
1916	1*	91	63	.591
1917	2	90	62	.592
1918	1*	75	51	.595
1919	6	66	71	.482
1920	5	72	81	.471
1921	5	75	79	.487
1922	8	61	93	.396
1923	8	61	91	.401
1924	7	67	87	.435
1925	8	47	105	.309
1926	8	46	107	.301
1927	8	51	103	.331
1928	8	57	96	.373
1929	8	58	96	.377
1930	8	52	102	.338
1931	6	62	90	.408
1932	8	43	111	.279

* World Champions

Yr.	Pos.	W	L	Pct.
1933	7	63	86	.423
1934	4	76	76	.500
1935	4	78	75	.510
1936	6	74	80	.481
1937	5	80	72	.526
1938	2	88	61	.591
1939	2	89	62	.589
1940	4	82	72	.532
1941	2	84	70	.545
1942	2	93	59	.612
1943	7	68	84	.447
1944	4	77	77	.500
1945	7	71	83	.461
1946	1	104	50	.675
1947	3	83	71	.539
1948	2	96	59	.619
1949	2	96	58	.623
1950	3	94	60	.610
1951	3	87	67	.565
1952	6	76	78	.494
1953	4	84	69	.549
1954	4	69	85	.448
1955	4	84	70	.545
1956	4	84	70	.545
1957	3	82	72	.532
1958	3	79	75	.513
1959	5	75	79	.487
1960	7	65	89	.422
1961	6	76	86	.469
1962	8	76	84	.475
1963	7	76	85	.472
1964	8	72	90	.444
1965	9	62	100	.383
1966	9	72	90	.444
1967	1	92	70	.568
1968	4	86	76	.531
Total		5192	5189	.499

ANGELS

Yr.	Pos.	W	L	Pct.
1961	8	70	91	.435
1962	3	86	76	.531
1963	9	70	91	.435
1964	5	82	80	.506
1965	7	75	87	.463
1966	6	80	82	.494
1967	5	84	77	.522
1968	8	67	95	.414
Total		614	679	.474

WHITE SOX

Yr.	Pos.	W	L	Pct.
1901	1	83	53	.610
1902	4	74	60	.552
1903	7	60	77	.438
1904	3	89	65	.578
1905	2	92	60	.605
1906	1*	93	58	.616
1907	3	87	64	.576
1908	3	88	64	.579
1909	4	78	74	.513
1910	6	68	85	.444
1911	4	77	74	.510
1912	4	78	76	.506
1913	5	78	74	.513
1914	6	70	84	.455
1915	3	93	61	.604
1916	2	89	65	.578
1917	1*	100	54	.649
1918	6	57	67	.460
1919	1	88	52	.629
1920	2	96	58	.623
1921	7	62	92	.403
1922	5	77	77	.500
1923	7	69	85	.448
1924	8	66	87	.431
1925	3	79	75	.513
1926	5	81	72	.529
1927	5	70	83	.458
1928	5	72	82	.468
1929	7	59	93	.388
1930	7	62	92	.403
1931	8	56	97	.366
1932	7	49	102	.325
1933	6	67	83	.447
1934	8	53	99	.349
1935	5	74	78	.487
1936	3	81	70	.536
1937	3	86	68	.558
1938	6	65	83	.439
1939	4	85	69	.552
1940	4	82	72	.532
1941	3	77	77	.500
1942	6	66	82	.446
1943	4	82	72	.532
1944	7	71	83	.461
1945	6	71	78	.477
1946	5	74	80	.481
1947	6	70	84	.455
1948	8	51	101	.336
1949	6	63	91	.409

1950	6	60	94	.390
1951	4	81	73	.526
1952	3	81	73	.526
1953	3	89	65	.578
1954	3	94	60	.610
1955	3	91	63	.591
1956	3	85	69	.552
1957	2	90	64	.584
1958	2	82	72	.532
1959	1	94	60	.610
1960	3	87	67	.565
1961	4	86	76	.531
1962	5	85	77	.525
1963	2	94	68	.580
1964	2	98	64	.605
1965	2	95	67	.586
1966	4	83	79	.512
1967	4	89	73	.549
1968	8	67	95	.414
Total		5289	5091	.510

INDIANS

Yr.	Pos.	W	L	Pct.
1901	7	54	82	.397
1902	5	69	67	.507
1903	3	77	63	.550
1904	4	86	65	.570
1905	5	76	78	.494
1906	3	89	64	.582
1907	4	85	67	.559
1908	2	90	64	.584
1909	6	71	82	.464
1910	5	71	81	.467
1911	3	80	73	.523
1912	5	75	78	.490
1913	3	86	66	.566
1914	8	51	102	.333
1915	7	57	95	.375
1916	6	77	77	.500
1917	3	88	66	.571
1918	2	73	56	.566
1919	2	84	55	.604
1920	1*	98	56	.636
1921	2	94	60	.610
1922	4	78	76	.507
1923	3	82	71	.536
1924	6	67	86	.438
1925	6	70	84	.455
1926	2	88	66	.571
1927	6	66	87	.431
1928	7	62	92	.403
1929	3	81	71	.533
1930	4	81	73	.526
1931	4	78	76	.506
1932	4	87	65	.572
1933	4	75	76	.497
1934	3	85	69	.552
1935	3	82	71	.536
1936	5	80	74	.519
1937	4	83	71	.539
1938	3	86	66	.566
1939	3	87	67	.565
1940	2	89	65	.578
1941	4	75	79	.487
1942	4	75	79	.487
1943	3	82	71	.536
1944	5	72	82	.468
1945	5	73	72	.503
1946	6	68	86	.442
1947	4	80	74	.519
1948	1*	97	58	.626
1949	3	89	65	.578
1950	4	92	62	.597
1951	2	93	61	.604
1952	2	93	61	.604
1953	2	92	62	.597
1954	1	111	43	.721
1955	2	93	61	.604
1956	2	88	66	.571
1957	6	76	77	.497
1958	4	77	76	.503
1959	2	89	65	.578
1960	4	76	78	.494
1961	5	78	83	.484
1962	6	80	82	.494
1963	5	79	83	.488
1964	6	79	83	.488
1965	5	87	75	.537
1966	5	81	81	.500
1967	8	75	87	.463
1968	3	86	75	.534
Total		5474	4930	.526

TIGERS

Yr.	Pos.	W	L	Pct.
1901	3	74	61	.548
1902	7	52	83	.385
1903	5	65	71	.478
1904	7	62	90	.408
1905	3	79	74	.516

1906	6	71	78	.477
1907	1	92	58	.613
1908	1	90	63	.588
1909	1	98	54	.645
1910	3	86	68	.558
1911	2	89	65	.578
1912	6	69	84	.451
1913	6	66	87	.431
1914	4	80	73	.523
1915	2	100	54	.649
1916	3	87	67	.565
1917	4	78	75	.510
1918	7	55	71	.437
1919	4	80	60	.571
1920	7	61	93	.396
1921	6	71	82	.464
1922	3	79	75	.513
1923	2	83	71	.539
1924	3	86	68	.558
1925	4	81	73	.526
1926	6	79	75	.513
1927	4	82	71	.536
1928	6	68	86	.442
1929	6	70	84	.455
1930	5	75	79	.487
1931	7	61	93	.396
1932	5	76	75	.503
1933	5	75	79	.487
1934	1	101	53	.656
1935	1*	93	58	.616
1936	2	83	71	.539
1937	2	89	65	.578
1938	4	84	70	.545
1939	5	81	73	.526
1940	1	90	64	.584
1941	4	75	79	.487
1942	5	73	81	.474
1943	5	78	76	.506
1944	2	88	66	.571
1945	1*	88	65	.575
1946	2	92	62	.597
1947	2	85	69	.552
1948	5	78	76	.506
1949	4	87	67	.565
1950	2	95	59	.617
1951	5	73	81	.474
1952	8	50	104	.325
1953	6	60	94	.390
1954	5	68	86	.442
1955	5	79	75	.513
1956	5	82	72	.532
1957	4	78	76	.506
1958	5	77	77	.500
1959	4	76	78	.494
1960	6	71	83	.461
1961	2	101	61	.623
1962	4	85	76	.528
1963	5	79	83	.488
1964	4	85	77	.525
1965	4	89	73	.549
1966	3	88	74	.543
1967	2	91	71	.562
1968	1*	103	59	.636
Total		5415	4994	.520

ATHLETICS†

Yr.	Pos.	W	L	Pct.
1955	6	63	91	.409
1956	8	52	102	.338
1957	7	59	94	.386
1958	7	73	81	.474
1959	7	66	88	.429
1960	8	58	96	.377
1961	9	61	100	.379
1962	9	72	90	.444
1963	8	73	89	.451
1964	10	57	105	.352
1965	10	59	103	.364
1966	7	74	86	.463
1967	10	62	99	.385
1968	6	82	80	.506
Total		911	1304	.415

TWINS

Yr.	Pos.	W	L	Pct.
1961	7	70	90	.438
1962	2	91	71	.562
1963	3	91	70	.565
1964	6	79	83	.488
1965	1	102	60	.630
1966	2	89	73	.549
1967	2	91	71	.562
1968	7	79	83	.488
Total		692	601	.535

YANKEES

Yr.	Pos.	W	L	Pct.
1903	4	72	62	.537
1904	2	92	59	.609

† Kansas City, 1955–67, incl. Oakland, 1968–.

1905	6	71	78	.477
1906	2	90	61	.596
1907	5	70	78	.473
1908	8	51	103	.331
1909	5	74	77	.490
1910	2	88	63	.583
1911	6	76	76	.500
1912	8	50	102	.329
1913	7	57	94	.377
1914	6	70	84	.455
1915	5	69	83	.454
1916	4	80	74	.519
1917	6	71	82	.464
1918	4	60	63	.488
1919	3	80	59	.576
1920	3	95	59	.617
1921	1	98	55	.641
1922	1	94	60	.610
1923	1*	98	54	.645
1924	2	89	63	.586
1925	7	69	85	.448
1926	1	91	63	.591
1927	1*	110	44	.714
1928	1*	101	53	.656
1929	2	88	66	.571
1930	3	86	68	.558
1931	2	94	59	.614
1932	1*	107	47	.695
1933	2	91	59	.607
1934	2	94	60	.610
1935	2	89	60	.597
1936	1*	102	51	.667
1937	1*	102	52	.662
1938	1*	99	53	.651
1939	1*	106	45	.702
1940	3	88	66	.571
1941	1*	101	53	.656
1942	1	103	51	.669
1943	1*	98	56	.636
1944	3	83	71	.539
1945	4	81	71	.533
1946	3	87	67	.565
1947	1*	97	57	.630
1948	3	94	60	.610
1949	1*	97	57	.630
1950	1*	98	56	.636
1951	1*	98	56	.636
1952	1*	95	59	.617
1953	1*	99	52	.656
1954	2	103	51	.669
1955	1	96	58	.623
1956	1*	97	57	.630
1957	1	98	56	.636
1958	1*	92	62	.597
1959	3	79	75	.513
1960	1	97	57	.630
1961	1*	109	53	.673
1962	1*	96	66	.593
1963	1	104	57	.646
1964	1	99	63	.611
1965	6	77	85	.475
1966	10	70	89	.440
1967	9	72	90	.444
1968	5	83	79	.512
Total		5815	4284	.576

SENATORS

Yr.	Pos.	W	L	Pct.
1901	6	61	72	.459
1902	6	61	75	.449
1903	8	43	94	.314
1904	8	38	113	.251
1905	7	64	87	.421
1906	7	55	95	.367
1907	8	49	102	.325
1908	7	67	85	.441
1909	8	42	110	.276
1910	7	66	85	.437
1911	7	64	90	.416
1912	2	91	61	.599
1913	2	90	64	.584
1914	3	81	73	.526
1915	4	85	68	.556
1916	7	76	77	.497
1917	5	74	79	.484
1918	3	72	56	.563
1919	7	56	84	.400
1920	6	68	84	.447
1921	4	80	73	.523
1922	6	69	85	.448
1923	4	75	78	.490
1924	1*	92	62	.597
1925	1	96	55	.636
1926	4	81	69	.540
1927	3	85	69	.552
1928	4	75	79	.487
1929	5	71	81	.467
1930	2	94	60	.610
1931	3	92	62	.597
1932	3	93	61	.604

1933	1	99	53	.651
1934	7	66	86	.434
1935	6	67	86	.438
1936	4	82	71	.536
1937	6	73	80	.477
1938	5	75	76	.497
1939	6	65	87	.428
1940	7	64	90	.416
1941	6	70	84	.455
1942	7	62	89	.357
1943	2	84	69	.549
1944	8	64	90	.416
1945	2	87	67	.565
1946	4	76	78	.494
1947	7	64	90	.416
1948	7	56	97	.366
1949	8	50	104	.325
1950	5	67	87	.435
1951	7	62	92	.403

1952	5	78	76	.506
1953	5	76	76	.500
1954	6	66	88	.429
1955	8	53	101	.344
1956	7	59	95	.383
1957	8	55	99	.357
1958	8	61	93	.396
1959	8	63	91	.409
1960	5	73	81	.474
1961	9	61	100	.379
1962	10	60	101	.373
1963	10	56	106	.346
1964	9	62	100	.383
1965	8	70	92	.432
1966	8	71	88	.447
1967	6	76	85	.472
1968	10	65	96	.404
Total		4744	5632	.457

Bibliography

Primary Sources

Unpublished Material

Allen, Lee. Notebooks containing statistical data on baseball players. MS, Office of the Historian, Baseball Hall of Fame, Cooperstown, N.Y.

Public Documents

Standard Oil Co. of Indiana v. *U.S.* 166 *Federal Reporter*, 376–96.

The Federal Base Ball Club of Baltimore, Inc. v. *National League of Professional Base Ball Clubs and American League of Professional Base Ball Clubs*. 259 U.S. 200, 42 Supreme Court 465.

U.S. House of Representatives. *Organized Baseball*. Report No. 2002 to accompany H.R. 95, 82 Cong., 2 sess. (1952).

———. *Organized Professional Team Sports*. Report No. 1720, 85 Cong., 2 sess. (1958).

———. *Telecasting of Professional Sports Contests*. Report No. 8757, 87 Cong., 1 sess. (1961).

Books

Axelson, Gustav. *"COMMY": The Life Story of Charles A. Comiskey*. Chicago, Reilly & Lee, 1919.

Cobb, Tyrus R. *Busting 'Em*. New York, E. J. Clode, 1914.

———, and Al Stump. *My Life in Baseball. The True Record*. New York, Doubleday, 1961.

Claudy, C. H. *The Battle of Baseball*. New York, The Century Co., 1912.

Evans, William. *The Billy Evans Course on Umpiring*. Privately published. Spalding Collection, New York Public Library.

Evers, John J., and Hugh S. Fullerton. *Touching Second: The Science of Baseball*. Chicago, Reilly and Britton, 1910.

Lieb, Frederick G., and Stan Baumgartner. *The Philadelphia Phillies*. New York, Putnam's, 1953.

McGraw, Mrs. John J. *The Real McGraw*. Ed. by Arthur Mann. New York, David McKay, Inc., 1953.

Ritter, Lawrence S. *The Glory of Their Times*. New York, Macmillan, 1966.

Sullivan, Mark. *Our Times: The United States, 1900–1925*, Vol. 3. New York, Chautauqua Press, 1931.

Sullivan, Ted. *History of the World's Tour, Chicago White Sox and New York Giants*. Chicago, Donahue Co., 1914.

Voigt, David Q. *American Baseball: From Gentleman's Sport to the Commissioner System*. Norman, University of Oklahoma Press, 1966.

PERIODICALS

1. Newspapers

Daily Globe. Boston, 1899–1906.

Eagle. Reading, Pa., 1964–68.

News. Cleveland, 1937.

Post. New York, 1964–68.

Times. New York, 1900–68.

Tribune. Chicago, 1917–22.

2. Sporting Journals

Baseball Digest. 1945–68.

Baseball Magazine. 1908–46.

Sporting Life. 1900–20.

The Sporting News. 1899–1968.

3. Baseball Guides

American League Red Book. 1962.

Baseball Bat Bag. 1921.

Baseball Register. 1960.

Napoleon Lajoie's Official Base Ball Guide. 1906–1908.
National League Green Book. 1964.
Reach's Official Base Ball Guide. 1900–39.
Spalding's Annual Base Ball Record. 1907–24.
Spalding's Official Base Ball Guide. 1900–39.
Spalding-Reach Official Baseball Guide. 1940.
The Baseball Blue Book. 1915–21.

4. Articles in Periodicals

A Club Owner. "The Base Ball Trust," *Literary Digest*, December 7, 1912.

Hodgson, James. "Digest of Laws Prohibiting Sports or Baseball on Sunday," New York Library Pamphlet, February, 1917.

Joss, Addie. "The Strenuosity of Pitching," *Baseball Magazine*, October, 1908.

O'Day, Henry. "A Big League Umpire's View," *Baseball Magazine*, June, 1908.

Sayre, A. "Fans and Their Frenzies: The Wholesome Madness of Baseball," *Everybody's Magazine*, September, 1907.

Sheridan, John. "Umpiring for Big Leaguers," *Baseball Magazine*, May, 1908.

Stallings, George, Jr. "I Was Buddy-Buddy With the Rip Roaring Players of My Dad's Teams," *Baseball Digest*, July, 1957.

Wilde, L. A. "Baseball and the Law," *Case and Comment*, August, 1912.

Reports

Baseball Advisory Council. *Professional Baseball in America*. Chicago, 1921.

Baseball Writers Association of America. *Constitution*, 1967.

Other Sources

Mrs. Grover Cleveland Alexander to Editor, *Time*, October 14, 1967.

National Broadcasting Company. "Today Show," June 9, 1967.

Voigt, David Q. Interview with Lee Allen, historian of Baseball Hall of Fame, Cooperstown, N.Y., July 26, 1967.

———. Interview with James Farrell, American novelist, November 9, 1967.

———. Interview with Curtis Simmons, baseball player and representative to the Players Association, November 12, 1967.

Secondary Sources

Unpublished Material

"Landis File." Uncataloged clippings. Office of the Baseball Commissioner, New York.

Curtis, Gerald R. "Factors That Affected the Attendance of a Major League Baseball Club." Master's essay. Graduate Division of the Wharton School, University of Pennsylvania, 1951.

Nichols, Edward J. "An Historical Dictionary of Baseball Terminology." Ph.D. dissertation, Department of English Literature, Pennsylvania State University, 1937.

Voigt, David Q. "Arthur 'the Great' Shires." 1967.

———. "Baseball's Pre-eminence in Popular Literature." Mimeographed. Author's file, 1967.

Books

Allen, Frederick Lewis. *Only Yesterday*. New York, Bantam Books, 1951.

———. *The Big Change*. New York, Bantam Books, 1961.

Allen, Lee. *The American League Story*. New York, Hill and Wang, 1962.

———. *The Hot Stove League*. New York, A. S. Barnes, 1955.

———. *The National League Story*. New York, Hill and Wang, 1961.

Allen, Mel, and Ed Fitzgerald. *You Can't Beat the Hours*. New York, Harper Bros., 1964.

Andreano, Alfred. *No Joy in Mudville*. Cambridge, Mass., Schenkman Pub. Co., 1965.

Asinoff, Eliot. *Eight Men Out: The Black Sox and the 1919 World Series*. New York, Holt, Rinehart and Winston, 1963.

Baltzell, E. Digby. *The Protestant Establishment*. New York, Random House, 1964.

Bardolph, Richard. *The Negro Vanguard*. New York, Vintage Books, 1961.

Barrow, Edward. *My 50 Years in Baseball*. New York, Coward-McCann, 1951.

Bealle, Morris A. *The Washington Senators*. Washington, Columbia Pub. Co., 1947.

Botkin, B. A., ed. *Sidewalks of America.* New York, Bobbs-Merrill Co., 1954.

Brosnan, Jim. *The Long Season.* New York, Dell Pub. Co., 1961.

Brown, Warren. *The Chicago Cubs.* New York, Putnam's, 1946.

Burnett, William R. *The Roar of the Crowd.* New York, Potter, 1964.

Daley, Arthur. *Times At Bat. A Half Century of Baseball.* New York, Random House, 1950.

Dean, Jerome H. (Dizzy). *Dizzy Baseball.* New York, Greenberg Publishers, 1952.

De Grazia, Sebastian. *Of Time, Work and Leisure.* New York, Anchor Books, 1964.

Farrell, James T. *My Baseball Diary.* New York, A. S. Barnes, 1957.

Fitzgerald, Ed, ed. *The Book of Major League Baseball Clubs: The American League.* New York, A. S. Barnes, 1952.

———. *The Book of Major League Baseball Clubs: The National League.* New York, A. S. Barnes, 1952.

Gallico, Paul. *Farewell to Sport.* New York, Alfred A. Knopf, 1938.

———. *Lou Gehrig: Pride of the Yankees.* New York, Grosset & Dunlap, 1942.

Gendell, Murray, and Hans L. Zetterberg. *A Sociological Almanac for the United States.* New York, Charles Scribner's Sons, 1964.

Gittlitz, Hy. *Don't Kill the Umpire.* New York, Grosby Press, 1957.

Graham, Frank. *Lou Gehrig, A Quiet Hero.* New York, Putnam's, 1942.

———. *The New York Giants.* New York, Putnam's, 1952.

———. *The New York Yankees: An Informal History.* New York, Putnam's 1943.

Greene, Laurence. *The Era of Wonderful Nonsense: A Casebook of the Twenties.* New York, Bobbs-Merrill Co., 1939.

Gresham, Matilda. *Life of Walter Quinton Gresham, 1832–1895.* 2 vols. Chicago, Rand-McNally, 1919.

Henry, Jules. *Culture Against Man.* New York, Random House, 1964.

Herskovits, Melville J. *Economic Anthropology.* New York, Alfred A. Knopf, 1952.

Hubler, Richard. *Lou Gehrig: Iron Horse of Baseball.* Boston, Houghton-Mifflin Co., 1941.

Hutchinson, William T. *Lowden of Illinois: The Life of Frank O. Lowden,* Vol. 1. Chicago, University of Chicago Press, 1957.

Jencks, Christopher, and David Riesman. *The Academic Revolution.* New York, Doubleday, 1968.

Kahn, James M. *The Umpire Story.* New York, Putnam's, 1953.

Klapp, Orrin E. *Symbolic Leaders: Public Dramas and Public Men.* Chicago, Aldine Pub. Co., 1964.

Lieb, Fred. *The Story of the World Series.* New York, Putnam's, 1949.

Lyman, Edward B. *Baseball Fanthology: Hits and Skits of the Game.* New York, privately printed, 1924.

McLuhan, Marshall. *Understanding Media: The Extensions of Man.* New York, McGraw-Hill, 1966.

Mann, Arthur. *Branch Rickey: American in Action.* Boston, Houghton-Mifflin Co., 1957.

Meany, Tom. *Baseball's Greatest Teams.* New York, A. S. Barnes, 1949.

Mencken, H. L. *The American Language.* New York, Alfred A. Knopf, 1935.

Mowry, George E., ed. *The Twenties: Fords, Flappers and Fanatics.* New York, Prentice-Hall, 1963.

Paige, Leroy (Satchel), and David Lipman. *Maybe I'll Pitch Forever.* New York, Doubleday, 1962.

Povich, Shirley. *The Washington Senators.* New York, Putnam's, 1954.

Rae, John B. *The American Automobile.* Chicago, University of Chicago Press, 1966.

Rice, Grantland. *The Tumult and the Shouting: My Life in Sport.* New York, Dell Pub. Co., 1954.

Rickey, Branch. *The American Diamond: A Documentary of the Game of Baseball.* New York, Simon and Schuster, Inc., 1965.

Schwed, Fred, Jr. *How to Watch a Baseball Game.* New York, Harper Bros., 1957.

Slate, Sam J., and Joe Cook. *It Sounds Impossible.* New York, Macmillan, 1963.

Smith, Robert. *Baseball's Hall of Fame.* New York, Bantam Books, 1965.

Spink, J. G. Taylor. *Judge Landis and Twenty-Five Years of Baseball.* New York, Crowell, 1947.

Tebbel, John. *The Compact History of American Newspapers.* New York, Hawthorne, 1963.

Turkin, Hy, and Sherley C. Thompson. *The Official Encyclopedia of Baseball.* New York, A. S. Barnes, 1956.

Veeck, William, Jr., and Ed Linn. *The Hustler's Handbook.* New York, Putnam's, 1965.

———. *Veeck as in Wreck.* New York, Bantam Books, 1963.

Wallop, Douglas. *The Year the Yankees Lost the Pennant.* New York, Pocket Books, 1958.

Articles and Periodicals

"Amazing Mr. MacPhail," *Newsweek*, June 24, 1940.

"Babe Ruth's $210,000 for Three Years of Swat," *Literary Digest*, March 19, 1927.

"Baseball Business from the Inside," *Colliers*, March 25, 1922.

"Baseball from the Bleachers," *Colliers*, May 8, 1909.

"A Baseball Manager Gives Sportswriters a Lecture," *Literary Digest*, February 19, 1938.

"Baseball Reporters Who Broke into Literature," *Literary Digest*, April 9, 1921.

"Baseball Shudders at the Home Run Menace," *Literary Digest*, April 9, 1921.

"Baseball's Integrity Mountain Signs Up," *Newsweek*, December 23, 1933.

"Base Stealing's Sensational Decline," *Literary Digest*, April 29, 1922.

"Batter Up, Batter Down—Beanball," *Literary Digest*, June 12, 1937.

"Big League Baseball," *Fortune*, August, 1937.

"Big Leaguers in Training," *Literary Digest*, March 30, 1912.

"Bill Veeck and the Cleveland Indians," *Business Week*, October 2, 1948.

Bloodgood, Clifford. "After the Game is Over," *Baseball Magazine*, January, 1946.

"Break Up the Yankees," *Colliers*, February 25, 1939.

Brougham, Harvey. "America's Erratic Judge: How Judge Landis Entered Into Public Life," *Overland Monthly*, April, 1921.

Camerer, David. "36 Years a Yankee," *Baseball Digest*, July, 1957.

Cartwright, Gary. "Confessions of a Washed-Up Sportswriter," *Harper's Magazine*, April, 1968.

Conlan, Jocko, and Robert Creamer. "Nobody Loves an Umpire," *Sports Illustrated*, June 26, 1965.

"Country Boys in the Big Leagues," *Literary Digest*, April 18, 1925.

"The Cubs: Baseball's Contribution to Successful Management," *Factory and Industrial Management*, October, 1929.

Daley, Arthur. "Fabulous Yankees Through Fifty Years," *New York Times Magazine*, March 9, 1952.

———. "Jocko Called 'Em" *New York Times*, September 12, 1967.

———. "The Big Frenchman," *New York Times*, February 10, 1959.

Demaree, A. "Grandstand Girls—Women and Baseball Don't Mix," *Colliers*, June 2, 1928.

"Doctored Baseballs," *Literary Digest*, September 22, 1923.

"Doctoring Our National Anthem," *Literary Digest*, February 19, 1938.

Drebinger, John. "Who Was the Hero of the '45 Series?" *Baseball Magazine*, December, 1945.

Durslag, Melvin. "When Will Sportscasters Be Allowed to Speak Up?" *T.V. Guide*, June 24, 1967.

Durso, Joseph. "Emmet the Great," *New York Times*, August 21, 1966.

Einstein, Charles. "The New Breed of Baseball Fan," *Harper's Magazine*, July, 1967.

"Fall of the House of MacPhail," *Saturday Evening Post*, April 17, 1943.

"The Federal League's Chances," *Literary Digest*, February 7, 1914.

"The First American Dictator," *The American Review of Reviews*, January, 1928.

Flaherty, Vincent X. "Miracle Move of the Dodgers—From Flatbush to Fantasia," *Baseball Register*, 1960. 3–21.

"Football or Baseball the National Game?" *Literary Digest*, December 6, 1924.

Ford, John. "The End of an Era," *Baseball Digest*, March, 1955.

"Fortunes Made in Base Ball," *Literary Digest*, July 20, 1912.

Frank, Stanley. "Corrupts! Debases! Exploits!" *T.V. Guide*, February 4, 1967.

Freeburg, Dwight. "Batter Number One," *Baseball Magazine*, January, 1942.

Fullerton, Hugh. "Baseball on Trial," *New Republic*, October 20, 1920.

———. "Baseball the Business and the Sport," *Review of Reviews*, April, 1921.

Furlong, William. "How Specialized Can You Get?" *New York Times Magazine*, August 14, 1966.

———. "Out in the Bleachers Where the Action Is," *New York Times Magazine*, July, 1967.

"Future Interleague Baseball Games," *Literary Digest*, July 22, 1930.

"The Golden Age of Sport," *Time*, June 2, 1967.

Gould, James. "The President Says, 'Play Ball,'" *Baseball Magazine*, January, 1942.

Graber, Ralph S. "Baseball in American Fiction," *The English Journal*, November, 1967.

Graham, Frank. "How New York Got Sunday Games," *Baseball Digest*, June, 1955.

———. "Kenesaw Mountain Landis," *Baseball Magazine*, February, 1945.

"Honesty in Baseball," *Literary Digest*, May 24, 1913.

Hornsby, Rogers. "Why Good Pitchers Are Easy to Hit," *Baseball Magazine*, April, 1919.

"How Tony Gives a Latin Tone to Our National Game," *Literary Digest*, July 2, 1932.

"I Hate the Yankees," *Life*, April 17, 1950.

" 'Inside' Baseball From an Owner's View-Point," *Literary Digest*, April 8, 1922.

"Is Professional Baseball A Sport?" *Literary Digest*, September 17, 1921.

"Joshing is Business in Baseball," *Literary Digest*, April 28, 1923.

Kiernan, John. "Big League Business," *Saturday Evening Post*, May 31, 1930.

"Kill Him," *Literary Digest*, May 22, 1937.

Kofoed, Jack, and Max Carey. "20 Greatest Players," *Esquire*, October, 1955.

Koppett, Leonard. "A Yankee Dynasty Can Never Come Back," *New York Times Magazine*, October 2, 1966.

Lardner, Ring. "Tyrus the Greatest," *American Mercury*, June, 1915.

"Lively Controversy Over the Lively Ball," *Literary Digest*, October 5, 1929.

"A Locker in the Living Room," *Time*, October 20, 1967.

"Love Those Yanks," *Life*, October 9, 1950.

Lukas, J. Anthony. "Down and Out in the Minor Leagues," *Harper's Magazine*, June, 1968.

McDermott, J. R. "The Psychology of a Slump," *Baseball Magazine*, July, 1913.

"Mack's Great Expectations," *Literary Digest*, March 8, 1913.

"The Mahatma," *Time*, December 17, 1965.

Mann, Arthur. "Baseball Reconverts," *Baseball Magazine*, June, 1946.

Merchant, Larry. "The Bleachers," *New York Post*, August 1, 1967.

Michener, James A. "Is the American Boy Quitting Baseball?" *Literary Digest*, July 12, 1930.

"A Million Dollar World Series," *The Digest*, October 9, 1939.

"Newspaper Fan," *Atlantic*, April, 1908.

"On the Difficulty of Being a Contemporary Hero," *Time*, June 24, 1966.

"The Passing of the Super Pitcher," *Literary Digest*, February 16, 1924.
"The Passing of Trick Pitching," *Literary Digest*, October 6, 1928.
"Play Ball," *Literary Digest*, April 17, 1937.
Phelon, William A. "The Great American Magnate," *Baseball Magazine*, January, 1913.
"President Hoover's Trials at the World Series," *Literary Digest*, November 12, 1929.
"The Radio in the Auto," *Literary Digest*, July 9, 1932.
Reynolds, Quentin. "Eddie Brannick, Secretary of the Giants," *Colliers*, May 1, 1937.
"The Rise of Basketball," *Literary Digest*, December 19, 1936.
Rosenblatt, Aaron. "Negroes in Baseball: The Failure of Success," *Transaction Magazine*, September, 1967.
"Rosy Twilight of the Vanished Ball-player," *Literary Digest*, April 21, 1928.
Sawyer, G. F. "Famous Big League Favorites in the Minors," *Baseball Magazine*, September, 1920.
Simons, Herbert. "Life of an Ump," *Baseball Magazine*, April, 1942.
Smith, Red. "The Fabulous Invalid," *Baseball Digest*, January-February, 1957.
"Some Presidential Ball Fans," *Literary Digest*, May 19, 1920.
"Stop Squawking—in Defense of the Yankees," *Colliers*, March 4, 1939.
Stump, Al. "Dames are the Biggest Headache," *Baseball Digest*, September, 1959.
"Them Phillies—How to Make Failure Pay," *Saturday Evening Post*, October 4, 1941.
Thompson, Lewis, and Charles Boswell. "Say It Ain't So, Joe," *American Heritage*, June, 1960.
"Thumbs Down on Night Baseball," *Literary Digest*, June 8, 1935.
Van Loan, C. "Baseball as the Bleachers Like It," *Outing*, September, 1909.
"The Vulnerable Star," *New York Times*, April 14, 1965.
"What Babe Ruth Does With His Money," *Literary Digest*, October 5, 1929.
"What Ball Players Read," *Literary Digest*, May 31, 1930.
"What is Babe Ruth Worth to the Yankees?" *Literary Digest*, March 29, 1930.
"When the Clock Strikes Forty," *Literary Digest*, March 10, 1934.
"Why is a Baseball Player," *Literary Digest*, June 12, 1915.

"Why the Yankees Win," *Nation*, September 17, 1938.

Williams, Ted and John Underwood. "Hitting Was My Life," *Sports Illustrated*, June 24, 1968.

Wolfe, Edgar F. "The Benevolent Brotherhood of Baseball Bugs," *Literary Digest*, July 7, 1925.

"Working More, Sleeping Less," *Time*, September 8, 1967.

Wrigley, William, Jr. "Owning a Big League Team," *Literary Digest*, September 13, 1930.

"The Yankees," *Fortune*, July, 1946.

"Yawkey of the Red Sox," *Literary Digest*, December 21, 1935.

"You've Got to Hand it to the Glove," *Baseball Digest*, March, 1959.

Miscellaneous

Mack, Gene. "Hall of Fame Cartoons, Major League Ball Parks," Spalding Collection, The New York Public Library.

Index